An Annotated Bibliography of HEALTH ECONOMICS

Western European Sources

This book is a companion volume to *An Annotated Bibliography of Health Economics, English Language Sources*, which was published by Martin Robertson, London, in 1977.

An Annotated Bibliography of HEALTH ECONOMICS

Western European Sources

ADRIAN GRIFFITHS

RAYMOND RIGONI

PIERRE TACIER

NICHOLAS PRESCOTT

Published for
Sandoz Institute for Health and Socio-Economic Studies, Geneva,
by
Martin Robertson • Oxford

First published in 1980 by Martin Robertson, Oxford

British Library Cataloguing in Publication Data

An annotated bibliography of health economics,
Western European sources.
1. Medical economics — Bibliography
I. Griffiths, A
016.3384'7'3621 Z6675.E2

ISBN 0-85520-246-7

Printed by J G Eccles Printers Ltd, Henderson Road, Inverness

Contents

Foreword

While health may be priceless, health care is certainly not without cost. Indeed, some European countries now spend close to one-tenth of their gross national product on health services. In the present economic climate, politicians are concerned about the tendency of health expenditure to rise year by year, particularly as it has not been demonstrated that the increased expenditure has brought about correspondingly greater health benefits or more equitable distribution of health services. On the contrary, health appears to be influenced at least as much by personal behaviour, and by measures in other sectors of the economy, as by organized health care.

Moreover, within the health sector it is economic and technological, rather than primarily health, factors that have been fuelling the growth of health care expenditure. Such factors include the often uncontrolled expansion of medical resources, the wasteful incentives of certain budgetary and finance systems, the proliferation of over-sophisticated technology, and rapid wage and salary increases. Given the size of the health sector, it is not surprising that activities in this field have had a major influence on levels of employment, price stability, the balance of payments, and other economic factors.

In parallel with the growing importance of the health sector, health economics — economics applied to the health field — has emerged as a new discipline. It is being increasingly called upon to broaden our understanding of the organization and behaviour of the health economy, and to help in making it more effective and efficient, so as to improve the health of all. As yet, the number of the health economists in Europe is relatively small, and claims for the success of their discipline must necessarily be modest; indeed, we still know little about how decisions regarding health care are made. It seems, however, that economic factors pertaining to the community at large are rarely taken fully into account.

The Regional Office for Europe of the World Health Organization has recently responded to this development by setting up a health economics programme which focuses on interdisciplinary health economics research, as one of the priorities for our overall activity in research promotion and development. This programme includes the development of a methodology for use in health administration, and the review of different patterns of health economics advice and training programmes.

One of the problems in this field is to improve communications between workers in different countries. Many are dealing with similar problems, and a considerable body of literature has already been published. However, because of the interdisciplinary nature of much of health economics research, and the varied backgrounds of the people involved, this literature is spread over a large variety of journals and other sources outside the specialist economic publications. International communication is also hindered by language barriers.

Among the first efforts to deal with this problem was the publication of *An Annotated Bibliography of Health Economics, English Language Sources*, by the Health Economics Group of the University of York. The present work represents a similar effort by the team of the Sandoz Institute for Health and Socio-Economic Studies, in Geneva. It draws together selected references from twelve Western European countries and provides a companion volume to the York publication.

The Regional Office for Europe is pleased to have been of help in enlisting additional contributors to this bibliography, so that more countries could be included. It is hoped that similar material can be made available from selected Eastern European countries over the next few years, since the *Abstracts of Books and Articles on Health Planning and Health Economics in Countries of Eastern Europe, 1965-1969* (EURO 4102) is now out-of-date.

I hope that not only health economists and general economists, but also health services researchers, health administrators, practising physicians, and nurses will find this Sandoz Institute bibliography useful in locating articles and books of special interest to them. After all, health economics is too important a subject to be left to economists alone.

LEO A. KAPRIO, M.D.
Regional Director
World Health Organization
Regional Office for Europe
Copenhagen

Introduction

The Institute of Economics in the University of York and the Sandoz Institute for Health and Socio-Economic Studies, in Geneva, set out to provide the first overall picture of the Western literature on health economics. Their objective has now been accomplished with the appearance of this book, the fourth in the bibliography series [1-3]. While the York team covered the Anglo-Saxon literature, the Sandoz Institute team reviewed material published in the various languages of Western European countries: Austria, Belgium, Denmark, the Federal Republic of Germany, Finland, France, Italy, Luxembourg, the Netherlands, Norway, Sweden, and Switzerland.

The Institute was assisted in its task by a number of European specialists in health and related disciplines. These included Professor Dominique Jolly, University of Paris, France; Dr Tiziana Baldone, Institute for Health Economics Research, Milan, Italy; Professor Denise Deliège-Rott, University of Louvain, Belgium; Assistant Professor Bengt Jönsson and Professor Ingemar Ståhl, University of Lund, Sweden; Dr Finn Kamper-Jørgensen, Assistant Programme Director, The Danish National Institute of Social Research, Copenhagen, Denmark; and Professor Manfred Pflanz, Professor Klaus Henke, and Dr Romuald Schicke, University of Hanover, Federal Republic of Germany.

We have not pursued uniformity as an end in itself, since we felt that the benefit of having specialists in each country select and summarize the main works in their own language would more than compensate for any resulting inconsistency in their conception of health economics or their styles of writing. Whether this was the best approach, each reader must decide for himself. As an interdisciplinary field covering several

[1]Culyer, A.J., Wiseman, J., and Walker, A. (1977) *An Annotated Bibliography of Health Economics, English Language Sources*, London: Martin Robertson, xvii + 361 pp.

[2]Jolly, D. with Jolly, C. and Tacier, P. (1977) *Economie de la santé, Bibliographie choisie et annotée, France. Une Synthèse de l'Institut Sandoz d'études en matière de santé et d'économie sociale*, Paris: Dunod, 247 pp.

[3]Baldone, T. (1978) *Economia sanitaria, Bibliografia selezionata e commentata*, Rome: Il Pensiero Scientifico, xvi + 94 pp.

specialized areas and skills, health economics is difficult to circumscribe. The definition accorded to it varies widely between countries, and even more so between individuals working in the field, who come from many different backgrounds.

The book is a select rather than an exhaustive bibliography, and our choice of what to include was necessarily subjective. We were, however, guided by certain criteria:

1. The national contributors were provided with a list of chapter headings. In those areas having a large number of relevant publications they were asked to select the major representative contributions, whereas in more sparsely worked areas they necessarily had to include whatever was available. This has inevitably led to some unevenness of quality.
2. Although hospital administration can be regarded as an integral part of health economics, it is a well-established discipline, taught and researched at universities and institutes in many countries. The abundant specialized literature on the subject would be sufficient to merit a separate publication. We therefore included only studies of a general nature.
3. Unlike our colleagues in York, we have included studies by governmental sources insofar as we had access to them, since they often represent a major contribution to health economics.
4. We have also included summaries of certain official publications by various international organizations, such as the World Health Organization, the Organization for Economic Cooperation and Development, the International Labour Office, and the World Bank.

As this was the first survey of its kind undertaken, the collection of data sometimes proved difficult. Certain important studies may in consequence have been inadvertently omitted. This is all the more likely since, in several continental countries, especially France, many works on health economics have appeared only as mimeographed documents. The Anglo-Saxon countries, in contrast, have a stronger tradition of formal publication.

The bibliography reveals that the areas covered by health economists, in the countries included, are remarkably similar, but that in many cases they depend at least as much on the individual interests of the investigators as on the importance and usefulness of the work for health planning. Some national features can nevertheless be discerned. In

France, there has been much more study than elsewhere on the utilization of hospital and other services, notably by the Centre de Recherche pour l'Etude et l'Observation des Conditions de Vie (CREDOC). In Denmark, the Federal Republic of Germany, and Finland, health economics is often dealt with by sociologists and specialists in preventive medicine; this explains the orientation of publications from these countries. In Sweden, many cost–benefit analyses in the field of hospital planning have been published, particularly by the Swedish Planning and Rationalization Institute of the Health and Social Services (SPRI), and there has been much emphasis on the cost of road traffic accidents. Overall, most publications are on empirical findings and few on theoretical studies.

We hope that our bibliography, drawn from virtually all the material published in Western Europe up to the end of 1976 (as well as some material published in 1977 and 1978), will be favourably received by the audience to whom it is addressed, notably health economists, administrators, and policy makers, and that it will help to foster international communication and collaboration. We are well aware that the amount of literature appearing each year in the field of health economics is so great that continuing coverage can be assured only by computer-based methods.

Three alphabetical indexes are appended to the bibliography: authors, titles of journals and periodicals, and names and addresses of publishers, journals, and periodicals cited.

Our warmest thanks go to the collaborators already mentioned; without their professional rigour this work could never have been completed. Encouragement and helpful advice have also come from Professor Guy Bäckman of the Åbo Akademi, Turku, Finland; Professor Maria Blohmke, director of the Department of Occupational and Social Medicine, University of Heidelberg, Federal Republic of Germany; Professor Antonio Brenna, director of the Institute of Health Economics Research, Milan, Italy; and our colleague, Dr Philip Selby, head of community medicine and epidemiology, of the Sandoz Institute.

We should also like to thank Mme Martine Zermatten for her cheerful assistance with the indexes and Mlle Chantal Scheidecker for her painstaking efficiency in checking and completing all the bibliographic details and the indexes, and preparing the final manuscript.

THE EDITORS

System of Classification

1. Entries are **classified** by topic in seven chapters, with further classification in subsections in Chapters II–V (see table of contents). Entries are listed in chronological order within chapters or subsections, and alphabetically within each year.
2. Annotated entries are **numbered** consecutively from the beginning to the end of the bibliography. All bold typeface numbers therefore refer to annotated entries.
3. Many references fall into several classifications. In such cases, the main annotated reference is numbered in bold typeface and the unannotated reference in other chapters or subsections carries the same number, in light typeface.
4. **Cross references** between related entries are given, where appropriate, beneath the annotation.
5. **Bibliographic details** are presented in a standard format.
   1. Papers published (a) in journals, (b) in other publications.
   2. Books, reports, theses, and other works, which are not part of a larger publication.

   The format is illustrated below.

   1 (a) **483** NIELSEN, G., MIKKELSEN, M., and WAMBERG, E. (1974) 'Cost–benefit analysis in prevention of mental retardation' ('Cost–benefit analyse af forbyggende åndssvageforsorg'), *Social Tidsskrift*, **50**, 9, 147–67.

   1 (b) **39** TSCHOPP, P. (1976) 'The role of health economics in future medical research and practice' ('Le rôle de l'économie de la santé dans la recherche et la pratique médicales de demain') in: RIGONI, R. (ed.) Health Economics, Proceedings of a Workshop, Coppet, 4 October 1975 (*Economie de la santé. Compte rendu d'un colloque, Coppet, 4 octobre 1975*), Geneva: Sandoz Institute for Health and Socio-Economic Studies, 28–36.

2 **18** BONAMOUR, P. (1974) Medicine in the World of Economics (*La médecine dans le monde économique*), Paris: Editions Médicales et Universitaires, 299 pp.

98 NATIONAL INSTITUTE FOR HEALTH AND MEDICAL RESEARCH (1972) Systematic Health Examinations (*Les examens systématiques de santé*) (Report of the French–Swedish seminar, Le Vésinet, 16–18 March 1971), Paris: Institut National de la Santé et de la Recherche Médicale, 129 pp. (mimeographed document).

6. All authors are **indexed** alphabetically, with the reference numbers of their annotated entries opposite their names. For **institutional authors** the name of the institution is given in English, and for government departments the name of the department is preceded by the name of the country, e.g., France, Ministry of Health. Almost all such authors publish their own material, and in this case the English translation of the name is cited in the list of addresses with a cross reference to the name in the original language (see 10 below).
7. **Composite names**, such as 'de Kervasdoue' or 'van Loon', are cited in alphabetical order of the first letter. However, since some countries cite such names under the first letter of the name after the particle, they are also indexed in this way with cross reference to the other citation. E.g., de Kervasdoue is cited under D — 'De Kervasdoue', and under K — '*Kervasdoue* (*see:* De Kervasdoue)'.
8. The **titles of organizations** are cited in full at least once in each entry for ease of reference, since abbreviations widely used in the country of origin may be unfamiliar to international readers. E.g., CREDOC is given in full: Centre de Recherche pour l'Etude et l'Observation des Conditions de Vie.
9. **Journals** cited in the bibliography are listed alphabetically on pages 294–8. Where journals have changed titles, both the old and the new title are listed. Old titles are given in italic type, followed by the new title in roman type.
10. **Publishers'** names are given in the original language. The addresses of journals, publishers, and in some cases editorial offices are listed alphabetically on pages 299–322.

An Annotated Bibliography of HEALTH ECONOMICS

Western European Sources

1 General Works

1965

1 Brenna, A. (1965) 'Economic aspects of health care' ('Gli aspetti economici della tutela della salute'), *Rivista Internazionale di Scienze Sociali*, **36**, 6, 563–83.

The starting point of this article is the controversy between supporters and opponents of the British National Health Service. It analyses the economic arguments normally advanced to justify public intervention in the field of health care, and then indicates the possible ways in which economics can be applied in this area. Inefficiency in the market for health care is essentially caused by three types of factors: the presence of external economies, consumer ignorance, and non-economic (humanitarian) factors which influence market behaviour. As a result of these characteristics, the application to health care of choice criteria derived from welfare theory are strongly criticized.

2 Zoellner, D. (1965) 'The economics of health care' ('Die Oekonomie der Versorgung mit Gesundheitsleistungen'), *Schmollers Jahrbuch für Gesetzgebung, Verwaltung und Volkswirtschaft*, No. 55, 171–98.

The health service market, the supply and demand for health services, and their characteristics are discussed and analysed.

1966

3 Bogs, W., Achinger, H., Meinhold, H., Neundoerfer, L., and Schreiber, W. (eds) (1966) Social Security, A Social Inquiry in the Federal Republic of Germany. Report of the Social Inquiry Commission (*Soziale Sicherung, Sozialenquete in der Bundesrepublik Deutschland. Bericht der Sozialenquete-Kommission*), Stuttgart, Berlin, Cologne: W. Kohlhammer Verlag, 354 pp.

Review and critical analysis of the entire social security situation in the Federal Republic of Germany, including old age insurance, health insurance, medical and social aspects of disability, family services, and public assistance.

4 Spek, J.-E. (1966) 'Economic and social aspects of health care' ('Samhällsekonomiska och sociala aspekter på sjukvàrden') in: Health Care Plan for Gothenburg, Appendix 2 (*Sjukvardsplan för Göteborg, Bilaga 2*), Gothenburg: Göteborgs Stadtskontor, 51 pp.

The article presents background material for the health care plan of the city of Gothenburg. It describes the organization of Swedish health care in terms of its functions and relevant legislation, and analyses its development during the period 1950–65. It then analyses the concepts of demand, need, and efficiency in health care. It recommends further research into the determination of the demand and need for health care, in order to improve the efficiency of planning.

1967

5 Brenna, A. (1967) 'Public and private choices in the health care sector' ('Scelta pubblica e scelta nel sistema di tutela della salute'), *Rivista Internazionale di Scienze Sociali*, **38**, 1, 44–54.

This paper relates to the debate provoked by Buchanan concerning externalities and public goods. The first part describes Buchanan's paper on 'The inconsistencies of the British National Health Service', and the second offers a critique of it. Brenna describes five models of health care systems, and analyses their relative efficiency in terms of their ability to secure market equilibrium and to guarantee Pareto optimal resource allocation. Public intervention on the supply side does not ensure attainment of both objectives; this is demonstrated in the case of the National Health Service (NHS). Public intervention is also required on the demand side. The author's criticisms concern, in particular, the inadequacy of Buchanan's model of political choice for interpreting the British experience. The most serious criticism is that Buchanan fails to understand the basic motive for creating the NHS, namely to improve the distribution of income.

1969

6 D'Iribarne, P. (1969) 'In search of rational health and social security policies' ('A la recherche de politiques rationnelles de santé et de sécurité sociale'), *Analyse et Prévisions*, **8**, 6, 725–36.

This study aims to determine the 'best' possible health policy, according to a definition satisfactory both to medical experts and to politicians. The author argues that efforts to improve an individual state of health may have related effects of varying significance to the community. Any 'rational' health policy must take account of this fact, and proceed from an analysis of objectives to the choice of the means.

7 SPEK, J.E. (1969) 'Medical care and economic research' ('Sjukvård och ekonomisk forskning'), *Socialmedicinsk Tidskrift*, **46**, 6, 306–11.

The purpose of the article is to outline possible applications of economic research to health and medical care. It reviews recent health economics research in England and the USA, and draws a distinction between basic, positive, and normative economic research in health and medical care. It points out that the best developed of these three areas is positive economic research, i.e., research into the cost and consumption of medical care. It concludes with an outline of some important problems to which economic analysis could be applied to facilitate rational decision making: (1) the goals of the health care system, (2) the design of the health care system, (3) the choice of a relevant information system, (4) the consistency of different goals, and (5) the methods of long-term planning.

1970

8 BONAMOUR, P., BROUN, G., and DARTIGUES, R. (1970) 'Health economics and French studies in health economics' ('L'économie de la santé et les travaux français d'économie sanitaire'), *Revue Française des Affaires Sociales*, **24**, 3, 33–62.

After first defining health economics and emphasizing its importance, the authors discuss the need for research in social security and planning. Health economics should facilitate the making of more rational choices, taking due account of objectives, possible projects, available resources, costs, and other constraints. The authors argue that there are two major categories of economic research in this field: studies aimed at determining the share to be assigned to the health sector in the economy as a whole, and those aimed at determining the shares to be assigned to each of its components.

1971

9 BRUNET-JAILLY, J. (1971) Essay on General Health Economics (*Essai sur l'économie générale de la santé*), Paris: Cujas, 897 pp.

An enormous collection of data on the development of the French health care system from about 1950 to 1968. The first part examines changes in the structure of production units in the health care system: the professions, the hospitals, and the pharmaceutical industry. The second part, which deals with special features of economic analysis of the health care system, presents studies of the remuneration of health professionals and of the financing of the first four French plans for health and social services, and a critical summary of early French studies of the regional distribution of medical personnel. These analyses show that the structure of supply is largely determined by technical and economic rather than specific health factors. The structure of demand is related to several factors, in particular the financing of medical expenditure. The author argues that economic factors have a much greater influence on demand than is generally admitted. The final part is devoted to some original analyses of the measurable effects of working conditions on health, and of the cost of inactivity due to sickness and accidents at work in France during the 1960s.

10 NATIONAL ALLIANCE OF CHRISTIAN MUTUAL INSURANCES (1971) Health Policy (*Politique de la santé*), Brussels: Alliance Nationale des Mutualités Chrétiennes, Série *Orientation Mutualiste*, **24**, 5, 191–253.

This work investigates aspects of health policy in the context of three main themes, selected for their relative importance in health policy, and for the urgency of finding effective solutions. The first concerns the appropriate level of investment in the health sector and its allocation between different sub-sectors. Although the importance of investment in personnel is recognized, only capital investment is considered. The second theme concerns the organization of medical care and the financing of medical consumption. The third theme deals with the institutional problems of health policy: how to prepare and implement an efficient and democratic policy; how to reach high-level decisions; and how consumers can participate in decision making. Problems related to these themes are set out, and a possible solution is proposed.

1972

11 GRIFFITHS, D.A.T. (1972) 'Economic evaluation in the health services', *Annales de la Société Belge de Médecine Tropicale*, **52**, 3, 215–34.

This paper reviews the contribution of the economist to health services evaluation. After enumerating the characteristics that differentiate the health care sector from other economic sectors, it goes on to consider, with examples, the key questions in planning and managing health services, and the economist's contribution to answering them. These questions include: How much money should the health sector receive? Who is to be treated for what condition? How should strategies be organized functionally and geographically? How does the time horizon affect choices and priorities? How are the standards of care to be measured and decided? What costs should be considered in resource allocation (including opportunity costs)? How should effects be measured and evaluated, and related to inputs (including the concepts of cost-effectiveness and cost–benefit analyses)?

12 SPEK, J.-E. (1972) 'Economics of medical care' ('Sjukvårdsekonomi') in: YSANDER, B. C. (ed.) Problems in the Economics of Public Administration (*Förvaltningsekonomiska Problem*), Stockholm: Jurist- och Samhällsvetareförbundet Förlags AB, 178–94.

The paper presents a general outline of economic analysis of health care systems. It first discusses the comparative development of health care expenditures and some health status indicators in Sweden. Public expenditure on health care increased from 1.0% to 6.5% of GNP over the period 1928–69. Mean life expectancy has increased over the last 200 years, but the decrease in mortality rates has occurred mainly in the younger age groups. For example, life expectancy at age 80 has not changed since the eighteenth century. The author concludes that the increase in health expenditures cannot be shown to have contributed significantly to the change in mean life expectancy. He then discusses the demand and need for health care, and concludes that these concepts require further research. Finally, the paper discusses the problems of efficiency and planning in the health care sector. It identifies the lack of appropriate output data and of economic incentives as major barriers to greater efficiency.

1973

13 PELICIER, Y. and MOUCHEZ, P. (1973) Summary of Medical Sociology and Economics (*Abrégé de sociologie et économie médicale*), Paris: Masson, 168 pp.

A summary intended to familiarize medical students with the basic notions of medical sociology and economics, in order to encourage future doctors to appreciate the importance of these disciplines.

14 RÖSCH, G. et al. (1973) Elements of Medical Economics (*Eléments d'économique médicale*), Paris: Flammarion, 195 pp.

A basic text on medical economics in France, containing a great deal of information collected by CREDOC (Centre de Recherches et de Documentation sur la Consommation) research workers. Four chapters deal with: economics and medical economics; microeconomics and the behaviour of economic agents; macroeconomic aspects and analysis of the medical care system; and forecasting for practical policy. A glossary and bibliography are included.

15 SCHOLLMER, J. (1973) Patient and Profit-Medicine. The Health Care System in the Federal Republic of Germany between Crisis and Reform (*Patient und Profitmedizin. Das Gesundheitswesen der Bundesrepublik zwischen Krise und Reform*), Opladen: Westdeutscherr Verlag, 280 pp.

A theoretical analysis of the patient's economic situation, and his dependence on supplier decisions due to his lack of inside market knowledge.

16 VOLKHOLZ, V. et al. (1973) The Health Care System in the Federal Republic of Germany, Project Analysis of the Health Care System (*Gesundheitssystem in der Bundesrepublik, Projekt Gesundheitssystem-Analyse*), Berlin: VSA-Verlag, 168 pp.

A theoretical analysis of the medical care system in the Federal Republic of Germany, including its economic aspects.

17 WAALER, H.T. (1973) 'Economic analyses of social services and health care – how relevant are they?' (*'Økonomiske analyser i sosial- og helsesektoren – hvor relevante er de?'), Sosialøkonomen*, **27**, 1, 47–50.

General problems in economic analyses of social services and health care are discussed.

1974

18 BONAMOUR, P. (1974) Medicine in the World of Economics (*La médecine dans le monde économique*), Paris: Editions Médicales et Universitaires, 299 pp.

An introductory health economics text intended particularly for the medical profession. Subjects covered include: medical consumption, demography, prevention, health indicators, the medical and paramedical professions, private medicine, hospitals, pharmacies, income redistribution and social security, national accounting, planning, and future trends.

19 DESTANNE DE BERNIS, G. (1974) 'Economics and health' ('Economie et santé), *Bulletin Trimestriel de l'Ecole Nationale de la Santé Publique*, **7**, 1, 3–40.

An economist's reflections on the importance of health economics, and the need for teaching it to future doctors. The author discusses, in particular, the relations between the health care system and the economy as a whole, and the inconsistencies created in the health system by its role in the social sector.

20 HERDER-DORNEICH, P. (1974) 'Health economics — a challenge to science' ('Gesundheitsökonomie — Vor einer Herausforderung an die Wirtschaft') in: VERBAND DER ÄRZTE DEUTSCHLANDS (HARTMANN-BUND) E.V. (ed), Health in a Free-Market Economy (*Gesundheit in der Wettbewerbswirtschaft*), Mainz: Kirchheim Verlag, 7–33.

This paper discusses the scarcity of resources in health care and the special characteristics of health goods and services. The guidance and control mechanisms in the health care market are analysed and discussed.

21 KAMPER-JØRGENSEN, F. (1974) Health Economics — From a Socio-medical Standpoint (*Sundhedsøkonomi — med socialmedicinsk sigte*), Copenhagen: University of Copenhagen, Institute of Social Medicine (Publication No. 3), 480 pp.

A comprehensive, research-oriented, health economics text. Contains the following chapters: (1) Health economics as a discipline, its definition and development; (2) Characteristics of the health market; (3) Health and disease, concepts and models; (4) Measurement of health and disease; (5) Demand theory, models and results; (6) Treatment of myocardial infarction, dynamic supply and demand considerations; (7) The health care sector and society; (8) Cost–benefit and cost-effectiveness analysis; and (9) The hospital as a producing unit.

22 SELBY, P. (1974) *Health in 1980-1990, A Predictive Study Based on an International Inquiry*, Basle: S. Karger, xi + 87 pp.

Discusses trends in health care up to the year 1990, based on an opinion survey conducted among 63 experts in 19 industrialized countries and on a three-day symposium attended by 16 of these experts. The first section, on health and disease, deals with major health problems, prevention, treatment, rehabilitation, the physical and social environment, the 'social drug', and the concept of health. The second section, on the organization of health care, covers health professions, health services, information, costs of health care, and the role of industry. The chapter on costs of health care includes a discussion of: rising costs, the need for rational choices in resource allocation, trends in systems of financing health care, relative expenditures on prevention, treatment and rehabilitation, and political pressures on the distribution of services. A relative increase is foreseen in expenditures on prevention, health education, and care of the elderly.
See 519

1975

23 Bonamour, P. and Jolly D. (eds) (1975) Education and Research in Health Economics: Report on the GERES Workshop, 12 April 1975, Paris (*L'enseignement et la recherche en économie de la santé, Compte rendu de la journée d'étude du Groupe d'étude et de recherche en économie de la santé du 12 avril 1975, Paris*), Paris: Dausse, 209 pp.

Provides an account of the present state of training in health economics for medical students and physicians. It considers how such training should be conducted and, in particular, offers a proposal for a complete curriculum for medical students. It then discusses the training of specialists in health economics, and reports on the work of various research teams that are beginning to be active in France. The final part deals with education and research in health economics in Sweden, Great Britain, Canada, and the United States of America.

24 Bonnevie, P. (1975) 'Health economics' in: Bonnevie, P., *Textbook of Social Medicine*, Copenhagen: Arnold Buscks, 51–4.

A brief introduction to the discipline of health economics.

25 Closon, J.P. (1975) Public Health Care and Social Security: An Economic Approach (*Santé publique et prévoyance sociale: une approche économique*), Louvain: Université de Louvain, Faculté des Sciences Economiques, Sociales et Politiques (PhD thesis, Nouvelle série des thèses de doctorat, No. 127), 105 pp.

The author identifies three particularly serious problems when health care is organized in a market system: illness is unforeseeable; the health of some individuals affects the welfare of others close to them; and supply and demand are not in equilibrium. These problems are considered in the context of general equilibrium theory. Policies to correct market failure are evaluated formally using general equilibrium theory. The author distinguishes between social security policies, of which prices and contribution rates are typical instruments, and public health care policies, which, he demonstrates, require much more precise instruments. Finally, some techniques applied to the organization of health care in Belgium are compared with theoretically optimal solutions. Concrete reforms in several areas are proposed.

26 Ehrlich, D.A. (ed.) (1975) *The Health Care Cost Explosion: Which Way Now?*, Berne: Hans Huber Verlag, 250 pp.

An international conference at the Henry Dunant Institute in Geneva, in 1974, brought together health officials of Western countries with diverse systems but common problems; representatives of the World Health Organization and of the principal caring professions; economists, sociologists, and other health services researchers; and experts from the pharmaceutical industry. The conference was intended to improve communication among these parties and to gain new insights into the problem of increasing health care costs. The discussions and reports from countries revealed areas for further study of cost-containment measures, and the effects of recent strategies. However, no attempt was made to draw up specific recommendations. This book is an edited version of the proceedings. The nine survey papers are:

1. Klarman, H.E. 'The economic determinants of health care expenditures', pp. 7–17.
2. Maxwell, R. 'The case for intervention', pp. 18–28.
3. Hastings, J.E.F. 'Hospital costs: implications for health care funding from Canadian experience', pp. 59–66.
4. Rexed, B. 'How Sweden plans for the 1980s', pp. 67–82.
5. Schlögell, R. 'Physicians' services: responsibilities and economic consequences', pp. 101–5.
6. Flahault, D. 'The new auxiliaries and their economic consequences', pp. 106–10.
7. Siderius, P. 'European studies of drug consumption', pp. 139–48.
8. Nowotny, O.H. 'The economics of the pharmaceutical industry', pp. 149–52.
9. MacLeod, G.K. 'The new health consumerism: a study in four countries', pp. 175–82.

All the papers include extensive bibliographies and suggestions for future research.

See 28, 124, 279, 634, 317, 183, 387, 331, 151

27 KAMPER-JØRGENSEN, F. (1975) 'Economic evaluation in the health care sector' ('Økonomisk vurdering i sundhedssektoren'), *Nordisk Medicin*, **90**, 1, 2–4.

This leading article introduces a series of papers on health economics in future issues of the journal. The future growth of the health care sector is questioned, and the need for economic analysis is emphasized. The discussion centres on the need for consciousness of prices, costs, and setting priorities, both within the health sector and between the health and other sectors. It is recommended that economic data be included in medical research and analysis, in order to illustrate the economic consequences of medical developments, and that the existing information system be used to make medical personnel aware of prices and costs in daily preventive, diagnostic, and therapeutic work. Priority setting is seen as a fundamental political issue that economic analysis may help to clarify.

28 KLARMAN, H.E. (1975) 'The economic determinants of health care expenditures' in: EHRLICH, D.A. (ed.) *The Health Care Cost Explosion: Which Way Now?*, Berne: Hans Huber Verlag, 7–17.

This paper comments on the growing share of GNP devoted to health expenditures whatever the political regime (with a few exceptions), the measures (e.g., health insurance) that curtail the operation of market forces in the health services industry, and the alternative measures that are being sought in order to bring health care expenditures under control.
See 26

29 LEON, J. (1975) Health and Society (An Analysis and Forecast of the Interrelations Between Social Classes, the State of Health, and the Consumption of Medical Services) (*Santé et société (analyse et réflexion prospective sur les interrelations entre le cadre social, l'état de santé et les consommations de soins)*), Paris: Prospective et Santé Publique, 116 pp. (mimeographed document).

The concept of health embraces a variety of highly complex ideas about such different entities as the individual, the group, and society. The complexity of the concept increases when one tries to determine the causes of a deficient state of health. There are two major types of causes, whose effects are nevertheless interrelated: direct, mechanistic causes, among which heredity plays a part; and indirect causes due to the environment, among which consumer habits play a major role. For a long time the mechanistic causes were considered of primary importance. This, together with the fact that they are easier to verify, explains why so many studies have been devoted to them. After first listing the different factors affecting health status, and then exploring their interactions, the author suggests the outline of a model covering all of these interrelations.

30 LEVY, E., BUNGENER, M., DUMENIL, G., and FAGNANI, F. (1975) Economics of the Health Care System (*Economie du système de santé*), Paris: Editions Sandoz, and Dunod, 354 pp.

The authors analyse the economics of the health care system in terms of three main sub-systems. First, they discuss the meaning and measurement of states of health, in terms of morbidity and mortality, and the factors that determine the appearance and progress of disease. Second, they discuss the organization and supply of health services, with emphasis on the difficulty of defining output. Third, they analyse the mechanisms of financing health expenditure, including social security and insurance schemes. The final chapter synthesizes the dynamic interrelations between these sub-systems, which constitute the health care system.

31 Paret, H. (1975) Attempt at an Economic Analysis of the Health Care System — Its Socio-Economic Maladjustment (*Essai d'analyse économique du système de santé — Son inadaptation socio-économique*), Paris: Université de Paris II, Faculté de Droit et des Sciences Economiques (state doctorate), 460 pp. (mimeographed document).

Examines the functional adaptation of health care system structures to the needs of the wider socio-economic systems of post-war, developed, capitalist countries. It considers the response of the health care system to increasing socio-economic demands and pressures, and examines the specific causes for the maladjustments identified, particularly in terms of inadequate system coherence and rising costs. It concludes that these diminish both short-term adaptability and long-term viability.

32 Rosenberg, P. (1975) Possibilities for Health Service Reform in the Federal Republic of Germany (*Möglichkeiten der Reform des Gesundheitswesens in der Bundesrepublik Deutschland*), Göttingen: O. Schwartz Verlag (Kommission für wirtschaftlichen und sozialen Wandel, Vol. 48), 362 pp.

This comprehensive account deals with all aspects of health services in the Federal Republic of Germany. Its basis is a systematic analysis of the German literature published since 1965. The author offers a description of nearly all reform proposals concerning medical institutions, public and private health insurance, financing, and planning. Medical education and professional training are also included. Of particular interest is a bibliography (classified by author and by subject), which fills more than a hundred pages. This book offers, at the same time, a systematic introduction to the German health care system.

33 Triomphe, A. (1975) Medical Economics (*Economie médicale*), Paris: Heures de France, 215 pp.

This book outlines the principal economic concepts applied in the field of health. Following an introduction concerned with the current emergence of problems related to the increase in medical care costs and to the average consumption of health goods and services (Fr. 1,374 per person in 1974), the author describes the methods of analysis, including national accounting and social indicators. This is followed by a study of health and demographic indicators. Final chapters describe the diversity of health service suppliers, and the determinants of medical consumption, and discuss the value of health. The author concludes with the hope that the health care system will be reoriented 'through a transformation of life styles and collective behaviour, as well as of the technological battle against disease'.

34 WHO (1975) *Health Economics. Report on a WHO Inter-regional Seminar,* Geneva: World Health Organization (Public Health Papers, No. 64), 44 pp.

A summary of a 1973 WHO inter-regional seminar in Geneva, Switzerland. Contains an introductory chapter outlining the aims of health economics; a chapter on the macro aspects of health economics, discussing reasons for trends in health care costs, their containment and monitoring, and the economic and social benefits of health care; and a chapter on the micro aspects of health economics, examining the relevance of the production function concept to the delivery of health services, the role of incentives in promoting efficiency, and the use of economics in programme evaluation. Concludes with recommendations by the seminar participants.

1976

35 DONZÉ, W. (1976) 'Socio-political aspects of health in Geneva, 1965-1975' ('Aspects socio-politiques de la santé à Genève, 1965–1975') in: RIGONI, R. (ed.) Health Economics. Proceedings of a Workshop, Coppet, 4 October 1975 (*Economie de la santé. Compte rendu d'un colloque, Coppet, 4 octobre 1975*), Geneva: Sandoz Institute for Health and Socio-Economic Studies, 11–17.

Four major parameters influenced the enormous increase in hospital expenditure in Geneva during the ten-year period 1965–75: inflation, staff costs, the age structure of the population, and hospital management. The author comments on each of these parameters, on the future role of the physician, and on the relative priorities that need to be established between medical practice and research.
See 38

36 FEDERAL REPUBLIC OF GERMANY (1976) Social Report 1976, the Federal Republic of Germany (*Sozialbericht 1976, Bundesrepublik Deutschland*), Bonn–Bad Godesberg: Bundesministerium für Arbeit und Sozialordnung (Drucksache No. 252/76), 83 pp.

This comprehensive social report covers social policies and expenditures from 1972 to 1976. Part A addresses the entire spectrum of social policies, including social security and rehabilitation. Part B presents and analyses the social expenditure budget.

587 GULDIMANN, J. (1976) The Limits of the Welfare State (*Die Grenzen des Wohlfahrtsstaates*), Munich: Beck-Verlag, 179 pp.

37 Herder-Dorneich, P. (1976) Growth and Equilibrium in the Health Care System. The Cost Explosion in Statutory Health Insurance and its Control (*Wachstum und Gleichgewicht im Gesundheitswesen. Die Kostenexplosion in der gesetzlichen Krankenversicherung und ihre Steuerung*), Opladen: Westdeutscher Verlag, 215 pp.

This book is an introduction to health economics. Starting with the present problem of the cost explosion in the health care system, the author forecasts future developments and discusses guidelines for development. In part two, the health care system and its elements are discussed, and the relationships between the participants in the health care system are analysed. In conclusion, five maxims for a rational health care policy are derived.

518 Jönsson, B. (1976) *Cost–Benefit Analysis in Public Health and Medical Care*, Lund: University of Lund, Department of Economics (Lund Economic Studies, No. 12) and Stockholm: Institutet för socialmedicinsk ekonomi, 141 pp. Also published in Swedish: (1977) *Sjukvårdsekonomi — sociala lönsamhetskalkyler inom hälso- och sjukvården*, Stockholm: AWE/Gebers, 180 pp.

38 Rigoni, R. (ed.) (1976) Health Economics. Proceedings of a Workshop, Coppet, 4 October 1975 (*Economie de la santé. Compte rendu d'un colloque, Coppet, 4 octobre 1975*), Geneva: Sandoz Institute for Health and Socio-Economic Studies, 98 pp.

The proceedings of a workshop organized for members of the Faculty of Medicine at the University of Geneva. The first part presents four papers:

1. Donzé, W. 'Socio-political aspects of health in Geneva, 1965–1975', pp. 11–17.
2. Mahler, H. 'The application of economic techniques to health planning, and its limits', pp. 18–27.
3. Tschopp, P. 'The role of health economics in future medical research and practice', pp. 28–36.
4. Jolly, D. 'The teaching of health economics', pp. 37–47.

The second part introduces a one-year survey of the causes and consequences of hospitalization in the Geneva Cantonal Hospital (1,966 beds). Its purpose is to identify the interrelationships between several factors in hospital admissions: factors associated with the hospital itself; social, psycho-social, medical, and public health factors; factors related to teaching; and economic factors.
See 35, 763, 39, 194.

39 Tschopp, P. (1976) 'The role of health economics in future medical research and practice' ('Le rôle de l'économie de la santé dans la recherche et la pratique médicales de demain') in: Rigoni, R. (ed.) Health Economics, Proceedings of a Workshop, Coppet, 4 October 1975 (*Economie de la santé. Compte rendu d'un colloque, Coppet, 4 octobre 1975*), Geneva: Sandoz Institute for Health and Socio-Economic Studies, 28–36.

The author argues that medicine must learn to forgo certain things in order to become more productive. He describes the purpose and means of medical production, touches on the concepts of 'macrosphere' (the allocation of resources in medicine in general) and 'microsphere' (the doctor's practice, whether private or hospital-based), and stresses the importance of marginal analysis. The 'globalization' of medicine is essential: health can no longer be achieved by the 'biological road' alone; it also requires understanding and control of social, psycho-social, and economic influences.
See 38

40 Van Gemert, H.G. and Werner, F.J.M. (1976) 'The meaning of economies in the health care sector in light of the 1%-norm' ('De betekenis van bezuinigingen in de gezondheidszorg in het kader van de 1%-norm'), *Economisch-Statistische-Berichten*, **61**, 3052, 452–3.

The considerably lower rate of real national income growth to 1980, forecast by the Dutch Central Planning Office, implies that continuation of growth in public expenditure would result in a fall in real income for the active population. The government therefore proposed to restrain real growth of public expenditure to 1%, allowing an increase in real income for lower income groups without causing further inflation. This paper analyses the possibilities and consequences of cuts in health care expenditure. It appears that a sectoral structural policy is more appropriate than economies through an insurance policy.

1977

41 Aebi, H. and Frey, U. (eds) (1977) Swiss Health Policy Today and Tomorrow (*Schweizerische Gesundheitspolitik heute und morgen*), Berne: Hans Huber Verlag, 99 pp.

Six chapters outline the peculiarities of the Swiss health care system and cover such subjects as: cooperative federalism and the health system, the economic aspects of the medical act, health policies and training policies, and the relationship between Switzerland and the World Health Organization.

42 Beske, F. (1977) 'Our health care system at the crossroads' ('Unser Gesundheitswesen am Scheideweg'), *Pharma Dialog*, No. 51, 31 pp.

Analyses expected cost trends in the health sector and its implied share of income in the Federal Republic of Germany. Explains the causes underlying the rise in costs, including the increase in demand.

43 Economic and Social Institute of the German Trade Union Congress (1977) Social Policy and Self-Government. The Democratization of the Social State (*Sozialpolitik und Selbstverwaltung. Zur Demokratisierung des Sozialstaates*), Cologne: Bund-Verlag (Studien zur Wirtschafts- und Sozialforschung des Wirtschafts- und Sozialwissenschaftlichen Instituts des Deutschen Gewerkschaftsbundes, No. 35), 277 pp.

Self-government of social security institutions is to be seen, not as an organizational problem, but as part of the democratization of society. The life situation of the insured has changed tremendously, and with it the concept of health problems and risks. The health insurance fund cannot restrict its activities only to payment for curative medicine. Self-government as a 'counter-power' of citizens has to deal with many other problems, such as environmental issues, working conditions, life style, rehabilitation, and improvement of the situation of the aged and the poor. The responsibility for this should be given not to a centralized administration, but to self-governing health insurance funds, and to community-based groups embracing self-governing bodies and citizens' representatives.

44 France, Ministry of Health and Social Security (ed.) (1977) 'Seminar on health economics in France, Paris, 14–15 January 1977' ('Colloque Economie de la Santé en France, Paris, 14–15 janvier 1977'), *Economie et Santé* (Supplement to the *Bulletin des Statistiques de Santé et de Sécurité Sociale*), No. 7, 88 pp.

A collection of all the papers submitted at this seminar. These report on health economics research undertaken in the ministries, by national and private research bodies, in faculties of medicine and economics, and in hospitals, and on the training in health economics provided in various faculties of medicine and economics in France.

645 Gygi, P. and Henny, H. (1977) The Swiss Health Care System (*Le système suisse de santé — Das schweizerische Gesundheitswesen*), Berne: Hans Huber Verlag, 328 pp.

45 Jolly, D. with Jolly, C., and Tacier, P. (1977) Health Economics: a Selected and Annotated Bibliography. — France. A compendium by the Sandoz Institute for Health and Socio-Economic Studies (*Economie de la santé: Bibliographie choisie et annotée — France. Une synthèse de l'Institut Sandoz d'études en matière de santé et d'économie sociale*), Paris: Dunod, 247 pp.

This book, the first of its kind in France, contains 310 summaries of books, articles, doctoral theses, and unpublished mimeographed documents dealing with health economics in France, selected from those that have appeared between 1965 and 1976. It is an enlarged version of the French contribution to this bibliography and adopts the same system of classification, with the addition of a selection on medical sociology. Four indexes of authors, research centres, journals, and publishers cited are included.

717 KOCHER, G. (ed.) (1977) Cost Reduction in the Health Care System (*Kosteneindämmung im Gesundheitswesen*), Solothurn: Verlag Konkordat der Schweizerischen Krankenkassen, 162 pp.

46 PFLANZ, M. and GEISSLER, U. (1977) 'Rapid cost expansion in the health care system of the Federal Republic of Germany', *Preventive Medicine*, **6**, 2, 290–301.

In the early 1970s, German health care costs expanded at an unprecedented rate of almost 20% per annum, or roughly twice the growth rate of the GNP. The Federal Statistics Office estimated total expenditures on health care in 1972 (including sickness payments, training, education, and medical research) at 11.4% of the GNP, or approximately US $630 per capita per year. Worldwide trends, as well as national factors, were responsible for this cost expansion. National factors consist mainly of the introduction of new benefits such as cancer screening programmes into statutory health insurance, new legislation concerning hospital financing, the separation of hospital and ambulatory care, and the fee-for-service system in ambulatory care. In the Federal Republic of Germany, it is commonly believed that preventive medicine is one way to check rapid cost expansion. However, few data exist to uphold such an assumption. In 1966, free antenatal care, including laboratory examinations, was introduced into statutory health insurance, but in the first years after introducing the programme infant mortality increased or remained the same; only in 1973 did the rate fall. In 1971, screening programmes for the early detection of infantile diseases and cancer were added. Screening for cardiovascular and metabolic diseases has been discussed, but is still to be finally decided upon; however, owing to doubts about the effectiveness of the programmes, enthusiasm for such measures is now fading.

47 VILMAR, K. (1977) 'A limit to charges — or a limit to medicine' ('Grenze der Belastbarkeit – auch Grenze der Medizin'), *Deutsches Aerzteblatt*, No. 18, 1213–23.

The author discusses the factors underlying trends in health care costs, in the light of the federal government's attempt to regulate spending on statutory health insurance in the Federal Republic of Germany.

1978

48 Baldone, T. (1978) Health Economics. A Selected and Annotated Bibliography. Italy. (*Economia sanitaria. Bibliografia selezionata e commentata. Italia*), Rome: Il Pensiero Scientifico, 94 pp.

This book, the first of its kind to be published in Italy, contains 175 annotated summaries of books and articles on health economics that have appeared in Italy between 1965 and 1977. Many of the entries are represented in this bibliography, according to the same system of classification. Four indexes of authors, research centres, journals, and publishers cited are included.

1979

49 BARRAL, E. (1979) Health Economics: Facts and Figures (*Economie de la santé: faits et chiffres*), Paris: Dunod, 360 pp.

Contains a general review of the problems of health economics, with extensive information on France and other countries. Its six chapters cover: world health and the demand for health; medical demography and medical supply; drugs and the pharmaceutical industry; hospital problems; sickness insurance and social security; and the profitability of health expenditures. The author argues that the slight increase in life expectancy among women and the decrease among men (10.3 years for men aged 65 in 1963; 9.4 years in 1970) is explained, not by zero marginal productivity of health expenditures, but by the fact that the pathogenic life style in industrialized countries cancels out scientific progress. Every year, 360,000 persons are injured in road accidents and at work. Alcoholism causes 20,000 cases of cirrhosis of the liver annually; taking into account the morbidity it causes (accidents, mental illness, etc.), it ranks third among causes of death in France, after cardiovascular diseases and cancer. The same may be said of tobacco smoking (600 cigarettes per person in 1938 in France, 1,500 in 1974). To reform the organization of the medical profession or hospitals would be to treat the symptoms but not the causes. What is needed is comprehensive prevention.

II Demand and Need for Care

1. Demography, Morbidity

1969

50 Gilliand, P. (1969) Demographic Ageing and Hospital Planning (*Vieillissement démographique et planification hospitalière*), Lausanne: Département Cantonal de l'Intérieur, Service de la Santé Publique, 342 pp.

An ageing population increases the economic dependency ratio in general, and makes heavy demands on health services in particular. Part one of this study, based on the Canton of Vaud, Switzerland, develops this demographic phenomenon as the necessary basis for planning, relating population to production, consumption, needs, and objectives. Part two summarizes the supply and demand of hospital and medical services, and discusses distribution inequalities and other factors that affect the choice of objectives and health service strategies. A factorial analysis shows that, in Switzerland, demand is largely determined by supply. Part three examines general and psychiatric hospitalization in the Canton of Vaud in 1950–60 and 1966, and the effect of the ageing population. The detailed analysis covers utilization rates by sex, age, diagnosis, and length of stay. Part four analyses the needs of the elderly, including a survey of an urban elderly population. Part five synthesizes the preceding sections and discusses their integration in hospital planning and policy making, including assessment of cost and staff implications.
See 57, 770.

1970

51 Brunet, A., Brams, L., and Fagnani, F. (1970) 'Factor analysis of morbidity reported in a population survey' ('Analyse factorielle de la morbidité déclarée dans une enquête de population'), *Bulletin de l'Institut National de la Santé et de la Recherche Médicale*, **25**, 4, 853–84.

Factor analysis of data obtained in a survey of 1,500 families in a district in the department of Aisne, in France, during November 1966 to November 1967. Data were collected on socio-economic variables, and on variables characterizing health problems (e.g., number of illnesses, number of work absences). The results of the analysis bring out the relative importance of socio-economic variables in explaining health problems, and the way in which families use medical services to resolve them, in different age groups. The effect of socio-economic conditions is greater in extreme age groups (children and the elderly), and among inactive and dependent persons.

1973

422 MIZRAHI, A., MIZRAHI, A., and RÖSCH, G. (1973) 'A morbidity indicator' ('Un indicateur de morbidité'), *Consommation*, No. 3, 7–56.

1974

52 DEJOURS, C. (1974) Study of Morbidity in France on the Basis of a Survey of Medical Consumption in 1970 (*Etude de la morbidité en France à partir d'une enquête sur la consommation médicale en 1970*), Paris: Centre de Recherches et de Documentation sur la Consommation, 151 pp. (mimeographed document).

This study analyses the frequency, by age and sex, of illnesses reported in a representative sample survey of 23,000 individuals in France. The survey, undertaken in four successive periods of three months, gives an approximation of morbidity experienced in France during 1971. Tables give the breakdown, by age (11 age groups) and sex, of the number of illnesses on the first day of the survey, the number during the survey, the percentage occurring in each age group, and the number of items of pharmaceutical consumption corresponding to the number of acute and chronic illnesses reported. A detailed study of 22 classes of illness is included. A large number of tables and graphs are presented.
See 79, 80, 84, 89, 91, 106, 134, 143.

53 MIZRAHI, A., MIZRAHI, A., and SANDIER, S. (1974) 'Demographic factors and the increase in items of medical consumption' ('Les facteurs démographiques et la croissance des consommations médicales'), *Consommation*, No. 1, 27–73.

A study of the variation in medical consumption by age and sex. After showing that these variables are important factors in the differential use of medical care, an attempt is made to evaluate the extent to which they explain differences in the level or trend of medical consumption, in two populations with different demographic structures. The analysis is based on French and American data obtained from household surveys, and the national accounts (for the USA). In both countries the heaviest consumers are infants and the elderly and, to a lesser extent, women of child-bearing age. The relative importance of hospital services is increasing; admission rates vary considerably by age and sex, but precise observations are lacking in France. Medical services for non-hospitalized patients follow similar consumption curves in both countries, but the increase with respect to age among adults is greater in France. The system of admissions is different in the two countries, since Medicare gives better coverage for hospital than other services. It is argued that increases due to age should be taken into account in the study of consumption trends, and that statistical sources should be improved to make it possible to construct health accounts by age. Numerous graphs and tables, and a bibliography, are included.

753 POLDERMANS, J.D.G. (1974) 'Some remarks on the implications for future health care facility needs of the latest population forecast in 1973' ('Enige opmerkingen inzake de toekomstige behoefte aan enkele voorzieningen in de gezondheidzorg, mede aan de hand van de nieuwste bevolkingsprognose 1973'), *Tijdschrift voor Sociale Genees-kunde*, **52**, 20, 715-19; **52**, 21, 761-5; and **52**, 22, 833-8.

1975

54 HARNI, A.-L. (1975) 'Regional variations in the development of illness in Finland', *British Journal of Preventive and Social Medicine*, **29**, 4, 249–57.

Investigates the prevalence of morbidity causing work incapacity in the population of working age in Finland.

55 KJELDSEN, K. (1975) 'Evaluation of the impact of various diseases on mortality', *Bulletin of the World Health Organization*, **52**, 3, 369–75.

This study compares and evaluates methods for measuring the importance of various diseases from the point of view of their lethal effects and significance for life expectancy. Three methods of evaluation are used: the percentage of all deaths due to the disease (method A); the gain in life expectancy that would occur if the disease were eradicated as a cause of death (method B); and the change in the ratio between productive and non-productive groups that would result from eliminating the disease as a cause of death (method C). The analyses are based on the total number of deaths in Denmark in 1969 and 1971. According to (A), one-third of all deaths was caused by heart diseases, one-fourth by cancer, and one-tenth by stroke. The results of method (B) were in agreement with those of method (A): the greatest gain in life expectancy was obtained by eliminating heart diseases; cancer ranked second, and accidents third for men and fourth for women. Method (C) yielded contrasting results. The result of eliminating most diseases would be an increase in the proportion of persons of non-productive age. This was most marked for heart diseases. The most important exception to this rule was accidents: if these were eliminated, the distribution of the population in the productive and non-productive age groups would remain stable.

1976

56 De Kervasdoue, J. Billon, F., and Marcovich, A. (1976) The Production of Knowledge and Social Needs: the Case of Cancer and Lung Research in France (*La production des connaissances et les besoins sociaux: le cas des recherches sur le cancer et le poumon en France*), Paris: Ecole Polytechnique, Centre de Recherches en Gestion, 53 pp. (mimeographed document).

This work, presented on 28 June 1976 at the PAREX Congress in Vienna (PAREX: European association of research workers interested in scientific problems, founded by the Universities of Paris and Essex), analyses the relations between the social demand for medicine, as measured by morbidity and mortality statistics, and the size of the research effort, in the fields of cancer and respiratory diseases. Noting the absence of a quantitative relationship between mortality and/or morbidity and the number of research workers, and observing a qualitative difference between the kind of laboratories working in pneumology and those concerned with cancer, the authors attempt to explain these findings in terms of three hypotheses: economic, sociological, and historical and institutional. The latter appears to best explain the differences in the development of the two disciplines.

57 Gilliand, P. (ed.) (1976) Medical Demography in Switzerland, Public Health Care and Prospects 1900–1974–2000 (*Démographie médicale en Suisse, santé publique et prospective 1900–1974–2000*), Lausanne: Office de Statistique de l'Etat de Vaud, 290 pp.

This four-part analysis begins with statistics from 1900 to 1974 on: doctors,

medical students, hospital staff, certificates and diplomas granted, insured population, medical and hospital provision, consumption and expenditures, doctor provision rates by canton, and international comparisons. Part two considers likely prospects and projections for Switzerland, including life expectancy, mortality, and the implications of ageing. Part three examines the relationships between the nature of the medico-social security system, the economics of the health care sector, population and medical demography, and health. It is concluded that Switzerland faces an unprecedented increase in medical manpower density, doubling its present level by the year 2000. The scenario for 1990–2000 covers likely economic constraints, prevention and health maintenance, the distribution of curative services, and cultural and socio-economic adaptations, including employment and education policies. Finding no close parallel to the Swiss situation in other countries, the analysis emphasizes the increasing importance of economic imperatives, and the need for a flexible, innovative approach.
See 50, 770.

2. Human Capital/Investment Approach to the Demand for Health Care

1964

58 Mizrahi, A. and Mizrahi, A. (1964) 'A model of medical expenditures applied to survey data' ('Un modèle des dépenses médicales appliqué aux données d'une enquête'), *Consommation*, No. 1, 3–35.

This study investigates a model, developed on the basis of the 1960 French national survey, intended to isolate the relative effects on medical consumption of age, sex, and some socio-economic characteristics (income, size of household, type of insurance). The significant socio-economic variables are those expressing daily activity and the expenses associated with it: size of family for women, and socio-occupational category for men.

1965

59 Magdelaine, M., Pequignot, H., and Rösch, G. (1965) 'A mathematical model of the consumption of medical services' ('Un modèle mathématique de la consommation de soins médicaux'), *Presse Médicale*, **73**, 22, 1319–21.

French medical consumption was studied in 1960 by CREDOC–INSEE survey (Centre de Recherches et de Documentation sur la Consommation – Institut National de la Statistique et des Etudes Economiques). This paper explains the biological, psychological, and social hypotheses underlying a mathematical model developed from the survey data. The aim was to investigate the relationship between the known distribution of expenditures for medical services among the various categories of the population, the potential expenditure, and the threshold (the level at which the potential expenditure appears in the form of real consumption). Some preliminary results are reported, e.g., the effect of socio-economic characteristics of households on potential expenditure and threshold.

60 MIZRAHI, A. and MIZRAHI, A. (1965) 'A model of medical expenditures (simultaneous effects of two or more socio-economic characteristics)' ('Un modèle des dépenses médicales (effets simultanés de deux ou plusieurs caractères socio-économiques)'), *Consommation*, No. 1, 60–75.

Eliminating the effects of age and sex, the authors analyse the simultaneous effects on medical consumption of two or more socio-economic variables. The effect of household size is considerable among agricultural and manual workers, but very slight among non-manual workers. The effect of socio-occupational category is definitely greater in large families. The effect of urbanization appears to be independent of the other variables, and greater than expected. The effect of income is very slight, except among large, low-income families. The analysis reveals the existence of a group of persons belonging to large, agricultural, uninsured, and low-income families, whose consumption of medical services is seriously inadequate.

1967

557 BRENNA, A. (1967) 'Health care and economic development' ('Tutela della salute e sviluppo economico') in: ECONOMICS INSTITUTE, UNIVERSITA CATTOLICA DEL SACRO CUORE (ed.), World Economic Problems in the Light of *Populorum Progressio (I problemi dell'economia mondiale alla luce della* Populorum Progressio), Milan: Vita e Pensiero, 233–49.

61 SANDIER, S. (1967) 'The development of radiology — an example of the dissemination of a technique and a form of consumption' ('Le développement de la radiologie — exemple de diffusion d'une technique et d'une consommation'), *Consommation*, No. 4, 67–75.

This research into radiological consumption was initiated in 1965, when the consumption level already represented 0.3% of the total consumption of private individuals, 2.8% of total medical consumption, and 12.8% of expenditures for doctors' services; a twentyfold increase in volume since 1938. The study covered new ground in measuring the development and dissemination of a technical medical procedure over a period of time, in different parts of France and in other countries, and in attempting to evaluate the degree of risk associated with its use.

1969

62 Broyelle, J., Brams, L., Courtecuisse, N., Fagnani, F., Grumbach, E., Poisson, N., Sarfati, R., and Rabah, L. (1969) 'Study of the health needs of a population' ('Recherche sur les besoins de santé d'une population'), *Bulletin de l'Institut National de la Santé et de la Recherche Médicale*, **24**, 3, 27–34.

The purpose of this study is to determine the extent to which public health facilities are adapted to the needs of the population. The analysis is based on a survey of 1,500 families and their medico-social services in the district of Soissons (Aisne), France. In twelve weeks, 8,082 health problems (WHO classification) were reported among the 3,829 persons surveyed. Tables are presented, giving the categories of illnesses and the effect on the reported morbidity of living conditions, age, sex, and socio-occupational class. Finally, the means used to meet the needs of the population surveyed are analysed.

1972

63 Andersson, Å. (1972) 'Health care and social policy in the perspective of distribution theory' ('Hälsovård och socialpolitik i ett fördelningsteoretiskt perspektiv'), *Sosialøkonomen*, **27**, 1, 27–34.

The problems of the social and health care sectors are discussed in terms of the economic theories of distribution and human capital formation. The lack of information in some socio-economic groups concerning health problems is discussed and elucidated empirically. To deal with the distributional problem, a discriminatory price system is suggested for the health care sector, setting zero prices for the under-privileged and increasingly higher prices for well-informed and resource-rich consumers.

64 Destanne de Bernis, G. (1972) 'Is the notion of need in economic analysis necessarily unacceptable to physicians?' ('La notion de besoin en analyse économique est-elle nécessairement inacceptable pour les médecins?'), *Cahiers de Sociologie et de Démographie Médicales*, **12**, 3, 94–8.

This paper describes the difficulties involved in economic analysis of the concept of need, in political economy in general and in the field of health in particular. The author explains the different kinds of need in health and the different social, political, and psychological influences which determine whether or not a need is felt, whether or not it is expressed, and whether or not it results in medical consumption, particularly in view of the available supply of services. Emphasis is placed on the role of the medical profession in determining the actual need for services, knowledge of which is essential for planning purposes.

1973

65 Andersson, Å. (1973) 'A new policy of income and wealth distribution' ('En ny fördelningspolitik'), *Ekonomisk Debatt*, **1**, 2, 246–54.

A welfare distribution policy must take account of relative endowments of human, as well as physical and financial, capital. Health and knowledge constitute the two most important forms of human capital. Data from recent studies are presented, which demonstrate the unequal endowment of health and health information capital. The possibility of using a discriminatory price system to achieve equality is discussed.

66 International Centre for Social Gerontology (1973) Workshop on the Medical and Pharmaceutical Expenditures of the Elderly (*Colloque sur les dépenses médicales et pharmaceutiques des personnes âgées*), (organized with the assistance of the Centre de Recherches et de Documentation sur la Consommation), Paris: Centre International de Gérontologie Sociale, 172 pp. (mimeographed document).

A collection of reports prepared by health economists (particularly researchers of the Centre de Recherches et de Documentation sur la Consommation) and physicians, dealing with the following subjects: the share of medical consumption by the elderly in total expenditure; the share of medical consumption by the elderly in total medical consumption; social and economic determinants of medical consumption by the elderly; the consumption of pharmaceuticals by the elderly; the share of the elderly in total consumption of hospital services; the consumption of psychiatric services by the elderly; and the expenditure by the elderly on physical rehabilitation.

67 Roche, L. (ed.) (1973) Health Economics — The Trend in Biological Treatments (Documents of the first meeting of French medical economists, Lyon, March 1973) (*Economie de la santé — Evolution des actes en B (Actes de la première réunion d'économie médicale française, Lyon, Mars 1973)*), Paris: Masson (Collection de médecine légale et de toxicologie médicale), 214 pp.

The following problems are dealt with: the trend in biological treatments and their cost; the distribution of services and the cost of sickness; the price per day and hospital investments; the prevention of cardiovascular diseases and its economic aspects; the cost of abortion; improving the efficiency of information systems in a children's hospital; limiting the increase in hospital pharmaceutical consumption; the psychological, social, and economic aspects of X-ray diagnosis.

1974

68 Couder, B. and Sandier, S. (1974) 'Comparison between projections of the consumption of medical services made by the VIth Plan (1970–1975) and its recent trend (1969–1972) (the case of physicians' services)' ('Comparaison des projections faites par le VIe Plan (1970–1975) et de l'évolution récente (1969–1972) de la consommation de soins médicaux (exemple de soins de médecins)'), *Cahiers de Sociologie et de Démographie Médicales*, **14**, 1, 1–4.

Before forecasting social security expenditures under the VIIth French Plan, the authors compare the forecast consumption of medical services under the VIth Plan with its actual values during 1969–72. Only physicians' services, which accounted for 17% of all medical services in 1969, are considered. The expected annual rate of increase of each of the descriptive parameters of the consumption of physicians' services (the number of visits, consultations, etc.) is compared with the actual rate.

69 Couder, B. and Sandier, S. (1974) 'The consumption and production of medical radiology' ('La consommation et la production de radiologie médicale'), *Concours Médical*, **96**, 5, 753–61.

Radiological consumption is (with laboratory analysis) one of the fastest growing items of medical consumption in France, increasing at an annual rate of 10% over the period 1959–72. The authors analyse this phenomenon in detail, and examine some economic aspects of the production and consumption of medical radiology. In 1972, 28% of radiological procedures were done in public hospitals and 72% in the private sector. Radiologists (1,700 in number) administered 65% of all radiological procedures; the other main providers were gastro-enterologists (5%), pneumologists (3%), dentists (6%) and rheumatologists (3%). Numerous graphs are included, together with some European comparisons.

70 DURIEZ, M., FOULON, A., and MATTHYS, M. (1974) Trends in Final Medical Consumption 1950–1974 (Provisional Results) (*Evolution de la consommation médicale finale 1950–1974 (résultats provisoires)*), Paris: Centre de Recherches et de Documentation sur la Consommation, 34 pp. (mimeographed document).

Particular attention is given to the trends during 1960–74 in ambulatory and domiciliary services, the value and volume of the components of medical consumption, the structure of financing, and the relative increase in different services. The major observations include: a steady increase in medical consumption, both in value (14.5% per annum) and in volume (7.4% per annum); an increase in medical expenditure as a proportion of GNP, from 2.9% in 1950 to 6.2% in 1974; a constant trend, particularly since 1960–61, in the increasing importance of hospitalization in the health system (38% of health expenditure in 1950, 42.6% in 1974); an increasing share of social security in total financing, from 44.4% of medical consumption in 1950 to 69.4% in 1974.

71 DURIEZ, M., FOULON, A., and MATTHYS, M. (1974) National Medical Consumption (Estimates for 1971, 1972, 1973, and the Trend during 1970–1974) (*La consommation médicale nationale (évaluations 1971–72–73 — évolution 1970-1974)*), Paris: Centre de Recherches et de Documentation sur la Consommation, 34 pp. (mimeographed document).

Four aspects of national medical consumption in France are analysed, on the basis of national accounts statistics for 1971, 1972, and 1973: its relative importance in the economy as a whole, its financing, its structure, and its suppliers. A provisional estimate is made for 1974. Medical consumption rose from Fr. 903 per person in 1970 to Fr. 1,535 in 1974, an average annual increase of 15.2%. The corresponding increase in volume, estimated at 9% per annum, demonstrates the effect of price inflation on the increase in nominal expenditure. Medical consumption as a proportion of GNP increased from 5.6% in 1970 to 6.2% in 1973, and as a proportion of household expenditure from 9.7% to 10.3% over the same period. Social security financed 65.2% of national medical consumption in 1970, 67.1% in 1973, and 69.4% in 1974. Public financing (state plus social security) increased from 70.5% to 71.6% over the same period. The trend in the structure of medical services shows a continuing increase in hospital relative to ambulatory services.

72 GIBERT, F. and LETOURMY, A. (1974) Health, Environment, and Medical Consumption: Development and Estimation of a Model on the Basis of Mortality Statistics (*Santé, environnement, consommations médicales: un modèle et son estimation à partir des données de mortalité*), Paris: Centre de Recherche sur le Bien-être, 59 + 139 pp. (mimeographed document).

The proposed model is intended to help solve the problem of the overall effectiveness of health services. The model comprises two types of equation, expressing for a given population unit (a French department in 1968): the level of a health indicator as a function of medical consumption indicators (including GP consultations, hospital days, different types of services, pharmaceuticals), and environmental indicators describing life style (alcoholism, cigarette smoking, nutrition, housing, transport, work, social isolation) and the physical environment (pollution, urbanization, climate, industrialization); the level of each medical consumption indicator as a function of the health indicator, supply indicators (personnel and equipment), and other medical consumption indicators (e.g., the number of radiological consultations determining the choice of therapy). After considering the various possible representations of these variables characterizing the population of a department, the author concludes that health status is best expressed in terms of a comparative mortality rate, principally because of the non-availability, heterogeneity, or ambiguity of the other data.

73 MICHEL, C. (1974) 'General causes of the increase in health insurance expenditures for health services' ('Les causes générales de l'accroissement des dépenses de l'assurance maladie en matière de soins de santé'), *Droit Social*, No. 1, 57–64.

An analysis of factors underlying the increase in health expenditures, including the changing age composition of a population, the increase in living standards, and the increase in the supply of services. The author argues that medical progress is the fundamental cause of increased medical consumption and its cost, one manifestation of which is the increased cost of diagnosis and treatment. Data on the increase in health expenditure in several countries are presented. The author concludes that health policies need to be formulated that give increasing responsibility to public authorities.

74 Vaerness, K. (1974) 'Women's participation in the labour market and expenditure in the health and social welfare sectors' ('Kvinners yrkesaktivitet og utgifter i helse- og sosialsektoren'), *Sosialøkonomen*, **28**, 4, 11–16.

Unpaid work still plays an important role in care within the family. The increase in the number of women entering the labour market may, however, lead to an increase in the demand for care provided by the health and social services. As a result, an increase in health care expenditures may be expected, as women shift from working at home to employment in the regular labour market.

1975

75 Söderström, L. (1975) Activities and Welfare (*Aktiviteter och välfärd*), Lund: University of Lund, Department of Economics (Report 1975:7), 25 pp. Also: (1976) *Variable Human Capital and the Value of Time*, Lund: University of Lund, Department of Economics (Report 1976:4), 13 pp.

Using the theory of the allocation of time, developed by De Serpa, and the theory of variable human capital, formulated by Grossman, a mathematical model combining these approaches is formulated. An individual has a set of capabilities which constrain the number of activities that can be performed during a unit of time. These capabilities change over time owing to the ageing process, but can also be changed by different inputs of health and medical services. The individual is assumed to maximize a dynamic utility function, resulting in an optimal programme for consumption and shadow values for time and capability constraints. The author criticizes the common assumption that the value of time at work is (approximately) equal to the marginal wage. It is also necessary to take account of the direct utility and human capital components of the value of time used.

1977

76 Uhde, A.L. (1977) *On the Optimal Allocation of Resources to Health Care; Implications for Cost–Benefit Analysis*, Bergen: University of Bergen (Economic papers, No. 1), 241 pp. (mimeographed document).

The dissertation begins with a general introductory review of some important issues in health economics. In the following chapters, alternative macroeconomic models with two or three sectors are developed, to study optimal resource allocation using different dynamic optimization techniques. The results obtained from the macro-models are compared with conventional benefit–cost studies. Finally, the models are used to study the economic impact of a prospective health programme: mass screening for cervical cancer.

1978

650 RUTTEN, F.F.H. and HOOIJMANS, E. (1978) *Financing Medical Care and its Impact on Medical Consumption in the Netherlands*, Leiden: Rijksuniversiteit Leiden, Centrum voor Onderzoek van de Economie van de Publieke Sector (Report 77.03); Leidschendam: Ministerie van Volksgezondheid en Milieuhygiëne, 25 pp.

3. Demand and Need for Health Care

1967

77 BRASK, B.H. (1967) 'The need for hospital beds for psychotic children' ('Behovet for hospitalspladser til psykotiske børn'), *Ugeskrift for Læger*, **129**, 46, 1560–70.

This paper presents the results of a prevalence survey of chronic psychotic and borderline psychotic syndromes, commencing before the age of 10 years, in children under 15 years of age in the county of Århus, Denmark. It was found that 6–7 per 10,000 children required hospital admission for approximately six months, while 3–4 per 10,000 were considered to require a longer period of admission, averaging six years with a range of 2–12 years. On this basis, the need for beds for psychotic children is estimated at approximately one per 6,000 children, or 200 beds in the whole of Denmark, i.e., 4–5 times the existing number. It seems desirable that three-quarters of the beds be established in small hospital treatment homes, attached to larger departments for child psychiatry, this being the most suitable form of long-term treatment for most psychotic children.

1968

78 Brunet-Jailly, J. (1968) 'Some characteristics of medical consumption in the EEC countries' ('Quelques caractéristiques de la consommation médicale dans les pays de la CEE'), *Economie et Sociétés*, **2**, 11, 2343–76.

Analysis of a family budget survey, carried out in 1963–64 and covering approximately 42,000 households in the then six Common Market countries. The author demonstrates the existence of a relation between medical consumption and income in all of the countries, but its precise form varies between the countries. Differing organizational features determining the price of medical goods and services, and the initial and final expenditure of households, may help to account for this variation.

440 Fabre, F. and Grandmont, J.M. (1968) Early Detection of Cancer of the Cervix (*Le dépistage précoce du cancer du col de l'utérus*), Paris: Centre de Recherches Mathématiques pour la Planification, Vol. I, 78 pp. and Vol. II, 78 pp.

79 Guillot, C., Mizrahi, A., and Mizrahi, A. (1968) 1965–1966 Pilot Survey of Medical Services. Part 1: Methodological Results (*Enquête pilote 1965–1966 sur les soins médicaux. Fascicule 1: résultats méthodologiques*), Paris: Centre de Recherches et de Documentation sur la Consommation, 66 pp. (mimeographed document).

Explains the methodology of a random sample survey of 400 households in the Paris area, carried out over six months during 1965–66; the survey data were supplemented by information from social security files. The purposes of the survey were: to obtain accurate estimates of household medical consumption; to collect information on the reimbursements, consultations, and visits to physicians contracted to the social security scheme; and to verify certain household data. Numerous tables, sample questionnaire forms, and extracts from social security documents are included.
See 52, 80, 84, 89, 106. 134, 143.

80 Guillot, C., Mizrahi, A., Mizrahi, A., and Rösch, G. (1968) 1965–1966 Pilot Survey of Medical Services. Part 3: Morbidity and its Relationship to Use of Medical Services (*Enquête pilote 1965–1966 sur les soins médicaux. Fascicule 3: La morbidité et ses relations avec le recours aux soins*), Paris: Centre de Recherches et de Documentation sur la Consommation, 117 pp. (mimeographed document). Also:

(1971) 'Morbidity in a population and its relationship to use of medical services' ('La morbidité d'une population et ses relations avec les recours aux soins médicaux'), *Revue d'Epidémiologie, Médecine Sociale et Santé Publique*, **19**, 4, 311–51.

The main factor in the growth of medical consumption, as revealed by this household survey in Paris, is technical progress. Many alternative treatments and repeated consultations have become possible for any given type of service. Medical services have become more technical in character, illnesses are treated that formerly were not, the number of recognized illnesses has increased (through improved detection and availability of services), and the number of existing illnesses has increased owing to the survival of the chronically ill. This part of the report analyses the morbidity reported in the sample population by age and sex, disease classification and duration, resulting disability, and according to the treatment services utilized. An annex compares the survey data with those of the French national survey of 1960.
See 52, 79, 84, 89, 91, 106, 134, 143.

81 HYRENIUS, H. (1968) 'A new way of simulating illness' ('Ett nytt sätt att simulera sjukdom'), *Socialmedicinsk Tidskrift*, **45**, 9, 498–500.

The author describes the use of stochastic models, developed in demography and epidemiology, to construct simulation models of different types of diseases. Simulation models, it is argued, are necessary to describe the structure of disease, as a background for planning and economic analysis of medical care.

1969

82 BRAUER, E., HJERMIND, P., and MACKEPRANG, B. (1969) 'Medical requirements in the old people's town' ('Afpasset patientpleje i De gamles by'), *Ugeskrift for Læger*, **131**, 20, 893–902.

Requirements for diagnostic and therapeutic medical assistance are assessed in a cross-sectional analysis of 1,487 patients (971 females and 516 males) in the old people's town, in January–February 1967. First, approximately 7% of the patients required medical assistance for acute disease; there were no significant differences by age or sex. Second, 40% of the patients required medical assistance for chronic disease; this requirement did not vary with age among males, but it diminished with age among females; females required slightly more frequent assistance than males. Finally, the distribution of requirements by various disease groups and by five requirement categories are reviewed.

83 FOULON, A. (1969) Medical Consumption in the Paris Area (*La consommation médicale de la région parisienne*), Paris: Centre de Recherches et de Documentation sur la Consommation, 25 pp. (mimeographed document).

Presents preliminary estimates, derived from several sources, of the various components of medical consumption in the Paris area for 1965. Its two chapters analyse medical consumption by type of service, and the trend in consumption of technical procedures in public hospitals under the social security system during 1962–66.

84 GUILLOT, C., MIZRAHI, A., MIZRAHI, A., and VILLENEUVE, A. (1969) 1965–1966 Pilot Survey of Medical Services. Part 2: The Determinants of Medical Consumption (*Enquête pilote 1965–1966 sur les soins médicaux. Fascicule 2: Les facteurs conditionnant la consommation médicale*), Paris: Centre de Recherches et de Documentation sur la Consommation, 110 pp. (mimeographed document).

Of those sampled in the Paris household survey, 92% were covered by social insurance, 53% by private insurance, and 3% by none (the latter percentage increased with age: 18% of elderly men, and 23% of women aged over 70 years, were not covered). Average expenditure on non-hospital services during the survey was Fr. 137, distributed as follows: pharmacies Fr. 56, physicians Fr. 42, and dentists Fr. 20. Shares in total health care expenditure were unequally distributed: 40% of the sample accounted for 1% of the total, 10% for 50% of the total, and 1% for 15% of the total. Health care expenditure varied with age and sex. For example, the level of expenditure by individuals aged over 60 years was double that of individuals aged between 10 and 40 years. Aggregating all age groups, expenditure by women was 50% greater than that of men, but the structure of consumption was very different: for example, men were hospitalized more frequently and for longer periods than women. Socio-economic variables explained some of the consumption differentials: the low-income group 'under-consumed' by 15%; the large-household group 'under-consumed' by 35%; non-working persons consumed about 40% more than the upper professional classes; and persons without insurance coverage, mostly elderly persons, 'under-consumed' by 30%. In general, health care expenditure increased with the amount of coverage.
See 52, 79, 80, 89, 91, 106, 134.

85 KALIMO, E. (1969) Determinants of Medical Care Utilization (*Lääkintäpalvelusten käyttöön vaikuttavat tekijät*), Helsinki: The Social Insurance Institution, Research Institute for Social Security, 253 pp.

This report, based on a large sample survey carried out in 1964, investigates the reasons why persons seek care for illness in different ways. Multivariate techniques are used to identify the influence of different psychological, sociological, and economic factors. The study was carried out prior to the introduction of the health insurance scheme in Finland, and has since been followed up by studies after the reform.

86 MICHEL, C. (1969) The Medical Consumption of the French (*La consommation médicale du Français*), Paris: La Documentation Française (Notes et Etudes Documentaires, No. 3584), 55 pp.

A detailed study of medical consumption in France in 1969, based on data from the National Federation of Social Security Organizations. The author first discusses the definition of health, and then analyses total medical consumption, its relation to total household consumption, and the various components of medical consumption — surgical, radiological, hospital, dental, and pharmaceutical. Data on daily benefits paid during sickness absence are presented. The concluding chapter discusses the determinants of medical consumption, including socio-professional characteristics, income, type of insurance cover, and cost of medical services.

1970

87 DENMARK, GOVERNMENT OF (1970) Health Visiting. First Report of a Committee Appointed by the National Health Service of Denmark on Health Visiting and Home Nursing (*Sundhedsplejerskeinstitutionen, betænkning I*), Copenhagen: Statens Trykningskontor (Betænkning No. 573), 98 pp.

This report analyses the development of the existing system of health visiting in Denmark, and concludes that a compulsory system should be introduced. All counties should establish public health nursing agencies providing nursing services to meet the needs of children and others; particular importance is attached to cooperation with GPs. Relevant research and economic analysis are summarized. A five-page English summary is included. The proposed system was adopted in 1974.

88 FOULON, A. (1970) 'Health services in Sweden and France (1960–1967)' ('Les services médicaux en Suède et en France (1960–1967)'), *Consommation*, No. 4, 3–31.

This study compares health services in Sweden and France in terms of general demographic data, the organization of health services, health sector expenditure, and sources of finance during 1960–67. Several features emerge: supply of health services is greater in Sweden; direct intervention by public authorities is greater in Sweden, in both current and capital expenditure; facilities, particularly hospitals, play a larger part in total Swedish health expenditure; expenditure on health services is 50% greater in Sweden than in France; both countries experience a similar average rate of growth in total health care expenditure; the public sector share of total expenditure is increasing in both countries, but more rapidly in Sweden.

89 MIZRAHI, A. and MIZRAHI, A. (1970) 1965–1966 Pilot Survey of Medical Services. Part 4: An Indicator of Morbidity — Analysis of Risks of Death and Incapacity (*Enquête pilote 1965–1966 sur les soins médicaux. Fascicule 4: Un indicateur de morbidité — analyse des risques vitaux et d'incapacité*). Paris: Centre de Recherches et de Documentation sur la Consommation, 61 pp. (mimeographed document).

Part 4 of the analysis of the Paris household survey deals with a morbidity indicator applied to the 1,000 persons (400 households) sampled. The indicator is evaluated in two dimensions: the risk of death and the risk of incapacity (activity restriction). These two characteristics of an individual's pathological state are disaggregated into ordinal categories: five for the risk of death, and eight for incapacity. The study attempts to describe and measure the effect of demographic variables on morbidity, the trend in the use of different treatments, and the duration of confinement to bed. Analysis of the clientele of different medical services, according to the risks the patients confront, is considered a useful approach. The influence of age on morbidity is significant, but that of sex is more difficult to identify and interpret. Young subjects are clearly concentrated in classes of low risk and low incapacity; adults gradually move towards the high-risk and high-incapacity categories typically occupied by the elderly. The relation between the risk of death and the risk of incapacity, which is very high in children, tends to decrease with age.
See 52, 79, 80, 84, 91, 106, 134, 143.

90 PANNIER, R. (1970) Man – Medicine – Community — The Place of Medicine in Present Day Society (*Mens – Geneeskunde – Gemeenschap — De plaats van de geneeskunde in het huiding maatschappelijk bestel*), Brussels: Arscia uitgaven n.v., Presses académiques européennes, 466 pp.

Subjects dealt with in this book include: problems of public health care, the development of individual health care in Belgium (1952–67) and the EEC countries (1952–66), financial trends, the causes of increased expenditure on medical insurance, and the organization of health care. The author argues from financial considerations that health care should no longer be regarded as a primary need, and that the rapid rate of growth of health insurance, relative to national income, puts into question the validity of the concept of health insurance. The book concludes with data on the growth of medical care:

volume of nursing days, expenditure on medical services in Belgium and the EEC, medical consumption, the number of accidents, etc.

1971

91 Guillot, C., Mizrahi, A., and Mizrahi, A. (1971) 1965–1966 Pilot Survey of Medical Services. Part 5: Nature and Prices of Medical Consumption in the City (*Enquête pilote 1965–1966 sur les soins médicaux. Fascicule 5: Nature et prix des consommations médicales de ville*), Paris: Centre de Recherches et de Documentation sur la Consommation, 67 pp. (mimeographed document).

Part 5 of the analyses of the 1965–1966 Paris survey describes the medical services. Of all consultations with physicians, 70% were given by GPs, and almost half were in the patient's home; specialists practise primarily in their consulting rooms, hospitals, or dispensaries, and rarely in the patient's home. 80% of consultations were paid for in full by households and 14% were completely free. The cost of a consultation with a GP not involving additional services (e.g. X-ray) was Fr. 20 in the patient's home, and Fr. 13.50 elsewhere; the corresponding charges for specialists were Fr. 52 and Fr. 29. Additional services were required in one out of eight GP consultations, and one out of three specialist consultations. The average cost of a prescription made out by a GP was Fr. 36, and by a specialist Fr. 45. Of all auxiliary consultations, 96% were given by nurses and physiotherapists, and 93% were prescribed by a physician. Approximately 55% of nurses' visits and 8% of physiotherapeutic treatments were paid in full by households; the remainder involved no charge to the household. 61% of nurses' work was performed in the patient's home, while 72% of the work of physiotherapists was carried out in their consulting rooms.
See 52, 79, 80, 84, 89, 106, 134, 143.

92 SPRI (1971) Methods of Measuring Medical Care Consumption (*Metoder att mäta vådefterfrågan*), Stockholm: The Swedish Planning and Rationalization Institute of the Health and Social Services (SPRI Report 10/71), 35 pp. + appendix 61 pp.

In order to facilitate prediction of the need for medical care, SPRI has started to develop forecasting methods. This report describes the results of a study of medical care consumption in Östergötland county, in Sweden. Results are presented showing how resources are utilized, and how medical care consumption differs with age and sex, at different types of clinics and in different types of health care.

1972

93 Brenna, A. and Lucioni, C. (1972) 'Health expenditures: primary care' ('Spesa sanitaria: la medicina di primo intervento'), *Economia Pubblica*, **2**, 5/6, 3–12.

This analysis of data on health service expenditure, provided by the major health insurance agencies, indicates a marked increase in the consumption of health services in Italy during 1966–70, both in absolute terms and relative to national income and public expenditure as a whole. The authors attribute this increase primarily to an increase in unit costs, and to the growth in demand for health services. In view of the key role of GPs in transforming health needs into effective demand for health services, the authors argue that expenditure on health services could be contained if GPs attempted to select cases in need of first- or second-level care.

94 Couder, B., Rösch, G., and Sandier, S. (1972) 'The consumption of medical services will continue to increase rapidly' ('La consommation de services médicaux continuera à croître rapidement'), *Economie et Statistique*, No. 37, 3–19.

Summary of a CREDOC (Centre de Recherches et de Documentation sur la Consommation) study for the Health Committee of the VIth Plan in France. The authors analyse the increase in medical consumption in terms of the relative increase in hospital services, their cost, and medical services for ambulatory and home patients. The analysis emphasizes the dependence of the health care sector on public policy and financing, the complexity of the health services system, and the problem of optimal resource allocation to different services within the sector.

308 Denmark, Government of (1972) Home Nursing. Second Report of a Committee Appointed by the National Health Services on Health Visiting and Home Nursing (*Hjemmesygeplejen, betækning II*), Copenhagen: Statens Trykningskontor (Betænkning No. 648), 147 pp.

95 Denmark, Government of (1972) Maternity Care (*Fødselshjælpens tilrettelæggelse*), Copenhagen: Statens Trykningskontor (Betænkning No. 633), 90 pp.

This report analyses the existing Danish maternity care system, composed mainly of private midwives, private GPs, and public hospitals. It is recommended that: the counties assume overall responsibility for the system within a five-year planning framework; midwives become public employees and be grouped into 'midwifery centres'; and deliveries be institutionalized.

Economic and other effects of the proposed system, which was later implemented, are analysed.

96 HOLST, E. and SCOCOZZA, L. (1972) 'Utilization of general practitioners from a socio-medical standpoint, a sample survey among the adult population in Roskilde' ('Lægekontaktfrekvensen i socialmedicinsk belysning. Stikprøveundersøgelse blandt den voksne befolkning i Roskilde'), *Ugeskrift for Læger*, **134**, 22, 1187–94.

This utilization survey was based on a postal questionnaire sent in November 1969 to 1% of the adult population of Roskilde, in Denmark, selected by date of birth. The frequency of contact with GPs was higher among women without training or with a short school education; it was not related to type of health insurance, but was lower among respondents with annual incomes over D.Kr. 50,000. People who were unable to consult their GPs during working hours included 21% of persons paid weekly, but only 4% of those paid monthly. People who forfeited pay by consulting their GPs during working hours included 57% of employees paid weekly, but only 5% of those paid monthly (and officials). Of those sampled, 27% stated they had felt the need to consult their GPs but had not done so. The frequency of consultation by nine specified symptoms did not vary with conditions of employment or length of school education.

97 LETOURMY, A. (1972) 'Health, environment, and medical consumption' (Santé, environnement et consommation médicale'), *Revue Economique* (special number: Economie de la Santé), **27**, 3, 402–32.

The problem of evaluating the effectiveness of medical consumption is approached by the formulation and estimation of an econometric model. The model is constructed on the basis of simple socio-economic and epidemiological hypotheses, and is estimated with data from French departments in 1968, using the mortality rate as an indicator of health status. The estimated model assigns the major role in determining the mortality rate to life style and environment, and almost none to medical services. At the same time, medical consumption appears to be determined primarily by the availability of medical resources. Some arguable features of the approach are discussed, particularly the representation of health status by the mortality rate. The author concludes by advocating a broader conception of evaluating the effectiveness of health services, taking into account the results of the model, and suggests a new and less technical approach to health problems.

98 NATIONAL INSTITUTE FOR HEALTH AND MEDICAL RESEARCH (1972) Systematic Health Examinations (*Les examens systématiques de santé*) (Report of a French-Swedish seminar, Le Vésinet, 16–18 March 1971),

Paris: Institut National de la Santé et de la Recherche Médicale, 129 pp. (mimeographed document).

This booklet contains sixteen reports, by various authors. They emphasize the importance of primary prevention, health education, and the detection of high pathological risks using computerized systems rather than systematic health examinations. They recommend the systematic application of interdisciplinary cost-effectiveness and cost–benefit analyses in choosing intervention strategies.

99 SVANE, O. (1972) Assessment of the Needs for Care of the Elderly (*Vurderinger af ældres behov for pleje og omsorg*), Copenhagen: Socialforskningsinstituttet (Publication No. 56), Teknisk Forlag, 321 pp.

The need of the elderly for institutional places and for nursing and care in their own homes was assessed on the basis of interviews with 4,200 elderly people, in the capital and two large provincial towns, during 1967–69. Interviewers, GPs, and social welfare authorities also assessed the elderly's needs. About 10% of those aged 70 years and over were considered to need institutional placement. Of those aged over 70 years and living in their own homes, it was estimated that about 25% needed home help and about 2% home nursing. There were differences both in the assessments of the four types of assessor, and between the assessments of need in the five areas; the causes of these differences are analysed. The major conclusion is that the supply of welfare services by a municipality is of vital importance in assessing total need: an increase in supply will result in new groups of elderly people being considered to be in need.

100 VAN PRAAG, B.M.S. (1972) Development of a Macro-Model of a Health Care System (*Ontwikkeling van een macro-rekenmodel gezondheidszorgsysteem*), Leiden and Leidschendam: Rijksuniversiteit Leiden and Ministerie van Volksgezondheid en Milieuhygiëne, Bureau Lange Termijn Planning, 53 pp.

This report lists the possibilities and limitations of econometric analysis of the health care sector. The research objective, its framework, and its scope of application are discussed in turn. The final volume discusses a supply and demand model in detail, and presents an aggregate model of the health care sector. No empirical results are given.

1973

101 BEHETS-CAPPAERT, L. and VERMOST, L. (1973) Socio-cultural Determinants of Health and Illness Behaviour, Vol. I: A Review of the

Literature (*Socio-kulturele determinanten van ziekte- en gezondheids-gedrag*, Vol. I: *Een literaturanalyse*), Leuven: Katholieke Universiteit Leuven, Sociologisch Onderzoeksinstitut (Report 1973/4), 194 pp. (mimeographed document).

VERMOST, L. (1979) Determinants of Health Behaviour, Vol. II: Contribution to Preventive Cancer Research, An Empirical Research (*Determinanten van gezondheidsgedrag*, Vol. II: *Participie aan preventieve kankeropsporing, Een empirisch onderzoek*), Leuven: Katholieke Universiteit Leuven, Sociologisch Onderzoeksinstitut (Report 1978/1), approx. 270 pp.

The work investigates the socio-cultural factors determining illness behaviour and medical consumption in Belgium. Recourse to medical care is considered the ideal response to illness. But research indicates that medical and lay 'rationality' do not always coincide. This raises the question of the optimal use of health care, and thus the problem of differential illness behaviour (at the curative level) and health behaviour (at the preventive level), expressed in differential consumption behaviour (at both levels). Factors other than strictly pathological factors may account for this, certainly in the preventive area. This project is concerned with the social determinants of health behaviour, and in particular with participation in a preventive programme of cancer screening for women.

102 CHAPALAIN, M.-T. et al. (1973) 'The economic benefit of systematic detection of illness and handicaps in childhood and adolescence' ('L'intérêt économique des dépistages systématiques d'affections et de handicaps dans l'enfance et l'adolescence'), *Economie et Santé* (supplement to the *Bulletin des Statistiques de Santé et de Sécurité Sociale*), No. 4, 90 pp.

In 1969 and 1970, the French government implemented measures aimed at providing systematic health screening in early childhood, with emphasis on early detection of chronic illness and prevention of educational maladjustment (particularly disturbances in behaviour and physical development). The first part of the study evaluates the economics of detecting handicaps by health screening in early childhood; the benefits are compared with the cost of screening plus additional examinations. The second part attempts to show that the benefit of detection, at school age, of certain illnesses and maladjustments is sufficient to offset the cost of the school health system. The final part contains relevant legislation and regulations currently in force in France.

103 HUYGEN, F.J.A. and DE MELKER, R.A. (1973) 'Referral of patients by the family doctor' ('Over het verwijzen door de huisarts'), *Medisch Contact*, **28**, 46, 1299–302.

This paper analyses data on patient referrals and hospital admissions from the authors' practice, two other practices, and a local health insurance fund in Nijmegen (the Netherlands). 11.1% of fund patients were referred to specialists, compared with 24.6% and 22.9% in the two sets of practices; 13.7% of fund patients were referred to laboratory and X-ray departments, compared with 4.2% and 1.3%; and 4.5% of fund patients were admitted to hospital, compared with 6.7% and 8.6%. Analysis of insurance fund data for some 70 general practices showed a positive correlation between patient referral and admission rates.

104 LENOIR, C. and SANDIER S. (1973) Trends in the Structure of Medical Services for 1959–1972. The General System of Social Security and Health Insurance (*Evolution de la structure des soins médicaux 1959–1972. Régime général de Sécurité sociale, assurance maladie*), Paris: Centre de Recherches et de Documentation sur la Consommation, 85 pp. (mimeographed document).

The purposes of this study are to investigate the structure and trends in the components of medical consumption in France, and to relate the trend in health insurance expenditures to its various determinants. Two parts analyse recent trends between 1970 and 1972, and trends over a longer period (estimated nominal and real expenditure during 1959–72, known expenditure during 1968–72, and coverage by health insurance during 1968–72). An annex gives detailed health insurance data for 1971 and 1972. Observations include: a decrease in the rate of growth of medical consumption during 1970–72 compared with 1968–70, particularly for pharmaceuticals and hospital services, but not for 'technical' services; a change in the structure of medical services in favour of technical procedures; a change in the major role of the physician, from a supplier of services to a prescriber of drugs; and an increase in the relative importance of hospitalization in the structure of medical services.

105 LHERMITTE, F. and HATTON, F. (1973) Health Examinations: Definition, Basic Data, Present Situation (*Les examens de santé: définition, données de base, situation actuelle*), Paris: Haut-Comité Médical de la Sécurité Sociale (Report), 62 pp. (mimeographed document).

A critical review of the present state of French preventive medicine for various client groups and types of risk. It concludes that the largely separate programmes (for mothers and children, schoolchildren, workers, the military, blood donors, the elderly, etc.) would be more effective and economic under an integrated policy of prevention, with systematic evaluation using computerized information systems.

106 MIZRAHI, A. and MIZRAHI, A. (1973) 1965–1966 Pilot Survey of Medical Services. Part 6: Medical Consumption and Recognized Morbidity

(*Enquête pilote 1965–1966 sur les soins médicaux. Fascicule 6: Consommation médicale et morbidité ressentie*), Paris: Centre de Recherches et de Documentation sur la Consommation, 52 pp. (mimeographed document).

Part 6 of the analysis of the Paris pilot survey analyses reported and recognized morbidity by age, sex, and socio-economic variables, and investigates differential medical consumption in relation to recognized morbidity. Men and women of the same age, and experiencing similar morbidity, use medical services to a similar extent but of a different type: women make greater use of non-hospital services. On the other hand, the use of services in relation to given morbidity decreases systematically with age. Holding age and morbidity constant, considerable differences exist in medical consumption according to socio-economic class, size of family, educational attainment, and insurance coverage. Social inequalities are evident both in the recognition of morbidity, and in medical consumption in response to morbidity.
See 52, 79, 80, 84, 89, 91, 134, 143.

679 NYMAN, K. and KALIMO, E. (1973) *National Sickness Insurance and the Use of Physicians' Services in Finland*, Helsinki: The Social Insurance Institution, Research Institute for Social Security (E 76/1973), 13 pp.; *Social Science and Medicine*, **7**, 7, 541–53.

107 PRIMS, A. and QUAETHOVEN, P. (1973) 'The cost of medical and paramedical care. Research into, and analysis of, the factors determining the increase in cost of medical and paramedical care' ('Le coût des soins médicaux et para-médicaux. Recherche et analyse des facteurs qui déterminent l'accroissement du coût des soins médicaux et para-médicaux'), *Revue Belge de Sécurité Sociale*, **15**, 4, 433–540.

This survey identifies six factors, characterized by 77 parameters, that determine medical consumption: the health of the population; medico-technical developments (considered to be largely responsible for increasing consumption); the organization of health care; socio-economic variables; cultural/demographic variables, including the education of family heads, population age and sex, degree of urbanization, and migration; and behavioural variables. Analysis of the effectiveness and efficiency of medical organization raises questions about future trends in medical consumption.
See 126.

108 VAN PRAAG, B.M.S., VAN DER GAAG, J., and RUTTEN, F.F.H. (1973) Supply–Demand Relations in the Health Care Sector (a Preliminary Survey) (*Vraag–aanbod relaties in de sektor gezondheidszorg (eerste* *verkenning)*), Leiden: Rijksuniversiteit, Economisch Instituut, 52 pp.

This report presents an econometric analysis of supply of and demand for health services in the Netherlands, by hospital catchment area and by health insurance fund coverage area. The dependent variables are clinical consumption in general hospitals, referral of patients insured by health insurance funds, and specialist treatment. The explanatory variables are age structure, degree of urbanization, supply of medical goods and services, and fee scales. Extensive literature references are included.

1974

109 CHRISTIANSEN, U. (1974) 'Demand for emergency health care and regional systems for provision of supply' in: PERLMAN, M. (ed.) *The Economics of Health and Medical Care*, London: Macmillan, 248–71.

In 1971, a proposal for a new emergency care system for Greater Copenhagen (1.3 million inhabitants) was submitted to the local authorities in the area by a committee of experts. The proposed system would contain emergency wards with beds, centres for traumatic surgery, coronary care units, modern emergency ambulances, a central referral office having radio contact with all ambulances for the purpose of giving medical advice, and clinics for minor casualties. The proposal was based upon a casualty survey in the area during November 1968, covering all hospitals, to which 16,500 patients were admitted through the casualty departments. Extensive information was collected for each patient: identification; time, place, and type of accident; diagnosis; ambulance response and duration of journey. The proposal was evaluated by a model assigning patients to the new system, and a linear simulation model for the location and number of ambulances, based upon an evaluation of the value of the patient's time and his condition. The location and number of hospitals were determined by political decisions, dating back to the beginning of the 1960s.

110 LEBART, L., SANDIER, S., and TONNELLIER, F. (1974) 'Geographic aspects of the system of medical services' ('Aspects géographiques du système de soins médicaux'), *Consommation*, No. 4, 50 pp.

This study analyses data on 173 variables describing the supply of and demand for health services, the rate and causes of mortality, and the socio-economic environment in the French departments. The following conclusions emerge from the results: industrialization and a poor climate have an adverse effect on health; the supply of health services is an important determinant of medical consumption; admissions to public hospitals are closely related to morbidity, analysed on the basis of causes of death, while ambulatory services and private sector hospitalization are more related to the level of development of the department; the mortality rate is a poor indicator of the effectiveness of medical services, in view of the great regional variation in mortality rates; two kinds of substitution between medical services seem possible: private sector hospitalization could substitute for home visits, and the technical level of private sector medicine would vary inversely with the rate of admission to public hospitals.

111 LECOMTE, T. (1974) Medical Consultation: Production and Consumption. Based on the 1970 Survey of Medical Consumption (*Les séances de médecine: production et consommation. D'après l'enquête de 1970 sur les consommations médicales*), Paris: Centre de Recherches et de Documentation sur la Consommation, 63 pp. (mimeographed document).

Analyses the structure of the supply of and demand for medical consultations in France on the basis of the 1970 INSEE–CREDOC survey (Institut National de la Statistique et des Etudes Economiques — Centre de Recherches et de Documentation sur la Consommation). 73% of consultations are given by GPs, 27% by specialists; 32.5% occur in the home, 67.5% elsewhere. The most frequently consulted specialists are radiologists, ophthalmologists, ENT specialists, and paediatricians. Radiological consultations are most frequent among the elderly, and paediatric consultations most frequent among younger children. Of GP consultations, 43% occur in the patient's home, as compared with 4.4% of specialist consultations. More than 20% of all consultations involve some associated treatment: 13% for GPs and 43% for specialists, with 80% for cardiologists. The most frequent associated treatments are injections, vaccinations, nursing care, radioscopy, and electrocardiograms. The major reasons for consultation are cardiovascular pathology (11%), digestive pathology (10%), musculo-skeletal disorders (9%), and acute ENT pathology (9%). Half of all individuals seek a consultation of their own accord. Three-quarters of prescribed consultations are given by the physician himself; cardiologists, surgeons, and urologists depend on referrals. Of those questioned, 38% consulted a physician during the last three months of the survey, 32% a GP, and 12% a specialist. Age and sex are important determinants: the number of consultations is high among young children (particularly girls), decreases in adults, and rises again among the elderly. 10% of consumers consult a GP or specialist more than three times every three months.

112 LECOMTE, T., MIZRAHI, A., and MIZRAHI, A. (1974) 'Distribution of non-hospital medical consumption in the population in 1970' ('Diffusion des consommations médicales de ville dans la population en 1970'), *Consommation*, No. 3, 31–80.

An analysis of non-hospital medical consumption in 7,400 households representative of the population of France according to: level of social security coverage, level of education, occupation, sex, age, size of household, income, and region. The results suggest that non-hospital medical consumption is fairly evenly distributed between social classes, with respect to GP services, to nursing services and to pharmaceuticals, since it is generally accessible to the whole population. As the technical level of medical services increases, however, their distribution becomes less equitable and biased in favour of the higher social classes.

752 LEMPERS, F.B. (1974) A Health Care Model for the Netherlands (*Een model voor de gezondheidszorg in Nederland*), The Hague: Centraal Planbureau, 43 pp.

113 PUROLA, T., KALIMO, E., and NYMAN, K. (1974) *Health Services Use and Health Status under National Sickness Insurance*, Helsinki: The Social Insurance Institution, Research Institute for Social Security, 317 pp.

This report summarizes, in English, a number of studies undertaken by the Research Institute for Social Security. In 1964, a national health insurance scheme was introduced in Finland. A sample survey was carried out in 1964, before the reform, and repeated in 1968. This report concentrates on the results of the 1968 survey, and on comparisons between these and the 1964 results; it also contains a description of the health services system in Finland. The insurance scheme increased consumption, which was one of its political goals. There is little evidence that it increased perceived sickness, or the length of sickness episodes. The use of medical care increased mostly in the under-privileged groups.

114 VAN DER GAAG, J., RUTTEN, F.F.H., and VAN PRAAG, B.M.S. (1974) *Do Different Financing Systems Cause Different Demands in the Health Care Sector?*, Leiden: Rijksuniversiteit, Economisch Instituut (Report 74.01), 18 pp.

This report investigates two questions: whether comprehensive risk insurance implies equality of treatment between patients; and which instruments could substitute for the price mechanism in controlling health care expenditure. The first section describes the situation in the Netherlands. The second section defines six variables describing medical consumption, specifies the equations relating them to a set of exogenous variables, and presents the results.

115 VAN HEDDEGEM, P. (1974) 'Social security needs: a provisional inventory' ('Les besoins en matière de sécurité sociale: un inventaire provisoire'), *Revue Belge de Sécurité Sociale*, **16**, 9, 857–900.

The author provides a systematic survey of past investigations of social security needs. He then describes the different types of persons in need, and the nature of their health care needs.

1975

116 Boisen, E. (1975) 'The emergency medical service in Copenhagen in 1974. A pilot study in production analysis, with comments' ('Københavns laegevagt 1974. En kommenteret pilotstudie i produktionsanalyse'), *Ugeskrift for Læger*, **137**, 34, 1961–9.

The study describes emergency medical services in Copenhagen. It analyses 421 requests for home visits by the doctor on call, in terms of the reason for the request and of the distribution of patients by age, sex, and health insurance category. Most requests concerned children aged under one year, and women of child-bearing age in the non-paying insurance groups. The sex differential was attributable, not to sex-specific disease, but to the generally greater morbidity experienced by women. Men dominated only in cardiovascular disease. Purely medical problems comprised 70% of cases, while socio–medical problems, with which the doctor was not equipped to cope, were frequently present in the remainder. Purely medical problems were present in 97% of cases in the paying group.

117 Bouckaert, L. et al. (1975) Expensive Medicine? Economic Aspects of Health Care in Belgium (*Dure geneeskunde? Ekonomische aspekten van de gezondheidszorg in België*), Leuven: Werkgroep Alternatieve Ekonomie, 112 pp.

The author's distinguish between 'needs' and 'means' in health care and investigate, on the basis of a survey, the extent to which means are used below capacity or inefficiently, in Belgium. Paucity of data made their task difficult. Four themes are dealt with: supply and demand, price determination, financing, and alternatives.

118 Closon, J.P. (1975) 'Influence of national health insurance on the accessibility of care and on income distribution' ('Influence de l'assurance maladie invalidité sur l'accessibilité des soins et sur la distribution des revenus'), *Orientation Mutualiste*, **28**, 3–4, 186–207.

Compulsory health and disability insurance, quality requirements, restrictions on the practice of medicine, etc., modify the market mechanism in health care, on both the production and the consumption side. Analysis of a sample of 2,475 families from the same health insurance fund in the area of La Louvière

(Belgium) reveals that compulsory insurance affected the distribution of health care, and to some extent contributed to a redistribution of income. Families with higher and lower incomes make very different use of the different types of health care, particularly of hospital care. This suggests a need for medical education, preventive medicine, and diversification of services. A redirection of effort is inevitable, but its guidance requires more accurate information.

119 DJUKANOVIC, V. and MACH, E.P. (eds) (1975) *Alternative Approaches to Meeting Basic Health Needs in Developing Countries*. Geneva: World Health Organization (Non-Serial Publications), 116 pp.

This joint WHO/UNICEF study argues the need for radical change in the provision of health services, in order to meet basic health needs in developing countries. It identifies features of conventional health services that have impeded progress towards this basic objective, and presents a series of case studies of new approaches that have been introduced, either at national or project level. These examine: the health service systems in Bangladesh (including the Savar project and Jurain nutrition project), China, Cuba, Tanzania, and Venezuela (the 'simplified medicine programme'); the Ivanjica health programme, in Yugoslavia; the Jamkhed comprehensive rural health project, in India; the use of village health workers and trained traditional birth attendants in the Department of Maradi, Niger; Ayurvedic medicine in India; and the use of two-way radio in North-Western State, Nigeria. The study emphasizes the fundamental change in resource allocation and community involvement required by these new approaches, and concludes with recommendations to WHO and UNICEF. Annexes review WHO and UNICEF policies and illustrate simple, intermediate, and more advanced delivery systems.

120 ESCHER, M. and BEYERLE, F. (1975) Morbidity and Mortality Statistics for Switzerland (*Morbiditäts- und Mortalitätsstatistiken der Schweiz*), Aarau: Schweizerisches Krankenhausinstitut (Schriftenreihe No. 2), 117 pp.

This is a systematic compilation of morbidity and mortality statistics for Switzerland. The data from various sources were classified according to comparable criteria, for analysis and planning in the health care system. The many tables and graphs give information on mortality and morbidity currently available from federal and private insurance agencies, based on analysis of data from practising physicians and of data on hospitalization. Where possible, time-series data are also provided.

121 FESTEN, H. (1975) 'Feasibility aspects of cost containment in health care' ('Mogelijkheden en onmogelijkheden tot kostenbewaking in de gezondheidszorg'), *Acta Hospitalia*, **15**, 2, 84–109.

The author describes trends in the cost, resources, and utilization of health care in the Netherlands since World War II. He emphasizes the enormous regional differences within the Netherlands, and argues that these are largely explained by over-consumption, made possible by the health insurance financing mechanism, and by a lack of incentives to suppliers and consumers to search for the most economic alternative for specific health care problems. He rejects, as myths, price inelasticity of demand for health care, and the claim that patients do not determine demand. He advocates as possible measures to contain costs: reducing the bed/population ratio, strengthening ambulatory and primary care services, making adequate provisions to meet psychosomatic needs, and establishing health services on a regional and integrated basis, planned and guided by central authorities.

122 GOMMERS, A., DELIEGE, D., and LESLIE-GREGOIRE, M.L. (1975) Medico-Social Needs of an Aged Population (*Les besoins médico-sociaux d'une population âgée*), Brussels: Université de Louvain, Ecole de Santé Publique, 130 pp.

This book presents the methodology and results of an investigation into the health and socio-economic status of the elderly, and estimates the implied need for medical and social services and public utilities.

123 LENOIR, C. and SANDIER, S. (1975) 'The consumption of medical services in the French departments in 1973' ('La consommation des soins médicaux dans les départements français en 1973'), *Concours Médical*, **97**, 16, 2795–803.

A study of the regional distribution of medical consumption and its components in the departments of France. The consumption of medical services, estimated at Fr. 69 billion, or Fr. 1,300 per person, in 1973, varied by up to 3 times its mean value. The differential structure of consumption is analysed in terms of hospital services, and ambulatory and domiciliary services. Within the latter category, the authors distinguish between services requested by patients themselves, and services prescribed by physicians. Data concern either all individuals, or those covered by the social security system (72.4% of the population in 1973).

124 MAXWELL, R. (1975) 'The case for intervention' in: EHRLICH, D.A. (ed.) *The Health Care Cost Explosion: Which Way Now?*, Berne: Hans Huber Verlag, 18–28.

The author reviews the causes of increasing national health care expenditures, and argues that priorities should not be left to emerge from natural forces; there is a need and a justification for rational intervention in the allocation of health care sector resources.

See 26

125 NYMAN K. (1975) Dental Care Consumption and Dental Status (*Hammaslääkärin palvelusten käyttö ja hampaiden kunto*), Helsinki: The Social Insurance Institution, Research Institute for Social Security, 198 pp.

A study of the determinants of dental care consumption and dental status, based on survey data for the adult population of Finland. The primary aim of the survey was to collect basic data for health planning and decision making. On the basis of a theoretical model, an attempt was made, using multivariate analysis, to identify the relation between: consumption of dental care and social, economic, and demographic variables; age-specific levels of dental status and the same social variables; and the level and changes in dental status and the consumption of dental care.

126 PRIMS, A. and QUAETHOVEN, P. (1975) 'The cost of medical and paramedical care. Scientific research methods and an outline of the basic statistical material' ('Le coût des soins médicaux et paramédicaux. Méthode de recherche scientifique avec indication du matériel statistique de base'), *Revue Belge de Sécurité Sociale*, **17**, 5, 432-593 and **17**, 6–7, 609–69.

This third report on a large-scale research project describes the selection of 37 parameters to construct a model of medical consumption in Belgium. It considers the statistical data available for such a model and describes the area, covering 77,000 families near Mechelen, that was selected for a survey.
See 107.

127 SANDIER, S. and THAURONT, A. (1975) Comparisons of Medical Consumption in Three Population Groups: Agricultural Labourers; Farmers; Persons Protected by the General Social Security System (Preliminary Results) (*Comparaisons des consommations médicales pour trois populations: salariés agricoles; exploitants agricoles; personnes protégées par le régime général de Sécurité sociale (résultats préliminaires)*), Paris: Centre de Recherches et de Documentation sur la Consommation, 39 pp. (mimeographed document).

Medical consumption in these three French population groups is analysed in terms of its level and structure, sources of finance, and trends during 1965–73. All items of medical consumption, except GP visits, are lower among the agricultural groups than among persons covered by the social security system. The extent of the differential varies with the type of service: large for technical services and small for GP visits and pharmaceutical expenditure. However, the three groups share a common feature in the structure of consumption, in their large and increasing share of hospitalization and their decreasing share of pharmaceutical expenditure. Analysis of sources of finance shows that the rate of insurance coverage is highest for agricultural labourers and lowest for farmers.

128 Sandier S. and Thauront, A. (1975) Trends in Medical Consumption and its Structure during 1959–1974 (General System of Social Security — Health Insurance) (*Evolution de la consommation médicale et de ses structures 1959-1974 (Régime général de la Sécurité sociale — assurance maladie)*), Paris: Centre de Recherches et de Documentation sur la Consommation, 129 pp.

The six chapters deal with: scope and methodology; consumption of medical services in France in 1974; the trend in medical consumption; trends in the structure of medical consumption; distribution of diagnostic techniques and services; and the share of health insurance in medical consumption during 1968–74. Observations for 1974 include: medical consumption continued to increase in real terms; the structure of the increase in medical consumption reflected its previous trend, with a relative increase in hospitalizations and technical services; while the share of physicians in the value of production continued to decrease relative to other producers, averaging Fr. 28 (for consultations or visits) compared with Fr. 93 (Fr. 11 for laboratory analyses, Fr. 12 for auxiliary services, and Fr. 70 for pharmaceuticals), their importance is increasing as the process of medical care is becoming longer; the share of health insurance in medical consumption is increasing, with a shift in consumption toward services that carry no charge to the patient (88% in 1974).

129 Smets-Desmedt, C. (1975) Differential Medical Consumption. A Tentative Statistical Analysis (*La consommation médicale différencielle. Essai d'analyse statistique*), Brussels: Université de Louvain, Ecole de Santé Publique, 211 pp.

This survey analyses the rates of reimbursement of services supplied by the Christian and Socialist health insurance federations in Belgium. The population covered, 5.5 million, is broken down into categories of beneficiaries, according to their politico-religious affiliation and occupational status. Comparison of averages reveals that the volume of consumption varies between the Christian and Socialist federations, that the nature of services utilized differs between blue and white collar workers, and that the volume of medical consumption varies between areas. Regression analysis reveals a non-linear relation between the volume of services reimbursed and the volume of services offered (medical density index), which is not equally significant for all types of services and which varies according to the category of beneficiary. The results show that medical supply and consumption are generally lower in the Flemish than in the Walloon regions. Finally, the possibility of substitution between specialist and GP services is demonstrated in a group of Flemish regions.

1976

130 BERFENSTAM, R., BERG, B., and SMEDBY, B. (1976) Medical Care Utilization in the Tierp Area 1973 (*Sjukvårdskonsumtion i Tierpsområdet 1973*), Stockholm: The Swedish Planning and Rationalization Institute of the Health and Social Services (SPRI Report 4/76), 53 pp.

This study describes the contacts made by the population in the Tierp area of Sweden (21,000 inhabitants) with different kinds of health and medical care services, during April and May 1973. Different levels of care are studied, as well as different diagnostic groups. The results are compared with those of a similar study undertaken in 1971. No less than 46% of the population had some form of registered contact with health services during the period investigated. The proportion varied greatly with sex and age, the lowest proportion being observed for men aged 15–44 years, and the highest for women over 75 years of age.

131 BLOHMKE, M. (1976) 'How do utilization and demand for medical services change with increasing supply?' ('Wie ändern sich Inanspruchnahme und Bedarf an ärztlichen Leistungen durch den Patienten bei steigendem Angebot?'), *Der Praktische Arzt*, No. 21, 4281–8.

Defines the objective medical indicators for demand and utilization of medical services. Possibilities for meeting medical demand with the available financial means are discussed.

132 CENTRAL OFFICE FOR STATISTICS OF THE NETHERLANDS (1976) The Physically Handicapped in the Netherlands 1971/72. Part 3: Demographic and Physical Data; Special Facilities; Supply of Medical and Social Services (*Gehandicapten wel geteld; lichamelijk gehandicapten 1971/72*), The Hague: Centraal Bureau voor de Statistiek, 69 pp. + appendix 194 pp.

This comprehensive study contains six parts (of which only part 3 has been published). These are: (1) Basic data; (2) Justification for the survey; (3) Housing; (4) Care, general daily vital functions, public transport, leisure time; (5) Getting a job, being employed, retiring, working in one's own home, going to school/university, training, and financial situation; (6) General attitudes, opinions, and retrospective view.

133 DENMARK, GOVERNMENT OF (1976) Dental Health Status of the Danish Population and Dental Care (*Betænkning om befolkningens tandsundhedsstatus og tandlægevæsenet, afgivet af en af sundhedsstyrelsen nedsat*

embedsmandsgruppe verdrørende tandlægevæsenet), Copenhagen: Statens Trykningskontor (Betænkning No. 756), 81 pp.

The report of a working group established to analyse oral health status and the dental care system in Denmark. All relevant research is reviewed, including studies relating to need and demand, the effectiveness of the dental care system, and the economics of the dental care sector. A clear correlation between health and social class in the adult population (served by private dentists on a co-payment basis) is found. The system of public dental care clinics for children is evaluated, and found largely to eliminate class differentials and to be an efficient preventive measure. The total cost of dental care is estimated at D.Kr. 1.5 billion (or about 14% of total health expenditure in Denmark), of which about 60% is borne privately. The need for dental care is analysed and organizational changes are proposed. An extensive list of literature references is included.

194 May, A.R. (1976) *Mental Health Services in Europe. A Review of Data Collected in Response to a WHO Questionnaire*, Geneva: World Health Organization (Offset Publication, No. 23), 59 pp.

134 Mizrahi, A. and Mizrahi, A. (1976) The 1970 Survey of Medical Consumption (A Summary of Studies Undertaken by the CREDOC Division of Medical Economics on 31 December 1975) (*L'enquête de 1970 sur les consommations médicales (Une synthèse des travaux effectués par la Division d'Economie Médicale du CREDOC au 31.12.1975)*), Paris: Centre de Recherches et de Documentation sur la Consommation, 109 pp. (mimeographed document); *Consommation*, No. 2, 67 pp.

Describes four types of research undertaken on the basis of the 1970 INSEE–CREDOC survey (Institut National de la Statistique et des Etudes Economiques — Centre de Recherches et de Documentation sur la Consommation) in France, which followed a pilot survey carried out in 1965–66: analysis of the demographic and socio-economic determinants of medical consumption; analysis of the composition of medical consumption (pharmaceuticals, physicians' services, radiology, laboratory analyses, and hospitalization), and the illnesses responsible; analysis of places of delivery of medical services, methods of payment, and real prices; and detailed analysis of morbidity, including reported morbidity and illness leading to medical consumption or incapacity. The survey data also yielded information on the number of individuals covered by different social security and private insurance schemes in 1970.
See 52, 79, 80, 84, 89, 91, 106, 143.

417 NASCHOLD, F. (1976) 'Structural factors affecting the growth of cost in the health care system' ('Strukturelle Bestimmungsfaktoren für die Kostenentwicklung im Gesundheitswesen'), in: Yearbook for Critical Medicine (*Jahrbuch für kritische Medizin*), Vol. 1, Berlin: Argument-Verlag. 196-207.

135 PRIMS, A. and QUAETHOVEN, P. (1976) 'Analysis of factors determining the consumption of medical care' ('Analyse des facteurs qui déterminent la consommation des soins'), *Gestions Hospitalières*, No. 159, 761–74.

The amount of care required is determined by several factors, which may be summarized in five main groups: (1) Medical factors and the evolution of medical techniques. The physical or psychic need for medical assistance, and technical progress in response to this need, are obvious determining factors. (2) The organization of health services, in terms of the supply of doctors and hospitals and the system of health insurance. (3) Social and economic factors, including prices and incomes, the social and professional group involved, and the type of health insurance (which contributes to the determination of prices to the consumer). (4) Cultural and demographic factors, involving social, cultural, and demographic variables and age, sex, education, residential area, etc. (5) Behavioural factors, which transform the consciousness of need into an active search for help.

136 SCHWARZ, E. and Hansen, E.R. (1976) 'Utilization of dental services in the adult Danish population 1975' ('Udnyttelse of tandplejen i den voksene danske befolkning 1975'), *Community Dentistry and Oral Epidemiology*, **4**, 6, 221–6.

Lack of information on the dental behaviour of adults in Denmark has become a major problem in the national planning of dental services. The purpose of this study was to establish the pattern of utilization of dental services among adult Danes (aged 15 years and over). A three-stage cluster sampling design, covering the total adult population of Denmark, was used to draw a representative sample comprising 1,600 persons. Household interviews by trained interviewers were carried out. Of the adults interviewed, 58% reported yearly dental visits in the last five years, 32% had not seen a dentist or only when in pain, and 10% went irregularly. Differences according to place of residence, age, sex, occupation, and school dental care were found. Of those who had not seen a dentist: 63% reported bad teeth or were edentulous, with or without dentures; 10% reported fear; 9% had good teeth; and 5% reported economic difficulties. The most frequent treatments at the latest dental visit were cleaning and filling for the regular patients, and extractions and dentures for the non-regular patients. A multiple classification analysis revealed that the number of teeth was the strongest predictor for utilization of dental services, with the following other predictors in descending order: age, occupation, place of residence, economic status, sex, and school dental care. These variables explained 58% of the variation in utilization.

137 SPRI (1976) Total Medical Care Consumption in a Defined Population Group (*Total sjukvårdskonsumtion i en definierad befolkningsgrupp*), Stockholm: The Swedish Planning and Rationalization Institute of the Health and Social Services (SPRI Report 12/76), 49 pp.

As part of Malmöhus County Council's work on health care planning, the consumption of health care and the number of sickness registrations (i.e. applications for sickness benefits) among the 16,000 inhabitants of the Dalby medical district, outside Lund (Sweden), were studied for the period April 1973–March 1974; the results were compared with those of a similar study in 1969. The average annual number of visits to outpatient care facilities was 2.0 to physicians, 0.1 to the specially trained nurse for hypertension and diabetes, and 0.1 for health care subject to charge — a total of 2.2 visits. During the study period, 56% of the population visited physicians in outpatient care, approximately 10% made 6 or more visits, and this group accounted for nearly half of all visits. The 20–66 years age group averaged 0.8 sickness registrations and 9.0 sick registration days per inhabitant per year. The whole population averaged 0.1 admissions and 1.2 bed-days per year. As in outpatient care, the infectious diseases dominated the diagnosis pattern for persons under 20 years of age. In the age group 20–60 years, diseases of the digestive tract were responsible for most admissions and most bed-days. As expected, heart and circulatory diseases dominated in the group aged 60 and over. Of the average of 1.0 visits per inhabitant to the general hospital, it was estimated that about 20% could be dealt with by an expanded primary care sector.

138 Van Der Gaag, J., Van Praag, B.M.S., Rutten, F.F.H., and Van de Ven, W. (1976) *Aggregated Dynamic Demand Equations for Specialist Outpatient Medical Care*, Leiden: Rijksuniversiteit, Economisch Instituut (Report 76.06), 18 pp.

A system of aggregated dynamic demand equations for specialist health care is estimated from a time-series (13 years) of cross-section data (11 regions). A time-wise, auto-regressive, regionally correlated model and an error-component model are presented. The dependent variables are the number of patients entering the second level of medical care (hospital outpatient specialist care) and the amount of care per patient. The explanatory variables include: alternative levels of health care, socio-economic and demographic variables, and the type of insurance. The model is recursive, and formally equivalent to two sets of seemingly unrelated regressions. A multi-stage estimation procedure yields consistent estimates of the model. The estimation results show clear substitution possibilities between the different levels of care, and a significant effect of the type of insurance on health care demand.

1977

139 DAHLBERG, L. (1977) 'Why does the (Swedish) consumption of medical care grow? Outline of an answer' in: DAHLBERG, L., *Empirical Studies in Public Planning*, Gothenburg: University of Gothenburg, Department of Economics (Memorandum No. 67), 32 pp.

A system of demand functions for medical care in Sweden is estimated for the period 1960–73. It is first shown that population changes have had only a minor impact on demand, and that disposable income and consumer price (out-of-pocket price, time price in queues, sickness benefits, and wages) are the major explanatory variables. The demand effects of changes in these variables are investigated theoretically, and the relationships between the corresponding demand elasticities are stated. The expected relative sizes of the demand elasticities are determined and then empirically estimated. The findings suggest that the observed growth of health care consumption is explained mainly by a fall in out-of-pocket prices, and by improvements in sickness benefits. Some of the growth is explained by population changes and the rise in wage levels. The slight decrease in ordinary working time, and the increase in the time price of medical services, have worked in the opposite direction and counteracted the growth of health care consumption attributable to other variables.

140 FAURE, H., SANDIER, S., and TONNELLIER, F. (1977) Regional Analysis of the Relations Between the Supply and Consumption of Medical Services (the Private Sector) (*Analyse régionale des relations entre l'offre et la consommation de soins médicaux (secteur privé)*), Paris: Centre de Recherche pour l'Etude et l'Observation des Conditions de Vie, 174 pp.

An attempt to identify the extent to which medical consumption is related to the supply of physicians in the private sector, in France, in order to evaluate the possibility of improving the balance between supply and demand by controlling the regional distribution of physicians. The analysis is based on detailed data for 1974 and trends during 1971–75. The results confirm the existence of considerable regional inequalities in the consumption of physician services, particularly specialist services. It appears that GPs adjust their supply of services to match demand, and that a rapid increase in the supply of GPs would not significantly affect consumption. On the other hand, the consumption of specialist services is significantly and positively related to the supply of specialists. These relationships differ between regions: the findings suggest that the elasticity of consumption with respect to the supply of GPs is greater than zero in some regions, while in others the elasticity of consumption with respect to the supply of specialists is close to zero.

141 Henke, K.D. (1977) Public Health Expenditures and Distribution, A Contribution toward Measuring and Influencing Group-Specific Welfare in the Health Care Sector (*Öffentliche Gesundheitsausgaben und Verteilung. Ein Beitrag zur Messung und Beeinflussung des gruppenspezifischen Versorgungsniveaus im Gesundheitsbereich*), Göttingen: Vandenhoeck und Ruprecht, 242 pp.

Opens with a theoretical chapter on input–output relations in health services. Questions and elements of a production function for health are discussed, and a group-specific concept for measurement in the health care sector is developed. The author then analyses the empirical basis for his theoretical concept, and examines health status, service utilization, and other welfare elements, by income classes and regions of residence. Owing to the lack of German data, US material is often used instead. Proposals are made for measuring objectives of health policies. In the final chapter, policy actions are analysed with regard to the supply and utilization of health services, and for an incentive-oriented influence on health behaviour.

142 Kruse, U. (1977) 'The influence of external factors on the growth of costs in the health care system' ('Der Einfluss externer Faktoren auf die Kostenentwicklung im Gesundheitswesen'), *Soziale Sicherheit*, **26**, 3, 72–7.

The author stresses the significance of preventive medicine as a guide to behaviour for both the physician and the patient, and pays particular attention to the role of welfare associations.

143 Mizrahi, A. and Mizrahi, A. (1977) The Effect of Socio-Economic Factors on Hospitalization (*Influence des facteurs socio-économiques sur l'hospitalisation*), Paris: Centre de Recherche pour l'Etude et l'Observation des Conditions de Vie, 92 pp.; *Consommation*, No. 2, 5–58.

A study based on the 1970 INSEE-CREDOC survey (Institut National de la Statistique et des Etudes Economiques — Centre de Recherches et de Documentation sur la Consommation) of 7,392 households (23,196 individuals) representative of the French population. It first analyses variations in the value, quantity, and sector of hospitalization (total medical expenditure and the share of hospitalization; frequency of admission and number of days of hospitalization, per person per year, public and private) according to each of a set of socio-economic variables: income, size of household, and area of residence. It then analyses the joint effect of different pairs of the same variables. The results show that the consumption of hospital services varies considerably with socio-economic variables. In general, the lower socio-economic groups experience long hospital stays, mostly in public general hospitals, while the higher socio-economic groups experience short stays, largely in private clinics. For example, the mean length of stay for the lowest income group is 24 days; only 37% of these stays occur in private clinics. On the other hand, the mean hospital stay is only 13 days for the highest income group, 61% of stays taking place in private clinics. Moreover, within both the public and private sectors the length of stay is always shorter for the higher socio-economic groups. This contrast, between hospitalization in the higher and lower socio-economic groups, is associated with a significant decrease in the total volume of hospitalization, measured in terms of expenditure or number of days, as living conditions improve; such hospital services appear to substitute for ambulatory and domiciliary services among the lower socio-economic groups, given that total medical expenditure varies little with living standards.

See 52, 79, 80, 84, 89, 91, 106, 134, 143.

144 VALKONEN, T. and NOTKOLA, V. (1977) *Influence of socioeconomic and other factors on the geographic variation of mortality in Finland, Sweden and Norway*, Helsinki: University of Helsinki, Department of Sociology (Research Report No. 105), 30 pp.

Attempts to identify the most important determinants of geographic variations in mortality. The standard of living is an important determinant of the mortality level; genetic and cultural factors may also be relevant explanatory variables.

1978

145 VAN DER GAAG, J. (1978) *An Econometric Analysis of the Dutch Health Care System*, Leiden: Rijksuniversiteit, Economisch Instituut (PhD thesis), 180 pp.

The purpose of this monograph is to build an econometric model of the Dutch health care system, with special emphasis on the interrelations between the different levels of medical care provided. After a short review of the relevant literature in Chapter 2, and a description of the Dutch health care system in Chapter 3, the consumption of primary health care is analysed in Chapter 4 using data on some 10,000 patients from a group practice in Ommoord,

Rotterdam. Chapters 5–8 analyse the development of medical care consumption in the 70% of the Dutch population that is publicly insured. Using data per province, covering the period 1960–72, a block-recursive, six-equation model is developed and estimated. Specialized inpatient and outpatient care, and the costs of pharmaceutical treatment, are the endogenous variables. Chapter 9 uses this model to predict future developments during 1976–85, given certain assumptions about the exogenous variables. The final chapter discusses policy implications of the estimation results, and offers suggestions for further research.

III Supply of Health Services

1. Productivity, Price Indices

1970

307 THIEMEYER, T. (1970) 'Socio-political and economic problems of physicians' fees' ('Sozialpolitische und ökonomische Probleme ärztlicher Honorargestaltung'), *Sozialer Fortschritt,* **19**, 5–6, 101–5.

1971

146 FEDERATION OF SWEDISH COUNTY COUNCILS (1971) Hospital Productivity and its Determinants (*Lasarettens produktivitet och faktorer som påverkar denna*), Stockholm: Svenska Landstingsförbundet (EA-report 14/71), 81 pp.

Presents empirical estimates of productivity differences between 72 Swedish non-teaching hospitals. Numbers of visits, admissions, and bed-days are used as output measures; 28 of the hospitals deviated more than 10% from average productivity (cost). Regression analysis is used to explain cost differentials between hospitals, by such variables as density of doctors, average length of stay, proportion of long-term care, and drug consumption. Hospitals with higher than average productivity are shown to have relatively more beds in long-term care, and shorter than average length of stay. Hospitals with lower productivity (higher costs) have a higher density of doctors and a higher drug consumption. No evidence is found that unit costs are correlated with hospital size, nor that higher costs per bed-day decrease the average length of stay. Of the observed variation in costs, 45% is explained by differences in average length of stay, but failure to standardize for case-mix makes it difficult to interpret this result.

147 GUILLAUMONT, P. (1971) 'Health and production' ('Santé et production'), *Revue d'économie politique*, **81**, 1, 1–35.

Relations between health and production analysis are studied with reference to the problems of economic development. The tools of production analysis may be applied to health production; this leads to research into health indicators and into relations between health factors (substitutability and complementarity). Different criteria of medical efficiency, as well as the way they are used, are indicated. Then the place of health in production is analysed. Production functions do not usually include health among production factors. Health can, in fact, be introduced, either as a specific factor or by way of other factors; in view of this, various hypotheses are suggested, according to the level of development. After a few remarks on the economic value of health, some concepts concerning the economic efficiency of health are expounded, and related to the concepts already defined concerning medical efficiency. To conclude, the importance of relations between health, other human resources, and development is underlined.

1973

148 Brenna, A. (1973) 'Hospitals' ('Ospedali') in: Stefani, G. (ed.) Public Enterprises (*La produttività delle imprese pubbliche*), Milan: Franco Angeli, 419–64.

The author first outlines the institutional arrangement of public hospitals within the Italian health care system. He then attempts to define the concept of physical productivity for use in hospital management; to formulate a practicable method for calculating productivity so defined; to test this method for several hospitals and to evaluate its validity and operational applicability; and, in light of the results, to make concrete proposals for establishing a mechanism for systematic measurement of hospital productivity in Italy.

1974

249 Coppini, G. (1974) 'Control of the productivity of hospital expenditure' ('Modalità di controllo della produttività della spesa sanitaria nel settore ospedaliero'), *I Problemi della Sicurezza Sociale*, **19**, 4, 431–56.

149 Frerichs, G. (1974) 'Reorganization of drug law and drug market' ('Zur Neuordnung des Arzneimittelrechts und des Arzneimittelmarktes'), *Pharma Dialog*, No. 34, 25 pp.

The author surveys the present situation in the drug market from producers through wholesalers to pharmacies. After considering the development of costs and marketing concessions, he offers suggestions for reorganizing the drug market.

1975

270 BRENNA, A. (1975) 'The economic aspects of the short stay' ('La degenza breve: aspetti economici'), *Rivista degli Ospedali*, **7**, 6, 370–4.

150 JÖNSSON, B. (1975) 'How do drugs influence the economy of the health care sector?' ('Vad betyder läkemedel för sjukvårdsekonomin?') *Svensk Farmaceutisk Tidskrift*, **79**, 12, 639–48.

Argues that health care planning tends to neglect the importance of patients' time, and the productivity contribution of drugs, in health care sector productivity. Productivity growth is commonly assumed to be very low in labour-intensive sectors such as health. Yet the introduction of new techniques, enabling substitution of drug therapy for expensive capital and labour inputs, can substantially increase health sector productivity, in the form of superior medical outcomes and/or lower costs of care.

151 MACLEOD, G.K. (1975) 'The new health consumerism: a study in four countries' in: EHRLICH, D.A. (ed.) *The Health Care Cost Explosion: Which Way Now?*, Berne: Hans Huber Verlag, 175–82.

The four countries selected for study were Denmark, Great Britain, the Federal Republic of Germany, and the USA; the former two governments with a high degree of centralization, and the latter two with strong federal-state relationships. The study identifies three phases of health care consumerism (direct, institutionalized, and indirect) and outlines the differences and similarities between the four countries.
See 26

152 TOMEAZZI, A. (1975) 'The difficulties of public expenditure control in the health sector' ('Sulle difficoltà di esercitare il controllo della spesa pubblica nel settore sanitario'), *Rivista Internazionale di Scienze Economiche e Commerciali*, **22**, 2, 193–9.

The author attempts to identify the factors responsible for the continuing increase in health sector expenditure, and to explain why it is so difficult to contain. The explanatory variables are of two types: factors that affect the overall demand for health services, and factors responsible for the continued increase of costs (particularly labour costs). The author attributes the difficulty of controlling health care expenditure to the difficulty of applying cost–benefit analysis to the health care sector. This is due both to structural factors (characteristics of the production of health services) and to socio-political factors (such as the attitudes of policy makers and health personnel, particularly doctors).

1976

37 Herder-Dorneich, P. (1976) Growth and Equilibrium in the Health Care System. The Cost Explosion in Statutory Health Insurance and its Control (*Wachstum und Gleichgewicht im Gesundheitswesen. Die Kostenexplosion in der Gesetzlichen Krankenversicherung und ihre Steuerung*), Opladen: Westdeutscher Verlag, 215 pp.

153 Herder-Dorneich, P. (1976) Systems analysis and system policy of drug supply ('Systemanalyse und Systempolitik der Arzneimittelversorgung'), *Pharma Dialog*, No. 45, 35 pp.

Using cybernetic or feedback theory, the author argues that inadequate control mechanisms are largely responsible for the various cost increases in areas such as drugs and hospital and ambulatory care. Suggestions are made to eliminate such inadequacies in specific areas.

154 Jonsson, M. (1976) 'Measuring health care' ('Att mäta sjukvård'), *Läkartidningen*, **73**, 23, 2189–92.

The author discusses different output and productivity related measures: average utilization, average treatment time, number of admissions per bed per year, and the proportion of empty beds. Productivity changes may be illustrated by combining these measures in monograms.

1977

717 Kocher, G. (ed.) (1977) Cost Reduction in the Health Care System (*Kosteneindämmung im Gesundheitswesen*), Solothurn: Verlag Konkordat der Schweizerischen Krankenkassen, 162 pp.

2. Manpower, Medical and Paramedical Demography, Training

1966

155 SANDIER, S. (1966) 'Estimate of medical needs on the basis of forecasts of the trend in demand' ('Estimation des besoins en médecins à partir des prévisions d'évolution de la demande', *Cahiers de Sociologie et de Démographie Médicales*, **6**, 2, 106–12.

Estimates the need for doctors on the basis of a sample survey of medical consumption and social security statistics. Presents a general model relating three parameters: the demand for medical services, the number of doctors, and the productivity of doctors.

1967

156 BUI-DANG-HA, D. and R. LEVY, D. (1967) 'Demographic structure and interval before specialization in some specialties' ('Structure démographique et intervalle de spécialisation dans quelques spécialités'), *Cahiers de Sociologie et de Démographie Médicales*, **7**, 1, 5–14.

A breakdown by age, sex, and length of time between qualifying as a doctor and qualifying as a specialist, in the following fields in France: anaesthesiology, cardiology, dermato-venereology, gastro-enterology, neuro-psychiatry, paediatrics, and rheumatology. Paediatrics and rheumatology have a relatively high proportion of female specialists (26% and 49.3%). All of the specialties manifest a decreasing time interval between qualifying as a doctor and as a specialist, reflecting a tendency to begin specialized study earlier.

1969

157 BUI-DANG-HA, D. (1969) 'The doctors' Europe' ('L'Europe des médecins'), *Cahiers de Sociologie et de Démographie Médicales*, **9**, 1, 76–84.

After noting the difficulties associated with inter-country comparisons, the author compares the medical density in several European countries. France, the Netherlands, and Great Britain share a similar density, which is far exceeded by Belgium and the Federal Republic of Germany, which in turn are exceeded by Italy.

158 Couder, B. and Rösch, G. (1969) 'Past, present, and future trends in the number of doctors in France, Europe, and the USA' ('Situation, évolution et perspectives des effectifs de médecins en France, dans les pays d'Europe et aux USA'), *Cahiers de Sociologie et de Démographie Médicales*, **9**, 2, 112–19.

Presents data on physician/population ratios in Europe and the USA during 1950–65, and on the trend in the annual number of new medical graduates per 100,000 population during 1955–65.

159 Quaethoven, P. (1969) 'The financial status of the hospital doctor in Germany, France, and the Netherlands' ('Het financieel statuut van de ziekenhuisgeneesheer in Duitsland, Frankrijk en Nederland'), *Acta Hospitalia*, **9**, 2, 122–63.

The financial status of the German hospital doctor depends on the category to which he belongs. In France, most health services are state-run; doctors practising in these services are salaried. Doctors working in teaching hospitals are paid both by the hospital and by the Ministry of National Education. All of these doctors are entitled to fees from (limited) private practice. The payment system in the Netherlands differs in the important role of the health insurance funds. Fees are charged per service and are usually paid directly by the insurance fund. Thus France uses a salary system, the Netherlands a fee-for-service system, and Germany a mixed system.

1970

160 Bui-Dang-Ha, D. (1970) 'The age structure of the French medical profession' ('La structure d'âge du corps médical français'), *Cahiers de Sociologie et de Démographie Médicales*, **10**, 3, 136–41.

The index relating the number of active physicians to the number of persons in the same age group in the population in France in 1970 was highest for the age group born between 1923 and 1927: 317 per 100,000.

161 Bui-Dang-Ha, D. and Laurent, G. (1970) 'Present structures of the medical profession' ('Structures actuelles de la profession médicale'), *Cahiers de Sociologie et de Démographie Médicales*, **10**, 3, 99–116.

An analysis of the structure of the medical profession in France in 1969. Of the 60,459 physicians studied, 7,461 were women and 20,904 were specialists. Observations include: the average age of female physicians is much lower than that of male physicians, and females are more inclined towards specialization than general practice.

162 FOULON, A. (1970) The Professional Earnings of Private Physicians According to Tax Revenue Data. Structure, Turnover, and Incomes in 1966 (*Les recettes professionnelles des médecins libéraux d'après les sources fiscales. Structure, chiffre d'affaires, revenus 1966*), Paris: Centre de Recherches et de Documentation sur la Consommation, 75 pp. (mimeographed document).

A comparative analysis of total and per capita earnings of physicians in France in 1966. Estimates are given of the value and structure of earnings, in terms of professional expenses, net income, and the number of services supplied, by category of practitioner.

163 R. LEVY, D. (1970) 'The medical situation' ('La conjoncture médicale'), *Cahiers de Sociologie et de Démographie Médicales*, **10**, 3, 117–35.

Analysis of the supply of physicians in France between 1966 and 1969, including the percentage of doctors contracted to the social security scheme (88.2% in 1969) and the increasing percentage of specialists (47.6% in 1969).

164 COSTARGENT, G. (1970-1971) Employment in the Health and Social Sector (*L'emploi dans le secteur sanitaire et social*), Paris: Université de Paris I, Panthéon-Sorbonne (PhD thesis), 111 pp. (mimeographed document).

In 1971, labour costs represented 60% of the total costs of health institutions and more than 89% of the cost of the social services in France. This work analyses the structure and conditions of employment in the health and social services sector.

1971

165 ANRYS, H. (1971) The Medical and Paramedical Professions in the Common Market. Fields of Activity, Access, Professional Rules, and the Major Ethical Problems of Our Time (*Les professions médicales et paramédicales dans le Marché Commun. Champ d'activité, accès, règles professionnelles, ainsi que les grands problèmes contemporains éthiques*), Brussels: Larcier, 762 pp.

An extensive work covering the original six member states of the Common Market. Its eight chapters describe: historical development, medical services, the medical profession, the quasi-medical professions (dentists and midwives), the paramedical professions, the role of the professional organizations in legislation and deontology, professional rules, and modern medicine. Each chapter surveys the situation in each member state and presents comparative statistics. It concludes with abstracts of several original texts, including the International code of medical ethics, the Charter of Hospital Doctors of the EEC, and the Italian code of deontology.

166 FOULON, A. and SANDIER, S. (1971) 'Economic study of the work of the physician' ('Etude économique de l'activité du médecin'), *Consommation*, No. 3, 27-83.

Physicians' services were valued at Fr. 6.4 billion, or 1% of GNP, in France in 1969; moreover, physicians play a fundamental role in determining the other components of medical consumption. These figures justified a detailed analysis of doctors contracted to the social security scheme (87% of all physicians, 93% of the total volume of physicians' services, and 81% of the total value of physicians' services in 1969) during the period 1962–69. The study analyses the level and structure of employment and output, price indices, productivity, professional resources, and nominal and real income.

167 ORENBUCH, J. and BALA-DOSSOGNE, M. (1971) Nursing Personnel, Career Profiles, Motivations, and Aspirations (*Le personnel de nursing, profils de carrière, motivations et aspirations*), Brussels: Université Libre de Bruxelles, Institut de Sociologie, 267 pp.

This survey defines the career of a registered nurse and investigates the development of the nursing career after qualification, the motivations underlying career choices, working conditions and nurses' attitudes towards them, and the nurse's role in the delivery of health care. It proposes measures to eliminate the current gap between supply and demand.

168 FAURE, H., GEORGE A., and ROCHEFORT, C. (1971–1974) Survey of the Behaviour of Private Physicians with Respect to Property (*Enquête sur les comportements patrimoniaux des médecins exerçant en pratique libérale*); Vol. I: Economic Functioning of the Offices of Private Physicians (*Fonctionnement économique des cabinets des médecins libéraux*), Paris: Centre de Recherche Economique sur l'Epargne, Centre de Recherches et de Documentation sur la Consommation, Confédération des Syndicats Médicaux Français (out of print document); Vol. II: Available Income — the Savings and Property of

Physicians (*Les revenus disponibles — l'épargne et le patrimoine des médecins*), Paris: Centre de Recherche Economique sur l'Epargne, Centre de Recherches et de Documentation sur la Consommation, Confédération des Syndicats Médicaux Français, 52 pp. (mimeographed document); Vol. III: Professional Activities — Structure of Property (*Les activités professionnelles — structures des patrimoines*), Paris: Centre de Recherche Economique sur l'Epargne, Centre de Recherches et de Documentation sur la Consommation, 86 pp. (mimeographed document).

These three volumes analyse the economic situation of French doctors in private practice. The analyses cover three main aspects: medical activities by type, working time, and number of patients; the expenses involved (postgraduate training, installation and equipment, professional and staff costs, taxes, household expenses, insurance, and provision for retirement); and income generated from fees and other sources. These income and expenditure patterns are examined over the doctors' working lives. The three volumes are supplemented by extensive tables.

739 WHO (1971) *Planning and Programming for Nursing Services*, Geneva: World Health Organization (Public Health Papers, No. 44), 123 pp.

1973

236 Duhart, J. and Charton-Brassard, J. (1973) 'Hospital reform and nursing care by medical prescription' (Réforme hospitalière et soins infirmiers sur ordonnance médicale'), *Revue Française de Sociologie* (special number on medical sociology), Vol. 14, 77–101.

169 Jolly, D. (1973) Continuous Medical Training and the Productivity of Human Investment in the Medical Practitioner (*La formation médicale continue et la rentabilité de l'investissement humain chez le praticien*), Paris: Université de Paris I, Panthéon-Sorbonne (PhD thesis), 240 pp. (mimeographed document).

The author reviews the availability of post-university training for doctors in France in 1972 (organized by volunteers and undertaken by only one third of all doctors) and in other countries (particularly the USA and the USSR), describes the different techniques for delivering such training, and analyses the reasons why doctors do or do not choose to undergo it. He proposes that post-university training should be organized and coordinated at national, regional, and local level, and made compulsory throughout the doctor's career: every doctor should be required to complete a certain number of continuous training units each year. He suggests that such training should be financed by the educational insurance funds provided for by the 1970 legislation concerning adult education. Finally, the author considers the social productivity of the proposed investment. A bibliography and a list of post-university training organizations in France in 1972 are included.

170 Orenbuch, J. and Lambert, S. (1973) The Supply of Nursing Personnel in Belgium. Recruitment and Abandonment of Careers. Motivations and Attitudes (*L'offre de personnel soignant en Belgique. Recrutement et abandons de la carrière. Motivations et attitudes*), Brussels: Université Libre de Bruxelles, Institut de Sociologie, 317 pp.

Analyses the supply of nursing personnel in the health sector in Belgium on the basis of a sample questionnaire survey that investigated the situations, motivations, and attitudes underlying the career options chosen. The survey also made it possible to construct career profiles.

1974

171 Brenna, A. (1974) 'Teaching health economics in medical schools' ('L' insegnamento di economia sanitaria nella facoltà di medicina'), *Rivista degli Ospedali*, **6**, 1, 39-46.

The author examines the importance of introducing health economics into medical schools, and then illustrates the aims of training in health economics, a possible curriculum for a health economics course, and methods of teaching. An appendix reports on relevant experience in England and France.

172 Bui-Dang-Ha, D. (1974) 'World trends in medical manpower, 1950-2000', *World Health Statistics Report*, **27**, 2, 84–108.

On the basis of observations for the period 1950–70, this paper projects future changes in medical manpower at both world and regional (Africa, Asia, Europe, and Latin America) level. Assuming a 'medium' future rate of population growth, it projects the rate of growth and implied absolute change in the number of physicians in each decade between 1970 and 2000. These projections are based on three alternative assumptions about the future rate of growth of the physician/population ratio (medical density): zero, constant at the 1960–70 rate, and changing over the projection period.

173 Cooreman, J. (1974) 'Private dental surgeons in France from 1966 to 1976' ('Les chirurgiens-dentistes libéraux en France de 1966 à 1976'), *Cahiers de Sociologie et de Démographie Médicales*, **14**, 2, 23–32.

The first part of the study analyses the number and age–sex structure of private dental surgeons in France between 1966 and 1976; the second part analyses entries into, and exits from, the profession. It concludes with a demographic forecast up to 1 January 1976.

174 Deliege, D. (1974) 'The medical profession in expansion. Consequences for the nation' ('Le corps médical en expansion. Conséquences pour la Nation'), *Revue Belge de Sécurité Sociale*, **16**, 5, 487–505.

Forecasts a 60% increase in Belgium's medical manpower, from 16,000 in 1973 to over 25,000 by 1985. Students and universities will face falling teaching standards, young doctors entering practice will face increasing competition, and the state and the public will face growing health sector expenses. Young doctors are advised to choose non-hospital careers, and more open, rational planning is advocated, based on need, together with an imaginative use of less costly, non-hospital strategies of care.

175 Kästli, S. (1974) 'Survey of the economic situation of licensed nursing personnel and of some other personnel in Swiss hospitals, 1972–1974' ('Enquête sur la situation économique du personnel infirmier diplômé et de quelques autres professions en milieu hospitalier suisse, 1972–1974'), *Revue Suisse des Infirmières*, **67**, 12, 441–5.

The first survey of its kind in Switzerland, undertaken by the Swiss association of licensed nurses. Notwithstanding the paucity of official Swiss statistics, the survey clearly demonstrates the existence of significant regional and professional disparities in the salaries of nursing and other qualified paramedical personnel.

176 Lenoir, C. and Sandier, S. (1974) 'Professional earnings of contract physicians' ('Ressources professionnelles des médecins conventionnés'), *Concours Médical*, **96**, 8, 1297–304.

The authors analyse the gross and net pre-tax earnings from private practice of physicians contracted to the social security scheme, and compare them with other occupational groups in France. In 1972 their average annual gross earnings were Fr. 182,400, representing an aggregate share of 14% of total medical consumption. Between 1966 and 1972, physicians' earnings increased at a slower rate than the general level; the still slower rate of growth of specialists' earnings reduced the absolute differential between the two groups.

177 Nijhuis, H. (1974) Model of Planning of Nurses' Work; General Overview of the Report regarding Future Health Services and Personnel Needs (*Planningsmodel over de voorspelling van de personeelsbehoefte een verpleegafdeling*), Eindhoven: Technische Hogeschool (Ziekenhuis Research Project, Report No. 11), 48 pp.

This report on planning nurses' work on the basis of patients' needs presents a method for teaching nurses to predict the duration of their work over both short (one day) and longer (one month) periods. The method is tested in three nursing departments in two hospitals. The test showed a probability of incorrect prediction between 0.001% and 8.5% in the different departments for the short period. Further research is recommended into the application of the method to daily reallocation of nursing personnel. The initial test of predictions for the one month period used the number of nursing days per group of operations; predictions were based on historical data and operations were grouped by different patient needs for nursing care. This approach did not yield reliable results.

410 Seffen, A. (1974) 'The income of doctors and incomes policy' ('Arzteinkommen und Honorarpolitik'), *Arbeit und Sozialpolitik*, **28**, 10, 359–64,

1975

178 Bartels, H. (1975) 'Health service occupations, 1974' ('Berufe des Gesundheitswesens 1974'), *Wirtschaft und Statistik*, No. 11, 735–7.

Statistical report for the Federal Republic of Germany indicating the availability of the various health professions in the different sectors for 1974: hospitals, ambulatory services, public health, and pharmaceutical services.

179 Bui-Dang-Ha, D. (1975) Specialization in the French Medical Profession (*La spécialisation dans la profession médicale française*), Paris: Centre de Sociologie et de Démographie Médicale, 224 pp. (mimeographed document).

This study was done for the Ministry of Public Health (Fougère Committee) in connection with the reform of medical studies under the directives of the European Economic Community. It reports on the successive stages in medical training and their implications for the supply of specialists. After defining the terms 'specialist' and 'consultant', which vary between countries, the paper attempts to quantify the extent of specialization, using the criteria applied by the Council of the Order of Physicians in granting the certificate of special studies, and analyses the statistical relationships between internship at university hospital centres and the process of specialization. (The French system now allows two options for specialist training: through the certificate of special studies, or by internship.) The key stages of the specialist training programme are then considered in more detail, and the intake of newcomers in 1954, 1959, 1964, and 1972 are used to examine supply trends by specialty. The paper concludes with policy and research recommendations.

180 Christensen, S.C. and Jørgensen, J. (1975) 'An account of employment of doctors in Denmark in November 1974' ('Opgørelse af lægernes beskæftigelse, november 1974'), *Ugeskrift for Læger*, **137**, 28, 1601–7.

The number of Danish doctors in November 1974 was calculated to be 11,275, an increase of 11% since November 1972. The number of doctors in general practice increased by 275 (12%) from 1972 to 1974. During the same period, the number of Danish doctors employed abroad rose from 850 to 1,150, of whom 550 were in Sweden. Within hospital services, the increase was greatest among doctors in subdivided and mixed hospitals, followed by larger hospitals with less than 800 beds, and was least in the large hospitals with more than 800 beds. In November 1974, there was one active doctor per 550 population, as compared with one doctor per 625 population in 1972, but there were large regional variations, from one doctor per 275 population in Copenhagen, to one per 950 in the County of Roskilde. From 1972 to 1974, the number of specialists recognized increased by 11% and the number of junior doctors, in trainee appointments for specialist education, increased by 170. This is considered to represent potential over-production of medical specialists.

181 Deliege, D. (1975) 'Mobility of health workers, consequences of the E.E.C. directives. Lecture for the 24th fellows' seminar of the American College of Hospital Administration, Brussels, 30 September 1975' in: *Health Services Systems in the E.E.C., Proceedings of the A.C.H.A. Seminar*, Washington, DC: US Department of Health, Education, and Welfare (No. HRA 76–638), 168–94 (mimeographed document).

An analysis of the directives of the European Economic Community concerning the opening of European frontiers, with comments on the probable consequences of these new regulations, especially for the migration of doctors.

182 Faure, H. and Sandier, S. (1975) Activity and Earnings of Private Medical Auxiliaries, 1969–1974 (*Activité et chiffre d'affaires des auxiliaires médicaux libéraux 1969–1974*), Paris: Centre de Recherches et de Documentation sur la Consommation, 75 pp. (mimeographed document).

This report analyses the level and structure of employment and earnings of private medical auxiliaries in France from 1969 to 1974. It estimates that in 1972 they included 12,900 nurses, 13,698 physiotherapists, 1,939 midwives, 1,893 chiropodists, and 1,350 speech therapists and orthoptists, and that they increased by 9.5% a year from 1967 to 1974. Total earnings increased by 18.5% annually from 1968 to 1974, or 10.4% adjusted for inflation. Volume of services increased by 12.1% annually. The report concludes that the number of orthoptists and speech therapists has increased rapidly, that physiotherapists have high gross earnings, and that the very rapid increase in spending for auxiliaries does not increase their purchasing power.

183 Flahault, D. (1975) 'The new auxiliaries and their economic consequences' in: Ehrlich, D.A. (ed.) *The Health Care Cost Explosion: Which Way Now?*, Berne: Hans Huber Verlag, 106-10.

Although highly qualified health personnel will always be in demand, there is a growing need for health auxiliaries, particularly (but not only) in developing countries. These can be divided into two categories: the multi-purpose type at the front line, such as the 'feldsher' or the barefoot doctor, and the specialized type, such as the 'measurers' who are needed in laboratories to assist the physician and his technicians. The author comments on the economic consequences of this new approach in health care.
See 26

184 Harichaux, M. (1975) The Payment of the Physician (*La rémunération du médecin*), Paris: Université de Paris II (state doctorate), Vol. I, 239 pp.; Vol. II, 518 pp. (mimeographed document).

In the first part the author discusses the characteristics of the main methods of payment of doctors, the development of these methods under the influence of social legislation, and the basis of the distinctions drawn between them. In the second part he discusses the advantages and disadvantages of the various methods.

185 Kaufmann, R. (1975) The Shortage of Nursing Personnel and Cost Expansion in the Health Care System (*Pflegepersonalknappheit und Kostenexpansion im Gesundheitswesen*), Aarau: Schweizerisches Krankenhausinstitut (Schriftenreihe No. 3), 178 pp.

Using a systems theory approach, the author analyses cause and effect relationships between the increase in hospital costs and the shortage of nursing personnel. Factors internal and external to the health care system are discussed, and control mechanisms are proposed both for hospital and for domiciliary care. Some of the proposals are formulated and tested by the Delphi method.

186 LAMBERT, S. (1975) Psychiatric Nursing Personnel, Vol. II: Demand for Personnel (*Le personnel soignant psychiatrique*, Vol. II: *La demande de personnel*), Brussels: Université Libre de Bruxelles, Institut de Sociologie, 125 pp.

Discusses the present problem of recruiting psychiatric nurses in the hospital sector in Belgium, and the virtual non-use of them outside the hospital sector. The roles of psychiatric nurses are studied in detail, with reference to the policy of restructuring the system of psychiatric care. The author then discusses the causes underlying the scarcity of psychiatric nurses: the special nature of psychiatric work, the difficulty of finding employment, prejudicial attitudes, the material and moral devaluation of the profession, and the poor organization of psychiatric hospitals. The final chapter considers possible measures to correct the scarcity of nurses.
See 188

187 MIZRAHI, A. and MIZRAHI, A. (1975) The Supply of Medical Services: Location and Density of Personnel (*L'offre de soins médicaux: implantation et densité des personnels*), Paris: Centre de Recherches et de Documentation sur la Consommation, 128 pp.

The authors analyze the number and accessibility of different suppliers of medical services in 161 communities in six major areas of France. The results show that the residents of 36% of the communities are unable to obtain the services of a GP locally. In the suburbs of the big cities the density of specialists is very low, compared with isolated towns of similar size. The most evenly distributed practitioners are GPs and non-hospital nurses. Dentists, midwives, and physiotherapists occupy an intermediate position. Specialists and hospital nurses are more highly concentrated in the big cities.

188 ORENBUCH, J. (1975) Psychiatric Nursing Personnel, Vol. I: Supply of Personnel, Recruitment and Career Structure, Motivations and Attitudes (*Le personnel soignant psychiatrique,* Vol. I: *L'offre de personnel, recrutement et profils de carrière, motivations et attitudes*), Brussels: Université Libre de Bruxelles, Institut de Sociologie, 347 pp.

The author identifies the potential supply of psychiatric nursing personnel, and investigates the career structure of the psychiatric nurse, the different types of job changes (permanent and temporary), and the important components of a career. Finally, he discusses the question of job satisfaction and attitudes.
See 186

189 STEPHAN, J.C. (1975) Essay on the Economic Role of the French Medical Unions. Concerning the Medical Service and its Value (*Essai sur le rôle* *économique des syndicats médicaux français. A propos de l'acte médical et de sa valeur*), Paris: Université de Paris I, Panthéon-Sorbonne, Librairie Arnette (PhD thesis), 234 pp.

Using data from the nineteenth century to the present, this study analyses the success of the French medical trade unions in defending the economic interests and status of physicians. It argues that the increasing trend for medical service costs to be borne by the state and other third party agencies will be paralleled by a tendency for the medical unions to conform to the model of skilled salaried workers' unions in general.

1976

190 DELIEGE, D. and LEROY, X. (1976) Medical Practice, its Conditions and Obligations (*L'exercice de la médecine, modalités et servitudes*), Leuven: Nauwelaerts, 138 pp.

Analyses the results of a survey of Belgian doctors' allocation of time: the amount of time they devote to different types of services, and the way they organize night and week-end duties. The hypothesis that the ratio of doctors to population is a poor indicator of medical supply was not confirmed. Although the number of hours worked by doctors varies greatly at the individual level, their overall level of activitiy does not vary regionally.

191 DELIEGE-ROTT, D., LIEVENS, J., and ZEEGERS-DOOREMAN, C. (1976) *Medical Doctors in the Nine Countries of the Common Market*, Brussels: CIACO, 335 pp.

A large comparative survey of the supply and earnings of doctors in Europe. Each chapter deals with one of the nine countries and includes: a review of the numbers and types of doctors, a survey of the various payment systems, an analysis of available data on the cost of doctors' services and an estimate of doctors' average earnings. The estimates are based on a variety of sources. The final estimates for the nine countries are converted into three European currencies and compared internationally. Using recent purchasing power parities, the conclusions are that: the level of earnings is lowest in Great Britain, 20%–40% higher in Ireland and Italy, 50%–100% higher in Belgium, France and Denmark, and 200%–250% higher in Luxembourg, Germany, and the Netherlands.

192 FRIIS-HASCHE, E., HOLMSTRUP, P., HØFFDING, J., JOHANNESEN, L., KJELDSEN, K., and SCHWARZ, E. (1976) 'Dental care in Denmark in 1974. I. The dentists'; '. . . II. The patients'; '. . . III. The treatments'

('Tandplejen i Danmark 1974. I. Tandlægerne'; '. . . II. Patienterne'; '. . . III. Behandlingerne'), *Tandlægebladet*, Vol. 79, 477–82; Vol. 80, 29–34, and 67–72.

These three papers analyse the results of a questionnaire survey of a representative 10% sample of all Danish dentists. The first part analyses the distribution of dentists according to sex, sector of employment (public or private), whether or not actively working, whether working in Denmark or abroad, number of years since graduation, and region of practice. The second part analyses all the patients seen on a given day by age, sex, place of residence, occupation, and time of visit (in or out of normal working hours). The final part analyses the dental services given to these patients by type and number, sector of treatment (public or private), and health insurance group

193 General Practitioners Organization (1976) 'Statistics on general practice as of 31 December 1975' ('Praksisoplysninger 31.XII.1975'), *Ugeskrift for Læger*, **138**, 3005–16.

Extensive data on GPs are given annually by the General Practitioners Organization. The distribution of the total number of GPs is analysed according to: age, sex, region, size of practice (number of patients), type of practice (group or single), average assistance per week by other personnel, and type of additional work (e.g. nursing home, children's institutions).

57 Gilliand, P. (ed.) (1976) Medical Demography in Switzerland, Public Health Care and Prospects, 1900–1974–2000 (*Démographie médicale en Suisse, santé publique et prospective 1900–1974–2000*), Lausanne: Office de Statistique de l'Etat de Vaud, 290 pp.

294 Hacquart, G. (1976) Economic Aspects of the Hospital Service Unit (*Aspects économiques de l'unité de soins hospitalière*). Paris: Editions Médicales et Universitaires (Collection Economie et Santé, No. 4), 336 pp.

194 Jolly, D. (1976) 'The teaching of health economics' ('L'enseignement de l'économie de la santé') in: Rigoni, R. (ed.) Health Economics, Proceedings of a Workshop, Coppett, 4 October 1975 (*Economie de la santé. Compte rendu d'un colloque, Coppet, 4 Octobre 1975*), Geneva: Sandoz Institute for Health and Socio-Economic Studies, 37-47.

The author, a physician with an economics PhD, emphasizes the need for better interdisciplinary communication to advance the progress of health economics, and argues the need to integrate a simple health economics course into the medical curriculum.
See 38

195 May, A.R. (1976) *Mental Health Services in Europe. A Review of Data Collected in Response to a WHO Questionnaire*, Geneva: World Health Organization (Offset Publication, No. 23), 59 pp.

The survey demonstrates the feasibility of conducting an international inquiry into the broad general aspects of the organization of manpower and material resources in mental health services. It points to the need to establish standard criteria and definitions applicable in all regions of WHO, and indicates that, to overcome the limitations of even well-developed national health information systems, certain apparently simple data can as yet be collected only at a local community level. What emerges is a series of imprecise yet recognizable patterns for the organization of services and the deployment of their resources, depending on the cultural, social and economic pressures that influenced their development. An investigation has been initiated by WHO in nine European countries into the operation of mental health services in small community areas, to collect more precise details about the distribution of various categories of staff and patients in the component parts of the service, and about the outcome of different treatment patterns in different patient groups. An important objective will be to establish norms and indicators of adequate acceptable service, and to evaluate the effectiveness of operational procedures. A practical result of the present survey has been the organization of an annual series of courses on the collection, interpretation, and application of mental health statistics, attended by psychiatrists, statisticians, and administrators, and designed to explore the use of statistics in monitoring and planning services. It is proposed that the material presented here be updated as appropriate, to determine the trends in development of mental health services over the next few years.

1977

645 Gygi, P. and Henny, H. (1977) The Swiss Health Care System (*Le système suisse de santé — Das schweizerische Gesundheitswesen*), Berne: Hans Huber Verlag, 328 pp.

196 Italian Federation of Regional Hospital Associations (ed.) (1977) Hospital Manpower and the Italian Health Reform *(Il personale ospedaliero nella riforma sanitaria)*, Rome: Federazione Italiana Associazioni Regionali Ospedaliere (Quaderni di *Ospedali d'Italia*), 201 pp.

The first part of this volume analyses hospital manpower in Italy according to size of hospital, function, and salary structure. The second part considers recent legislation concerning the Italian health system reform and its implications for the quantity and quality of hospital manpower.

3. Hospitals, Clinics, Stationary Care

1964

197 SPRANZI, A. (1964) Cost Variability (*La variabilità dei costi*), Milan: Antonio Giuffrè, 102 pp.

This book examines the relationship between costs and the efficiency of production in hospitals, using information obtained from a survey of Italian hospitals. Two major issues are analysed: the determination of the prices to be charged for the various hospital services provided, and the measurement of the efficiency of hospital production. To explain variability in costs between hospitals, and to evaluate productive efficiency, it is necessary to improve the collection of data on costs in hospitals, and to define appropriate units of output for specific hospital departments. These units should take into account the patterns of illness treated.

1965

198 EYSKENS, M. (1965) 'Principles of market analysis in the hospital sector' ('Elementen van markt-analyse in de sector van het ziekenhuis-wezen'), *Acta Hospitalia*, **5**, 4, 295–309.

Argues that the increasing tendency for hospital care to be removed from the free market, in the modern welfare state, needs to be taken into account in analysis of the supply of and demand for health care.

1966

199 GIRERD, R., GUERRE, J., PEQUIGNOT, H., and PORTOS, J.L. (1966) 'A systematic study of the patients attending hospital for a consultation' ('Etude systématique de la clientèle d'une consultation hospitalière'), *L'Hôpital et l'Aide Sociale à Paris*, **7**, 38, 231–48 and **7**, 40, 469–503.

The results of a survey of patients consulting at Broussais Hospital in Paris are presented in these articles. The first article analyses demographic and social characteristics of 3,258 patients and the pattern of their illnesses. Various aspects of hospital administration are then examined: the percentage of hospitalized patients, the number of consultations per patient, and relations with town doctors. The second article analyses the medical data of the survey. Since Broussais Hospital specializes in cardiology, particular attention is given to cardiovascular disorders, although tuberculosis, cancer, obesity, diabetes, and digestive diseases are also examined. Numerous tables show the distribution of illness by cause and by age and sex of patient.

1967

200 FRANCE, MINISTRY OF PUBLIC HEALTH, FORECASTING DIRECTORATE, INVESTMENT PROFITABILITY DIVISION (1967) Methods of Applying Cost–Benefit Analysis. The Treatment of Fractures in Two Wards of the Paris Public Assistance Service (*Notes sur les méthodes d'application de calculs coûts/avantages aux services hospitaliers. Exemple du traitement des fractures dans deux services de l'Assistance Publique de Paris*), Paris: Ministère de la Santé Publique, 64 pp. (mimeographed document).

After a description of research objectives and the general principles of cost–benefit analysis, a comparison is made of the treatment of leg fractures in the wards of two Paris hospitals, a general surgical ward of 120 beds and an orthopaedic surgical ward of 150 beds. The methodology of estimating costs of treatment is defined, and then cost estimates are made. The average cost of treatment is found to be lower in the orthopaedic ward. The patients' degree of invalidity and other non-economic factors are taken into consideration in assessing the benefits of treatment.

1968

599 FOULON, A. (1968–1969) The Economic Accounts of Public Hospitals, 1961–64 (*Les comptes économiques des hôpitaux publics 1961–1964*), Paris: Centre de Recherches et de Documentation sur la Consommation, Vol. I (1968), 67 pp.; Vol. II (1969), 95 pp. (mimeographed documents).

1969

201 CHALAVET, S. (1969) 'Hospitals and hospital planning' ('L'hôpital et la planification hospitalière') in: DEGARDIN, M. (ed.) '3rd national meeting of public hospitals, Paris, 17–21 November 1969, on hospitals in the nation' ('3e Assises nationales de l'hospitalisation publique, Paris, 17 au 21 novembre 1969, sur l'hôpital et la nation'), *Revue Hospitalière de France*, **33**, 225, 1449–78.

Report of the third national meeting on public hospitals, held in Paris in November 1969. After a definition of hospital planning, a survey is made of its use in France prior to 1966. The Vth National Plan (1965–1970) and the conclusions of the Committee on Health and Social Services are then discussed. Finally, three topics related to hospital planning are examined: the definition of general health policy, the definition and quantification of needs, and the definition of a specific policy.
See 202, 203

202 DEGARDIN, M. (ed.) (1969) '3rd national meeting of public hospitals, Paris, 17–21 November 1969, on hospitals in the nation' ('3e Assises nationales de l'hospitalisation publique, Paris, 17 au 21 novembre 1969, sur l'hôpital dans la nation'), *Revue Hospitalière de France*, **33**, 225, 1189–618.

In France, public hospitals are an important component of the health care system. In 1969, ten million patients were treated in their 500,000 beds. This report on a meeting devoted to public hospitals contains information on the following topics: national policy on hospitalization; hospitals and the patient; hospitals and the doctor; hospitals and education; hospitals in the national economy; hospital management; hospital planning; hospitals and psychiatry; rural hospitals; and institutions for the aged and for maladjusted children.
See 201, 203

203 DUNAND, J.P. and BRUNET-JAILLY, J. (1969) 'The hospital in the economy' ('L'hôpital dans l'espace économique') in: DEGARDIN, M. (ed.) '3rd national meeting of public hospitals, Paris, 17–21 November 1969, on hospitals in the nation' ('3e Assises nationales de l'hospitalisation publique, Paris, 17 au 21 novembre 1969, sur l'hôpital dans la nation'), *Revue Hospitalière de France*, **33**, 225, 1335–430.

In the first part of this report, prepared for the third national meeting on public hospitals, J.P. Dunand discusses economic aspects of hospital services: their supply and demand, their price structure, and their role in the economy as a whole. J. Brunet-Jailly then describes alternative means of integrating the hospital in the economy: first, through the use of market mechanisms and second, through rational planning of scarce resources. This report also discusses the problems of applying standard economic concepts to health activities, and the development of hospital economics.
See 201, 202

50 GILLIAND, P. (1969) Demographic Ageing and Hospital Planning (*Vieillissement démographique et planification hospitalière*), Lausanne: Département Cantonal de l'Intérieur, Service de la Santé Publique, 342 pp.

204 GROOT, L.M.J. (1969) 'Pricing hospital services in Belgium and the Netherlands' ('Tarifering van ziekenhuisdiensten in Belgie en Nederland'), *Acta Hospitalia*, **12**, 4, 323–49.

Compares the system of hospital pricing in Belgium and the Netherlands. Hospital price legislation represents only a part of legislation covering overall hospital organization in Belgium, while in the Netherlands it has been only the first step to such legislation. In Belgium, pricing regulations only apply to hospitals owned by the Ministry of Public Health, but in the Netherlands they cover all hospitals. In Belgium, the state subsidizes hospital costs in some cases; in the Netherlands costs must be fully recovered by hospital revenue. In Belgium, annual hospital price adjustment is based on the retail price index; in the Netherlands, it is based on a schedule sensitive to specific price movements, e.g. wages and equipment costs.

205 PEREZ, R. (1969) 'Hospital planning' ('La programmazione ospedaliera'), *Bolletino dell' economia pubblica*, No. 11, 15–20.

The objectives of the 1968 Law no. 132 were to reorganize the hospital system and to establish principles for hospital planning. This article analyses the planning section of the law, and the responsibilities of different levels of government (parliament, central and regional government) in the field of hospital planning.

206 VÄÄNÄNEN, I., BÄCKMAN, G., PERÄLÄ, J., and VAUHKONEN, O. (1969) Study of Hospital Use by Regression Models (*Väestön sairaulankäytön selittäminen ja ennakoiminen regressiomallien avulla*), Helsinki: The Finnish Hospital Federation, 98 pp.

This study explores the use of regression models for estimating the needs for hospital services in 21 Finnish Central Hospital areas, up to 1980.

1970

207 ADVANCED SCHOOL FOR HOSPITAL ADMINISTRATION (1970) The Microeconomic Aspects of Hospitals (*Gli ospedali: aspetti economico-aziendali*), Milan: Vita e Pensiero, xiii + 699 pp.

This book is based on a lecture course for hospital administrators, given in Milan in 1969, concerning managerial problems generated by the Italian hospital reform of 1968. Among the topics covered were: the economic interpretation of the public hospital as a producer of services, and the organization of administrative services within the hospital. Among the specific managerial problems examined were: the analysis of cost structures and pricing policy for hospital services; the management of financial resources of the hospital (liquidity, real-estate, and stockholdings); the planning of purchases and inventory control; and the control of the efficiency of the production of health care services.

208 BERESFORD, J.C. and GRIFFITHS, D.A.T. (1970) 'Hospital costing for planning and management' ('Etablissement du prix de revient des hôpitaux en Angleterre et au Pays de Galles'), *Revue Hospitalière de France*, **34**, 234, 1467–75; English language version (1970) in *The Hospital*, **2**, 66, 48–53.

The fallacy of using cost per inpatient week as an indicator of hospital efficiency is demonstrated by examining the relationship between cost per week, cost per case, and throughput. The case is developed for high tempo hospitals offering more intensive treatment during a shorter stay. Allied with this is the need for a more precise definition of the type of care a particular hospital, of whatever type, is meant to provide.

604 BOSERUP, H. (1970) 'The expansion of hospitals from an economic point of view' ('Udbygningen af sygehusvæsenet i samfundsøkonomisk belysning'), *Ugeskrift for Læger*, **132**, 40, 1897–901 and **132**, 50, 2415–22.

540 BRENNA, A. (1970) 'Reflections on economic efficiency in the health care sector, with particular reference to hospitals' ('Alcune considerazioni in materia di efficienza economica del settore sanitario con particolare riguardo al comparto ospedaliero'), *I Problemi della Securezza Sociale*, **25**, 3, 425–64.

209 CAPPELLI, A., GUGLIOMELLA, G. PELLICELLI, G., and SCANAGATTA, A. (1970) Methodology of Hospital Planning (*Elementi di metodologia della programmazione ospedaliera*), Rome: Federazione Italiana Associazioni Regionali Ospedaliere, xv + 212 pp.

In the authors' opinion, the development of the Italian hospital system has been uncoordinated, and inadequate attention has been given to geographical and demographic realities. Consequently, it is vital that hospital service planning be improved. The connection between hospital planning and general economic planning is examined, and methodologies for hospital planning, based on already existing official data, are outlined. These planning techniques would enable the determination of effective and potential demand for hospital services, and would facilitate the calculation of regional needs for hospital beds, and the analysis of the degree of utilization of existing facilities.

210 DEDONI, G. (1970) 'The hospital problem: some solutions' (Il problema ospedaliero: prospettive di soluzioni'), *I Problemi della Sicurezza Sociale*, **25**, 3, 479–88.

After a statistical examination of recent increases in the volume of hospital treatment, and the growing deficits of the health insurance agencies, the author concludes that the incorrect formulation and implementation of the 1968 law on hospitals are responsible. He argues that it can be remedied either through the creation of a state-supported hospital system, which provides services free of charge, or by reforming the current system through the creation of a national hospital fund.

211 GRIFFITHS, D.A.T. (1970) 'Planning and operational research in the hospital services' ('Planification et recherche opérationnelle dans les services hospitaliers'), *Revue Médicale de Bruxelles*, **26**, 9, 527–47.

Reviews the implications of medical progress for hospital planning and management in general, then provides a series of illustrations of the use of operational research methods at various levels. At district level, the illustration given deals with decisions about the size and location of acute and supporting hospitals, to ensure good access and reduce travel costs. At hospital level, the relationship between throughputs of cases and costs is analysed, and it is shown that a more discriminating use of expensive acute hospitals, with appropriate support from cheaper non-acute hospitals, would produce significant economies. At the department and ward level, the major reasons for needless hospital stays are quantified, and a mathematically based decision making model is described for improving bed occupancy while coping with both waiting list and unprogrammed emergency admissions. Finally, a mathematical approach is demonstrated for reducing variation in nurse staffing demands, through the flexible use of staff across larger nursing units.

212 HERDER-DORNEICH, P., GERDELMANN, W., and KOETZ, W. (1970) Doctors' Incomes and Improvements in Hospital Financing (*Honorarreform und Krankenhaussanierung*), Berlin: Erich Schmidt Verlag, 124 pp.

Deficits in hospital budgets are examined, and proposals are made for a subsidy programme that would enable costs to be covered.

213 LODEON, M.C. (1970) Investigation of Qualitative Criteria for Assessing the Management of Hospital Services (*Recherche de critères qualitatifs permettant d'apprécier la gestion des services hospitaliers*), Paris: Ministère de l'Economie et des Finances, Division de la Prévision, Département des Biens Collectifs, 21 pp. (mimeographed document).

An attempt is made in this study, prepared for the Office of the General Commissioner for the Plan, to define criteria for evaluating the management of hospital services. The author examines the following topics: staff efficiency; investment in personnel; the relationship between investment and the productivity of personnel; measures of daily production; and investment in equipment. The use of better criteria should enable hospitals to improve management and to obtain various economic benefits.

214 PROPERSI, A. (1970) 'The management of public hospitals' ('La gestione programmata della azienda ospedaliera pubblica'), *Ospedali d'Italia*, **7**, 9, 809–32; **7**, 10, 933–51; and **7**, 11, 1055–76.

In Italy, the 1968 hospital reform law provided the legislative framework for hospital planning at both the regional and national level. This law was a response to the acute need for the development of a regional hospital system within the available economic resources. After discussing the general issues, the author examines the various decision systems used by business firms, and evaluates their relevance to the management of public hospitals.

215 ROCHAIX, M. and MAILLARD, C. (1970) 'The control of financial management in public hospitals' ('Le contrôle de gestion financière à l'hôpital public'), *Techniques Hospitalières*, **25**, 296, 79–85.

Adequate control of the financial management of public hospitals is of great importance, because it ensures that expenditures and receipts will be brought into balance by the end of the business year. The forecasting of expenditures and receipts makes it possible to control the future development of administrative accounts. The authors explain financial control techniques in detail, and discuss the difficulties of their application. They conclude that these supervisory tools are of great value in modern hospital management.

1971

216 BOYER, R. (1971) An attempt to Analyse the Dynamics of Hospital Costs (*Essai d'analyse de la dynamique des coûts hospitaliers*), Paris: Université de Paris I, Panthéon-Sorbonne, Faculté de Droit et de Sciences Economiques (PhD thesis), 317 pp.

Hospital costs increased at an annual rate of 15.6% (at current prices) in France, between 1950 and 1969. The author identifies certain factors causing the inflation of hospital costs: the increase in daily volume of hospital services (6%); the rise in the general price level (4.9%); structural changes in hospital costs (1.5%); the increase in hospital admissions (1.4%); and demographic growth (1%). A comparison is made of the influence of these factors in the public and private sectors for the period 1962–69. The author also investigates whether the increase in hospital costs is the result of changed needs, caused by demographic and social factors, or variations in incomes, prices, and kinds of insurance. He goes on to examine whether the increase in costs can be explained by factors relating to the functioning of the hospital system. He concludes that the main reason for this increase is the radical transformation of hospital services through the utilization of intensive techniques.

217 BRUNET-JAILLY, J. (1971) 'An economic study of the cost of hospitalization' ('Elément pour une étude économique du coût de l'hospitalisation'), *Techniques Hospitalières*, **26**, 304, 39-48.

After discussing the special features of hospital costs according to economic theory, this article shows that the discrepancy in average daily costs between wards cannot be explained solely by the variation in cases treated. A method of analysis that might be fruitfully used is then described. The primary indicator would be the average cost per hospitalized patient calculated for homogeneous units. This could be supplemented by other indicators measuring treatment techniques and results. The author believes that a cost-benefit analysis using the indicators described would greatly improve hospital management.

218 COURQUET, J. (1971) The Hospital Today and Tomorrow (*L'hôpital aujourd'hui et demain*), Paris: Editions du Seuil (Collection Société), 143 pp.

Among the topics discussed in this book are: the current problems of hospitals; hospital management; the question of hospital–university medical staff; hospital costs; and the health map (carte sanitaire). Examples are given from several foreign countries. The book contains many simple statistical tables and graphs.

219 FRANCE, MINISTRY OF PUBLIC HEALTH (1971) The Hospital (*L'hôpital*), Paris: La Documentation Française (Collection Pour une politique de santé, Vol. III), 227 pp.

This book contains two reports on hospital reform, as well as the text of the Hospital Act of 31 December 1970. The first report is a comprehensive review of important hospital problems, including those related to the structure and operation of the public hospital service, the planning and installation of hospital equipment, the cost of hospital care, and hospital fees. The second report examines the question of how to humanize the hospital environment and considers current policy recommendations.

220 FRANCE, MINISTRY OF PUBLIC HEALTH, GENERAL INSPECTORATE FOR SOCIAL AFFAIRS (1971) Hospitalization (*L'hospitalisation*), Paris: Ministère de la Santé Publique, Inspection Générale des Affaires Sociales, 301 pp. (mimeographed document).

This is a critical assessment of public and private hospitalization in France, based on data from 1969 to 1971. Certain defects in the hospital system are revealed, and a number of reforms of hospital policy are suggested. The four chapters of the report deal with: the medical performance of the public hospitals; their administrative and financial operations; a comparison of public and private hospitalization; and the relationship between health establishments and the reimbursement agencies.

221 JEAN, P. and GRABARSKY, J.M. (1971) Seminar on the Cost of Hospitalization, 29 June — 3 July 1970, General Summary Record (*Séminaire sur le coût de l'hospitalisation, 29 juin — 3 juillet 1970, Compte rendu général des travaux*), Rennes: Ecole Nationale de la Santé Publique (no pagination, mimeographed document). Also: 'Seminar on the cost of hospitalization, Rennes, 29 June — 3 July 1970' (Séminaire sur le coût de l'hospitalisation, Rennes, 29 juin — 3 juillet 1970'), Summary report, *Bulletin Trimestriel de l'Ecole Nationale de Santé Publique*, **3**, 1, 57-74.

Report of a seminar held by the National School of Public Health in Rennes in 1970. The authors state that hospital care expenditures are absorbing an increasing share of the French health budget. To cover the cost of future demand for hospitalization, better use needs to be made of available resources. The goals and efficiency of the current hospital system are questioned. The use of cost–benefit analysis to improve hospital organization is called for, although the authors recognize the difficulties of applying this technique, such as ascertaining true costs, and correctly estimating benefits.

222 KOCK, S.E. (1971) 'Can the hospital economy be rationalized?' ('Kan sjukhusekonomin rationaliseras?'), *Ekonomiska Samfundets Tidskrift*, **24**, 4, 263–90.

Presents data on the structure and costs of the Finnish health care sector, and discusses methods of economic research applicable to it.

223 MAILLARD, C. (1971) The Application of Modern Management Methods to Public Hospitals (*Essai d'application des méthodes de management à*

l'hôpital public), Aix: Université d'Aix-Marseille, Faculté de Droit et Sciences Economiques (LlD thesis), 552 pp. (mimeographed document).

The author argues that modern management techniques should be introduced in public hospitals, because their present administrative methods are inadequate in the light of socio-economic changes in the hospital sector, and the technical transformation of the service distribution system. The experiment with new management methods, carried out in the regional hospital centre in Nîmes from 1960 to 1970, is described in detail. The possibility of extending such methods to all hospital units is then evaluated. Finally, obstacles that might hamper the development of better hospital management are outlined and ways to overcome them suggested.

224 Pellicelli, G. (1971) 'Italian and foreign experiences in hospital planning' ('Esperienze italiane e straniere sulla programmazione aziendale ospedaliera'), *Ospedali d'Italia*, **8**, 4, 397–410.

This article develops a hospital planning model based on British and American experience. Different levels of responsibility and decision making are identified: the strategic level, at which decisions are taken about the relationship between the hospital and the general health care system (the Ministry of Health and regional authorities); the administrative level, at which decisions are made about the organizational structure of the hospital; and the operational level, at which decisions are taken about the provision of hospital services.

225 Ramond, M. (1971) 'Hospital charges and price accuracy' ('Tarifs hospitaliers et vérité des prix'), *Statistiques et Etudes Financières* (Série orange, No. 4), 6–11.

This study attempts to develop an improved method for calculating the cost of hospital services. The author suggests that prices should be determined on the basis of the following cost components: fixed costs, costs for specific medical services, and a time-dependent cost function that would exhibit diminishing costs per bed-day as the length of stay in hospital increased. The proposed system of charges should include various adjustments, which would take into account factors such as the type of patient accommodation.

226 Rochaix, M. (1971) 'Fixed capital formation in the public hospital. An attempted critical analysis and search for elements of an overall policy' ('La formation de capital fixe à l'hôpital public. Essai d'analyse critique et recherche d'éléments d'une politique globale'), *Revue Hospitalière de France*, **35**, 245, 1179–215.

The preservation and expansion of hospital capital stock are discussed in this article. The author is interested in the relationship between the utilization of fixed capital and investment. He analyses how the present accounting system describes this relationship in public hospitals. Through a detailed examination of the interaction between utilization and investment, he attempts to show how the public hospital system could be expanded in a rational manner.

227 SPRI (1971) A Model for Estimating Expenditures and Costs in Health Care — An Application (*Modell för att beräkna utgifter och kostnader inom hälso- och sjukvården — räkneexempel*), Stockholm: The Swedish Planning and Rationalization Institute of the Health and Social Services (SPRI Report 20/71), 25 pp.

Presents a model capable of estimating hospital care expenditure in a county in Sweden. Given a specified need for care, the model can be solved for required resources, expenditures, and taxes.

228 Various Authors (1971) 'Paris hospitals' ('Les hôpitaux de Paris'), *Revue Hospitalière de France*, **35**, 239, 389–434.

A description of the hospital sector of the Paris Public Assistance Service, based on documents provided by the Director-General. It has a total capacity of 44,518 beds, a medical staff of 6,557 (including 2,714 working full time), a non-medical staff of 54,533, and expenditure, in 1969, of Fr. 2,702, 871, 220. Information is given on: number and categories of hospitals, services offered, patients treated, equipment, organization, investment, and hospital expenditure. Numerous annotated tables on economic features of the Paris hospitals, and their develoment from 1959 to 1969, are provided.

739 WHO (1971) *Planning and Programming for Nursing Services*, Geneva: World Health Organization (Public Health Papers, No. 44), 123 pp.

1972

229 Brenna, A. and Cesarini, F. (1972) Contributions to the Lombardy Hospital Plan — Economic and Financial Aspects (*Contributi per il Piano Ospedaliero della Lombardia – Gli spetti economico-finanziari*), Milan: Giunta Regionale della Lombardia, Assessorato alla Sanità, 105 pp.

This study, intended as a basis for the formulation of the regional hospital plan, examines the economic and financial aspects of hospitals in Lombardy. Factors that determine hospital expenditure, such as demand, supply of services, and costs, are analysed. Forecasts of expenditures up to 1975 are made. Finally, the current financial situation of hospitals in the region, and their methods of financing activities, are evaluated.

230 GRECO, J., FONTENAILLE, C., and WEILL, J. (1972) 'Concerning the economic profitability of a CHU' ('A propos de la rentabilité économique d'un C.H.U.'), *Gestions Hospitalières*, No. 114, 229–327.

Since their creation in 1958, university hospital centres (CHU) have been responsible for the treatment of the sick, teaching, and research. The authors argue that the financial resources of the CHU are insufficient to ensure the attainment of these three objectives. Moreover, because of obsolete administrative regulations these inadequate resources are used inefficiently. The budget of a CHU is studied and disaggregated into expenditures on hospital care, teaching, and research. The article concludes with suggestions for reducing expenditures and increasing resources.

231 IMBERT, J. (1972) French Hospitals (*L'hôpital français*), Paris: Presses Universitaires de France (Collection Thémis), 96 pp.

In this comprehensive guide to hospitals in France, a wide variety of topics is discussed: the structure of the public hospital service, the administrative and financial characteristics of hospitals, and problems with personnel (administrative, technical, paramedical, and medical staff). Published after the 31st December 1970 Act on hospital reform, it contains extracts of hospital reform legislation and regulations.

232 JONSSON, EGON and JONSSON, T. (1972) 'Efficiency and measures of efficiency in health care' ('Effektivitet och effektivitetsmått inom sjukvården'), *Läkartidningen*, **69**, 47, 5509–15.

A critical review of efficiency measures in hospital planning, including utilization (bed occupancy) rates, average length of stay, number of bed-days, cost per patient and cost per bed-day. The authors point out that the different measures are not consistent. An increase in the bed occupancy rate is usually associated with an increase in average length of stay. A decrease in average length of stay is usually associated with an increase in cost per bed-day.

233 JONSSON, EGON and JONSSON, T. (1972) 'Average length of stay in hospital as a measure of the efficiency of hospital care' ('Medelvårdtiden som effektivitetsmått för den slutna vården'), *Läkartidningen*, **69**, 48, 5660–8.

The authors critically analyse the use of average length of stay in hospital as a measure of efficiency, and investigate average length of stay by specialty (general medicine and general surgery), rather than by diagnostic category. Analysis of data from five Swedish hospitals reveals significant variation in average length of stay, both between hospitals and over time for all hospitals. Different explanations for variations in average length of stay between specialties over time are examined; age is estimated to explain more than 50% of the observed variation.

234 Minvielle, D., Morando, B., and Tordeux, J. (1972) 'A comparative study of average lengths of stay in clinics and hospitals' ('Etude comparée des durées moyennes de séjour en clinique et à l'hôpital'), *Revue Française des Affaires Sociales*, **26**, 2, 3–14.

The lengths of stay of patients hospitalized for surgery, in 8 public hospitals and 14 private clinics in the Auvergne area, are compared in this article. An analysis is made of the files of 402 patients in public hospitals and 541 in private clinics during three different periods in 1968. For each patient the waiting time between admission and surgical operation was determined, as were the total length of stay in the ward, the number of operations, and the hospital services received. The average length of stay was 21 days in public hospitals as opposed to 9.4 days in private clincis. The number and type of operations performed, and the structure of illness, were responsible for this difference.

777 Smedby, B., Kjellström, T., and Berfenstam, R. (1972) The Utilization of Hospital Care (*Sjukhusvårdens konsumenter*), Stockholm: The Swedish Planning and Rationalization Institute of the Health and Social Services (SPRI Report 18/72), 69 pp.

1973

148 Brenna, A. (1973) 'Hospitals' ('Ospedali') in: Stefani, G. (ed.), Public Enterprises (*La produttività delle imprese pubbliche*), Milan: Franco Angeli, 419–64.

671 Commission of the European Communities (1973) Synthesis of Three Investigations of the Main Items of Health Insurance Expenditure Covered by Social Security (*Rapport de synthèse concernant trois études sur les principaux postes des dépenses de l'assurance maladie couvertes par la sécurité sociale*), Brussels: Commission of the European Communities, General Directorate of Social Affairs (Report No. V/396/73–F), 38 pp. (mimeographed document).

235 COMMISSION OF THE EUROPEAN COMMUNITIES (1973) The Cost of Hospitalization under Social Security (*Le coût de l'hospitalisation dans la sécurité sociale*), Brussels: Commission of the European Communities, General Directorate of Social Affairs (Report No. V/456/73–F), 55 pp. (mimeographed document).

Argues that inter-country differences in hospitalization rates and length of stay are less marked than differences in the availability of medical resources. Concludes that further analysis requires development of specific indicators for each country of: consumption of hospital care, the real daily cost of hospital services, and the social security share in these costs.

236 DUHART, J. and CHARTON-BRASSARD, J. (1973) 'Hospital reform and nursing care by medical prescription' ('Réforme hospitalière et soins infirmiers sur ordonnance médicale'), *Revue Française de Sociologie* (special number on medical sociology), Vol. 14, 77–101.

French hospitals are experiencing serious problems with their nursing staff, such as shortages of staff in the wards, recruiting difficulties, and resignations after a few years of service. The authors have used a CORDES (Comité d'Organisation des Recherches Appliquées sur le Développement Economique et Social) survey of 2,215 nurses, in 58 French hospitals and 11 training schools, in their examination of the role of the hospital nurse. Among the topics studied are: the social relations between doctors and nurses, the division of work, and the discrepancy between the theoretical and actual medical responsibilities of nurses. It is suggested that the practice of nursing care by prescription could solve some of the problems.

237 FOULON, A. (1973) Hospital Prices and Costs in Seven EEC Countries (*Les prix et les coûts hospitaliers dans sept pays de la C.E.E.), Paris: Centre de Recherches et de Documentation sur la Consommation, 57 pp. (mimeographed document).*

The prices per bed-day in hospitals of seven European countries are compared in this study. Considerable differences exist, but this is due in part to national variations in the methods of calculating costs. Hospital prices cover all expenditures in the Netherlands and Great Britain, but only partial costs in the Federal Republic of Germany, the balance being covered by subsidies. In Italy, prices cover total expenditure for care and accommodation, but in France and Luxembourg medical fees are billed separately in public hospitals. In Belgium, and in French private hospitals, the total cost includes charges for nursing care, medical treatment, pharmaceuticals, accommodation, management, and depreciation. The author argues that a valid comparison of hospital costs should take all cost elements into account.

238 France, Ministry of Public Health and Social Security (ed.) (1973) 'Public hospitalization in France' ('L'hospitalisation publique en France'). *Revue Française des Affaires Sociales* (special issue), 177 pp.

Presents a comprehensive survey of public hospitals in France. After a description of the regulations, the capacity, design, construction, and costs of hospitals are discussed. The role of public hospitals in the French hospital system overall, and in the economy, are examined. Finally, questions related to regionalization, the health map, hospital management, and computerization are considered.

239 Kock, S.E. (1973) Simulation of Hospital Activities (*Simulering av sjukhusfunktioner*), Helsinki: Svenska Handelshögskolans Publikationer, 45 pp. (mimeographed document).

Discusses the use of simulation models in hospital planning and describes different models applied to ambulatory clinics, X-ray departments, and laboratories.

779 Kohler, F. (1973) 'The economic and organisational aspects of health care in Europe and their influence on hospital management', *Hospital and Health Services Review*, **69**, 8, 296–302.

240 Leclercq, J. (1973) 'The health map or the programming of equipment' ('La carte sanitaire ou la programmation des équipements'), *Cahiers de Sociologie et de Démographie Médicales*, **13**, 1, 16-21.

The 'health map' is a tool for analysing the distribution of medical resources over a geographical region. The author uses it to study the distribution of hospital services, both public and private. He believes that there is an adequate quantity of equipment in French hospitals at present, but that better use could be made of it. A computer model is described, which would facilitate the rational programming of medical investment for a given geographical pattern of demand for services.

241 Maillard, C. (1973) 'A study of the daily activity in a hospital' ('Etude de l'activité journées d'un établissement hospitalier'), *Techniques Hospitalières*, **29**, 337, 81–9 and **29**, 338, 65–72.

The pattern of activity in a hospital over time is examined in this study. The author finds that weekly, monthly, and seasonal cycles exist. These cycles can be incorporated into a model to forecast the activity of hospitals. Examples of the application of such a model are given. Although further research is needed in this area, the author believes that the use of activity models can improve the utilization of hospital resources. They will also facilitate the decentralization of hospital management.

242 VAUHKONEN, O. and BÄCKMAN, G. (1973) Hospital Activities in the 1960s (*Sairaalalaitos 1960–luvulla*), Helsinki: The Finnish Hospital Federation, 165 pp. (mimeographed document).

An account of the Finnish hospital sector during the 1960s, including data on different measures of hospital output, sources of finance, costs, and the increased consumption of health care. Incorporates several articles dealing with aspects of hospital research, such as forecasting. References to research undertaken by the Finnish Hospital Institution are given.

243 VETERE, C. (1973) 'Modern management techniques for the health care sector' ('Moderne tecniche di gestione per l'assistenza sanitaria'), *Ospedali d'Italia*, **10**, 8, 645–9.

The use of modern management techniques in the Italian health care system is made difficult by the extreme rigidity of administrative rules binding health care agencies (hospitals, health insurance agencies, and local government agencies). The application of rational managerial methods occurs infrequently. It is seen mainly in hospitals that have studied staff work efficiency, the profile of patients, and the cost of hospital services.

1974

547 AARBY, P. (1974) Evaluation of the Effectiveness of the Hospital (*Effektivitetsvurdering af sygehuse*), Copenhagen: Institutet for Organisation og Arbejdssociologi, (Series Nyt fra Samfundsvidenskaberne, No. 74–12) 23 pp.

244 BLOX, J.T. (1974) Review of Literature on Cost Containment Systems for Hospitals (*Literatuuronderzoek kostenbeheersingssystemen in ziekenhuizen*), Eindhoven: Technische Hogeschool (Ziekenhuis Research Project, Report No. 15) 24 pp.

A review of literature on hospital cost containment systems in the USA, the UK, Sweden, France, and the Netherlands. Argues that further development of these systems must give special attention to the units for measuring different hospital operations, to the development of a flexible budgeting system, and to the applicability of responsibility accounting.

245 Borgquist, L. (1974) Organization of the Public Health Service (*Organisationsnivåer inom sjukvården*), Lund: University of Lund, Department of Business Administration (PhD thesis), 121 pp.

The author investigates aspects of the Swedish hospital system related to medical technology, and economic and social conditions, through a case study of fractures of the neck of the femur. The considerable increase in the number of the elderly has led to an increase in the number of such fractures, and to a greater bed occupancy in acute wards. Despite improved technology, resource scarcity is as apparent now as it was ten years ago. Further, the disappearance of the mixed-generation family has diminished the availability of non-hospital care for the elderly. These factors affect the organization of hospitals.

246 Canaletti, F. and Dodaro, E. (1974) 'Principles of hospital organization' ('Principi di organizzazione dell'ente ospedaliero'), *Ospedali d'Italia*, **11**, 8, 30–43.

As a result of the 1968 reform, Italian public hospitals have been changed in status from charitable institutions to productive enterprises. This has raised management problems for hospital administrators. To resolve these problems, a radical reorganization of health care facilities is required. The authors examine the medical and administrative functions of hospitals, and, taking account of current legislation, propose several organizational reforms.

109 Christiansen, U. (1974) 'Demand for emergency health care and regional systems for provision of supply' in: Perlman, M. (ed.) *The Economics of Health and Medical Care*, London: Macmillan, 248–71.

247 Ciucchi, G. (1974) 'Structures and perspectives of the hospital financial situation' ('Strutture e prospettive della situazione finanziaria ospedaliera'), *Ospedali d'Italia*, **11**, 11, 35–53.

The weak financial situation of the public hospitals in Italy prior to 1974, due to the insolvency of the health insurance agencies, stimulated the transfer of the responsibility for hospital care provision to the regional authorities. Each region was to be assigned a portion of the national hospital fund to support its system. To determine whether the fund would meet the financial needs of the hospitals, the author analysed data on expenditure for 85% of the Italian public hospitals. Particular attention was paid to: the size and admission capacity of the hospital network: the financial situation of hospitals in 1973 and 1974; forecasts of increases in operating costs for 1975; and problems relating to the proper distribution of the national hospital fund.

248 Comet, P. and Piganiol, R. (1974) Public Hospitals (*L'hôpital public*), 3rd edition, Paris: Berger-Levrault (Collection l'Administration Nouvelle), 200 pp.

The three major reforms of the French hospital system (in 1941, 1958, and 1970), which have given the public hospital a new role, are examined. The first section discusses the place of the hospital in the total public hospital system, the use of the 'health map', the development of treatment technology, and the standardization of installations. The second part covers hospital administration and finance. Finally, the psychological, technical, and administrative aspects of the doctor–patient relationship in the public hospital are considered.

249 Coppini, G. (1974) 'Control of the productivity of hospital expenditure' ('Modalità di controllo della produttività della spesa sanitaria nel settore ospedaliero'), *I Problemi della Sicurezza Sociale*, **19**, 4, 431–56.

This article examines expenditure, especially on hospital care, by Italian health insurance agencies between 1963 and 1972. The rate of growth of these expenditures is so high that it cannot be sustained in the future. Proposals are made for controlling the productivity of expenditure in the hospital sector, in order to contain costs effectively.

250 Cordurier, P. (1974) Prices per Day (*Les prix de journée*), 3rd edition, Paris: Berger-Levrault (Collection L'Administration Nouvelle), 160 pp.

This is the first comprehensive study of French laws and regulations concerning the determination of daily hospital prices. The author discusses how hospitals develop price proposals, the role of local government in approving prices, and the disputes that can arise between hospitals and the government on price policy. The appendices contain documents on regulations and decisions of the Social Assistance Council.

251 European Club of Health (1974) The Cost of Public Health Care in Europe: Hospitalization (*Le coût de la santé publique en Europe: l'hospitalisation*), Paris: Club Européen de la Santé, pp. 120 (mimeographed document).

Participants from France, the Federal Republic of Germany, Great Britain, Austria, Sweden, and Switzerland attended a two-day consultation in Strasbourg, France, in May 1974. The increase in expenditures on hospitals (40% of total health expenditures in France in 1973, 66% in Great Britain) was discussed. It was concluded that this increase was due more to an improvement in the quality of care and accommodation than to increased activity. Hospital operating costs in general, and wages (70% of hospital expenditures in France in 1973) in particular, are increasing most rapidly. Analyses of the six initial countries of the European Economic Community examined the differences in the methods of financing hospital care and the difficulties associated with cost comparisons. The relationship between hospital prices and costs, and cost reduction schemes, was also considered.

252 Ferry-Pierret, J. and Karsenty, S. (1974) Medical Practices and the Hospital System (*Pratiques médicales et système hospitalier*), Paris: Centre de Recherche sur le Bien-être, 113 pp. + appendixes (mimeographed document).

The authors of this document are critical of standard models of hospitals, particularly those that portray it as a business enterprise, or as a rational enterprise attempting to attain certain technical objectives. They argue that it is necessary to take into account the wide variety in the behaviour and goals of the 'actors' (patients, doctors, technical staff) in the hospital 'scenario'. The historical development of hospital specialization, and its negative consequences for the various actors are described. The socio-economic consequences of uncontrolled hyperspecialization of hospital services are criticized. The authors conclude with a forecast of the nature of the hospital of the future (1995–2000).

253 Gadreau, M., Majnoni D'Intignano, B., Chevailler, J.C., Mougeot, L., and Dagras, G. (1974) The Costs of Hospitalization in the Psychiatric Field (*Les coûts de l'hospitalisation en milieu psychiatrique*), Paris: Centre National de la Recherche Scientifique (Collection des Actions Thématiques Programmées — Sciences Humaines), 106 pp.

Three psychiatric wards in the Burgundy and Franche-Comte regions were examined in this multidisciplinary study of the costs of hospital care of psychiatric patients. The authors consider not only the direct costs of medical care and accommodation, but also indirect administrative costs and depreciation. The relationship between the average cost per day and length of stay is analysed. Demographic and disease characteristics of patients in the region are evaluated.

254 Gauthier, P., Grenon, A., Omnes, L., and Perchat, J.Y. (1974) Management Analysis in the Hospital (*L'analyse de gestion à l'hôpital*), Paris: Heral, 135 pp.

Members of the Directorate of Hospitals in the French Ministry of Public Health have produced this book on modern hospital management. After a survey of management objectives and methods, several specific managerial techniques that can improve hospital performance are described.

255 Henny, H.M. (1974) The Cost Structure of Swiss Hospitals (*La structure des coûts dans les hôpitaux suisses*), Aarau: Institut Suisse des Hôpitaux, 36 pp. (also available in German).

Analyses the trend in the structure of current costs in the Swiss hospital system from 1950 to 1971, in both absolute and relative terms. The data cover almost all the major hospitals in Switzerland. Between 1950 and 1971: the share of labour costs in current expenditure increased from 44.3% to 66.6%; the share of medical supplies increased from 7.3% to 9.2%; the share of food decreased from 21.8% to 5.8%; total current expenditure increased from Sw.Fr. 192 million to Sw.Fr. 1,800 million, at an annual rate of increase reaching more than 20%.

256 JUHL, T. (1974) Hospital Planning — Problems and Practice (*Sygehusplanlægning — problemer og praksis*), Copenhagen: Institut for Organisation og Arbejdssociologi (Series Nyt fra Samfundsvidenskaberne), 36 pp.

This monograph discusses various problems related to estimation of the demand for medical care. It introduces a demand model in the context of a discussion of the concepts of demand and need, and analyses the applicability to hospital planning of a simple supply–demand mechanism. It then describes a concrete supply–demand based forecasting model, and its application in the development of a master plan for the Copenhagen County Hospitals; possible ways of developing the forecasting model are suggested.

257 KARLSEN, S. (1974) Cost Analysis of General Hospitals (*Kostnadsanalyse av somatiske sykehuse*), Trondheim: Norsk Institutt for Sykehusforskning, 40 pp. + appendix (mimeographed document).

The aim of the study was to construct a hospital cost measure superior to the ususal cost per bed-day measure. A cost index was constructed, which varied with patient turnover, hospital size, and the number of long-term beds.

258 KARNER, A. (1974) 'Cost trends in Austrian hospitals' ('Die Kostenentwicklung im Krankenhaus in Österreich'), *Österreichische Krankenhaus-Zeitung*, Vol. 15, 27–9.

This article surveys cost trends in Austrian hospitals and identifies causal factors.

259 KARSENTY, S. (1974) 'The planning of hospital equipment or the ambiguities of medical production as a means of satisfying health requirements' ('La planification des équipements hospitaliers ou les ambiguîtés de la production médicale comme moyen de satisfaire les "besoins de santé"') in: NIZARD, L., Planning in French Society (*La planification dans la société française*), Grenoble: Presses Universitaires de Grenoble (Collection Etat et Société), 308–14.

Increases in technology and in specialization in the modern hospital create a sociological environment in which it is difficult to plan rationally the acquisition of hospital equipment. The author claims that doctors and administrators now want the latest equipment, irrespective of whether there is a medical need for it.

260 LETOURMY, A. (1974) An Economic Model of the Hospital (*Modèle économique de l'hôpital*), Paris: Centre de Recherche sur le Bien-être, 122 pp. (mimeographed document).

Twenty-six economic studies of hospitals in North America and France have been surveyed in this document. The first part examines the results of the modelling of hospital operations, the patient mix, and the hospital as a medical service production unit. The inflation of hospital costs is studied in the second part. The last section evaluates a number of theories of hospital behaviour derived from neo-classical economics and the sociology of organizations.

261 MAJNONI D'INTIGNANO, B. (1974) 'Hospital investments, selection criteria and constraints' ('Les investissements hospitaliers, critères de choix et contraintes'), *Economie et Santé* (supplement to the *Bulletin des Statistiques de Santé et de Sécurité Sociale*), No. 5, 5–38.

This is a summary of a doctoral thesis in economics, which discusses ways of improving the choice of hospital investments and the distribution of their benefits. The author differentiates between investments that affect health and those that affect management, and develops the selection criteria for each type. He believes that economic analysis of investments is necessary, and that this can help to attain the moral, ethical, and social objectives of the hospital service.

262 PERCHAT, J.Y. (1974) 'The economic function of the hospital' ('La fonction économique de l'hôpital'), *Revue Trimestrielle de Droit Sanitaire et Social* (special number: Hospitalisation publique et privée. Problèmes et perspectives), **10**, 37–38, 41–54.

After surveying French health care expenditures and finance at the macroeconomic level, the author shifts his attention to the behaviour of public hospitals. He analyses their physical characteristics and performance indicators and then looks at their financial side. Operating and investment budgets are described and analysed. An attempt is made to develop an indicator of hospital product, expressed in terms of days of hospitalization.

263 RHENMAN, E. (1974 *Managing the Community Hospital: Systems Analysis of a Swedish Hospital*, Farnborough: Saxon House, 304 pp.

Also: (1969) The District Hospital (*Centrallasarettet*), Lund: Studentlitteratur, 275 pp.

Examines the hospital as an organizational system and analyses the factors influencing the outcome of the system. Different proposals to increase hospital efficency by changing its organizational structure are discussed.

264 SCHRIJVERS, A.J.P. (1974) 'A survey of costs in two outpatient departments in the Netherlands' ('Kostenberekeningen van twee ambulatoria in Nederland'), *Het Ziekenhuis*, **4**, 2, 80–3.

Compares the cost of nursing an ambulatory patient in a conventional and in a 'low-care' outpatient department. Data from two Dutch hospitals indicate that 24% fewer personnel are required in the 'low-care' department. Very low capital expenditure is needed to add a 'low-care' department to an existing hospital.

265 SIMON, J.M. (1974) Five Exercises in Economic Analysis in a Hospital Environment: The Cost of the Little Frenchman Born at Antoine Béclère / Hidden Beds in Surgery / Economic Waste / Learn to Know Medical Services in order to Prescribe More Effectively / Give Everyone the Proper Medicine. (*Cinq exercices d'analyse économique en milieu hospitalier: Le coût du petit Français né à Antoine Béclère / Des lits cachés en chirurgie / Le gâchis économique / Connaître les actes médicaux pour mieux les prescrire / A chacun ses médicaments*), Paris: Editions de l'Assistance Publique de Paris, 76 pp.

These five studies in hospital economics were made by students of the National School of Administration. In the first, Planning Programming and Budgeting Systems techniques are used to examine the benefit derived from increased frequency of prenatal consultations and the preventive hospitalization of the pregnant woman. The second argues that improved pre-operative appointments, and staff meetings in the surgical ward, would allow additional treatment of emergency cases. In the third study, an examination of dosages of prescribed drugs in the paediatrics department of a hospital revealed no possible economies. Finally, the files of patients admitted to a cardio-thoracic ward and a rheumatology ward were analysed, to estimate the costs of various forms of treatment. The objective was to improve the economic effectiveness of prescription policy.

266 SONRIER, A. (1974) Management and Hospital Finance (*Gestion et finances hospitalières*), 2nd edition, Paris: Berger-Levrault, 324 pp.

The financial repercussions of the French Hospital Act of 31 December 1970 are examined in detail. Among the topics covered are: loans, depreciation, finance, investments, invoicing for services, the balance-sheet, the equipment programme, prices per bed-day, the annual report on the financial situation, and management control. Each chapter contains statistical examples, which illustrate the method of analysis used. For example, there is a study of recent developments in the financing of regional health centres.

267 VARIOUS AUTHORS (1974) Regional Hospital Planning (*Programmazione regionale ospedaliera*). Florence: Le Monnier, xiii + 223 pp.

This book contains the proceedings of a recent conference on regional hospital planning, a subject that has acquired particular significance in Italy since Law no. 386 was passed in 1974. This law transferred hospital administration from the central to the regional authorities. Its importance is assessed. The experiences of two regions, Tuscany and Lombardy, which have prepared their hospital plans, are examined. As well as health care issues, political, legal, institutional and economic aspects of hospital planning in these regions are considered.

1975

268 BAUHOFER, F. (1975) 'Hospital systems in Europe' ('Krankenhaussysteme in Europa'), *Österreichische Krankenhaus-Zeitung*, **16**, 9, 457–71.

The differences between the various hospital systems in Europe are considerable, mainly for historical or purely local reasons. Since hospitals throughout the world have adopted similar measures (e.g. computer centres, cost accounting) to overcome problems of hospital management and organization, similarities of the various hospital systems have tended to emerge. Differences are mainly confined to the extent of government control or involvement in the organization of hospital systems. With reference to Robert Maxwell's book, *Health Care, the Growing Dilemma*, the author divides the hospitals in Southern and Western Europe into five major groupings according to the degree of government involvement. He adds, however, that all groups are subject to change, since most countries are either experimenting with new models, or are actually reforming their hospital systems. The final part analyses the French, British, Scandinavian and Russian hospital systems.

689 BLOHMKE, M. (1975) The cost of Health Care Systems, Social Ecology, and Social Medicine (*Kosten des Gesundheitswesens, Sozialökologie und Sozialmedizin*), Stuttgart: A.W. Gentner Verlag (Schriftenreihe Arbeitsmedizin, Sozialmedizin, Präventivmedizin, Vol. 56), 135 pp.

See 413, 584

269 BLOX, J.T. and THEEUWES, J.A.M. (1975) 'Cost containment in hospitals' ('Kostenbeheersing in ziekenhuizen'), *Acta Hospitalia*, **15**, 2, 128–45.

Containment of hospital operating expenditure is one means of restraining the rising cost of health care. It requires well-balanced decisions on the use of production inputs, and the submission of the resulting expenditure to those responsible for the decisions ('responsibility accounting'). This paper discusses the major problem of specifying the standards that underlie these expenditure estimates. Determination of standards for diagnostic activities presupposes standardization of procedures undertaken by specialists, but this area of 'medical audit' has yet to make real progress. The problems of determining standards for other activities in various service centres (laboratory, X-ray, nursing, kitchen, etc.) are similar to those encountered in industrial organizations. For such activities it is necessary to determine the optimal use of production inputs for each activity, within a single standard, or several standards applicable to different levels of activity, for the relevant budget period.

270 BRENNA, A. (1975) 'The economic aspects of the short stay' ('La degenza breve: aspetti economici'), *Rivista degli Ospedali*, **7**, 6, 370–4.

The author examines the possibilities for reducing average length of stay and number of admissions in Italian hospitals. He lists the conditions under which investments in plant (reception departments, day hospitals, etc.) to reduce hospital stays can be economically justifiable. The author argues that such investments should be made only when excess admission capacity does not exist at both the hospital and regional level. Such a prerequisite is not satisfied in most regions of Italy.

271 BUI-DANG-HA, D. (1975) 'Analysis of some trends in the development of hospital equipment in Europe' ('Analyse de quelques tendances de l'évolution de l'équipement hospitalier en Europe'), *Cahiers de Sociologie et de Démographie Médicales*, **15**, 3, 122–40, and *World Health Statistics Report*, **28**, 9, 364–86.

Each year, a WHO questionnaire is sent to member states requesting statistical information about their hospitals and other medical establishments with beds. This study is based on replies received during the period 1969–70. The author calculated time-series of the ratios of hospital beds (total and by specialization) to population for each country. He then examined levels and trends of hospital bed densities, and made various types of international comparisons.

272 CIUCCHI, G. (1975) 'Hospital expenditure between 1974 and 1975. Analysis, controls, and trends' ('La spesa ospedaliera nel biennio 1974–75. Analisi, controllo, prospettive'), *Ospedali d'Italia*, **12**, 11, 7–100.

This analysis aims to provide regional and central government decision making bodies with aggregated data on the current hospital situation. Topics covered in the article are: facilities and their capacities, the financial burden of hospitals, and future prospects.

273 Coppini, G. (1975) 'An economic function for controlling and distributing hospital expenditure' ('Una funzione economica per il controllo e la ripartizione della spesa ospedaliera'), *I Problemi della Sicurezza Sociale*, **30**, 2, 215–35.

The growth rate of health care expenditures of the social security system is so high that it could threaten orderly economic development in Italy. Costs of hospital treatment are increasing very rapidly and are most difficult to control. The author examines a sample of public hospitals and tries to establish a functional relationship for each between the principal expenditure items of the hospital budget and three variables (capacity, utilization, and case-mix). It is thereby possible to determine the appropriate level of hospital expenditure. This 'economic function' approach can be used both for forecasting and budgeting in individual hospitals. It could also be used by agencies responsible for the control and inter-regional distribution of hospital expenditure.

274 Dahlberg, L. (1975) 'Hospital days as an output measure' ('Vårddagar som pretationsmått'), *Läkartidningen*, **72**, 33, 3056–8.

The number of hospital or treatment days is commonly used as an output measure. The author shows that the average cost per bed-day decreases with the duration of the sickness episode. The use of bed-days as an output measure will therefore give a misleading index of efficiency.

550 Danish Hospital Institute (1975) An Analysis of Resource Consumption in Hospital Health Care (*En Analyse af sygehussundhedsvæsendets ressourceforbrug*), Copenhagen: Danish Hospital Institute, 45 pp. (mimeographed document).

275 Eyskens, M. (1975) 'Hospital care in the mixed economy system' ('Het ziekenhuiswezen in de gemengde economie'), *Acta Hospitalia*, **15**, 3, 184–213.

Hospital care represents an excellent test area for observing the functioning of the mixed economy system, where public and private initiative co-exist. One of the major difficulties is that hospital services partially escape the rules of the market (in the output market the provision of health care is governed by legitimate social reasons, while the input market frequently remains subject to market disciplines). Additionally, the hospital sector faces conflicts between economic rationality and social utility, especially in periods of inflation and lagging economic growth. From a microeconomic viewpoint, application of marginal cost rules to hospitals must be preferred, in principle, to average cost regulations, if hospitals are to be left with some flexibility in self-financing. Macroeconomic data emphasize the prominent place of hospital care in social policy.

276 FOULON, A. and MATTHYS, M. (1975) National Health Accounts, the Price of Medical Goods and Services, Vol. III: The Price Per Day in Public Hospitals, 1968–1974 and 1950–1974 (*Comptes nationaux de la santé, les prix des biens et des services médicaux, Tome III: Le prix de journée des hôpitaux publics 1968–1974 et 1950–1974*), Paris: Centre de Recherches et de Documentation sur la Consommation, 39 pp. (mimeographed document).

The report begins with a discussion of methodology. Trends in daily hospital prices, from 1968 to 1974, according to type of hospital and category of service, are then examined. A comparison is made between the trend in average hospital prices per day, and daily social security expenditures in the period 1969–74. Finally, the report studies the trend in the price of public hospitalization from 1950 to 1974.

277 GADREAU, M. (1975) Hospital Prices (*La tarification hospitalière*), Paris: Editions Médicales et Universitaires (Collection Economie et Santé, No. 1), 416 pp.

This book examines the continuing rise in hospital costs. The first section discusses the hospital market and the theory of public hospital pricing. The second part is an analysis of hospital prices in France from the 'Ancien Régime' to the present day. The current method of hospital price determination, based on the 'price per day' concept, is criticized for not reflecting the true cost of services given to the patient. Incorrect hospital prices hamper rational decision making. The book concludes with suggestions for future reform.

278 HANAU, C. (1975) 'Current expenditure of, and the real resources employed by, four European hospitals — problems of efficiency' ('Spesa corrente e risorse reali impiegate per il funzionamento di quattro ospedali europei— Problemi di efficienza'), *I Problemi della Sicurezza Sociale*, **30**, 6, 825–75.

Outlines the economic problems linked with the evaluation of the efficiency of health services in general, and of the hospital system in particular. The study compares two university polyclinic hospitals (S. Orsola of Bologna and Istituti Ospedalieri of Modena) and two foreign hospitals (Kantonsspital of Zurich and Sygehus of Odense). The Zurich hospital differs from the other three in having much more highly specialized facilities and workload. The amount and distribution of current expenses for the various items in the balance-sheet are then examined, and allowance made for the differences in price levels of hospital inputs. It is clear that the Italian hospital spends less on equipment than the others. Personnel, the biggest component of operating expenses, is analysed separately by type of staff. Hospital output is divided into ambulatory and inpatient services, including both admissions and hospital bed-days. The input/output ratio, although to be considered with some reserve, is high in the S. Orsola hospital, medium in the Odense Sygehus, low in the Istituti Ospedalieri of Modena; the two Italian hospitals show a ratio of medical staff to hospitalizations that is respectively two and three times higher than that of the Danish hospital, and even exceeds the ratio for the highly specialized Zurich hospital.

279 HASTINGS, J.E.F. (1975) 'Hospital costs — implications for health care funding from Canadian experience' in: EHRLICH, D.A. (ed.) *The Health Care Cost Explosion: Which Way Now?*, Berne: Hans Huber Verlag, 59–66.

Presents and interprets data on various aspects of the increase in health care expenditure in Canada from the mid-1950s to the early 1970s. Suggests that long-term success in developing a rational health care system requires coordinated planning and resource allocation, together with renewed emphasis on health promotion, prevention, and environmental protection.
See 26

280 JUHL, T. (1975) 'Criteria for need and forecasting methods in hospital planning' ('Behovskriterier og prognosemethoder i sygehusplanlægningen'), *Danmarks Amtsråd*, Vol. 2, 18–24.

Introduces a demand model, discusses the concepts of need and demand, and evaluates the application to hospital planning of a simple supply–demand model. A concrete supply–demand based forecasting model and its use in practical hospital planning are described, and possible ways of developing it are suggested.

281 KARLSEN, S. (1975) Cost Analysis of General Hospitals (*Kostnadsanalyse av somatiske sykehus*), Vol. II, Trondheim: Norsk Institutt for Sykehusforskning, 58 pp. + appendix (mimeographed document).

Begins with a discussion of hospital outputs and then analyses the relation between costs, categories of patients, and the complexity and duration of treatment. The importance of these factors in explaining cost variations is not clear from the statistical analysis, and it is suggested that budgeting and administrative procedures might provide a better explanation of observed cost differentials.

282 LIESS, M. (1975) The Cost of Illness in Hospital — Two Methodological Approaches (*Le coût de la maladie à l'hôpital — Deux approches méthodologiques*), Paris: Université de Paris I, Panthéon-Sorbonne (PhD thesis), 210 pp. (mimeographed document).

This thesis examines two alternative methods of determining hospital cost structure. The first consists of directly evaluating the cost of illness at the level of the hospital care unit. The second is an indirect method of evaluation based on the approach of R.G. Evans and H.D. Walker. After describing these two methods, the author discusses the results of a 1972 survey of 44 hospital wards of the Paris Public Assistance Service.

283 LINDAHL, O., WANTULOK, J., and LINDWALL, L. (1975) 'Methods of comparing treatment costs in identical medical clinics in different hospitals' ('Metod för jämförelse av sjukvårdskostnader mellan samma specialiteter på olika sjukhus'), *Landstingens Tidskrift*, **62**, 4, 37–42.

Total costs for different clinics in four regional hospitals in Sweden are disaggregated and analysed. Elimination of fixed costs made it possible to attribute cost differentials to efficiency differentials. The authors propose some changes in the statistical system.

284 MOUGEOT, L. (1975) A Study of Local Hospital Services (*La localisation hospitalière — Etude positive et normative*), Dijon: Université de Dijon, Faculté des Sciences Economiques et de Gestion (PhD thesis), 423 pp. (mimeographed document).

In the author's opinion, decisions about the provision of local hospital services are as important as those concerned with investment and price determination. The first section examines the effect of distance on the consumption of hospital services. The second section studies the economic factors that affect the provision of local hospital services. In the third section, a model that can be used to locate a complex of hospital establishments is proposed. It is then applied to the Franche-Comte region.

285 PERSSON, E. (1975) 'Hospital costs over 50 years' ('Sygehusomkostningernes udvikling gennem 50 år'), *Tidsskrift for Danske Sygehuse*, **51**, 1, 10–18.

Data presented for Danish hospitals include expenditure, average cost per patient day, number of hospitalized patients, and manpower. These are discussed with particular emphasis on the ten-year period 1961-71.

286 Roggen, H. (1975) 'Pricing problems of Belgian hospitals. Ten years' experience' ('De prijsbepaling in de Belgische ziekenhuizen. Tien jaar ervaring'), *Acta Hospitalia*, **15**, 4, 289–322.

Price setting is one of the major problems of the Belgian hospitals. Prices are fixed by the Ministry of Public Health. Only in exceptional circumstances, when the normal price is proved to be insufficient, can it be increased to cover hospital costs. This paper attempts to isolate statistical relationships between prices and other characteristics. The results show a significant relation between higher prices and local government hospitals, large hospitals, hospitals with several different departments, and hospitals with intensive care units. They also reveal a significant relation between prices and hospitals with only one department, and hospitals with the four basic departments (surgery, internal medicine, paediatrics, and obstetrics). The prices of services for internal medicine and paediatrics are increasing while the prices of obstetric services are decreasing. The size of the departments appears to be particularly important. Differentiated rather than uniform prices are therefore required, according to the specific function of each hospital.

287 Rutten, F.F.H., Van der Gaag, J., and Van Praag, B.M.S. (1975) The Hospital in Health Care. An Econometric Analysis of the Use of Hospital Beds (*Het ziekenhuis in de gezondheidszorg*), Leiden: Stenfert Kroese b.v., 117 pp.

The first part of this report uses econometric results to estimate the effects on clinical consumption of expected health care sector developments, in the context of the Secretary of State's proposal to restrict the number of hospital beds to 4 per 1,000 population in the Netherlands. The second part describes the method of data collection and analyses clinical consumption in total, and by age, sex and type of insurance.

412 Schwemin, B. and Stollenwerk, H.H. (1975) 'The economic effects of a constant nursing rate' ('Die wirtschaftlichen Auswirkungen des linearen Pflegesatzes'), *Die Ortskrankenkasse*, **57**, 18, 678–86.

413 Swertz, P. (1975) 'Hospital cost problems' ('Kostenprobleme des Krankenhauses') in: Blohmke, M. (ed.), The Cost of Health Care Systems, Social Ecology, and Social Medicine (*Kosten des Gesundheitswesens, Sozialökologie und Sozialmedizin*), Stuttgart: A.W. Gentner-Verlag, (Schriftenreihe Arbeitsmedizin, Sozialmedizin und Präventivmedizin, Vol. 56), 49–57.

288 Van Aert, J.H. and Van Montfort, A.P.W.P. (1975) 'Basic investigation of hospital costs' ('Het Basisonderzoek Kostenstruktuur Ziekenhuizen'), *Het Ziekenhuis*, **5**, 22, 560–3.

The basic investigation of hospital costs project was set up by the Foundation for Medical Registration to gain insight into a number of patient and hospital characteristics. The 89 participating hospitals are categorized into 4 four function groups (from group 1, local hospitals, to group 4, hospitals with the most complex functions and facilities). A number of variables are then compared for each of the function groups separately: patient age groups per diagnosis category per function group; total personnel per 100 beds; investment costs per bed; average number of beds; duration of stay per diagnosis group per function group; and complicated operations per 100 admissions. The general trend seems to be that, in line with expectations, the function groups 3 and 4 do seem to deal with the more difficult patient groups and that the more common diagnosis groups dominate in function groups 1 and 2. Further research will focus on testing this hypothesis and quantifying this trend. The conclusions reached will provide an important indication of the extent to which hospital facilities can further be rationalized by internal division of labour.

784 Van der Gaag, J., Rutten, F.F.H., and Van Praag, B.M.S. (1975) 'Determinants of hospital utilization in the Netherlands', *Health Services Research*, **10**, 3, 264–77. Also: *An Inquiry into the Determinants of Hospital Utilization, with Reference to Government Intervention, The Dutch Case*, Leiden: Rijksuniversiteit Leiden, Economisch Instituut, 28 pp. (mimeographed document).

289 Various Authors (1975) 'Special issue on the health care sector' ('Speciale sanità'), *Prospettive Sociali e Sanitarie*, **5**, 17/18, 1–34.

Special issue of the journal devoted to the present organization of the Italian health care system, and the potential for the creation of a national health service. Use is made of data from a survey by the Associazione Nazionale Aiuti ed Assistenti Ospedalieri and the Institute for Research in Health Economics. Evaluation of the proliferation of recent health reform legislation shows that it has had little effect. A strategy for solving the problems without the introduction of a national health service is outlined. These problems include the financing of hospital activities, contract renewal between the medical profession and the health insurance agencies, the definition of drugs to be distributed free of charge, and methods for calculating drug prices. Finally, information is given on the regional distribution of health services and personnel. An assessment is made of the performance of regional authorities in the health sector.

1976

788 BLANPAIN, J.E. (1976) 'Survey of medical organization patterns in hospitals' ('Overzicht van samenwerkingsverbanden'), *Acta Hospitalia*, **16**, 1–2, 84–91.

290 BRUNET-JAILLY, J. (1976) 'The distribution of costs between public hospitals' ('La dispersion des coûts entre hôpitaux publics'), *Revue Economique*, **27**, 3, 506–52.

Although theorists have been convinced for some time that it is impossible to treat a hospital as a business firm, business enterprise models are still frequently and mistakenly used in health economics. This article sets out the reasons why this practice should be abandoned, and then analyses the variables that explain the distribution of hospital costs. The results, very different from those obtained in Canada in comparable conditions, show little relation between the resources available to hospitals and the tasks demanded of them by their patients.

291 CHALAVET, S. (1976) Hospital Cost Price (*Le prix de revient hospitalier*), Paris: Editions Médicales et Universitaires (Collection Economie et Santé, No. 2), 260 pp.

The author, who was in charge of the Central Office of Costs and Statistics of Paris Hospitals from 1968 to 1975, believes that operating accounts provide the information necessary for understanding the economic performance of hospitals. These accounts facilitate the correct determination of cost price, and are therefore important, both in studying individual estalishments, and in forming a health policy at the national macro-economic level. However, his experience has shown that there are numerous defects in the accounting system, which must be eliminated in order to improve management and planning of the hospital system.

292 EICHHORN, S. (1976) 'The structure and organization of hospital managements' ('Struktur und Organisation des Krankenhausmanagements') *Zeitschrift für Organisation*, **45**, 7, 364–70.

The author analyses the traditional structure and organization of hospitals in the Federal Republic of Germany, and suggests modifications that would lead to more effective functioning.

790 EMBRECHTS, G. (1976) Growth and Evolution of Hospital Organizations (*Groei en Evolutie van Zuejebgyusirgabusatues)*, Antwerp: Rijks-

universitair Centrum, Leerstoel Bijzondere Sociologie (thesis in applied economics), 220 pp.

293 Goisis, G. (1976) Returns to Scale and Economic Efficiency in the Production of Hospital Services (*Rendimento di scala ed efficienza economica nella produzione di servizi ospedalieri*), Milan: Antonio Giuffrè, xi + 168 pp.

The objective of this study was to identify the factors that determine the cost structure of hospitals. In the Lombardy region, 105 public hospitals were grouped according to size, and their production and cost functions were estimated for 1972 and 1973. These functions revealed many characteristics of the production process in the hospital sector. It was found that the average variable cost curve begins to slope upwards in the 300-350 bed range. In the final section of the book, determinants of the demand for hospital care are discussed.

294 Hacquart, G. (1976) Economic Aspects of the Hospital Service Unit (*Aspects économiques de l'unité de soins hospitalière*), Paris: Editions Médicales et Universitaires (Collection Economie et Santé, No. 4) 336 pp.

The cost of personnel (more than 60% of total hospital costs), the demand for their services, and the utilization of their labour within the hospital unit need further study, according to the author. Duplication of tasks and improper use of personnel increase costs and staff dissatisfaction. Patients should be classified according to their degree of dependence, so that the volume of direct care needed and consequently the work load of the staff could be calculated directly. Nurses in France would thereby be able to devote more than the present 30% of their labour to direct care of patients. Information on five hospital units in France, and from several foreign countries, is analysed. The foreign studies revealed that the amount of labour available in a hospital unit depends more on its architectural structure, its internal organization, and the organization of the hospital than on the number and type of patients present.

295 Iuele, R. (1976) 'Hospital care by the National Institute of Health Insurance between 1950 and 1974' ('L'assistenza ospedaliera del'Istituto Nazionale per l'Assicurazione contro le Malattie nel periodo 1950–1974'), *I Problemi della Sicurezza Sociale*, **31**, 5, 494–527.

Responsibility for hospital care in Italy passed from the social insurance agencies to the regional authorities, under Law no. 386 in 1974. This article presents an economic and statistical balance-sheet, for the period 1950 to 1974, of the hospital management experience of l'Istituto Nazionale per l'Assicurazione contro le Malattie, the major Italian health insurance agency. Trends in hospital expenditure are identified and an analysis is made of expenditure components. It is argued that the system used to finance hospital care must be improved, and that more effective control of the organisations providing hospital services is needed.

296 JONSSON, EGON and MARKE, L.Å. (1976) 'Financial aspects of computerized tomography' ('Datortomografi — ekonomiska synpunkter'), *Läkartidningen*, **73**, 32, 2609–14.

This article surveys the financial aspect of using computerized tomography instead of other diagnostic methods. The authors conclude that the use of computerized tomography should result in considerable savings on health service expenditure in Sweden.

297 MIZRAHI, A. and MIZRAHI, A. (1976) Hospitalization According to the 1970 Survey of Medical Consumption (*L'hospitalisation d'après l'enquête de 1970 sur les consommations médicales*), Paris: Centre de Recherches et de Documentation sur la Consommation, 84 pp.

LECOMTE, T. MIZRAHI, A., and MIZRAHI, A. (1976) 'Hospitalization and its place in medical expenditure in 1970' (L'hospitalisation et sa place dans les dé médicales en 1970'), *Consommation*, No. 3, 43–82.

During the 1970 INSEE–CREDOC survey (Institut National de la Statistique et des Etudes Economiques — Centre de Recherches et de Documentation sur la Consommation) of French medical consumption, 647 cases of hospital patients were examined. These papers use the survey information to make standardized comparisons of public and private hospitals of all types. The average length of stay in a public general hospital was 17.4 days and in a private clinic 11.4 days. The most important causes of hospitalization in public general hospitals were accidents, injuries, and pregnancies; in private clinics they were diseases of the digestive tract and pregnancies. The most common surgical operations in public general hospitals were to treat fractures, while in clinics appendectomies occurred most frequently. Women were hospitalized more often than men in the 16-39 year age group, because of maternity; over the age of 50, however, more men than women were hospitalized. Clinics usually treated young adults, whereas the elderly and children were mainly cared for in public hospitals. In 1970, the survey found annual expenditure on hospitalization was Fr. 206 per person, or 35% of total per capita medical expenditure. Half of all medical expenditure for children under two years was spent on hospitalization. This proportion dropped to a minimum for those aged between 40 and 64, and then rose sharply.

298 SCHLAUSS, H.-J. (1976) 'Cost containment: price linkage in hospitals' ('Kostendämpfung: pretiale Lenkung am Krankenhaus?'), *Der Deutsche Arzt*, No. 12, 26–7.

The author argues that hospital costs can be contained only if legal provisions are made to ensure that financial security of the hospital, and laws concerning hospital cost-setting mechanisms are correctly applied.

299 SELIN, T. and PERSSON, E. (1976) 'The development of hospitals in Sweden, Denmark, Finland, and Norway during the 1960s', *Tidsskrift for Danske Sygehuse*, Vol. 52, 116–22.

This article outlines trends in the development of hospitals in Sweden, Denmark, Finland, and Norway during the 1960s and early 1970s. The population, gross national product, and expenditure for social services are tabulated for each country, together with the number of hospitals, their capacities, and their production. The annual costs of the hospitals and their staffs are also presented. The running costs of the hospitals for each country are increasing at two to three times the rate of growth of the gross national product. This is due to the fact that the prices of the resources for public health services have increased more rapidly than other prices, and that the quality of medical care has improved. Denmark and Finland appear to have been more successful than Sweden in keeping down the running costs of the hospital system.

300 SPEK, J.E. and THORBURN, T. (1976) Analysis of Cost Relationships in International Health Care Delivery (*Analys av kostnadsförhållanden inom utomlänssjukvården*), Gothenburg: University of Gothenburg, Department of Economics (Memorandum No. 63), 203 pp. + appendix 14 pp.

Discusses the development of a basis for pricing in the Swedish health care system, when patients from one country are treated in hospitals in another country. In order to set prices covering all hospital costs, the authors estimate the costs of different treatments on the basis of a sample of patients' records. A pricing system for inter-country health care deliveries is suggested and discussed.

301 SPRI (1976) Computerized Skull Tomography — Economic Aspects (*Datortomografi av skallen — ekonomiska beräkningar*), Stockholm: The Swedish Planning and Rationalization Institute of the Health and Social Services (SPRI Report 9/76), 28 pp.

Discusses economic aspects of substituting computerized tomography (CT) for other diagnostic methods. The new technique reduces the need for pneumoencephalograms (1 per 3,700 inhabitants) and cerebral angiograms (1 per 700 inhabitants) performed annually in Sweden at an average cost respectively of Sw.Kr. 3,500 and 2,200. The corresponding cost of a CT head scan is Sw.Kr. 300-350. The introduction of CT scanning is expected to reduce the number of pneumoencephalograms by 70% and of cerebral angiograms by 50%, yielding an annual expenditure saving of about Sw.Kr. 15 million.

765 SPRI (1976) *Hospital Buildings 3. Cost Projection Method. Linear Regression Analysis*, Stockholm: The Swedish Planning and Rationalization Institute of the Health and Social Services (SPRI Report 10/76), 21 pp.

302 SPRUYT, M. (1976) The Evolution of Costs in the Hospital Sector in Belgium (*Kostenentwikkeling van het ziekenhuiswezen in België*), Antwerp: Rijksuniversitair Centrum (PhD thesis in applied economics), 109 pp.

Emphasizes the problem of sub-optimal use of acute hospital beds and considers possible corrective measures. Concludes with some forecasts and a discussion of 'health villages'.

641 VAN MONTFORT, A.P.W.P. and SPAAN, J.M. (1976) 'Hospital costs from 1971 to 1974' ('Kosten over 1971 t/m 1974 van ziekenrichtingen'), *Het Ziekenhuis*, **6**, 4, 98–100.

303 WIPF, M. (1976) 'Calculation of hospital costs' ('Die Kostenrechnung in den Spitälern'), *Das Schweizer Spital — L'hôpital suisse*, **40**, 2, 2–3.

The Veska committee (Vereinigung Schweizerischer Krankenhäuser) for cost calculation in hospitals published a handbook for cost accounting in hospitals, in 1976. It serves both as an instruction manual and an aide memoire in implementing cost accounting in Swiss hospitals. The author reports the presentation of the first volume to the Conference of Swiss Sanatoria Directors. The conference recommended that: the use of the Veska accounting method should be made compulsory; the method should be introduced in all Swiss hospitals; and the performance evaluation method worked out by Veska should be adopted by the cantonal governments.

1977

304 BRUCKENBERGER, E. (1977) 'Cost reduction through increased complexity in the health care system' ('Kostensenkung durch Erhöhung der

Komplexität im Gesundheitswesen'), *Arzt und Krankenhaus*, **2**, 3, 11–25.

The author argues that the development of special facilities (e.g. hostels) for the care of patients after intensive hospital treatment would lead to savings in the hospital sector.

645 GYGI, P. and HENNY, H. (1977) The Swiss Health Care System (*Le système suisse de santé – Das schweizerische Gesundheitswesen*), Berne: Hans Huber Verlag, 328 pp.

143 MIZRAHI, A. and MIZRAHI, A. (1977) The Effect of Socio-Economic Factors on Hospitalization (*Influence des facteurs socio-économiques sur l'hospitalisation*), Paris: Centre de Recherche pour l'Etude et l'Observation des Conditions de Vie, 92 pp.; *Consommation*, No. 2, 5–58.

594 SCHRÄDER, W.F. and VOLKHOLZ, V. (eds) (1977) Regional Analysis of Medical Care (*Regionale Analyse der Medizinischen Versorgung*), Berlin: Technische Universität Berlin, Berliner Arbeitsgruppe Strukturforschung im Gesundheitswesen (Schriftenreihe No. 2), 307 pp.

4. General Practice, Physician Practice, Community Care

1964

305 LIEFMANN-KEIL, E. (1964) 'On the economic importance of physicians' activities' ('Ueber die volkswirtschaftliche Bedeutung der ärztlichen Tätigkeit'), *Bundesgesundheitsblatt*, No. 7, 177–81.

Questions of the economic and social costs relevant to the health care sector are discussed with reference to physicians' activities, and the economic consequences of extended longevity are analysed.

1970

306 LINDEN, R. (1970) 'The structure of costs in general practice' ('Die Kostenstruktur der Allgemeinpraxis'), *Zeitschrift für Allgemeinmedizin*, **46**, 8, 406–8.

The cost structure of general practice is analysed and discussed, and a cost distribution sheet is suggested as a basis for facilitating comparisons between practices.

90 Pannier, R. (1970) Man — Medicine — Community — The Place of Medicine in Present-Day Society (*Mens — Geneeskunde — Gemeenschap — De plaats van de geneeskunde in het huiding maatschappelijk bestel*), Brussels: Arscia uitgaven n.v., Presses académiques européennes, 466 pp.

307 Thiemeyer, T. (1970), 'Socio-political and economic problems of physicians' fees' ('Sozialpolitische und ökonomische Probleme ärztlicher Honorargestaltung'), *Sozialer Fortschritt*, **19**, 5–6, 101–5.

The fee system is a pricing system that has to serve four goals: (1) to regulate the supply of physicians' services in ambulatory care according to time and place; (2) to manipulate, stimulate, or limit the demand for physicians' services; (3) to determine the share of the scarce economic good (physicians' services) in the economy, and the income of physicians relative to other occupations; (4) to determine whether the demanding person has to contribute to the financing of health services beyond his insurance premiums. The functions of fees are to be seen as part of a policy of production and distribution. The physician in the Federal Republic of Germany can manipulate three factors: number of permanent patients, number of cases, and number of acts performed. The salaried physician has no incentive to increase any of these. With a fee-for-service, however, the physician may manipulate all three; in addition, his productivity influences his income. The conclusion is that the income of the physician has to be linked to the general costs of living and the inflation rate. Otherwise, the economy has to face many undesired effects of a fee policy.

1972

93 Brenna, A. and Lucioni, C. (1972) 'Health expenditures: primary care' ('Spesa sanitaria: la medicina di primo intervento'), *Economia Pubblica*, **2**, 5/6, 3–12.

308 Denmark, Government of (1972) Home Nursing. Second Report of a Committee Appointed by the National Health Services on Health Visiting and Home Nursing (*Hjemmesygeplejen, betækning II*), Copenhagen: Statens Trykningskontor (Betænkning No. 648), 147 pp.

This report analyses the system of home nursing, including its economic aspects. It recommends a publicly run community system, providing home nursing services in close cooperation with the local GP and social services. The report includes relevant research. The proposed system was later implemented.

309 ROEMER, M.I. (1972) *Evaluation of Community Health Centres*, Geneva: World Health Organization (Public Health Papers, No. 48), 42 pp.

This report aims to clarify the various meanings of 'health centres', to review the literature on their evolution, and to suggest future studies. Chapter I reviews the functional definitions of health centres from their historical background to the present, then considers developing countries, before concluding with the functions of an integrated primary health centre. Chapter II considers various approaches to evaluating primary health centres, based on: resource provision, services provided, quality of services, health improvements achieved, and cost. Chapter III recommends research into practical delivery methods for primary care, staffing and operational policy, and measurement of effectiveness in changing health status. It suggests that research design for programme evaluation should be multi-centre and multi-country; it should involve areas with clearly differentiated inputs of health centre services; and it should apply specific criteria for measuring health improvement, based on well-kept birth and death records, and sample surveys of the population, over a period of at least three years.

1973

671 COMMISSION OF THE EUROPEAN COMMUNITIES (1973) Synthesis of Three Investigations of the Main Items of Health Insurance Expenditure Covered by Social Security (*Rapport de synthèse concernant trois études sur les principaux postes des dépenses de l'assurance maladie couvertes par la sécurité sociale*), Brussels: Commission of the European Communities, General Directorate of Social Affairs (Report No. V/396/73-F), 38 pp. (mimeographed document).

310 DELIEGE, D. (1973) Remuneration of Doctors: What Are the Official Rates in Europe? (*Les rémunérations des médecins: Quels sont les tarifs officiels en Europe?*), Brussels: Université de Louvain, Ecole de Santé Publique, 16 pp.

Compares doctors' earnings in the six initial countries of the European Economic Community. The average official salary is calculated for the beginning and end of the main salaried careers (public health officers, university professors and assistants, and health insurance fund doctors). The potential earnings of professional doctors are estimated on the basis of fees-for-services in different specialties in the different countries. On average, fees vary by up to 100% between the countries, and even more between the individual specialties. The implication is that there is no European consensus on the relative value of particular services.

239 KOCK, S.E. (1973) Simulation of Hospital Activities (*Simulering av sjukhusfunktioner*), Helsinki: Svenska Handelshögskolans Publikationer, 45 pp. (mimeographed document).

1974

311 BLUECHEL, K. (1974) The White Sorcerers, the Billion Dollar Sickness Business (*Die weissen Magier, das Milliardengeschäft mit der Krankheit*), Munich — Vienna: Bertelsmann, 432 pp.

A critical discussion of the factors that have led to the present social role and significance of physicians, such as the doctor shortage, the growth in demand for the services of the health system, etc.

408 GREFFER, M. (1974) 'The provision of medical services at stable prices' ('Medizinische Leistungen zu konstanten Preisen'), *Arbeit und Sozialpolitik*, **29**, 1, 13–18.

312 WORKING PARTY OF THE SOCIETY FOR SOCIAL PROGRESS (1974) The Changing Position of Doctors in the Distribution of Income, Physicians' Earnings, the Payment System, and Physicians' Services (*Der Wandel der Stellung des Arztes im Einkommensgefüge, Arzteinkommen, Honorierungssystem und ärztliche Tätigkeit*), Berlin: Duncker & Humblot (Schriften der Gesellschaft für Sozialen Fortschritt, Vol. 20), 139 pp.

The first part of the report deals with the income distribution of physicians in the Federal Republic of Germany, the development of their income levels, and the influence exerted upon them. The second part is devoted to a discussion of the system of fee schedule and the reimbursement of physicians, from the political perspective. Finally, individual contributors discuss the problems of physician reimbursement, income growth, productivity factors in the determination of income, and selected cost factors in private practice.

1975

313 Bjerkelund, C. (1975) 'Doctors and priorities in the health service' ('Legene og prioriteringen i helsevesenet'), *Nordisk Medicin*, **90**, 4, 105–8.

Argues that doctors and research workers demand resources without comparing their benefits and costs. Emphasizes the potential of cost–benefit analysis as a tool for rational decision making in the health sector.

314 Herder-Dorneich, P. (1975) 'The theory of "double dynamics" in the earnings of doctors' ('Die These von der "doppelten Dynamik" der ärztlichen Einkommen'), *Sozialer Fortschritt*, **24**, 5–6, 121–5.

The author critically analyses the theory of 'double dynamics' in physician reimbursement. 'Double dynamics' is defined as the increase in the physician's income arising from an increase in the number of services provided coupled with increases in fee schedules.

315 Metze, I. (1975) 'Problems of medical income and their reform' ('Probleme der Ärztehonorierung und ihre Reform') in: Lampert, H., Current Problems in Health Policy in the FRG (*Aktuelle Probleme der Gesundheitspolitik in der BRD)*, Berlin: Duncker & Humblot (Schriften des Vereins für Sozialpolitik, Neue Folge, Vol. 82), 29–94.

Incomes of doctors in private practice were, in 1971, more than six times higher than the average income of employed workers, and three times higher than the income of doctors working in administration, with an extremely low variance. The paper analyses the determinants of doctors' incomes in private practice. It finds that the quantity of services produced rose 5.7% per year between 1959 and 1971, while the number of doctors increased by only 0.6%, and other personnel by under 2.6% per year. The main reason is the rise in labour productivity. During the same period the price per service rose by 5.3% per year. Because costs per service also rose by 5.2%, net income increased by 10.2%. The shortage of doctors, combined with the competition for better services for their clients among different health insurance funds, supported the doctors' demand to replace the former lump-sum-payment by a fee-for-service system. The strong market position of doctors was also supported by price differentiation, according to the income of the clients of the funds, and by region. The rise in income of private practitioners obliged the government to modify payment methods to doctors in hospitals and administration, in order to reduce the disparity with private practitioners. The paper ends with a model to calculate the rise needed in medical service prices to maintain the relative income position of doctors.

316 NIEUWENHUIS, A. (1975) The Referral of Patients to Hospitals by Family Doctors (*Het verwijzen van ziekenhuispatienten door de huisarts*), The Hague: Centraal Planbureau, 16 pp.

The 70% of the Dutch population who have compulsory health insurance receive free specialist care only if they have been referred by a GP. The number of referrals per 100 compulsory insured has increased from 24.3 in 1953, to 45.7 in 1971. This paper attempts to identify the determinants of referral and to estimate their relative importance.

317 SCHLÖGELL, R. (1975) 'Physicians' services: responsibilities and economic consequences' in: EHRLICH, D.A. (ed.) *The Health Care Cost Explosion: Which Way Now?*, Berne: Hans Huber Verlag, 101–5.

Argues that physicians alone are not responsible for the rise in health care costs and discusses the role of other factors, including political promises, demographic and social change, and technical progress in medicine.
See 26.

414 WOLLNY, G. (1975) 'The income of doctors and Gross National Product' ('Arzthonorar und Bruttosozialprodukt'), *Die Ortskrankenkasse*, **57**, 19, 713–22.

1976

191 DELIEGE-ROTT, D., LIEVENS, J., and ZEEGERS-DOOREMAN, C. (1976) *Medical Doctors in the Nine Countries of the Common Market*, Brussels: CIACO, 335 pp.

791 HATTINGA-VERSCHURE, J.C.M. (1976) 'The influence of physician payment systems and medical staff organization on the quality of health care' ('Betekenis van betaalsystemen en samenwerkingsverbanden voor de kwaliteit van zorgen'), *Acta Hospitalia*, **16**, 1–2, 153–62.

792 HECKMAN, J. (1976) 'Payment systems and ethics' ('Betaalsystemen en ethica'), *Acta Hospitalia*, **16**, 1–2, 74–83.

1977

645 Gygi, P. and Henny, H. (1977) The Swiss Health Care System (*Le système suisse de santé — Das schweizerische Gesundheitswesen*), Berne: Hans Huber Verlag, 328 pp.

318 Rutten, F.F.H. and Van der Gaag, J. (1977) 'Referrals and demand for specialist care in the Netherlands', *Health Services Research*, **12**, 3, 233–49.

Three independent sets of data are analysed to investigate the determinants of referrals from general practitioners to specialists, the demand for specialist care, and the rapid increase in referrals and use of specialists in the Netherlands. Individual determinants of demand are examined with data from a three-man group practice; macro-analyses are conducted on cross-section data from all service areas of the Dutch Sickness Fund Organization for 1971 and 1973, and cross-section time-series data from all provinces for the period 1960 to 1972. Regression coefficients are estimated for socio-economic and supply of care variables, which explain the number of referrals to specialists, and the amount of care given by specialists. Results are discussed in the light of Feldstein's classification of three types of care, in which, for some types, the physician is seen as generating the demand for care. The authors conclude that demand for specialist outpatient care is largely supply-determined, and that general practitioners substitute for specialists; they also suggest that the dual physician payment system in the Netherlands (capitation for legally insured patients and fee-for-service for privately insured patients) contributes to increased use of specialist care.

5. The Pharmaceutical Industry

1964

319 Ravazzi, G. (1964) 'Structure and problems of the Italian pharmaceutical market' ('Strutture e problemi del mercato farmaceutico italiano'), *Rivista Internazionale di Scienze Economiche e Commerciali*, **11**, 10, 928–82.

The author analyses the production, distribution, and consumption of Italian pharmaceuticals. Among the issues discussed are: industrial concentration, scientific research, patent registration of new drugs, price structure, health insurance, and consumption of pharmaceutical products. The author argues that the Italian pharmaceutical industry has problems similar to those found in other countries, such as many small production units, an ever-increasing burden of distribution costs, and pharmaceutical over-consumption.

1968

320 BARRAL, E. (1968) Structural Analysis of the Pharmaceutical Industry in France (*Analyse structurale de l'industrie pharmaceutique en France*), Paris: Université de Paris, Faculté de Droit et des Sciences Economiques (PhD thesis), 796 pp. (3 volumes) (mimeographed documents).

The first chapter discusses the various determinants of demand for pharmaceuticals: biological, demographic, psycho-sociological, socio-economic, and technical. The second analyses supply. The French pharmaceutical industry is then compared with foreign pharmaceutical industries. The third chapter assesses the economic consequences of pricing policies in different countries, and examines the drug policies of their social security systems. The fourth chapter evaluates the impact on the French pharmaceutical industry of outside competition, particularly from the European Economic Community. Material and manpower resources used in pharmaceutical research are described in the fifth chapter. The author concludes by asserting that, in the future, pharmaceutical product competition will be replaced by price competition, which will eventually expedite the restructuring of the European pharmaceutical industries.

321 MEDUSA, G. (1968) 'Drug prescription policy under the Italian health insurance system. Influence of organizational patterns in health insurance on the development of drug consumption' ('Aspetti e problemi dell'assistenza farmaceutica in Italia. Influenza dei modelli organizzativi della protezione sociale sullo sviluppo dei consumi farmaceutici'), *Economia e Lavoro*, (special number: The pharmaceutical problem in the context of social security), **2**, 5, 563–609.

Production costs, prices, and the demand for pharmaceutical products are influenced by the organization of the health care system and by economic and legal features of the pharmaceutical industry. A comprehensive strategy to solve problems in the pharmaceutical market is required. Health insurance agencies should use a variety of methods to manipulate demand for medicines. For example, a proportional or fixed fee could be charged for every prescription, with the exception of essential medicines. Further, a government agency should be created to administer the production, purchase, and distribution of essential medicines. Finally, it is argued that better patent protection, and the entry of public enterprises into the pharmaceutical sector, would yield substantial benefits.

322 SABA, A. (1968) 'The pharmaceutical industry: structure, production, and role of the public enterprise' ('Il settore farmaceutico: strutture produttive, produzione e ruolo dell'impresa pubblica'), *Economia e Lavoro*, (special number: The pharmaceutical problem in the context of social security), **2**, 5, 611–29.

This article begins with an examination of the principal problems caused by the economic and institutional structure of the Italian pharmaceutical sector. Possible strategies for state intervention are then outlined. The author argues that the improvement of patent protection, the entry of public enterprise into the sector, and the elimination of very small production units would improve the industry. Particular importance is attached to the development of public enterprise, which would have two major goals: the creation of active centres for scientific research, and the concentration of productive capacity.

323 VARALDO, R. (1968) The Role of Scientific Research in the Economics of the Pharmaceutical Industry (*La ricerca scientifica nell'economia delle aziende farmaceutiche*), Pisa: Colombo Cursi, 294 pp.

This book discusses the role of research in the Italian pharmaceutical industry. The relationship between science and industry, and the research policies of the pharmaceutical producers, are discussed. A correlation is made between the size of the company and the amount of research it carries out, and the Italian industry is examined in detail. The effect on management of competition in the pharmaceutical market for new products is evaluated. In order to avoid obsolesence in this sector, and extensive research programme is called for.

1969

324 ANONYMOUS (1969) 'Economic analysis of moderate centralization of pharmaceutical production' ('Økonomisk analyse vedr. mild centralisering'), *Archiv for Pharmaci og Kemi*, Vol. 76, 517–33.

Report of a meeting organized by the Danish pharmacists' association in 1969, to discuss centralization of production of drugs prepared in pharmacies. The discussion was based on an investigation into the possible economic consequences of centralization.

325 Medusa, G., Petralia, S., and Inghilesi, M. (1969) 'Prescription drugs and health care reform' ('Il problema farmaceutico e la riforma sanitaria'), *I Problemi della Sicurezza Sociale*, **24**, 6, 971–1005.

The authors present a detailed examination of certain aspects of the consumption, distribution, and production of pharmaceuticals. The distortions in this market are discussed. Recent health care, and legislative and economic policies related to pharmaceuticals are evaluated. It is argued that the improvement of patent protection and the development of public pharmaceutical enterprises should be encouraged.

326 OECD (1969) *Pharmaceuticals*, Paris: Organization for Economic Cooperation and Development (Series Gaps in Technology, Vol. 5), 149 pp.

Analyses by a group of experts of the microeconomic aspects of the pharmaceutical sector in Western developed countries, including production and productivity, labour inputs, investments, company size and economies of scale, price trends, etc. Priorities, and research and development investments, receive special attention in a separate chapter.

327 Sweden, Government of (1969) The Pharmaceutical Industry (*Läkemedelsindustrin*), Stockholm: Esselte AB (Statens Offentliga Utredningar), 298 pp.

During the 1960s, the government committee on concentration in private industry analysed a number of industrial sectors in Sweden. This report describes the structure of the pharmaceutical industry and analyses market performance, research and development, and pricing policies. A theoretical chapter by Guy Arvidsson confronts the empirical studies with a theoretical analysis of optimal pricing policy and research and development.

1971

328 Centre for Pharmaceutical Research (ed.) (1971) Pharmaceutical Research at a Turning Point, Proceedings of a Study Day, Villa Miani, Rome, 22 October 1971) (*La ricerca farmaceutica al bivio, Atti della giornata di studio, Roma — Villa Miani, 22 ottobre 1971*), Rome: Centro per Ricerce Farmaceutice, 150 pp.

Proceedings of a conference on pharmaceutical research. The following topics are discussed: methods of financing research; criteria for rational allocation of resources; the links between pure and industrial research; the responsiveness of research to health policy; and the impact on the research programme of prices and the demand for pharmaceutical products. The intervention of the state in the pharmaceutical sector is considered. Regulations on experimentation, registration of drugs, and price determination are evaluated.

329 KASTNER, F. (1971) 'Problems of drug cost inflation for the statutory health insurance scheme' ('Probleme der Arzneikostenentwicklung in der gesetzlichen Krankenversicherung'), *Pharma Dialog*, No. 4, 26 pp.

The problems of rising trends in the cost of providing drugs and medication under the statutory German health insurance scheme are discussed and examined at the level of both distribution and consumption.

330 LUCIONI, C. and MONTI, L. (1971) 'The planning and control of research projects in the pharmaceutical industry' ('La programmazione e il controllo dei progetti di ricerca nell'industria farmaceutica') in: VARIOUS AUTHORS, Industrial Research Projects (*I progetti di ricerca industriale*), Rome: Il Crogiolo, 277–84.

Since it is difficult to predict the biological effect of a chemical in man, a positive outcome in pharmaceutical research is intrinsically uncertain. Despite this, the authors claim that the programme evaluation review systems technique (PERT) can improve the management of research projects, particularly for those projects concerned with improving the production of medicines already in use. Introduction of PERT into project management requires an investment of about 1% of the total project cost, but it can reduce costs by 10–15% and shorten project time by 20–30%.

331 NOWOTNY, O.H. (1971) *International Drug Prices, Reasonable or Exorbitant?*, Basle: Hoffmann-La Roche, 55 pp.

This paper reviews the innovative role of the pharmaceutical industry and the concept of 'reasonable' prices in the context of efforts to improve health care at acceptable cost. Having considered the principal economic and other factors involved, including research costs and risks, market competition, clinical trends, and public policy, the author concludes that the industry makes a positive and economic contribution to health care improvement. He goes on to consider the future economics of the industry against the trend of increasing industrialization in the health sector, in both hospital and ambulatory care, and the possibility that this will contain rising labour costs.

A brief review of these issues is also given in: NOWOTNY, O.H. (1975) 'The economics of the pharmaceutical industry' in: EHRLICH, D.A. (ed.) *The Health Care Cost Explosion: Which Way Now?*, Berne: Hans Huber Verlag, 149–52.
See 26.

332 PHARMA INFORMATION (1971) Documentation on the Research-Based Pharmaceutical Industry (*Documentation sur l'industrie de recherche du médicament*), Basle: Pharma Information, 288 pp.

This book, published by a group of large Swiss research-based pharmaceutical firms, attempts to give an overall picture of the industry. Chapters cover drug pricing, industry profits, brands and specialties, licences, information and advertising, quality control, safety, research, 'molecular manipulation', risks, competition, the economic and social contributions of the pharmaceutical industry, and relations between drugs and health care costs.

1972

333 FRANCE, MINISTRY FOR INDUSTRIAL AND SCIENTIFIC DEVELOPMENT and MINISTRY OF PUBLIC HEALTH (1972) The Problems of the Pharmaceutical Industry — Towards a Health Policy Series, No. 21 (*Etude des problèmes de l'industrie pharmaceutique — Série: Pour une politique de santé*, No. 21), Paris: Ministère du Développement Industriel et Scientifique et Ministère de la Santé Publique, 107 pp. (mimeographed document).

Report produced by a joint ministerial committee formed in 1970, on the problems of the French pharmaceutical industry and the means by which a contractual relationship can be established between the industry and the public authorities. The economic and technical features of the industry and its relationship to the authorities are examined. Finally, the procedures for putting new drugs on the market are discussed, as well as social security policy on drug prices and reimbursement.

334 FRANCE, MINISTRY FOR INDUSTRIAL AND SCIENTIFIC DEVELOPMENT and MINISTRY OF PUBLIC HEALTH (1972) Pharmaceutical Research — Towards a Health Policy Series, No. 18 (*La recherche pharmaceutique — Série: Pour une politique de santé*, No. 18), Paris: Ministère du Développement Industriel et Scientifique et Ministère de la Santé Publique, 35 pp. (mimeographed document).

Future problems in pharmaceutical research are assessed in this report, produced by a joint committee of the Ministry for Industrial and Scientific Development and the Ministry of Public Health. The use of resources, the results of French pharmaceutical research, and a projection of its developments are discussed. Policy suggestions are made.

335 MEDUSA, G. and DE SANTIS, M. (1972) 'Drug Consumption and Expenditure in Italy' ('Il consumo e la spesa farmaceutica in Italia'), *I Problemi della Sicurezza Sociale*, **27**, 2, 219–46.

Using data collected by the National Institute of Health Insurance, the authors describe the negative features of the Italian pharmaceutical market. They discuss recent proposals for state intervention in this market. In terms of supply, these include patent protection, the development of public enterprises, and improved methods for fixing prices. In terms of demand, they include reform of the health system, improved public health education, and the specification of 'essential' pharmaceuticals.

336 RIEBEL, P. (1972) Costs and Prices (*Kosten und Preise*), Opladen: Westdeutscher Verlag, 119 pp.

An analysis of cost conditions in the pharmaceutial industry, with particular attention to cost structure and cost sharing. Extensive reference is made to drug price formation.

1973

337 FELDING, F. (1973) 'Industrial drug production in Denmark' ('Industrial medicinfremstilling i Danmark'), *Medicinsk Forum*, **26**, 3, 85–97.

The economics of the Danish pharmaceutical industry is described. The author argues that, over the next decade, the industry needs to invest heavily in research and development and in new capital stock if it is to compete successfully with other countries. Relevant data are presented.

338 VON MANGER-KOENIG, L. (1973) 'The responsibility of the pharmaceutical industry for the delivery of health care' ('Die Verantwortung der Pharma-Industrie für die gesundheitliche Versorgung der Bevölkerung'), *Pharma Dialog*, No. 22, 19 pp.

Various aspects of the supply of pharmaceuticals are discussed, and their relevance for the system of health care in the Federal Republic of Gemany is indicated.

1974

339 DEL FAVERO, A. and LOJACONO, G. (1974) Drugs, Health, and Profits in Italy (*Farmaci, salute e profitti in Italia*), Milan: Feltrinelli, 224 pp.

This book analyses the role played by the pharmaceutical industry in the decline of the Italian health care system. Because, in the authors' view, previous critiques of the industry are inadequate, this analysis also considers economic, institutional, and legal factors influencing the industry. The complexity of the Italian health care sector is due to the predominance of foreign capital in the pharmaceutical industry, the widespread use of health insurance to finance medical care, and the variety of authorities and institutions concerned with health.

340 DUPUY, J.-P. and KARSENTY, S. (1974) The Pharmaceutical Invasion (*L'invasion pharmaceutique*), Paris: Editions du Seuil, 269 pp.

Influenced by the writing of Ivan Illich, this book considers specific problems in the pharmaceutical field as well as general ones related to health, medicine, and the doctor–patient relationship. The authors criticize the profits made by the pharmaceutical industry, and the mechanism for fixing the price of drugs. They attack the over-consumption of drugs, and claim that all aspects of life have become excessively 'medicalized'. Much of this critique is based on a study of drug consumption made by a research team of the Centre de Recherche sur le Bien-être. In conclusion, a number of suggestions are made for improving the situation. These include: reducing the production of 'me too' drugs, nationalizing the marketing of pharmaceutical products, and determining the true cost of raw materials. In addition, medical activity and the role of the doctor need to be redefined.

341 FRANCE, MEDICAL HIGH COMMISSION OF THE SOCIAL SECURITY (1974) Drugs and Health Insurance (*Le médicament et l'assurance maladie*), Paris: Haut-Comité Médical de la Sécurité Sociale, 58 pp. (mimeographed document).

The first part of this report describes the complicated regulations that affect the development of new drugs at various stages. Basic and applied research, and ministerial authorization procedures before a new drug can be marketed or included on the list of drugs reimbursed by social security, are discussed. The report also examines the information received by doctors in public and private hospitals on pharmaceutical products and medical prescriptions. The pharmaceutical share of total health insurance payments since 1960 is studied. Although it amounted to 25% in 1972, it has since declined. Ways of preventing pharmaceutical over-consumption in the EEC, and of improving data banks, are suggested.

486 STOLZ, P. (1974) Economics of Psychotropic Drugs. A Cost–Benefit Analysis of Tranquilliser Usage in the Federal Republic of Germany in 1972. (*Psychopharmaka — volkwirtschaftlich analysiert, eine Kosten–Nutzen–Analyse der Verwendung von Tranquilizern in der Bundesre-*

publik Deutschland im Jahre 1972), Zurich: Schulthess Polygraphischer Verlag (Basler sozialökonomische Studien, Vol. 4), 70 pp.

1975

342 Blunden, K. (1975) Study of the Evolution of Concentration in the Pharmaceutical Industry in France (*Etude sur l'évolution de la concentration dans l'industrie pharmaceutique en France*), Brussels: Commission of the European Communities, 126 pp.

This study analyses the role in industrial concentration of research, manufacturing, international trade, distribution networks, the relation between producers and consumers, and the social security system. It then analyses the structure of supply in terms of the number, concentration, turnover, and market share of the pharmaceutical companies, and in terms of the number, share in turnover, and market share of the products. Finally, it describes the financial connections of the six major French groups, and of other groups with laboratories in France. Extensive data are included.

380 Consumers' Association (1975) Drugs: Advertising and Over–Consumption (*Les médicaments: publicité et surconsommation*), Brussels: Association des Consommateurs, 258 pp.

150 Jönsson, B. (1975) 'How do drugs influence the economy of the health care sector?' ('Vad betyder läkemedel för sjukvårdsekonomin?'), *Svensk Farmaceutisk Tidskrift*, **79**, 12, 639–48.

343 Mapelli, V. (1975) 'Foreign investments in the Italian pharmaceutical industry' ('Gli investimenti esteri in Italia nell'industria farmaceutica'), *L'Industria*, No. 3/4, 154–64.

This article is concerned with foreign investment in the Italian pharmaceutical industry and its share of the market. Foreign investment was at its height between 1956 and 1966, when many Italian pharmaceutical companies were bought up. This was due to the fragmentation of the Italian firms, the increased consumption of pharmaceuticals by people with health insurance, and the backwardness of research. Pharmaceutical companies with foreign capital operating in Italy are listed. It is asserted that this foreign investment has produced no significant benefits for Italy, in terms of increased employment or improved technology.

344 SIGVARD, J. (1975) The Pharmaceutical Industry (*L'industrie du médicament*), Paris: Calmann-Lévy (Collection Perspective de l'Economique), 344 pp.

The problems and strategies of the main pharmaceutical groups dominating the French market are analysed in this book. Topics examined include: scientific research, price policy, and marketing methods. The increasing concentration of the pharmaceutical industry, the internationalization of capital, and the international division of the market are predicted.

345 STÅHL, I. (1975) 'Should the pharmaceutical industry be nationalized?' ('Skall vi socialisera läkemedelsindustrin?'), *Ekonomisk Debatt*, **3**, 5, 300–9; and (1976) in: *Värt att veta om läkemedel*, Stockholm: B. Wahlströms, 75–99.

Analyses and discusses the economic structure of the pharmaceutical industry in terms of theoretical welfare economics. Analysis of research and development policy and its consequences for pricing behaviour in an international market, with trade and multinational firms. gives conclusions different from those of traditional welfare theoretical analysis of optimal investment in research and development. The author considers the policy implications of the importance of pharmaceuticals to productivity growth in the health care sector. He concludes that nationalization is neither a necessary nor a sufficient means of bringing about changes that economic analysis suggests are desirable.
See 351.

1976

346 BERGWALL, G. (1976) 'Our exports and imports of drugs' ('Vår export och import ov läkemedel') in: BERGWALL, G. (ed.) Drugs (*Om Läkemedel*), Stockholm: B. Wahlströms, 173–89.

Discusses the internationalization of the pharmaceutical market, with reference to the pharmaceutical market in Sweden. Specialization of pharmaceutical firms will increase imports from foreign firms, at the same time as domestic firms increase their exports.

347 BRENNA, A. (1976) 'The cost of pharmaceutical research' ('Il costo della ricerca farmaceutica'), *I Problemi della Sicurezza Sociale*, **31**, 3, 143–56.

Scientific research in the Italian pharmaceutical industry is inadequate and needs to be encouraged, according to the author. He proposes that a development plan for the industry should be drawn up by those engaged in research, and that government procedures related to industrial research should be rationalized. Further, he advocates state intervention to control price levels and to improve the industry.

348 DURIEZ, M. (1976) Pharmaceuticals in Germany and France (*La pharmacie en Allemagne et en France*), Paris: Centre de Recherches et de Documentation sur la Consommation, 84 pp.

Using statistics for 1974, this report compares French and German pharmaceutical production, industrial structure, turnover, international trade, and expenditure for research and marketing. Medical and pharmaceutical consumption by the respective populations is then studied on the basis of data from two international studies. One conclusion reached is that German prices are higher than French prices because there is less control of market mechanisms in Germany.

349 EDSTEDT, U. (1976) 'Pricing and price trends of drugs' ('Prissättning och prisutveckling på läkemedel') in: BERGWALL, G. (ed.) Drugs (*Om Läkemedel*), Stockholm: B. Wahlströms, 155–72.

Discusses the principles of pricing in a research and development intensive industry, and compares the trend in drug prices with the trend in the general consumer price index in Sweden. From 1968 to 1975, the general price index increased by 68%, while the retail drug price index increased by 53%. Finally, the product cycle, patent laws, and government intervention in the pharmaceutical industry are discussed.

415 KAUFER, E. (1976) The Economics of the Pharmaceutical Industry (*Die Oekonomik der pharmazeutischen Industrie*), Baden-Baden: Nomos Verlag, 231 pp.

350 LUCIONI, C. (1976) 'The determination of pharmaceutical prices in Italy' ('La fissazione del prezzo dei farmaci in Italia'), *Rivista di Economia e Politica Industriale*, **2**, 3, 405–27.

This article analyses the procedures used in Italy to determine pharmaceutical prices. The characteristics of the pharmaceutical industry are described, and the current method used to determine prices is criticized. The cost structure of the pharmaceutical sector is then analysed. Finally the new method for fixing prices, and its consequences for the pharmaceutical industry, are discussed.

351 MALMGREN, S. (1976) 'The pharmaceutical industry once more' ('Läkemedelsindustrin ännu en gång'), *Ekonomisk Debatt*, **4**, 2, 182–6.

This comment on an earlier article by Ståhl on the pharmaceutical industry considers the problems presented to research and development by increasing costs and the decreasing number of genuinely new drugs. Drug price indices are inherently downward biased because new drugs are generally not included. Competition increasingly takes the form of 'me too' drugs rather than the introduction of genuinely new formulations.
See 345.

352 MOEBIUS, K., SEUSING, E., and AHNEFELD, A. (1976) The Pharmaceutical Industry in the Federal Republic of Germany (*Die pharmazeutische Industrie in der Bundesrepublik Deutschland*), Tübingen: J.C.B. Mohr (Paul Siebeck), 139 pp.

An examination of the characteristics of production, supply and demand, and price structure in the pharmaceutical industry. The prices of pharmaceuticals in a number of countries are compared, and the implications for modifying the price structure of drugs in the Federal Republic of Germany are discussed from the authors' own perspective.

1977

353 BRENNA, A., LUCIONI, C., and ROSSI, F. (1977) 'A survey of the pharmaceutical industry and research' ('Industria farmaceutica e ricerca: i risultati di una indagine'), *Economia Pubblica*, **7**, 10, 10–20.

This article assesses a survey of the Italian pharmaceutical industry carried out between 1976 and 1977. All the major pharmaceutical companies took part, but only 20 out of 53 provided adequate information. Correlations are made between company size and variables such as research and development expenditures and the number of employees engaged in research. An attempt is made to evaluate the effectiveness of laboratories engaged in research.

354 INSTITUTE FOR RESEARCH IN HEALTH ECONOMICS (ed.) (1977) The Price of Pharmaceutical Products as a Means of Regulating the Pharmaceutical Sector (*Il prezzo dei farmaci quale strumento di politica del settore*), Milan: Associazione per l'Informazione Sanitaria, 219 pp.

Proceedings of a conference organized by the Institute for Research in Health Economics in Rome, 1977. The conference examined price determination of pharmaceutical products and its socio-economic and political implications. Drug prices are compared internationally, and the procedures used to determine pharmaceutical prices in the various countries are described.

355 OBERENDER, P. (1977) 'The West German pharmaceutical industry: a case study of the competition on the supply side of the market for drugs' ('Die pharmazeutische Industrie in der Bundesrepublik Deutschland. Eine Fallstudie zur Wettbewerbssituation auf der Angebotsseite des Arzneimittelmarktes'), *Jahrbuch für Sozialwissenschaften*, No. 28, 163–95.

The author analyses the increasingly entangled national and international links and relations among the leading pharmaceutical corporations. He finds that the overall drug market is fragmented into a number of separate, non-competing, therapeutic markets. This means that manufacturers do not compete on an industry-wide basis, and therefore concentration must be evaluated within the various therapeutic groups of drugs in which competition occurs. He concludes that the scope for competitive market processes in supply is already non-existent. This is explained by the constitutional peculiarities of the market and the nearly complete and instantaneous transparency of moves and countermoves in all important dimensions of competition. Transparency is more pronounced for such parameters of action as price, quantity, and advertising, than for product quality, and activity in research and development.

6. Consumption of Drugs

1964

319 RAVAZZI, G. (1964) 'Structure and problems of the Italian pharmaceutical market' ('Strutture e problemi del mercato farmaceutico italiano'), *Rivista Internazionale di Scienze Economiche e Commerciali*, **11**, 10, 928–82.

1968

321 MEDUSA, G. (1968) 'Drug prescription policy under the Italian health insurance system. Influence of organizational patterns in health insurance on the development of drug consumption' ('Aspetti e problemi dell'assistenza farmaceutica in Italia. Influenza dei modelli organizzativi della protezione sociale sullo sviluppo dei consumi farmaceutici'), *Economia e Lavoro*, (special number: The pharmaceutical problem in the context of social security), **2**, 5, 563–609.

1969

325 MEDUSA, G., PETRALIA, S., and INGHILESI, M. (1969) 'Prescription drugs and health care reform' ('Il problema farmaceutico e la riforma sanitaria'), *I Problemi della Sicurezza Sociale*, **24**, 6, 971–1005.

356 MOLITOR, B. (1969) 'Expenditure on drugs in social health insurance reform' ('Der Ausgabeposten "Arzneien" in der Reform der sozialen Krankenversicherung'), *Die Ortskrankenkasse*, **51**, 21, 625–9.

The volume of expenditure on drugs in the statutory health insurance scheme and some quantitative aspects of consumption are discussed, within the framework of the market for pharmaceutical products in the Federal Republic of Germany.

1970

357 CARLSEN, H., CHRISTENSEN, F., and HOLST, E. (1970) 'Drug consumption in Denmark' ('Lægemiddelforbruget i Danmark'), *Ugeskrift for Læger*, **132**, 43, 2037–44.

This paper describes the method and results of a combined questionnaire and interview undertaken in Elsinore in March 1969. Of the 339 individuals questioned, 63% responded to the questionnaire; 37% of these respondents took one or more drugs during the week of the investigation (43% if vitamin preparations are included). The quantity and type of drugs used are analysed by the sex, age, and residence of the users. 72 of the respondents were questioned by interview, and good agreement was found between the two survey methods (when vitamin preparations are excluded). The importance of further investigations into drug consumption is emphasized.

1972

358 DENMARK, GOVERNMENT OF (1972) Report on Subsidizing Drugs (*Betænkning om tilskud til Lægemidler*), Copenhagen: Statens Trykningskontor (Betænkning No. 659), 113 pp.

This report of a committee established by the Minister of Social Affairs considers possible changes in the drug subsidy provisions of the national health insurance scheme, in order to reduce public expenditure on drugs by D.Kr. 90

million. It recommends that the existing subsidy of 75% of the price of major drugs be changed in favour of a three-tier system: 80% subsidy of very important drugs, 50% subsidy of less important drugs and zero subsidy of drugs for which there is a tendency to over-consumption. Free provision of drugs to economically deprived groups is also recommended. These proposals were later adopted in a modified form.

359 EIKE, S. (1972) 'Who determines drug prices? Comments by the German Federal Union of the Pharmaceutical Industry' ('Wer bestimmt die Arzneimittelpreise? Bemerkungen des Bundesverbands der pharmazeutischen Industrie'), *Pharma Dialog*, No. 9, 22 pp.

The author examines the factors influencing price structure and the development of the pharmaceutical and other industries involved in marketing pharmaceutical products.

360 GROOT, L. (1972) 'Economic aspects of drug dispensing' ('De economische aspecten van de geneesmiddelenvoorziening'), *Acta Hospitalia*, **12**, 1, 46–55.

Discusses economic aspects of drug dispensing, on the basis of a survey of several Belgian hospitals, including: drug purchasing and prices, total costs, labour costs, and the floor stock of drugs. The author then analyses the economic efficiency of drug dispensing in hospitals.

361 LIEFMANN-KEIL, E. (1972) 'Some possibilities for improving the role of statutory health insurance in the drug market' ('Überlegungen zur Verbesserung der Position der gesetzlichen Krankenversicherung auf dem Arzneimittelmarkt'), *Bundesarbeitsblatt*, No. 9, 503–6.

The costs and sales of pharmaceuticals, and their component elements, are described and discussed. Some questions relating to demand and supply factors, and the role of statutory health insurance in the market for pharmaceuticals in the Federal Republic of Germany, are examined, and some changes are proposed.

335 MEDUSA, G. and DE SANTIS, M. (1972) 'Drug Consumption and Expenditure in Italy' ('Il consumo e la spesa farmaceutica in Italia'), *I Problemi della Sicurezza Sociale*, **27**, 2, 219–46.

1973

362 BUSCA, L. (1973) The Cost of Drug Consumption under Social Security (*Le coût de la consommation pharmaceutique dans la Sécurité sociale*), Brussels: Commission of the European Communities (Report No. V/442/73-F), 41 pp.

This report first examines drug consumption in terms of relevant legislation and regulations, and then studies the particular problems of exchange of information and advertising. Final observations concern price control, third-party payment, consumer cost-sharing, lists of reimbursable products, limitation of sale points, and advertising.

671 COMMISSION OF THE EUROPEAN COMMUNITIES (1973) Synthesis of Three Investigations of the Main Items of Health Insurance Expenditure Covered by Social Security (*Rapport de synthèse concernant trois études sur les principaux postes des dépenses de l'assurance maladie couvertes par la sécurité sociale*), Brussels: Commission of the European Communities, General Directorate of Social Affairs (Report No. V/396/73-F), 38 pp. (mimeographed document).

363 FORTH, W. (1973) 'Are drugs consumer goods?' ('Arzneimittel — Eine Konsumware?'), *Bild der Wissenschaft*, **10**, 12, 1432–9.

The author presents a social and economic analysis of consumer behaviour in relation to drugs, and of its implications for rising costs in the system of health care provision.

364 KIPPENBERG, P. (1973) 'Librium and Valium — a comparative study of prices in Britain, Germany, Austria, and Switzerland' ('Librium und Valium — Ein Preisvergleich zwischen Grossbritannien, Deutschland, Oesterreich und der Schweiz'), *Die Ortskrankenkasse*, **55**, 12, 376–83.

A comparision is made of the prices of Librium and Valium in Great Britain, the Federal Republic of Germany, Austria, and Switzerland. The differences are discussed.

365 LIEFMANN-KEIL, E. (1973) 'Retail sales in the market for pharmaceuticals — present and future' ('Der Arzneimittelvertrieb im Arzneimittelmarkt — Gegenwart und Zukunft'), *Deutsche Apotheker Zeitung*, **113**, 21, 800–3.

The author describes the pattern of distribution in the market for pharmaceuticals, and outlines possible future developments in the Federal Republic of Germany.

366 LIEFMANN-KEIL, E. (1973) The Drug Market in the Light of the Further Development in Statutory Health Insurance (*Der Arzneimittelmarkt im Rahmen einer Weiterentwicklung der gesetzlichen Krankenversicherung*), Frankfurt: Athenäum, 177 pp.

The drug market is characterized by the lack of relationship between the consumer and the provider. The consumer does not demand certain goods or services, but the attainment of certain states (feeling well, sleeping better, etc.). The transformation process assigns the function of prescribing to the doctor. It is he who determines the supply function rather than the consumer. Need is not an objective variable determining demand in the drug market, because need depends on the physician's definition of what is best for his patient. After considering the aspects of registration and control of pharmaceuticals, and of the processes by which information is disseminated, the author argues that all regulation of the drug market should focus primarily on the doctor. She suggests the establishment of a centre for disseminating information about the effectiveness and the price of drugs, in the hope that such information would enable and encourage physicians to act more rationally in terms of cost-effectiveness, and also from the point of view of the statutory health insurance. The book is based on a report made for the Federal Department of Labour and Social Affairs. The recommendation, for an independent drug information centre for physicians, was enacted in subsequent legislation.

367 PEDONE, A.P. (1973) 'A regional survey of trends in the prescription of drugs' ('Ricerca sull'andamento territoriale delle prescrizioni farmaceutiche'), *I Problemi della Sicurezza Sociale*, **28**, 3, 289–314.

Differences in prescription trends between the regions in Italy are widening over time. This is due to demographic and socio-economic factors, the method of payment for doctors' services, the professional status of the insured person, and whether he is an urban or rural resident. The different doctor/population ratios in the regions also play a role.

368 RAHNER, E. (1973) 'Controlling the price of drugs — gains and losses' ('Stop der Arzneimittelpreise — Gewinne und Verluste'), *Pharma Dialog*, No. 18, 44 pp.

An analysis of costs and prices in the drug market under price regulation in the statutory health insurance scheme in the Federal Republic of Germany.

369 SCHICKE, R.K. (1973) 'The pharmaceutical market and prescription drugs in the Federal Republic of Germany: Cross-national comparisons', *International Journal of Health Services*, **3**, 2, 223–36.

The pharmaceutical market, prescription drug costs, and consumption, in the Federal Republic of Germany and other countries, are examined. Depending on the level of development in the countries studied, either a per prescription cost push, or a cost increase pull from increased utilization, was found. In the Federal Republic of Germany a relatively high level of utilization was the main factor affecting the total per capita drug consumption cost.

1974

465 ALTER, U. and KLAUSING, M. (1974) 'Costs and benefits of drugs — the case of influenza and tuberculosis' ('Kosten und Nutzen von Arzneimitteln am Beispiel Grippe und Tuberkulose'), *Pharma Dialog*, No. 29, 33 pp.

370 ANDERSEN, A.H. and JOHANSEN, P.J. (1974) 'The consumption of drugs in Denmark' ('Medicinforbruget i Danmark'), *Ugeskrift for Læger*, **136**, 39, 2204–9.

An analysis of drug consumption in Denmark in 1971. Expenditure on prescription drugs amounted to D.Kr. 634 million, and on non-prescription drugs D.Kr. 164 million. Almost half of this expenditure was financed by public subsidy. Including hospital drug consumption, expenditure on drugs totalled D.Kr. 1 billion, or 0.71% of GNP. Analysed by therapeutic group, psychotropic drugs accounted for the largest share of total expenditure, at D.Kr. 109 million. It is estimated that every Dane is prescribed a dose of tranquilliser every second to third day, and an analgesic every eighth day. Changes in subsidies significantly alter the pattern of consumption, but not its total. The recent subsidy provisions are estimated to have resulted in a direct national saving of approximately D.Kr. 60 million. Regular follow-up reports on drug consumption (as proposed by WHO) are recommended.

371 DENMARK. GOVERNMENT OF (1974) Drug Distribution in Denmark (*Lægemiddeldistribution i Danmark*), Copenhagen: Statens Trykningskontor (Betænkning No. 725), 250 pp.

A comprehensive analysis of the drug distribution system in Denmark, and a description of the systems used in several other countries. The existing distribution system is based on private pharmacies operating under public licence. The effects of various alternative models are analysed, including: complete nationalization, a decentralized system run by local communities, and centralization in a single licensed private company.

340 Dupuy, J.P. and Karsenty, S. (1974) The Pharmaceutical Invasion (*L'invasion pharmaceutique*), Paris: Editions du Seuil, 269 pp.

372 Duriez, M. and Rösch, G. (1974) 'Drug consumption in France (1966–72)' ('La consommation pharmaceutique en France (1966–1972)'), *Semaine des Hôpitaux*, **50**, 2, 115–21.

National consumption of pharmaceutical products dispensed in pharmacies (about 11.3% of the total) from 1966 to 1972 is discussed. Dietetic, toilet, and cosmetic products are excluded from this study, as are medicines used in hospitals. Estimates of drug consumption in 1970 are made on the basis of several statistical sources: governmental expenditures, which account for 60% of the total expenditure on pharmaceuticals; the business turnover of the pharmaceutical industry; the business turnover of the pharmacies; the 1970 INSEE–CREDOC survey (Institut National de la Statistique et des Etudes Economiques — Centre de Recherches et de Documentation sur la Consommation) of medical services in France. On the basis of government data, yearly consumption is estimated to be Fr. 11,654,000; this is very close to the estimates calculated from the other sources.

341 France, Medical High Commission of the Social Security (1974) Drugs and Health Insurance (*Le médicament et l'assurance-maladie*), Paris: Haut-Comité Médical de la Sécurité Sociale, 58 pp. (mimeographed document).

373 Herder-Dorneich, P. (1974) 'The drug market in a socially oriented market economy' ('Der Arzneimittelmarkt in einer sozialen Marktwirtschaft'), *Pharmazeutische Zeitung*, **119**, 43, 1757–62.

The pharmaceutical market in a socially oriented free-market economy is discussed and an analysis made of its non-market aspects, price information, research, and other relevant factors.

374 Kippenberg, P. (1974) 'The profit margin of the pharmacist in considering additional discounts' ('Die Handelsspanne des Apothekers unter Einbeziehung der Zusatzrabatte'), *Die Ortskrankenkasse*, **56**, 6, 193–211.

The pharmacy profit margin, and discounts and rebates in the sale of pharmaceuticals, are discussed, raising questions of price formation and competition, at wholesale and producer levels, in the pharmaceutical market in the Federal Republic of Germany.

375 LANGELLA, L. (1974) 'Pharmaceutical services provided by the National Institute of Health Insurance' ('La farmaceutica dell'Istituto Nazionale per Assicurazione contro le Malattie'), *I Problemi della Sicurezza Sociale*, **29**, 5, 685–708.

Analysis of the consumption of drugs between 1946 and 1972 by people making use of national health insurance, including trends in: the number of patients whose insurance covers prescription medicines, the number of prescriptions provided by the national health insurance, the average yearly number of prescriptions per insured person, and the total expenditure on prescription medicines.

376 LECOMTE, T. (1974) 'Drug consumption in 1970 according to a household survey' ('La consommation pharmaceutique en 1970 d'après une enquête auprès des ménages'), *Consommation*, No. 2, 36 pp.

Report of the 1970 INSEE–CREDOC survey (Institut National de la Statistique et des Etudes Economiques — Centre de Recherches et de Documentation sur la Consommation) of 7,393 French households (23,197 people), to determine their consumption of pharmaceuticals and medical services. Per capita expenditure on pharmaceuticals was Fr. 168.52, of which prescription products accounted for Fr. 148.14. The number of unit sales per person was 18.14. Consumption was examined according to demographic, socio-economic, and medical factors. Quantities and costs of prescriptions, subdivided into 23 therapeutic categories, were determined, as were the average unit prices of the various medications.

377 LIEFMANN-KEIL, E. (1974) 'Consumer protection, incentives, and externalities in the drug market', in: PERLMAN, M. (ed.), *The Economics of Health and Medical Care*, London: Macmillan, 117–29.

This paper follows the new approach to the theory of demand (Becker and Lancaster) in analysing the costs of the efforts to protect the consumer, and the externalities generated by the regulations introduced to reduce other externalities.

378 SCHICKE, R.K. (1974) 'Pharmaceutical markets in a socio-economic perspective' ('Arzneimittelmärkte aus sozio-ökonomischer Sicht'), *Pharmazeutische Zeitung*, **119**, 37, 1415–20.

Drugs are classified into three categories according to the controls imposed on them. Socio-economic sub-optimization of drug provision and consumption are discussed. An international typology of pharmaceutical systems is proposed, together with a model of hypothetical systems.

379 SCHICKE, R.K. (1974) 'Socio-economic aspects of drug supply systems' ('Sozio-ökonomische Aspekte der Arzneimittelversorgungssysteme'), *Niedersächsisches Ärzteblatt*, **47**, 21, 776–80.

A study, from a historical perspective, of the evolution of drugs, the development of supply, and the formation and control of their prices.

1975

380 CONSUMERS' ASSOCIATION (1975) Drugs: Advertising and Over-Consumption (*Les médicaments: publicité et surconsommation*), Brussels: Association des Consommateurs, 258 pp.

The first part of this study deals with the pharmaceutical industry in Belgium, the over-consumption of psychotropic drugs, the causes of misuse of drugs, and the waste due to unused drugs and medication errors. The second part describes existing legislation on pharmaceutical advertising, and the influence of pharmaceutical firms on medical prescriptions.

381 GEMELLI, A. and NAZZARO, E. (1975) 'Causes of the rise in drug consumption and some solutions' ('I fattori di aumento del consumo farmaceutico e gli elementi per un possible contenimento'), *I Problemi della Sicurezza Sociale*, **30**, 5, 723–48.

The authors believe that psychological pressure on the consumer, and the behaviour of the pharmaceutical market, contribute to increasing demand for prescription drugs. Demand patterns for drugs, the doctor–patient relationship, and the proliferation of pharmaceutical companies and pharmacies in Italy are examined. Improved health education, state intervention in the production of pharmaceuticals, and rationalized criteria for the prescription of drugs are advocated as means of curbing pharmaceutical consumption.

382 GLISMANN, H.H. and SEUSING, E. (1975) 'Problems of international price comparisons — pharmaceutical products' ('Probleme internationaler Preisvergleiche — pharmazeutische Produkte'), *Die Weltwirtschaft*, No. 2, 176–90.

Methodological problems of international comparisons are analysed in the context of pharmaceutical products, and the implications for reliability in comparisons are discussed.

383 Jørgensen, N. (1975) 'Distribution of drugs' ('Medicindistribution'), *Archiv for Pharmaci og Kemi*, **132**, 1313–54.

Describes and analyses the distribution of drugs in Denmark, and a committee report on drug distribution in the future.

384 Lilja, J. (1975) The Physician's Choice of Drug Outside Hospitals and Ways of Improving it (*Läkares läkemedelsval ur samhällets synvikel*), Stockholm: Bonniers, 251 pp.

Analyses the physician's choice of drug in a defined therapeutic context, using the results of a questionnaire survey of 180 Swedish GPs (81% response). The survey collected information on relevant GP background variables and choice of drug in two therapeutic contexts, one describing a patient with adult-onset diabetes, and the other a patient with pneumococcal pneumonia. Few associations were found between choice of drug and the background variables, with the exception that recently qualified GPs chose a new and cheaper drug for pneumonia. Judged by medical and economic criteria, 65% of GPs made an unsatisfactory choice in the case of pneumonia. In the case of diabetes, the choice of biguanide, by 3% of the GPs, was considered by experts to be unsatisfactory; similarly judged, the worst choice of drugs was made by the older GPs. Several recommendations are discussed, including the provision of more information to doctors about the curative and side effects of drugs, and greater price competition.

385 Mach, E.P. and Venulet, J. (1975) 'The economics of adverse reactions to drugs', *WHO Chronicle*, **29**, 3, 79–84.

Reviews evidence on the frequency and importance of adverse reactions to drug therapy, and proposes a method for estimating the social cost due to such reactions, in order to encourage more rational use of drug therapy. The paper illustrates the method with a series of typical cases (deaths, malformations, permanent disabilities, hospital admissions, and extended stay in hospital) reported to the WHO drug monitoring centre. The social cost is calculated as the sum of treatment costs and the present value of lost earnings.

386 Rahner, E. and Teichner, H. (1975) 'Drug market and competition' ('Arzneimittelmarkt und Wettwerb'), *Pharma Dialog*, No. 39, 19 pp.

The authors present the results of an empirical study of the pharmaceutical industry in the Federal Republic of Germany, over the period 1966–74. Information is given about sales volume and market structure, and about changes in market shares, the number of pharmacologists, and significant drug groups.

387 Siderius, P. (1975) 'European studies of drug consumption' in: Ehrlich, D.A. (ed.) *The Health Care Cost Explosion: Which Way Now?*, Berne: Hans Huber Verlag, 139–48.

A survey of some European studies on the pattern and determinants of drug consumption.
See 26.

388 Sournia, J.C. and Arsac (Mrs) (1975) Drugs and Health Insurance (*Le médicament et l'assurance maladie*), Paris: La Documentation Française (Notes et Etudes Documentaires, Nos. 4195–4196), 88 pp.

The author evaluates the importance of expenditures on drugs in total French health care expenditure, and attempts to measure the influence of the social security reimbursement system on drug consumption.

1976

389 Carlizza, L. and Mei, V. (1976) 'The relationship between primary health care and the prescription of drugs' ('Relazione fra i sistemi di erogazione dell'assistenza medico-generica e la prescrizione farmaceutica'), *I Problemi della Sicurezza Sociale*, **31**, 4, 369–83.

The authors demonstrate that the consumption of pharmaceuticals increases considerably in a health care system financed by insurance payments. They argue that the pattern of pharmaceutical expenditure depends to a large extent upon the system (fee-for-service or capitation fee) used to finance the provision of health care.

348 Duriez, M. (1976) Pharmaceuticals in Germany and France (*La pharmacie en Allemagne et en France*), Paris: Centre de Recherches et de Documentation sur la Consommation, 84 pp.

390 Lenoir, C. and Sandier, S. (1976) Drug Consumption in France and the USA (*La consommation pharmaceutique en France et aux Etats-Unis*), Paris: Centre de Recherches et de Documentation sur la Consommation, 170 pp.

Drug consumption in France and the USA is compared. Although the Americans have a higher GNP per capita and spend more on health than the French, the per capita pharmaceutical expenditure is roughly the same in both countries. Consequently, the pharmaceutical share of total health care expenditure is lower in the USA than in France. Retail prices of pharmaceutical products are higher in the USA. However, increases in pharmaceutical price indices are similar, and less than those of general price indices, in both countries. American doctors prescribe medicines less often and choose from a narrower range of products, but recommend a higher number of doses. Variations in drug consumption caused by demographic factors are fairly similar in both countries, except when socio-economic factors are considered. Drug consumption in the USA, unlike France, increases with income and education.

391 NORD, D. (1976) Drug Consumption in the Federal Republic of Germany — A Behavioural Analysis of the Pharmaceutical Industry, the Physician and the Consumer (*Arzneimittelkonsum in der Bundesrepublik Deutschland, eine Verhaltensanalyse von Pharma-Industrie, Arzt und Verbraucher*), Stuttgart: F. Enke Verlag, 171 pp.

The relationship between the pharmaceutical industry, the prescribing physicians, and the consumers is discussed, and drug consumption is analysed.

418 NORD, D. (1976) The Costs of Progress in Drugs: the Analysis of Expenditure on Drugs in the Statutory Health Insurance Scheme, with Particular Reference to Important Groups of Drugs. (*Kosten des medikamentösen Fortschritts, Analyse der Arzneimittelausgaben der gesetzlichen Krankenversicherung, dargestellt am Beispiel wichtiger Arzneimittelgruppen*), Frankfurt: Medizinisch Pharmazeutische Studiengesellschaft, 71 pp.

392 SCHICKE, R.K. (1976) 'Socio-economic systems of pharmaceuticals', *Social Science and Medicine*, **10**, 6, 277–81.

This analysis traces and characterizes the broad historical development of drugs, including the relationship between mythological remedies, folk medicine, and scientifically developed medications in a social pharmaceutical system. The conceptual framework of the analysis consists of an attempt to classify this triad by stages of development, also pointing to the role occupied by marginal pharmaceutical doctrines and therapeutic sub-systems. Drugs are classified into three sub-systems: the illegal, the para-pharmaceutical, and ethical drugs. The corresponding social control mechanisms acting in each of the sub-systems are examined. It is concluded that socio-economic optimization of drug utilization is likely to be easier in systems offering wider choices and alternatives than in systems with centralized controls, given that most of the scientific discoveries and achievements have been accomplished in the stimulating free-market environment. A typology classifying provider systems of pharmaceuticals in different countries concludes the analysis.

393 Schicke, R.K. (1976) Social Pharmacology (*Sozialpharmakologie*), Stuttgart: W. Kohlhammer Verlag, 93 pp.

The author introduces social pharmacology as a social science of medicines. He then analyses drug relationships between supplier and consumer, using methods from sociology, economics, and organization and communication theory.

394 Westphal, E. (1976) 'The pharmaceutical market in the light of critical investigations' ('Der Arzneimittelmarkt im Lichte kritischer Untersuchungen'), *Die Ortskrankenkasse*, **58**, 18, 609–15.

A review of various aspects of the pharmaceutical market that warrant further research, such as supply, demand, competition, price formation, and international price comparisons.

1977

395 Del favero, A. (1977) The Pharmaceutical Problem (*Il problema dei farmaci*), Rome: Il Pensiero Scientifico, 235 pp.

This book deals with the therapeutic and socio-economic aspects of drugs. It discusses their effectiveness and correct usage, the relationship between drugs and health, the current and future role of drugs in health care, and pharmaceutical research. Ways of improving the social function of pharmaceuticals are proposed.

396 George, A. (1977) Drug Consumption in the United Kingdom (*La consommation pharmaceutique au Royaume-Uni*), Paris: Centre de Recherche pour l'Etude et l'Observation des Conditions de Vie, 148 pp.

This report describes the economic context of the British health care system. It compares British and French expenditures on pharmaceuticals from 1960 to 1974. Pharmaceutical price policy in Britain is discussed, and British and French prices are compared. The level of drug consumption in both countries is then considered. The author concludes that, during this period, expenditure was lower in the United Kingdom than in France in terms of value and percentage of the GNP. The British national health care system enables expenditure on health services and pharmaceuticals to be kept within acceptable limits.

645 GYGI, P. and HENNY, H. (1977) The Swiss Health Care System (*Le système suisse de santé — Das schweizerische Gesundheitswesen*), Berne: Hans Huber Verlag, 328 pp.

397 HERDER-DORNEICH, P. (1977) The Economics of Self-Medication (*Zur Oekonomik der Selbstmedikation*), Cologne: Bundesfachverband der Heilmittelindustrie, 29 pp.

The controversial issue of self-medication is discussed, in the context of trends since 1965 in the consumption of over-the-counter drugs, and of the cost of ethical as compared with over-the-counter drugs.

398 JÖNSSON, B. (1977) 'Information, control, and technology in connection with drug treatment' ('Hur skall vi förbättra den interna effektiviteten i läkemedelsterapin?'), *Svensk Farmaceutisk Tidskrift*, **81**, 14, 550–6.

The author poses two questions. What economic benefits will result from replacing drugs associated with high costs of supervision and information by drugs that are less demanding in these respects? What are the most efficient ways of improving the correspondence between drug prescription and drug intake in outpatient care? It is argued that the introduction of new drugs or dispensing schemes that require less supervision and information are important factors in productivity growth in medical care.

399 LENOIR, C. and SANDIER, S. (1977) Pharmaceuticals in the Health Care System in Sweden and France (*La pharmacie dans le système de santé, Suède/France*), Paris: Centre de Recherche pour l'Etude et l'Observation des Conditions de Vie, 215 pp.

This comparison takes into account national demographic, economic and medical characteristics. In Sweden, the geographic situation, medical infrastructure, and largely public-financed medical service have generated a hospital-based health care system. Consequently, in Sweden as compared with France, hospital shares of total health care expenditure and of total pharmaceutical expenditure are higher, but per capita drug consumption, in terms of quantity and value, is lower. Drug price-setting procedures are similar in both countries, but the level of prices is appreciably higher and increasing more rapidly in Sweden. The pharmaceutical share of total health care expenditure, and the importance of over-the-counter sales of medicines, are decreasing in both countries, but the hospital share of total consumption of pharmaceutical products is increasing.

IV Evaluating the Contribution of Health Services

1. The Evaluation of Life

1960

400 Abraham, C. and Thedie, J. (1960) 'The price of human life in economic decisions — a human capital approach' ('Le prix d'une vie humaine dans les décisions économiques — évaluation du capital humain'), *Revue Française de Recherche Opérationnelle*, No. 16, 157–67.

Presents a methodology for estimating the value of human life in economic decisions. Two main types of costs are considered. Economic costs include direct costs, such as transport, hospitalization, burial, policing and administration of justice, insurance, etc., and indirect costs, as represented by the net present value of lost economic output. Emotional costs include pain, grief, worry, loss of well-being and opportunity. In 1960, the authors arrived at a total *a priori* estimate of 150,000 francs for the average value of a human life.

1961

401 Rösch, G. (1961) 'Some extensions and implications of the valuation of human life' ('A propos du prix de la vie humaine; de quelques prolongements et ramifications en divers domaines'), *Revue Française de Recherche Opérationnelle*, No. 19, 125–38.

The author tries to solve the problem posed by the question: what does it cost the community to save a human life? After explaining the difficulties involved in integrating economic, medical, psycho-sociological, and moral data, the author offers a number of fundamental definitions. He concludes that the cost of a life is the expenditure that is technically necessary in order to save a life; the price of a life is the expenditure that one actually agrees to devote to saving a life; the cost of a man is the sum total of the expenditures on consumption, investment, and public services that are devoted to him. Finally, the author explains that the conclusions drawn in studies of this kind presuppose an analysis of the behaviour of individuals and societies when confronted with death.

1962

402 De Guenin, J. (1962) 'Concerning the price of a human life in economic decisions' ('A propos du prix d'une vie humaine dans les décisions économiques'), *Revue Française de Recherche Opérationnelle*, No. 23, 123–8.

A discussion of some basic issues in calculating the value of human life in economic decisions that reduce deaths or the risk of death. The author points out that value is essentially a collective phenomenon; it is only meaningful in one market at one given moment and it is an integral part of a whole, from which it cannot be separated. On the basis of the definitions and problems discussed, the author briefly describes possible methods for calculating the appropriate price of a life in economic decisions.

1965

403 Ståhl, I. and Ysander, B.C. (1965) 'How is human life valued?', *Läkartidningen*, **62**, 39, 3143–8.

The paper discusses methodological problems in the valuation of human life. It stresses that calculations must refer to a context of choice if they are to be meaningful. It elucidates some of the difficulties, using an example where the value is calculated as the present value of the individual's future income stream. The authors suggest the possibility of testing the consistency of valuations in different situations.

1967

404 Hellqvist, B., Juås, B., Karlsson, C., Mattson, B., and Thompson, S. (1967) Valuation of Personal Injuries. A Comparison of Explicit and Implicit Values (*Värdering av risken för personskador. En jämförande studie av implicita och explicita värden*), Karlstad: University College of Karlstad, Department of Economics (Memorandum No. 69), 434 pp.

The monograph starts with a theoretical and methodological discussion of the valuation of human life. Different approaches are thoroughly discussed. The major part treats implicit and explicit evaluation in Sweden, covering a broad field: work safety, fire safety, nuclear energy, and transport accidents including air, rail, sea, and road traffic. Sectoral studies are supplemented by an individual interview survey. Finally, the Swedish material is compared with similar studies in other countries. Explicit values are shown to be not significantly different from implicit values. The explicit values are evenly distributed between S.Kr. 100,000 and S.Kr. 2 million. The distribution of implicit values is bimodal, with the intervals S.Kr. 0-250,000 and S.Kr. 1-2 million. The high values for nuclear energy and aviation safety support the hypothesis that people are prepared to pay more to avoid catastrophes, even though the expected number of victims is the same.

405 MORLAT, G. and ROPARS, A. (1967) Research on the Cost of Protecting Human Life (*Recherches sur les coûts de protection de la vie humaine*), (provisional report, June 1967), Paris: Bureau Universitaire de Recherche Opérationnelle, 500 pp. (mimeographed document).

This report contains a number of theoretical observations on the formulation of decisions in medical economics. It uses simple theoretical models of the elements involved in the choices open to the community or to the authorities, for expressing their preferences. It discusses problems in the valuation of life, and the cost of protecting it, and also considers studies done on a number of special medical problems: artificial kidneys, anti-tuberculosis campaigns, the detection of phenylketonuria, the effectiveness of systematic vaccination, and the care of premature babies. Finally, the report contains the preliminary results of an analysis of demographic data, showing the influence on age-specific mortality rates of the volume of medical services consumed, as estimated by the studies of the Centre de Recherches et de Documentation sur la Consommation.

1970

406 LEBART, L. (1970) Research on the Cost of Protecting Human Life in the Medical Field (*Recherche sur le coût de protection de la vie humaine dans le domaine médical*), Paris: Centre de Recherches et de Documentation sur la Consommation, 162 pp. (mimeographed document).

Using statistical data for the years 1966 and 1967, the author tries to estimate the costs and consequences of various medical projects at a microeconomic or macroeconomic level. Part one, on microeconomic projects, contains analyses of: implicit prices; choices between future or present medical projects; renal dialysis; the dissemination of technical information; the costs of organ transplants; and the problem of choosing a public health approach appropriate to the general level of economic development, as exemplified by smallpox vaccination in the USA and measles vaccination in Senegal. Part two aims at a comprehensive treatment of the relations that may exist between the medical care provided for certain groups of individuals, and health characteristics, like life expectancy. The parallel development of such economic and health indicators as life expectancy and mortality rates, in France and the USA, are studied in relation to the level of development and the distribution of medical services. An analysis is made of different socio-economic groups; mortality and utilization of medical services by selected health and economic characteristics in various nations are compared, and the comparable data for French cities and departments are summarized.

1971

407 STEENSTRUP, J.E. (1971) 'Economic evaluation of human life is nothing new' ('Økonomisk vurdering af menneskeliv ingen nyhed'), *Danmarks Amtsråd*, **2**, 6, 5–8.

A general discussion of economic principles applied in health planning.

1972

11 GRIFFITHS, D.A.T. (1972) 'Economic evaluation in the health services', *Annales de la Société Belge de Médecine Tropicale*, **52**, 3, 215–34.

1974

408 GREFFER, M. (1974) 'The provision of medical services at stable prices' ('Medizinische Leistungen zu konstanten Preisen'), *Arbeit und Sozialpolitik*, **29**, 1, 13–18.

A consideration of various new methods of organizing the provision of medical services: group practices, shared practices, equipment sharing, medical technical centres, diagnosis and screening centres, and day care.

409 MATTSON, B. (1974) 'Some economic aspects of the evaluation of risks for human accidents', *Ekonomist Debatt,* **2**, 7, 412–16.

Discusses different aspects of the evaluation of risks of death and injury, and distinguishes between implicit and explicit evaluations of risk. The author points out that maximum technically possible safety cannot be a desirable goal for society, as this would be too demanding of scarce resources; there must be a trade-off between increased safety and other social goals. He criticizes the distinction between voluntary and involuntary risks, and proposes instead the use of the concepts of information, level of decision making, and transaction costs, defined as the costs of moving from one risk group to another.

410 SEFFEN, A. (1974) 'The income of doctors and incomes policy' ('Arzteinkommen und Honorarpolitik'), *Arbeit und Sozialpolitik*, **28**, 10, 359–64.

A summary of the study undertaken by the Committee of the Society for Social Progress, in Bonn. The study adopts a macroeconomic approach to the analysis of the changes that have taken place in the earnings of doctors, the position of physicians in the distribution of income, and the processes whereby incomes are negotiated.

1975

411 KAMPER-JØRGENSEN, F. (1975) Evaluation of Life in Health Economics Calculations (*Vurdering af menneskeliv i sundhedsøkonomiske beregninger*), Copenhagen: University of Copenhagen, Institute of Social Medicine, 33 pp.

Can an economic value be placed on the loss or gain of life? The conclusion, drawn from a survey and discussion of the methods used to answer this question, is that no single correct measure exists. However, the production loss approach can be applied in specific cases involving loss of life and disability. Examples of this approach are reviewed and its limitations emphasized.

412 SCHWEMIN, B. and STOLLENWERK, H.H. (1975) 'The economic effects of a constant nursing rate' ('Die wirtschaftlichen Auswirkungen des linearen Pflegesatzes'), *Die Ortskrankenkasse*, **57**, 18, 678–86.

The effects of a constant nursing rate on the patient's length of stay are analysed. Alternative forms of nursing rate (e.g., a decreasing nursing rate) and their effects on hospital administration are discussed.

413 SWERTZ, P. (1975) 'Hospital cost problems' ('Kostenprobleme des Krankenhauses') in: BLOHMKE, M. (ed.), The Cost of Health Care

Systems, Social Ecology, and Social Medicine (*Kosten des Gesundheitswesens, Sozialökologie und Sozialmedizin*), Stuttgart: A.W. Gentner Verlag (Schriftenreihe Arbeitsmedizin, Sozialmedizin und Präventivmedizin, Vol. 56), 49–57.

A discussion of hospitals' cost structure, building costs, nursing ratios, staffing costs, and financing. References are made to improvements by changing the structure of diagnosis, therapy, and care.
See 584, 689

414 WOLLNY, G. (1975) 'The income of doctors and Gross National Product' ('Arzthonorar und Bruttosozialprodukt'), *Die Ortskrankenkasse*, **57**, 19, 713–22.

The author discusses the issue of a fair income for doctors in private practice, and compares the growth of doctors' earnings with the growth of GNP.

1976

430 HEMMINKI, E., HEMMINKI, K., HAKULINEN, T., and HAKAMA, M. (1976) 'Increase in years of life after eliminating causes of death: significance for health priorities', *Scandinavian Journal of Social Medicine*, **4**, 1, 1-6.

415 KAUFER, E. (1976) The Economics of the Pharmaceutical Industry (*Die Oekonomik der pharmazeutischen Industrie*), Baden-Baden: Nomos Verlag, 231 pp.

Competition in the market for pharmaceutical products, the rate of industrial innovation, the structure of the industry, and price formation are discussed and analysed, with reference to the experience of other countries.

416 KUEHN, H. (1976) 'Some statistical reflections on cost inflation in the health care system' ('Statistische Ueberlegungen zur Kostenentwicklung im Gesundheitswesen') in: Yearbook for Critical Medicine (*Jahrbuch für kritische Medizin*), Vol. I, Berlin: Argument Verlag, 179–96.

Patterns are discerned in the data on expenditure under the statutory health insurance scheme, which enable an indicator of the growth in cost to be constructed. Due to unquantifiable factors, however, the indicator has no absolute validity.

417 NASCHOLD, F. (1976) 'Structural factors affecting the growth of cost in the health care system' ('Strukturelle Bestimmungsfaktoren für die Kostenentwicklung im Gesundheitswesen') in: Yearbook for Critical Medicine (*Jahrbuch für kritische Medizin*), Vol. 1, Berlin: Argument Verlag, 196–207.

Ideological aspects of the current national policy relating to the provision of health and welfare services are discussed. The prospects for an approach that differs from current economic and social models are explored.

418 NORD, D. (1976) The Costs of Progress in Medicine: the Analysis of Expenditure on Drugs in the Statutory Health Insurance Scheme, with Particular Reference to Important Groups of Drugs (*Kosten des medikamentösen Fortschritts, Analyse der Arzneimittelausgaben der gesetzlichen Krankenversicherung, dargestellt am Beispiel wichtiger Arzneimittelgruppen*), Frankfurt: Medizinisch Pharmazeutische Studiengesellschaft, 71 pp.

Trends in the cost of drugs within the statutory health insurance scheme in the Federal Republic of Germany are examined, with particular reference to important categories such as antibiotics, tranquillisers, antidiabetics, and cardio-vascular drugs. The changing composition of expenditure on these drugs is analysed.

2. Health Indices

1967

419 MAGDELAINE, M., MIZRAHI, A., MIZRAHI, A., and RÖSCH, G. (1967) 'A morbidity indicator applied to survey data on medical consumption' ('Un indicateur de morbidité appliqué aux données d'une enquête sur la consommation médicale'), *Consommation*, No. 2, 3–41.

The level of morbidity is treated as an explanatory variable in the determination of the consumption of medical services. After explaining the conceptual and practical difficulties of measuring morbidity, the authors describe a method for working out a characteristic indicator of the morbid state of an individual. Using the data of the 1960 CREDOC–INSEE survey (Centre de Recherches et de Documentation sur la Consommation — Institut National de la Statistique et des Etudes Economiques), the statistical technique is applied to medical consumption, by demonstrating morbidity as it is perceived and reported by the subjects themselves. Morbidity is evaluated in terms of seriousness of consequences, including: future morbidity trends, the degree of incapacity, and the risk of death (allowing for the duration of the pathological condition). Allowance is also made for the nature of the disorder, and the presence of multiple disorders of a major or minor kind. The results make it possible to study variations in the degree of morbidity according to age, sex, and socio-economic characteristics, and to estimate the relations between degree of morbidity and level of medical consumption. At the individual level, morbidity increases are accompanied by a marked increase in the quantity and type of medical consumption. For a given level of morbidity, however, the consumption of medical services decreases with age.

1971

420 WHO (1971) *Statistical Indicators for the Planning and Evaluation of Public Health Programmes*, Geneva: World Health Organization (Technical Report Series, No. 472), 40 pp.

This report of a WHO Expert Committee discusses the statistical system required for efficient health planning and evaluation. It reviews, and makes recommendations regarding: the types of health statistics required, methods of data collection, collaboration between health statisticians and planners, and training and research in statistical methods.

1973

421 Damiani, P. (1973) 'Measuring the level of health' ('La mesure du niveau de santé'), *Journal de la Société de Statistiques de Paris*, No. 2, 129–42.

The WHO definition of health is difficult to quantify in practice. Health can be partly measured by morbidity, using data on: the natural history of diseases, prolonged sickness absence, trends in disability pensions, and annual morbidity data from public aid organizations and from mortality statistics published by INSERM (Institut National de la Santé et de la Recherche Médicale). It is also possible to use data from population morbidity surveys. The USA has had the National Health Survey routinely since 1956; France has the INSEE–CREDOC surveys (Institut National de la Statistique et des Etudes Economiques — Centre de Recherches et de Documentation sur la Consommation) of 1970. Mortality, life expectancy, and more sophisticated composite indicators using variables correlated with mortality have also been used in measuring health. The author favours using life expectancy at birth as a simple crude indicator, supplemented, where possible, by morbidity data.

422 MIZRAHI, A., MIZRAHI, A., and RÖSCH, G. (1973) 'A morbidity indicator' ('Un indicateur de morbidité'), *Consommation*, No. 3, 7–56.

On the basis of a sample survey of consumption of medical services by 1,062 individuals, carried out by INSEE and CREDOC (Institut National de la Statistique et des Etudes Economiques — Centre de Recherches et de Documentation sur la Consommation) among households in the Paris area during the six winter months of 1965–66, an attempt is made to define a two-dimensional morbidity indicator. The indicator is constructed on the basis of the age and sex of the respondents, whether or not they are confined to bed, and the average number of ailments suffered during a period. In the second part, the study attempts to elucidate and measure the specific influence of social or economic factors on the morbidity indicator, and on medical consumption when morbidity is held constant. The results, though less clear, resemble those of the 1960 survey. Two findings of particular note are that a systematic decline in the consumption of medical services occurs with increasing age, and that sex has virtually no influence on consumption within each of the reported groups of morbidity.

1974

172 BUI-DANG-HA, D. (1974) 'World trends in medical manpower, 1950-2000', *World Health Statistics Report*, **27**, 2, 84–108.

423 DUPUY, J.-P. (1974) 'On the social rationality of health policies' ('Rationalité sociale des actions de santé'), *Revue d'Economie Politique*, **84**, 1, 45–79; also in: PERLMAN, M. (ed.) (1974) *The Economics of Health and Medical Care*, London: Macmillan, 481–509.

Paper presented to the 1973 Tokyo Congress of the International Economic Association, on health economics and medical care in developed countries. Part one seeks more refined indicators of the outcomes of health programmes than the global morbitity and mortality indicators that are generally used. Such indicators should be capable of revealing, not only the technical outputs of health projects (e.g., the prolongation of life and the healing of sickness), but also the non-technical, and in particular the psycho-sociological, effects. Part two deals with the consumption of drugs in a system of private medical practice. Here also, the purely technical and the non-technical effects (such as the relief of anxiety) are considered. Finally, pharmaceutical over-consumption is discussed, and particularly the large number of new drugs introduced, with corresponding obsolescence and psychological depreciation of the so-called old drugs.

424 France, Ministry of Public Health and Social Security (1974) Health Indicators (*Indicateurs de santé*) (a document written in preparation for the VIIth Plan), Paris: Ministère de la Santé Publique et de la Sécurité Sociale, 137 pp. (mimeographed document).

A collection of basic data on the state of health of the population and on the operation of the health care system. The data, broadly described as health indicators, are in three categories: indicators of health states, describing the health characteristics of the population (e.g., life expectancy, infant and perinatal mortality, main causes of death, and measures of morbidity); indicators of outputs of the health system (e.g., hospital outputs, medical services for private patients, medical consumption and health expenditure per head); indicators of inputs of the health care system (e.g., the personnel and equipment used for the production and distribution of medical services). The statistical data that make up these indicators are classified by stocks (e.g., amount of equipment, inpatient cost per day, and levels of staff) and by flows (e.g., expenditure on equipment and staff).

425 Klein-Beaupain, T. and Lefevere, G. (1974) Social Health Indicators: An Approach for Belgium (*Les indicateurs sociaux de santé: une approche pour la Belgique*), Brussels: Editions de L'Université de Bruxelles, pp. 223.

The first part attempts to define the concept of social indicators, with reference to work in the United States and France, and investigates the problems involved in constructing such indicators. It includes a study of health indicators adopted by the World Health Organization. The second part tentatively proposes health indicators for Belgium. A distinction is made between outcome and resource indicators, the former being the proper means of evaluating health status. The proposed indicators require further analysis of their validity and improved statistical data, particularly on morbidity and health resources.

426 WHO (1974) 'Health Trends and Prospects, 1950-2000', *World Health Statistics Report*, **27**, 10, 672–706.

This paper reviews the following aspects of mortality in both developing and developed countries over the period 1950–70: aggregate levels and trends in mortality; infant, perinatal, and early childhood mortality; sex, age, social class, urban–rural, and other differentials in mortality; and causes of death. The report concludes with a brief discussion of mortality prospects to the year

2000, and speculates that 'values of expectation of life at birth ranging between 60 and 65 in less-developed countries, and 75 to 80 in developed countries, should be attainable by the end of the century for the vast majority of the world population'.

1975

427 Chapalain, M.-T. (1975) 'The construction of new health indicators' ('La construction d'indicateurs nouveaux de santé'), *Cahiers de Sociologie et de Démographie Médicales*, **15**, 2, 69–73.

This research study expresses data compiled by doctors, during the routine examination of children, in the form of health indicators. The resulting health balance-sheets, drawn up by the Maternal and Child Welfare Service of the Primary Health Insurance Fund of the Paris area, were used to study the development of the 1,000 four-year-old children covered. The doctors themselves select the model for processing their data, which are fed into a master system by the programme budgeting analysts. It is essential to have this type of collaboration between doctors and Planning Programming, and Budgeting System analysts, in order that individual medical practice may be translated into social terms.

428 Dupuy, J.-P. and Karsenty, S. (1975) 'The concealed logic behind the growth of medical institutions' ('La logique cachée de la croissance de l'institution médicale'), *Futuribles*, No. 3, 179–203.

The authors demonstrate the extent to which the classical social indicators, such as measures of morbidity and life expectancy, are inadequate, in that the logic of medical decision making cannot be reduced to the logic of economic rationality. They try to show that this logic, created by the social and symbolic role of the medical institution in industrial societies, underlies two types of mechanism, and that this enables them to explain: why constantly increasing inputs are necessary to achieve constant, if not decreasing, returns relative to the objectives of the medical system, whether technical or non-technical; and why it is not inconsistent that every doctor, in his own field of clinical work, feels that his results are worthwhile, yet the overall effectiveness of medicine is minimal or at least difficult to demonstrate. Doctors' conceptions of personal efficiency are not easily combined into a comprehensive indicator. Indeed, doctors are often confused and irritated by aggregate data and statistical reasoning. To illustrate their argument, which resembles that of Ivan Illich, the authors use examples from private medical practice and the consumption of drugs, on the one hand, and the hospital consumption of laboratory services on the other.

429 Van de Voorde, H. (1975) 'Health indicators for life expectancy in the Louvain region', *Archives Belges de Médecine Sociale, Hygiène, Médecine du Travail et Médecine Légale*, **33**, 5, 316–30.

In 1974, in the region of Louvain, which consists of 21 municipalities with a total population of 130,000, research was done into life expectancy on the basis of a number of health indicators and the medico-social infrastructure, with the aim of developing a quality-of-life model to be applied to other parts of Belgium. Demographic data, causes of death, some biological parameters such as growth and age of menarche, the evolution of unemployment, and certain elements of the medico-social infrastructure were examined in this region, and compared with equivalent data for the whole country. The population does not differ obviously from the total Belgian population, although the birth rate, infant mortality rate, migration surplus, and tuberculin index show more favourable figures in the Louvain region. Because of the large number of university hospitals in this region, the parameters for the curative health service were deliberately omitted from the survey. Preventive health services, infant care, the number of day-nurseries, youth health care, and care and admission capacity for the aged are above the level of the national average. The total area of outdoor and indoor sports facilities, and the number of public swimming pools, are impressive. A large number of possible criteria for measuring the quality of life were left out of this study, either because it was impractical to use certain criteria as a test of well-being, or because comparable data did not exist.

1976

430 Hemminki, E., Hemminki, K., Hakulinen, T., and Hakama, M. (1976) 'Increase in years of life after eliminating causes of death: significance for health priorities', *Scandinavian Journal of Social Medicine*, **4**, 1, 1–6.

The theory of competing risks of death is applied to construct two indices: (1) the increase in the expectation of life as a function of age, and (2) the increase in the average number of years lived by a newborn up to various ages, when selected causes of death have been eliminated.

431 Jazairi, N.T. (1976) *Approaches to the Development of Health Indicators*, Paris: Organization for Economic Cooperation and Development, Social Indicator Development Programme (Special Studies No. 2), 58 pp.

This report on the development of health indicators in the OECD programme begins with a review of some past approaches to the measurement of health. It then explores indicators capable of monitoring the two fundamental social concerns of the OECD countries in the area of health: the probability of a healthy life through all stages of the life cycle, and the impact of health impairments on individuals. Within this framework it proposes and discusses possible indicators of the length of life, the healthiness of life, the quality of health care, the delivery of health care, and the degree of integration of the disabled into society.

432 JEANNERET, O. and RAYMOND, L. (1976) 'Health statistics on children of school age', *WHO Chronicle*, **30**, 3, 101–7.

This is a digest of an article by the same authors (*World Health Statistics Report*, **28**, 4, 1975, 140–53). The authors argue that health statistics on children of school age are important and have been too neglected in the past. In the absence of an ideal index of health, the classical indicators, mortality and morbidity, give enough information on the health status of children of school age. Better use should be made of available statistics.

433 KRASNIK, A. (1976) 'Health status in population groups, indicators of health and disease' ('Sundhedsstatus i befolkningsgrupper'), *Ugeskrift for Læger*, **138**, 23, 1417–25.

This paper presents different indicators of health and disease, and discusses the need for developing improved indicators, including those related to planning and the quality of life.

434 LOGAN, W.P.D. (1976) 'World health related indicators', *World Health Statistics Report*, **29**, 12, 682–97.

This paper presents the following series of vital and health statistics, estimated from various sources for recent years, for 20 continental regions. Demographic indicators: distribution of world population, world population density, annual rates of population growth, proportion of population under 20 years, and median age of population. Social indicators: urbanization, dietary energy supply, and gross national product. Vital statistics: crude birth rate, crude death rate, expectation of life at birth, and infant mortality. Health service resource indicators: physicians, nursing and midwifery personnel, and hospital beds per 10,000 population.

435 RUFF, J. (1976) Health Indicators (*Les indicateurs de santé*), 4th edition, Rennes: Ecole Nationale de la Santé Publique, 93 pp. (mimeographed document).

The first part of this study, designed for teaching, deals with the objectives of constructing a health indicator and the properties required of it, and attempts to classify indicators according to their basis, results, or development. The second part covers the methods by which the main indicators are calculated, and their use.

436 TAMBURI, G. and MOUTON, P. (1976) 'Social security indicators', *International Labour Review*, **114**, 2, 155–67.

Great hopes have been placed in social indicators, whether as means to action or as aids to knowledge, although there now seems to be a better awareness of their limitations and of the methodological and conceptual questions they involve. Attempts to develop suitable indicators in the field of social security deserve encouragement. In considering some of the special problems they raise at the international level, previous research is reviewed and certain questions of method, and the difficulties of using indicators to make inter-country comparisons, are discussed.

1977

437 HELBERGER, C. (1977) 'Objectives and results of health policy' ('Ziele und Ergebnisse der Gesundheitspolitik') in: ZAPF, W., Conditions of Life in the Federal Republic of Germany (*Lebensbedingungen in der Bundesrepublik Deutschland*), Frankfurt/Main: Campus, 677–743.

Outlines the objectives and problems of German health policy between 1950 and 1975, then examines empirical data for nearly all factors relevant to the field of health (health status and impairments, life expectancy, mortality, morbidity, psychic well-being; insurance and quality of medical services; economic efficiency of health services; working conditions; accidents; smoking and drinking habits). The data, obtained from official documents and surveys, are partly disaggregated by demographic and socio-economic characteristics. The work is part of a larger research project on social indicators.

141 HENKE, K.D. (1977) Public Health Expenditures and Distribution, A Contribution toward Measuring and Influencing Group-Specific Welfare in the Health Care Sector (*Öffentliche Gesundheitsausgaben und Verteilung. Ein Beitrag zur Messung und Beeinflussung des gruppenspezifischen Versorgungsniveaus im Gesundheitsbereich*), Göttingen: Vandenhoeck und Ruprecht, 242 pp.

594 SCHRÄDER, W.F. and VOLKHOLZ, V. (eds) (1977) Regional Analysis of Medical Care (*Regionale Analyse der Medizinischen Versorgung*), Berlin: Technische Universität Berlin, Berliner Arbeitsgruppe Strukturforschung im Gesundheitswesen (Schriftenreihe No. 2), 307 pp.

3. Estimating the Cost of Disease. Cost–Benefit Analyses and Cost–Effectiveness Analyses of Particular Health Care Programmes

1965

438 RAHNER, E. (1965) Cost–Benefit Analysis in the Health Service. An Attempt at an Economic Evaluation of Health Measures in the Federal Republic of Germany (*Kosten- und Ertragsanalyse im Gesundheitswesen. Versuch einer ökonomischen Beurteilung von gesundheitspolitischen Massnahmen in der Bundesrepublik Deutschland)*, Saarbrücken: Universität Saarbrüken (dissertation), 201 pp.

The first systematic outline of the problems of cost–benefit analyses in health services in the German language. The main problem in the analysis is the assessment of benefits. The concept of 'lost years of gainful employment' is suitable only for global analyses. It is preferable to use the 'average of expected years of gainful employment'. Here, both invalidity and mortality are included. The author is sceptical whether it is possible to reduce mortality and invalidity by more than 10% in the years ahead, and the cost of attaining this goal is unknown. The returns due to a reduction of premature death are diminishing. Therefore, health policy has to concentrate on reduction in morbidity and invalidity. In addition to this global analysis of costs and returns of resource allocation in health care, two cases are examined: poliomyelitis vaccination, and rehabilition programmes. The direct benefit: cost ratio is estimated as 0.44:1, but this rises to 2.7:1 if the whole economy and the effective employment rate are taken into account.

1968

538 BOGATYREV, I.D. and ROJTMAN, M.P. (1968) *Methods of Studying the Economic Benefits of Disease Control*, Copenhagen: World Health Organization, Regional Office for Europe (Original in Russian. Summary in English, No. EURO 0339/4), 5 pp.

439 Brenna, A. (1968) 'The application of cost–benefit analysis to health' ('L'applicazione dell'analisi costi e benefici sociali alla salute'), *I Problemi della Sicurezza Sociale*, **23**, 4, 509–32.

The author first examines why it is necessary to develop new methods for determining the amount of resources to be devoted to the health care sector. One reason is that the market mechanism operates inefficiently in allocating resources to this sector. The author then analyses approaches designed to guide political choices in the field of health. Two methods are considered: including expenditure on health care as an explanatory variable in models of economic development, and quantifying the costs and benefits to society of implementing a particular programme of health care. Both methods presuppose that the allocation of resources to health care represents, at least in part, an investment, in that it results in an increase in the supply of labour available to the economic system. It is concluded that cost–benefit techniques have value as instruments for guiding the policy maker only when they are applied to single health care programmes.

440 Fabre, F. and Grandmont, J.M. (1968) Early Detection of Cancer of the Cervix (*Le dépistage précoce du cancer du col de l'utérus*), Paris: Centre de Recherches Mathématiques pour la Planification, Vol. I, 78 pp. and Vol. II, 78 pp.

This cost–benefit study attempts to evaluate the effectiveness and desirability of a systematic mass screening programme for cancer of the cervix, in France. Costs are estimated, according to different stages of the disease, first of prevention, and then of treatment of the later stages by cone biopsy, hysterectomy, and radiotherapy. The benefits are largely determined by the years of life saved, valued at age-specific earnings rates; an imputed value for household labour is included. The authors conclude that mass screening for cervical cancer is socially profitable, and that examinations should be carried out every four years between the ages of 25 and 60.

441 Mattsson, B. (1968) The Economic Costs of Road Traffic Accidents (*Vägtrafikolyckornas samhällsekonomiska kostnader*), Stockholm: Statens Trafiksäkerhetsråd (Report No. 116), 220 pp.

The economic consequences of road traffic accidents in Sweden are estimated for the period 1961–65. Costs of deaths and injuries are thoroughly discussed, and a production loss approach is finally adopted. The report contains a comprehensive review of statistical data available for the estimation of social costs, as well as a discussion of different theoretical approaches. The total economic cost of road traffic accidents in 1965 is estimated at S.Kr. 1,337 million (1963 prices). Production loss accounts for S.Kr. 419 million, medical care for S.Kr. 38 million, property damage for S.Kr. 780 million, and administrative costs for S.Kr. 100 million.

442 WOLFSLAST, J. (1968) Cost–Benefit Analysis in the Health Care System (*Cost–Benefit-Analyse im Gesundheitswesen*), Hamburg: Weltarchiv, 229 pp.

The author emphasizes his opinion that the lack of exact cost–benefit analyses in health care is a luxury that the economy cannot afford. After a careful consideration of the calculation of costs, benefits, discounting, and constraints, some specific methods are discussed, e.g. the use of opportunity costs. The main basis of all cost–benefit analyses in health care is the assumption that the results of health programmes should be a reduction of losses of productivity, and a saving of future health care expenses. The examples given are prenatal care and rehabilitation. It is shown how such an analysis is made difficult by a number of possible medium-term and long-term effects; it is almost impossible to determine the net result of health programmes. In spite of this, the benefit–cost ratio of prenatal care is estimated at 5.2:1 or, considering the whole economy, at 20.3:1. The main constraint in cost–benefit analyses of rehabilitation programmes is the uncertainty of the future labour market. The benefit–cost ratio in rehabilitation is estimated at 1:3.1.

1969

443 JENSEN, A. (1969) *Operations Research in Screening and Diagnosis; Working Paper for the Seminar on the Uses of Operational Research in Health Services, Bucharest, 18-23 September 1969*, Copenhagen: World Health Organization, Regional Office for Europe (EURO 0408/8), 7 pp.

Discusses the application to overall medical planning of operations research techniques used in the planning of telephone systems.

444 RÖSCH, G. (1969) 'Economic aspects of the development of cardiac resuscitation' ('Aspects économiques du développment de la réanimation cardiaque'), (Seminar on cardiac and circulatory arrest), *Colloques de l'INSERM*, No. 4, 209–25.

An analysis of the statistical data on the diseases that can lead to cardiac arrest, and on the number of patients in the French population as a whole who are suitable subjects for cardiac resuscitation. Resuscitation is being used with increasing frequency, and its techniques are being constantly improved. The author describes the technical facilities and personnel that are needed to carry out cardiac resuscitation, and discusses the cost of cardiac resuscitation centres, in terms of the factors of production and the investment and operating expenses.

445 THOMPSON M. and SØRENSEN, B. (1969) 'The socio-economic significance of burns' ('Brandskaders samfundsøkonomiske betydning'), *Ugeskrift for Læger*, **131**, 37, 1575–7.

Estimates the economic significance of burns in the municipality of Copenhagen. On the basis of information about patients with burns during the financial year 1965-66, the total annual cost of burns per million inhabitants is estimated at D.Kr. 435 million, composed as follows: expenses directly attributable to treatment, D.Kr. 1,810,000; compensation, D.Kr. 600,000; loss of earnings, D.Kr. 1,940,000. In addition, burns cause 9-10 deaths per million inhabitants and significant disablement each year.

1970

446 MORLAT, G. (1970) 'A model for some medical decisions' ('Un modèle pour certaines décisions médicales') in: 'General equilibrium and growth model, demand for consumer goods and housing, medical-type decisions' ('Equilibre général et modèle de croissance, demande relative aux biens de consommation et du logement, décisions d'ordre médical'), *Cahiers du Séminaire d'Econométrie*, No. 12, 109–19.

The problem of choice for the medical profession is a difficult one, involving as it does the making of optimal decisions about the use of limited resources It is impossible to treat all patients in need of a particular technique, and therefore some decisions have to be taken about priorities and trade-offs. Applying experience gained with renal dialysis machines, the author proposes a model that contains the following variables: the prevalence of a given disease in a given population over a particular period; the value assigned to the preservation of human life; the probability of recovery, which is a function of biological factors specific to the patient and of the technical characteristics of the therapy; the probability of the biological factors within the population, and the cost of treatment. When either of two procedures may be used for treating a given disorder, the one for which net gain is maximized should be chosen. Furthermore, the author considers that the best possible use should be made of any technique that has proved to be reliable, and that research efforts should seek more effective and less expensive treatment, so that total expenditure is shared between therapy and research. The author defines the price of human life as the cost of adopting protective measures that the community agrees are necessary to save anonymous lives.

447 ØSTRE, S. (1970) 'Economic evaluation of road traffic accidents' ('Økonomisk vurdering av trafikkulykker'), *Sosialøkonomen*, **24**, 10, 5–12.

Discusses the problem of calculating a 'shadow' or implicit price for avoided deaths and injuries. This price should be equal for all projects. A simple model based on theoretical welfare economics is presented, and some data on the costs of road traffic accidents in Norway are discussed.

1971

448 CHRISTIANSEN, U. (1971) 'Operations research and economic models applied to hospital problems' ('Operationsanalyse og økonomiske modeller anvendt på hospitalsproblemer'), *Nationaløkonomisk Tidsskrift*, **109**, 1-2, 28–49.

This paper reviews: the state of the art in analysis of hospital cost and production functions (mainly in the United States and Great Britain); interpretation of capacity problems and queuing, using a Danish example; and the location of health care systems, using central place theory.

449 GERHARDSEN, R. (1971) Optimization Studies in Health Care — The Example of Treating Tuberculosis (*Optimaliseringsstudier i helsestellet – Et eksempel fra tuberkuloseomsorgen*), Oslo: Finansdeparttementet, Planleggingsavdelningen, 115 pp. (mimeographed document).

This paper illustrates how economic analysis may be used in the allocation of resources in medical care. Two different vaccination programmes are compared, using an epidemiological model developed by Waaler. The results suggest that the cost per man-year saved is lower for the programme with complete vaccination.

450 JONASSON, J. (1971) The Benefits of Health Care (*Hälsovårdens lönsamhet*), Stockholm: Statens Bakteriologiska Laboratorium, 144 pp + 4 appendixes.

The author discusses the methodology of estimating the social cost of disease. The costs and benefits of preventive measures against measles, rubella, hepatitis, poliomyelitis, influenza, and phenylketonuria (PKU) are estimated. A vaccination programme against measles is estimated to cost about S.Kr. 30 million in the initial phase and S.Kr. 4.5 million per year during subsequent years. The benefits, mainly in the form of reduced loss of production among employed women as a result of their children's illness, are estimated at S.Kr. 19 million per year. Production loss and treatment costs resulting from influenza are estimated at S.Kr. 20 million if 1% fall ill (the minimum alternative) and S.Kr. 360 million in the case of a severe epidemic. The costs of the Swedish screening and treatment programme for PKU is estimated at S.Kr. 2.7 million.

The social cost of the disease, if screening had not been carried out, is estimated at about S.Kr. 18 million per year, of which S.Kr. 16 million is treatment costs and S.Kr. 2 million production loss. The social cost averted by polio vaccination is estimated at S.Kr. 185.5 million at 1967 prices, comprising S.Kr. 106.5 million for treatment costs saved and S.Kr. 79 million for production loss avoided. A vaccination programme against rubella is estimated to yield a net benefit, but this result is particularly sensitive to the assumptions made.

775 LEVY-LAMBERT, H. and GUILLAUME, H. (1971) Rationalization of Budgetary Choices (*Rationalisation des choix budgétaires*), Paris: Presses Universitaires de France (Collection L'Economiste), 213 pp.

451 LIESS, M. and SOURNIA, J.C. (1971) 'Methodology of a longitudinal survey of the medical and socio-professional costs of chronic bronchitis' ('Méthodologie d'une enquête dynamique sur le coût médical et socio-professionnel de la bronchite chronique'), *L'Evolution Médicale* (special number on chronic bronchitis), **15**, 3–5, 309–14.

One of the objectives of this survey is to estimate the costs of specialized treatment for chronic bronchitis which is susceptible to early detection by systematic screening. A choice of priority objectives is considered. Medical criteria are selected for early diagnosis of respiratory disorders, in a population using hospitals and social hygiene dispensaries in several areas of France. The behaviour of the relevant variables through time is established from a random sample that is supervised and treated, compared with a control group that is observed only. The survey, planned over a five-year period, also aims to estimate costs, use of medical services, mortality, and the incidence of handicap. It is hoped that the use of a mathematical model will enable choices to be made, using multiple criteria, of the best form of treatment. In spite of the difficulties inherent in this kind of survey, it should, if strictly carried out, yield valuable and decisive information for determining the measures to be taken for the prevention, detection, and treatment of chronic bronchitis.

1972

452 BRÜNGGER, H. (1972) 'Health in cost–benefit analysis: the case of the new drug l-dopa', *Revue Suisse d'Économie Politique et de Statistique — Schweizerische Zeitschrift für Volkswirtschaft und Statistik*, **108**, 3, 347–75.

The introduction of the new drug levodopa, the first generally successful therapy against Parkinson's disease, is shown to be advantageous for

Switzerland. The author attempts to quantify the consumption aspects of health by means of a social indicator, the additional number of years of life saved by treating patients with levodopa. Two benefit categories that can be evaluated by market prices are identified: additional productive activity by cured patients, and relief of facilities such as long-stay hospitals and nursing homes.

453 ILLUMINATI, F. (1972) 'The cost of health: hospitalization, drugs, and relations between the medical profession and social security' ('Le coût de la santé: hospitalisation, médicaments, relations du corps médical avec la Sécurité Sociale'), *Revue Internationale de Sécurité Sociale*, **25**, 4, 408–28.

This study, which is focused on drugs and hospitalization, contains comparative data for the six countries that were members of the European Economic Community in September 1972, and for six other countries, including the United Kingdom and the Scandinavian countries.For these twelve countries, the trends in the cost of principal health benefits, and in the cost per person protected, are described, from 1962 to 1970. The author also studies the relations between the social security institutions and the medical profession. This problem is especially complex, since there are considerable differences between the systems adopted by institutions in different countries for granting both general and specialized medical benefits. The author stresses the importance of establishing a relationship based on confidence between both parties, and the need to preserve clinical freedom in the prescription of drugs.

454 KAMPER-JØRGENSEN, F. (1972) 'Cost–benefit analysis of proposals for mass examination for cancer of the cervix' (Cost–benefit analyse af forslag til folkeundersøgelsesprogram for livmodehalskraft'), *Ugeskrift for Læger*, **134**, 23, 1239–43.

A cost–benefit analysis of a proposed programme of a mass screening for cancer of the cervix in Denmark, offering a screening examination every third year to all women aged 30-49 years. A model comparing the existing tracing and therapeutic system for cancer of the cervix with a complete mass screening programme is constructed. Despite some uncertainties in the model, it is estimated that, over a 15-year period, the marginal cost of the proposed programme would be approximately D.Kr. 228 million and that the following benefits would accrue: about 800 deaths and about 1,200 cases of cervical cancer would be avoided; some 10,000 additional cases of cervical cancer at a pre-invasive stage would be identified; the health authorities would obtain contact with menopausal women; and a relative increase in welfare for the upper social classes would ensue. The marginal cost per avoided death is estimated at approximately D.Kr 280,000. Inclusion of the production gain due to reduced mortality yields a small net benefit for the programme.

455 Kamper-Jørgensen, F. (1972) The Social Cost of Road Traffic Accidents in Denmark 1967–1969 (*Trafikulykkernes samfundsmæssige omkostninger 1967–1969*), Copenhagen: University of Copenhagen, Institute of Social Medicine (Publication No. 1), 262 pp.

This book first describes the epidemiology of road traffic accidents and revises the official police data on traffic accidents (which are estimated to under-report the total by about 50%). The problems of estimating social costs are then discussed, with emphasis on the production loss approach. The total social cost of road traffic accidents in Denmark, both direct and indirect, is estimated at D.Kr. 2 billion for 1969. The cost per individual killed, seriously injured, or slightly injured averaged D.Kr. 270,000, D.Kr. 10,000, and D.Kr. 2,500 respectively. Finally, it is estimated that the use of seat belts by car drivers and front-seat passengers is socially profitable at usage rates greater than about 35%.

456 Levy, E., Lasserre, C., and Ravel d'Estienne, B. (1972) Influenza — A PPBS Study (*La grippe – Etude RCB*) (a dissertation on the research seminar on health economics – 1972), Paris: Université de Paris X, Nanterre, Unité d'Enseignement et de Recherche Sciences Economiques, 98 pp. (mimeographed document).

Influenza is one of the most serious communicable diseases, with important socio-economic repercussions. Every year it confines 10–40% of the population to bed for about ten days. Tens of millions of working days are lost, and medical and pharmaceutical expenditures amount to hundreds of millions of francs. Between 3,000 and 15,000 deaths from influenza occur annually in France. The Planning Programming Budgeting Systems study carried out by the authors includes: the present position (morbidity and mortality studies, with their respective costs); the objectives (the reduction of morbidity and mortality; possible measures to be taken (means of prevention, particularly vaccination, and means of treatment); possible programmes of action (whom to vaccinate, how to persuade people to be vaccinated, how and where to vaccinate them); evaluation of these measures from the viewpoint of effectiveness; and finally a cost–benefit study.

457 Veninga P. (1972) 'Costs of accidents and cost responsibility in road traffic' ('Ulykkeskostnader og kostnadsansvar i biltrafikken'), *Sosialøkonomen*, **26**, 10, 33–8.

The main problem is to develop a price system giving a better allocation and distribution of the costs and benefits of road traffic. The price the consumer is willing to pay to avoid accidents is probably far above the costs of injuries and material damage. However, these costs could be used as a first approximation for road user charges, and for insurance premiums. Some earlier Norwegian cost data are re-calculated.

1973

458 ALTER, U. (1973) 'Cost–benefit analysis of preventive medical measures agains poliomyelitis' ('Kosten–Nutzen–Analyse vorbeugender medizinischer Massnahmen gegen Poliomyelitis'), *Das öffentliche Gesundheitswesen*, **35**, 1, 50–3.

A tentative cost–benefit analysis of preventive measures against poliomyelitis, done by the Battele research institute for the Ministry of Youth, Family Affairs, and Health, of the Federal Republic of Germany.

459 FELDSTEIN, M.S., PIOT, M.A., and SUNDARESAN, T.K. (1973) *Resource Allocation Model for Public Health Planning. A Case Study of Tuberculosis Control* (supplement to Vol. 48 of the *Bulletin of the World Health Organization*), Geneva: World Health Organization, 110 pp.

The authors develop a model for public health planning, capable of simultaneously allocating resources both within and between disease control programmes, and of integration into more general development planning models. The health sector planning problem is formulated in the optimization framework of linear programming, and applied specifically to the allocation of resources within a tuberculosis control programme, using epidemiological data from the Republic of Korea. The objective function aggregates the present value of four types of benefit: reduction of temporary disability, of permanent impairment, of excess mortality (in four different age groups), and of income loss due to tuberculosis. The constraints express resource (budget, manpower, and bed-days), epidemiological, and demographic restrictions on the set of curative and preventive activities. Lacking relative social prices for the aggregated objective function, the authors calculate optimal solutions for the four partial objective functions corresponding to each type of benefit. The optimal activity content of the resulting sub-programmes is stable, and the implied pattern of resource use requires only limited hospital bed care, in contrast to the traditional pattern. The authors discuss the use of the model in planning and the sensitivity of its results to some of the parameter values, and recommend extending its optimization framework from a single-period to a multi-period planning horizon. The analysis is supported by exposition of its theoretical basis, including the relationship of health to economic development and approaches to establishing relative social values to weight the different types of benefit of health programmes.

460 FREOUR, P., TESSIER, J.F., LECOUBLET, D., SERISE, M., BERNADOU, M., and LABADIE, J.C. (1973) 'The cost of sickness' ('Le coût de la maladie'). Part 1, 'Importance and limitations of financial estimates'

(1e partie, 'Intérêt et limites des évaluations financières'). Part 2, 'Social costs: effect of the sickness of one individual on the other members of society, applications to the cases of an alcoholic tubercular patient and that of a non-alcoholic tubercular patient' (2e partie, 'Le coût social: incidence de la maladie d'un sujet sur les autres membres de la société, applications aux cas d'un sujet tuberculeux alcoolique et à celui d'un tuberculeux non alcoolique'), *Revue Française des Affaires Sociales*, **27**, 2, 31–58 and **27**, 4, 17–67.

In part one, the authors stress the importance of epidemiological studies, for the development of medical economics, which would make it possible to evaluate the financial and economic consequences of certain pathological conditions and show the burden they represent for the community. The authors take as examples two surveys carried out in Bordeaux, the first dealing with the comparative cost of tuberculosis among alcoholics and non-drinkers (1969 to 1971), and the second with the cost of serious forms of chronic bronchitis (1971). The results of these surveys allow the development of a methodology for calculating the cost of the sickness, which comprises medical cost and social cost. The latter is defined by the authors as 'the sum-total of the community's resources absorbed by sickness, of non-amortized personal investments, and of additional contributions which the individuals would have made to the community if they had not been partly or totally prevented from doing so by sickness, whether temporary or terminal'.

461 Jönsson, B. (1973) 'Cost–benefit analysis of care and activation measures for the elderly: some points of principle' ('Cost–benefit analys av vårdarrangemang och aktivering åtgärder för äldre: några principiella synpunkter') in: Zotterman, Y. (ed.) Retirement and Activation Measures for the Elderly (*Pensionering och Sysselsättning Aktivering av Äldre*), Stockholm: Allmänna Förlaget, 223–46.

The paper discusses the choice between income transfers, changes in prices, and changes in the supply of social services, to increase the welfare of the elderly. The possiblity of applying cost–benefit analysis to the choice between home and institutional care is outlined. The effect of different activation measures on the elderly is surveyed, and the possibility of applying economic analysis discussed. It is pointed out that activation measures can be intrepreted as an investment, which changes the need for, and the costs of, care in the future. No quantitative estimates are made, owing to the limited information available concerning the effect of different activation measures on the costs of care.

462 Lindholm, B. (1973) Benefits and Costs of Poliomyelitis Vaccination (*Poliovaccinets samhällsekonomiska lönsamhet*), Stockholm: Statens

Medicinska Forskningsråd, 78 pp. A summary under the same title appears in *Läkartidningen* (1973), **70**, 12, 1174–8.

A summary of a cost–benefit analysis, by the Swedish Medical Research Council, of the benefits and costs of poliomyelitis vaccination. The calculations are based on the assumption that the incidence of paralytic cases would have reached 1,000 if vaccination had not been undertaken. A prospective study of the paralytic cases in the Stockholm epidemic of 1953 makes it possible to calculate the benefits of the reduced prevalence of poliomyelitis achieved by immunization. It is calculated that the reduced costs of medical treatment, and the simultaneous increase in hours of productive work due to the immunization programme, amounted, at the beginning of the 1970s, to around S.Kr. 200 million per year. The reduction in treatment costs for the period 1958-77 are estimated at S.Kr. 1,865 million (1967 prices), while the loss of production is estimated at S.Kr. 850 million. The cost of the vaccination programme for the same period is about S.Kr. 225 million.

463 Malignac, G. (1973) 'Methodology of a research study on the cost of alcoholism' ('Méthodologie d'une recherche sur le coût de l'alcoolisme'), *Bulletin des Statistiques de Santé et de Sécurité Sociale*, **A**, 4, 5–12.

The paper tackles the methodological problems involved in calculating the cost of alcoholism, from a mathematical standpoint.

464 Moe, T. (1973) 'Cost-effectiveness analysis: useful tools in the public planning process?' ('Kostnads-effektiviseringsanalyser: nyttige hjelpemiddel i den offentliga beslutningsprocess?'), *Sosialøkonomen*, **27**, 1, 51–4.

A critical discussion of cost-effectiveness analysis. The main use of the method seems to be in providing a framework for structuring and analysing resource allocation problems. The ideas are elucidated with an example of different ways of treating tuberculosis.

107 Prims, A. and Quaethoven, P. (1973) 'The cost of medical and paramedical care. Research into, and analysis of, the factors determining the increase in cost of medical and paramedical care' ('Le coût des soins médicaux et para-médicaux. Recherche et analyse des facteurs qui déterminent l'accroissement du coût des soins médicaux et para-médicaux'), *Revue Belge de Sécurité Sociale*, **15**, 4, 433-540.

1974

465 ALTER, U. and KLAUSING, M. (1974) 'Costs and benefits of drugs — the case of influenza and tuberculosis' ('Kosten und Nutzen von Arzneimitteln am Beispiel Grippe und Tuberkulose'), *Pharma Dialog*, No. 29, 33 pp.

The costs and benefits of pharmaceutical intervention are examined. Cost–benefit calculations of the use of drugs to treat influenza and tuberculosis are carried out. For both diseases the intervention appeared to be worthwhile.

466 BORELLY, R. (1974) The Economics of Malaria — Essay on Health Economics (*L'économie du paludisme — Essai sur l'économie de la santé*), Grenoble: Université des Sciences Sociales de Grenoble (supplementary thesis), 217 pp. (mimeographed document).

This thesis, based on WHO documentation, examines the economics of anti-malaria campaigns throughout the world. The author studies the effects of the elimination of malaria on economic development. She then discusses the relationship between endemic malaria and economic under-development, and shows that it may be considered an integral part of under-development. Under-development conditions the transmission of malaria, and is a fundamental obstacle to the success of anti-malaria campaigns. The author analyses possible anti-malaria programmes using the cost–benefit method, while stressing that they must be closely integrated with general measures for the economic development of the countries in question.

467 BRODIN, H. (1974) Ulcer and Cost–Benefit Analysis (*Magsår och cost–benefit analys*), Lund: University of Lund, Department of Economics, 24 pp. (mimeographed document).

The paper compares two different surgical techniques in ulcer operations. Selective proximal vagotomy, a new surgical technique, is shown to give lower treatment cost, reduced sickness time, and reduced mortality, compared with ordinary resection. However, patients were not distributed randomly between the two techniques. Observations on the resection group commenced in 1960, and on the selective proximal vagotomy group in 1972. This suggests that the productivity increase shown by the study might be attributable to factors other than the change in surgical technique.

468 BRÜNGGER, H. (1974) Benefit–Cost Analysis as a Planning Tool in the Health Care System (*Die Nutzen-Kosten Analyse als Instrument der Planung im Gesundheitswesen*), Zurich: Schulthess Polygraphischer Verlag (Basler sozialökonomische Studien, No. 3), 251 pp.

This thesis reviews and discusses different approaches to evaluation in the health care sector. It introduces the concept of willingness to pay, and develops a model of health service decision making, adapting Arrow's general equilibrium model with uncertainty to curative services. It discusses the quantification of the state and duration of health. Finally, it examines the specific adjustments necessary to the approach described, if it is to be applied to projects other than curative health services.

469 Dahlberg, L. and Grenninger, C.M. (1974) Working Environment — Occupational Injuries — Health Care Expenditure (*Arbetsmiljö — Yrkesskador — Vårdkostnader*), Stockholm: Sveriges Kommunaltjänstemannaförbund, 140 pp.

The first chapters discuss the relationship between occupational injuries and economic development, and conclude that the number and severity of occupational injuries increases with the capital intensiveness of the industry. The number of sickness benefit days and occupational injuries, and their economic consequences, are estimated. Occupational injuries are estimated to have resulted in costs for 'protected employment' and medical care of S.Kr. 190 million and 220 million, respectively, in 1974. Finally, possible preventive measures and their likely benefits and costs are discussed.

470 Darbon, S. (1974) 'The social budget of disability' ('Le budget social de l'inadaptation'), *Economie et Santé* (supplement to the *Bulletin des Statistiques de Santé et de Sécurité Sociale*), No. 5, 69–87.

The purpose of this study is two-fold: to list the various financial flows directed towards handicapped persons, in order to study their magnitude and structure; and to suggest a means of linking these results to the conceptual framework of the national accounts. Owing to the difficulties of defining the limits of the field in question, any evaluation of a 'social budget of disability' can only be an approximate one. The author considers four categories of handicapped persons: those who are mentally weak or defective; motor defectives; sensorial defectives; and children with behavioural disorders. After examining existing information on which to draw up a social budget, the author makes many recommendations for accounting changes that would allow better understanding of the problems.

471 Davies, G.N. (1974) *Cost and Benefit of Fluoride in the Prevention of Dental Caries*, Geneva: World Health Organization (Offset Publications, No. 9), 91 pp.

On the basis of a number of trials in different countries, this report reviews the cost and benefits of alternative techniques of using fluoride in the prevention of dental caries. It presents estimated cost-benefit ratios for each trial of each technique, measuring cost as the undiscounted cost of intervention, and benefits as undiscounted savings either in the cost of dental treatment or in dentist man-hours over the trial period. The range of ratios estimated for each technique is as follows: fluoridation of community drinking water, 0.23 to 0.04; fluoridation of school water supply, 0.06; fluoride tablets, 0.91 to 0.05; professionally administered applications of fluoride solutions, 0.26 to 0.07 (toothbrushing) and 0.09 to 0.06 (mouth-rinsing). The author emphasizes the strict non-comparability of the estimated ratios both between and within techniques, and recommends further analyses within an agreed methodological framework.

472 DENMARK, GOVERNMENT OF (1974) 'Screening for tuberculosis' ('Betænkning om de kollektive tuberkuloseundersøgelser samt de i lovgivningen m.v. undersøgelser af enkeltpersoner ved ansættelse'), *Fra Sundhedsstyrelsen*, Vol. 6, 261–84.

This report, from the National Board of Health, discusses and analyses tuberculosis screening in the framework of cost–benefit analysis. It concludes that, in future, the coverage of screening should be reduced and concentrated on particular risk groups (this proposal was later adopted in Denmark). Epidemiological and economic data are presented.

473 ELO, O. (1974) 'Health and economic consequences of rubella', *Acta Universitatis Tamperensis*, Ser. A, Vol. 60, 27–44.

Various vaccination programmes for rubella were studied by benefit–cost methods. The differences in the benefit–cost ratios calculated were rather small. However, only tangible costs were included in the comparison. A preliminary conclusion is that the optimal programme comprises vaccination of girls before adolescence and all women after delivery, in addition to serological testing during pregnancy and abortion where necessary.

474 FLAMM, H., MATHAUSEN, H., KUNZE, M., and KUNZE, M.J. (1974) 'Problems of analysing the costs of illness — the case of bronchial carcinoma' ('Probleme der Kostenanalyse von Krankheiten am Beispiel des Bronchuskarzinoms'), *Das öffentliche Gesundheitswesen*, **37**, 3, 157–62.

The need for economic analysis of health care is emphasized. The concepts of direct, indirect, and social costs are discussed. Conservative estimates are made of the social costs of bronchial carcinoma.

475 GOKSTAD, A.C. and BUREN, G. (1974) 'Cost–benefit analysis of rehabilitation' ('Cost–benefit analys av en rehabiliteringsverksamhet'), *Socialmedicinsk Tidskrift*, **51**, 7, 483–93.

The article presents the results of a cost–benefit study of a rehabilitation clinic at Linköping regional hospital. It assumes that all future income of the cases treated can be attributed to the rehabilitation programme. On this assumption it has a pay-off period of about two years.

476 Guth, D. (1974) Children's Asthma — An Economic and Social Study (*L'asthme infantile — Etude économique et sociale*), Paris: Université de Paris X, Nanterre (PhD thesis), 325 pp. (mimeographed document).

After referring to medical data on children's asthma, the author studies the situation in 1970 (epidemiological surveys, morbidity and cost estimates of asthma in children and young adults), examines the financial costs of treatments, absenteeism, backwardness in school, daily allowances, and loss of earning power for families and the community. The second part of the study considers possible measures, classified in programmes: supporting programmes (training of doctors and paramedical personnel, information for families, health balance-sheets) and active programmes (desensitization and respiratory re-education, health cures, prevention, vocational training). These active programmes are considered in cost–benefit terms. In conclusion, the author points out that the sum-total of medical costs for asthmatic children in 1970 was approximately Fr. 176 millions. Drugs alone accounted for nearly half of the medical expenses, and thermal cures for a further fifth.

477 Johansson, L.Å. and Persson, J. (1974) The Social Costs of Cerebrovascular Disease — An Empirical Analysis (*Apoplexins samhällsekonomiska kostnader — an empirisk analys*), Gothenburg: University of Gothenburg, Department of Economics, 59 pp. (mimeographed document).

The social cost of cerebrovascular disease is estimated for the first year after the patient becomes ill. The analysis includes costs of inpatient care, outpatient care, social services, and loss of production. The total average cost in 1971 is estimated at S.Kr. 30,854, of which 48% represents costs of inpatient care and 46% loss of production.

478 Jonsson, Ernst (1974) Social Costs of Road Traffic Accidents, Occupational Injuries, and Diseases Caused by Tobacco Smoking (*Samhällskostnader för trafikolyckor, yrkesskador och sjukdomar orsakade av tobaksrökning*), Stockholm: Ekonomiska Forskningsinstitutet, 211 pp. Also: (1974) 'Social costs of road traffic accidents, occupational injuries, and diseases caused by tobacco smoking', *Landstingens Tidskrift*, **61**, 6, 23–7.

The report estimates the costs of medical care, losses of production, and reduced consumption due to illness, invalidity, and premature deaths caused by road traffic accidents, occupational injuries, and smoking-related diseases (coronary diseases, chronic bronchitis, and some cancers) in Sweden in 1970. The total costs of road traffic accidents were S.Kr. 1,445 million, of which S.Kr. 975 million was due to loss of production. Corresponding costs for occupational injuries were S.Kr. 1,011 million and S.Kr. 850 million, respectively. The social costs of smoking-related diseases were S.Kr. 500 million, of which loss of production accounted for S.Kr. 410 million. On average, the loss of production per person killed in road traffic accidents, occupational accidents, and smoking-related diseases was S.Kr. 400,000, S.Kr. 475,000, and S.Kr. 65,000, respectively. Net of consumption, the corresponding production loss was S.Kr. 135,000, S.Kr. 230,000, and S.Kr. 70,000, respectively.

479 Jonsson, Ernst (1974) Putting a Price on Occupational Injuries (*Sätt pris på arbetsmiljön*), Stockholm: Svenska Landstingsförbundet, 28 pp.

The external costs of occupational injuries that are not borne by employers are estimated at S.Kr. 1.1 million in 1970. The total revenue from compulsory injury insurance was S.Kr. 236 million in the same year. This averages only 20% of total social costs. The higher the social costs of occupational injuries in a particular branch of industry, the lower the revenue share. The author proposes a differentiated fee, based on differences in risk of injury between work-places, payable by employers to the occupational injury insurance scheme. This would provide an incentive for employers to implement preventive measures.

480 Jönsson, B. (1974) Health Economics — Cost–Benefit Analysis in Health and Medical Care (Sjukvårdsekonomi — cost–benefit analys inom hälso- och sjukvården), Stockholm: Institutet för Socialmedicinsk Ekonomi, 32 pp.

A general introduction to health economics and the use of cost–benefit analysis. Reviews some recent Swedish studies of the cost of certain diseases, and surveys different cost–benefit studies of tuberculosis to illustrate productivity change in the health sector.

481 Kemp, E. et al. (1974) 'Experience with home dialysis over a period of 19 months in Denmark' ('Nitten måneders erfaring med hjemmedialyse in Danmark'), *Ugeskrift for Læger*, **136**, 3, 136–41.

Six patients performed a total of 789 home dialysis treatments during a period of 19 months. The cost of installing the apparatus varied between D.Kr. 25,000 and D.Kr. 63,000, depending on the choice of apparatus and the extent of alterations. The operating cost of a single home dialysis treatment is estimated at approximately D.Kr. 600, or about half the cost of institutional dialysis. The annual saving with three weekly dialyses is estimated at nearly D.Kr. 100,000.

482 LEVY, E. and PARIENTE, R. (1974) 'Chronic respiratory insufficiency and its cost to French society' ('L'insuffisance respiratoire chronique et son coût pour la société française'), *Economie et Santé* (supplement to the *Bulletin des Statistiques de Santé et de Sécurité Sociale*), No. 5, 51–68.

An article based on the results obtained in a study done for the Commission of the European Communities, in 1972. The authors tried to develop physical and financial indicators with which to define the consequences of this group of diseases, which includes asthma, emphysema, and chronic bronchitis. They first define the criteria for clinical and histological diagnosis, and then discuss the cost of the disease, using the available statistics on morbidity and mortality. Their notion of cost is related to the resources mobilized by the medical sector to control the disease, and to losses, through sickness and death, in domestic and leisure activities. The study, based on 1969 data, shows that this group of diseases affected between 1.2 million and 2.5 million individuals, and caused more than 15,000 deaths. In addition, it cost the community nearly Fr. 3,000 million, of which Fr. 2,000 million were for treating the disease and Fr. 1,000 million for the consequences of the deaths.

483 NIELSEN, G., MIKKELSEN, M., and WAMBERG, E. (1974) 'Cost–benefit analysis in prevention of mental retardation' ('Cost–benefit analyse af forbyggende åndssvageforsorg'), *Socialt Tidsskrift*, **50**, 9, 147–67.

The births of approximately 20 children suffering from mongolism (Down's syndrome) could be prevented each year by amniotic fluid examination of 4,260 pregnant women aged 35 years and over. It is estimated that the social costs and benefits of screening balance for this age group, but that costs exceed benefits for younger age groups. The cost of amniotic fluid examination of all pregnant women aged 15-49 years is estimated to exceed its benefit by approximately D.Kr. 102 million (at 1971–72 prices). A ten-year course of diet treatment for phenylketonuria is estimated to yield a net social benefit of approximately D.Kr. 0.5 million per child.

484 PEDERSEN, K. (1974) 'Clinical and economic aspects of home dialysis' ('Hjemmedialyse, kliniske og økonomiske aspekter'), *Ugeskrift for Læger*, **136**, 46, 2579–85.

The operating cost of one home dialysis treatment is D.Kr. 370–440, compared with D.Kr. 2,405 for hospital dialysis and D.Kr. 1,800 for peritoneal dialysis. Home dialysis patients, the majority of whom are able to undertake full-time employment, save hospital travel expenses estimated at approximately D.Kr. 10,000 annually. The conclusion is that home dialysis is preferable to hospital dialysis whenever feasible.

485 SINTONEN, H. (1974) Cost Factors in Welfare for the Aged (*Vanhusten huoltokustannuksiin vaikuttavista tekijöistä*), Helsinki: Finnish Government Printing Centre (Official Statistics of Finland, Special Studies XXXII:40), 127 pp. + English summary 22 pp.

The study attempts to produce cost models that could be used in deciding which form of welfare (institutionalization or open community care) would be more economical in an individual case. In costing welfare, the concept of social costs is followed. After outlining a theoretical framework for finding relevant cost factors, the social costs of welfare for a sample of old people drawn from institutions and open community care are estimated. In developing models to explain the variance in these costs, principal component analysis, stepwise multiple regression analysis, and residual analysis are used. Also, some major cost items are analysed. Practical uses of the models are discussed.

486 STOLZ, P. (1974) Economics of Psychotropic Drugs. A Cost–Benefit Analysis of Tranquilliser Usage in the Federal Republic of Germany in 1972. (*Psychopharmaka — volkwirtschaftlich analysiert, eine Kosten–Nutzen-Analyse der Verwendung von Tranquilizern in der Bundesrepublik Deutschland im Jahre 1972*), Zurich: Schulthess Polygraphischer Verlag (Basler sozialökonomische Studien, Vol. 4), 70 pp.

This study of tranquilliser prescription, by general practitioners and specialists in internal medicine in the Federal Republic of Germany in 1972, reveals considerable cost–benefit implications when compared with alternative psychotherapeutic treatment.

1975

487 ARNOLD, H. (1975) 'Efficiency measurements in the health care system' ('Effizienzmessungen im Gesundheitswesen'), *Deutsches Aerzteblatt*, **72**, 33, 2319–37.

Economically viable medical measures are surveyed, and their efficiency estimated.

313 BJERKELUND, C. (1975) 'Doctors and priorities in the health service' ('Legene og prioriteringen i helsevesenet'), *Nordisk Medicin*, **90**, 4, 105–8.

689 BLOHMKE, M. (1975) The Cost of Health Care Systems, Social Ecology, and Social Medicine (*Kosten des Gesundheitswesens, Sozialökologie*

und Sozialmedizin), Stuttgart: A.W. Gentner Verlag (Schriftenreihe Arbeitsmedizin, Sozialmedizin, Präventivmedizin, Vol. 56), 135 pp.

See 413, 584

488 Brand, M., Escher, M., Menzl, A., and Horisberger, B. (1975) Cost–Benefit Analysis of Anti-depressant Drugs (*Kosten–Nutzen-Analyse Antidepressiva*), Berlin, Heidelberg, New York: Springer Verlag, 70 pp.

This study attempts to go beyond evaluation of purely economic consequences of medical procedures. The multidimensional analysis first discusses the epidemiology of depression, and then covers systematically: costs of treatment, costs of pharmaceuticals, benefits due to reducing length of hospital stay, and benefits due to an increase in the work force. The following topics are then discussed: medical and social advantages and disadvantages of anti-depressant drugs, long-term use of anti-depressants, influences of the distribution of incomes, and humanization of drug treatment. Future developments in the use of anti-depressants are assessed using the Delphi technique, on the basis of the experience and ideas of 21 leading psychiatrists.

489 Brunet-Jailly, J., Huard, P., and Liess, M. (1975) The Cost of Sickness in the Hospital Field: Methodological Approaches (*Le coût de la maladie en milieu hospitalier, approches méthodologiques*), Aix-en-Provence: Laboratoire d'Economie et de Sociologie du Travail, Centre National de la Recherche Scientifique, 272 pp. (mimeographed document).

This document consists of a number of studies on the theoretical and methodological problems of analysing the cost of sickness in French hospitals. The scope and volume of the information needed to carry out research of this kind is emphasized, e.g., the characteristics of hospital clientèle must be known accurately. Many theoretical and methodological problems remain unsolved. Among other things, the authors attempt to select a few basic hypotheses from the existing literature, in order to enable a model of hospital behaviour to be constructed that could be used in France.

490 Dahlberg, L., Berglund, G., Sannerstedt, R., and Werkö, L. (1975) 'Economic aspects of hypertension-related diseases' ('Nationalekonomiska aspekter på blodtryckssjukdom') *Låkartidningen*, **72**, 40, 3823–5.

The paper estimates the social costs of four hypertension-related diseases in Sweden. Of the total cost, estimated at S.Kr. 2.3 billion (1970 prices), S.Kr. 0.9 billion represents production losses due to premature death, S.Kr. 0.5 billion production losses due to sickness, S.Kr. 0.2 billion production losses due to premature payment of pensions, and S.Kr. 0.7 billion the cost of medical care.

491 ESTBORN, B. (1975) Cost-Benefit Analysis of Laboratory Tests (*Cost–benefit-problematiken inom klinisk kemi*), Stockholm: The Swedish Planning and Rationalization Institute of the Health and Social Services (SPRI Project 3019), 52 pp. (mimeographed document).

In Sweden, medical services account for about 7% of total medical care costs and about 15% of hospital costs. Between 1965 and 1972, the relative cost of medical services fell somewhat, mainly because X-ray costs decreased relative to medical care costs as a whole. The paper discusses the possibility of improving the efficiency of clinical chemistry with the help of cost–benefit analysis. It points out that laboratory results are an input to the medical decision making process, and that measurement of the benefits of laboratory tests requires a fundamental understanding of the way the results are used, including the implications of the time factor for the value of a laboratory result.

492 GOERTTLER, K., KOEHLER, C.O., WAGNER, G., and WANZEK, L. (1975) 'Results of the "cancer prevention week in Baden-Wurttemberg". An attempt at cost–benefit analysis' ('War die "Woche der Krebsvorsorge in Baden-Württemberg" ein Erfolg. Versuch einer Kosten–Nutzen-Analyse'), *Die Medizinische Welt*, No. 26, 961–71.

The problems associated with the assessment of preventive medical measures are discussed, and a cost–benefit analysis of a cancer prevention week is attempted.
See 533

493 HÖRTE, L.G. and JOHANNESSON, P.A. (1975) 'The social costs of suicides as compared with road traffic accidents' ('Självmordens samhällsekonomiska kostnader i jämförelse med trafikolyckor'), *Läkartidningen*, **72**, 8, 715–18.

The authors estimate the social cost of suicides using the production loss approach applied to road traffic accidents. On this basis, the cost of suicides in 1970 is estimated at S.Kr. 450 million, compared to the cost of road accidents which is estimated at S.Kr. 500 million. The authors point out that much greater political attention is given to measures to reduce road accidents than suicides. The article receives critical discussion elsewhere in the same journal (**72**, 8, 1415 and 1632–3).

494 JONSSON, ERNST (1975) 'Loss of future production and consumption due to premature deaths' ('Bortfall av framtida produktion och konsumtion vid dödsfall i förtid'), *Landstingens Tidskrift*, **62**, 2, 58–61.

A summary of a report presenting the value of the loss of production and consumption due to premature deaths caused by accidents and smoking-related diseases, for different age groups.

495 KARLSSON, C. (1975) 'Socio-economic aspects of work accidents and their prevention' ('Samhällsekonomiska aspekter på arbetsolycksfall och deras förebyggande'), *Socialmedicinsk Tidsdrift*, **52**, 3, 238–45.

The article presents an economic approach to the problem of work accidents and their prevention. The author argues that application of an economic approach, with careful analysis of costs and methods of resource allocation, can help political choices. He suggests the imposition of taxes on activities with high accident risks, calculated on the basis of social costs.

496 MATTSON, B. and THOMPSON, S. (1975) Medical Costs of Road Traffic Accidents in Sweden (*Vägtrafikolyckor och sjukvårdskostnader*), Stockholm: Liber Förlag, 281 pp.

It is estimated that 60,000–70,000 people are injured or killed annually in road traffic accidents in Sweden. Of these, 16,000 receive inpatient care and 1,200 die. The total cost of medical care for persons injured in road traffic accidents during a one-year period in Sweden is estimated using data from two hospitals. Costs of production loss, property damage, deaths, and suffering are not included. The results for the 265 inpatients registered in 1969 at the Department of General Surgery, Karlstad, and an estimated 850 outpatients (including those who did not need inpatient care) were: transportation S.Kr. 140,000, inpatient care S.Kr. 1,720,000, and outpatient care S.Kr. 400,000. Extrapolating to the national level, the total cost is estimated to be about S.Kr. 150 million at 1972 prices. Including the S.Kr. 71 million estimated for home care of injured persons, the total costs for medical care of road traffic accidents amount to S.Kr. 220 million per year.

497 MIZRAHI, A., MIZRAHI, A., and SANDIER, S. (1975) Prices and Standard Charges for Medical Services — 1960–1975 (*Les prix et les tarifs des services médicaux — 1960–1975*), Paris: Centre de Recherches et de Documentation sur la Consommation, 109 pp. (mimeographed document).

The authors construct prices per day, per case, and per service for hospitals in the public and private sectors, using household survey data and statistics from the Department of Social Security and the Ministry of Health. They examine the trend in prices per day from 1962 to 1975, and conclude that the prices of doctors' services to non-hospitalized patients vary according to where the consultation takes place, its duration, and the doctor's specialty. The price of the consultation is strongly related to the proportion of services rendered by specialists, surgeons, or radiologists. The authors also consider the prices of other medical services to non-hospitalized patients, such as dental care, nursing care, and physiotherapy.

498 NEUMANN, G. (1975) 'The costs of cancer screening' ('Die Kosten der Krebsfrüherkennung'). *Geburtshilfe, Frauenheilkunde*, Vol. 35, 615–18.

This paper calculates the costs arising from cancer screening, especially for early detection of cervical carcinoma.

499 OCELLI, R. (1975) Economic and Social Statistical Aspects of Hypertensive Disease in France (*Aspects statistiques économiques et sociaux de la maladie hypertensive en France*), Paris: Université de Paris I, Panthéon-Sorbonne (PhD thesis), 107 pp. (mimeographed document).

Report of a morbidity study of 24,426 patients with hypertensive disease, and a sample survey covering 4,000 persons representative of the general population concerning their views about their blood pressure. The author studies the direct costs of hypertensive disease, in terms of the use of medical services and of resultant work absenteeism, and the indirect costs, in particular those related to mortality. He conservatively estimates the cost of hypertension in the adult French population at Fr. 1,642 million per year.

500 PETERSEN, K. (1975) Cost–Benefit Analysis in Health Care (*Cost-benefit analyser inden for sundhedsvæsenet*), Copenhagen: Handelshøjskolen i København, 68 pp.

A general introductory discussion of the use of cost–benefit analysis in the health sector. Some methodological difficulties in identifying the effects of different programmes are discussed.

501 ROCHE, L. et al. (1975) PPBS in Health Matters (2nd meeting of the Lyons Association of Medical Economics, Lyons, 25 April 1974) (*RCB en matière de santé* (Actes de la 2e réunion de l'Association Lyonnaise d'Economie Médicale, Lyon, 25 avril 1974)), Paris: Masson (Collection Médecine Légale et Toxicologie Médicale), 155 pp.

The central topic of this work is the Planning Programming and Budgeting System, which is successively considered at the general level, the level of the medical profession (rationalization of education and role of the medical unions), the level of the economic cost of certain pathological states, and the level of hospitalization in general and in psychiatry in particular.

502 ROUSSSEAU, M. (1975) 'The "perinatality" programme — study — decisions — management — supervision' ('Le programme "Périnatalité" — Etude — Décision — Gestion — Contrôle'), *Cahiers de Sociologie et de Démographie Médicales*, **15**, 2, 60–5.

Summarizes the various elements of the PPBS study concerning problems of perinatality, begun in 1970 by the Studies and Planning Division of the Ministry of Health, with the collaboration of the Directorate-General of Health and of the Institut National de la Santé et de la Recherche Médicale. This study subsequently served as a basis for the preparation of the 'definitive perinatality programme' under the VIth Plan. In 1968, accidents during the perinatal period resulted in 21,000 deaths and 40,000 disabilities; for 1970, costs were estimated at Fr. 15,000 million, i.e., 2.5% of GNP. The goal proposed was to reduce the rate of perinatal mortality to 18 per 1,000 as compared to the 23 per 1,000 predicted by 1980. The author outlines the different phases of this PPBS programme (studies, decisions, management, and supervision).

503 SINTONEN, H. (1975) 'A cost-effectiveness approach in welfare for the aged' ('Kustannus-vaikuttavuusanalyysi vanhustenhuollossa'), *Kansantaloudellinen Aikakauskirja*, **71**, 4, 435–48.

A cost-effectiveness comparison of institutional and domiciliary care of the aged is carried out using the fixed effectiveness approach. Effectiveness is defined in terms of standard of care, and two individually varying standards are fixed: that prevailing in old people's homes, and that in domiciliary care. Calculations suggest that, in Finland, the average social cost of domiciliary care would be 1.7 times that of institutional care, if the standard of care is that prevailing in institutions. If the required standard is that of domicilary care, the average cost of institutional care is about 1.1 times that of domiciliary care. The sensitivity of results to various assumptions is tested.

504 SINTONEN, H. (1975) 'Reflections on cost–benefit/effectiveness analysis in health and social welfare' (*'Synpunkter på cost–benefit/effectiveness analysen i social- och hälsovården'*) in: RINGEN, A. (ed.) Research on Social Welfare and Social Policy (*Velferdsforskning og sosialpolitikk*), Oslo: Institutt for anvendt sosialvitenskapelig forskning (Report 75:1), 263–72.

The pros and cons of cost–benefit and cost-effectiveness analysis in health and social welfare are examined, and limits to their application are outlined. In particular, problems in the identification of objectives and effects of action taken in these fields are discussed.

505 STÅHL, I. (1975) 'Present state of cost–benefit analysis in medical evaluation' in: *Preventive Medicine — Rationale for the Use of Drugs* *and Vaccines* (Supplement No. 576 to *Acta Medica Scandinavica*), 129–34.

Cost–benefit analysis is presented as a technique based on theoretical welfare economics. Methods of estimating benefits using an insurance approach are discussed for chronic renal failure. It is proposed that the benefits of early detection and prevention be analysed in terms of insurance premiums for different risk groups.

506 WAALER, H.T. (1975) 'On benefit–cost analysis in health care' ('Om nytte-kostnadsanalyser i helsesektoren'), *Sosialøkonomen*, **29**, 3, 49–51.

The allocation of resources between preventive and curative activities is discussed with regard to the problems of time preference. The example considered is BCG vaccination, where the surplus of benefits over costs might change in future time periods.

507 WAALER, H.T. (1975) *The Use of Dynamic Models in the Epidemiology of Tuberculosis* (collection of articles published in 1968–74), Oslo: Universitetsforlagets Trykningscentral, 75 pp.

A deterministic mathematical model is constructed to study the epidemiology of tuberculosis in a closed population. The model, which uses a system of differential equations, and makes it possible to study the effects of curative and preventive activities. The future reduction in the number of life years with illness is aggregated, using a discount rate expressing the rate of time preference.
See 517

508 WALLER, Å. (1975) 'An investigation of road traffic accidents' ('En trafikolycksundersökning'), *Socialmedicinsk Tidskrift*, **52**, 4, 276–80.

All cases of road traffic accidents treated at the Karlstad district hospital are investigated with regard to a number of variables connected with the accident. The social costs of the 850 cases are estimated at S.Kr. 23 million.

1976

509 ANDREE, R., BERGSTRÖM, K., and BÅNG, H.O. (1976) 'Computer tomography, encephalography, and cerebral angiography: comparative costs' ('Datortomografi, encefalografi och cerebral angiografi — En kostnadsjämförelse'), *Läkartidningen*, **73**, 28–29, 2479–81.

Computer tomography has considerably increased the safety of examining the brain; it may reduce the use of encephalography and cerebral angiography, which are costly and risky procedures. The productivity of the different methods was investigated. Computer tomography has the highest fixed cost, but the lowest cost per examination when the volume of production is high. The total possible savings in costs depend, however, on the extent to which computer tomography can replace the other methods.

510 BØNSING, E. (1976) 'The cost of anaesthesia in view of possible economies' ('Omkostninger ved anæsthesi med henblik på mulige besparelser'), *Ugeskrift for Læger*, **138**, 21, 1282–4.

The costs of seven different types of anaesthesia are calculated, and recommendations concerning the choice of anesthesia in hospitals are made.

511 CHODKIEWICZ, J.P. (1976) Neurosurgical Emergencies in the Paris Area: Aetiological, Clinical, and Economic Considerations (*Les urgences neurochirurgicales de la région parisienne: considérations étiologiques, cliniques et économiques*), Paris: Université de Paris I, Panthéon-Sorbonne (PhD thesis), 191 pp. (mimeographed document).

This thesis attempts to draw up a balance-sheet of the way in which four neurosurgical wards have divided emergency cases in Paris among themselves, over a 15-year period. Estimates of the costs of treating emergency cases, and of the other activities of the wards, are made for each month in 1972. The author suggests the essential elements of a reform of the existing system.

512 FRIIS-HASCHE, E., HOLMSTRUP, P., HØFFDING, J., JOHANNESEN, L., KJELDSEN, K., and SCHWARZ, E. (1976) 'Dental care in Denmark in 1974, economic aspects' ('Tandplejen i Danmark 1974, Samfundsøkonimiske aspekter'), *Tandlægebladet*, Vol. 80, 103–7.

This paper presents the results of a questionnaire survey of a random sample of 426 Danish dentists in 1974. Services covered by the national health insurance scheme accounted for 83% of the number of services performed, mostly of a preventive or maintenance nature, but for only 54% of total expenditure on dental services. The remaining 17% of total services, mainly gold crowns, dentures, and bridge work, accounted for 46% of total expenditure. The direct cost of dental services totalled nearly D.Kr. 1 billion. The indirect costs (lost working time and travel expenses associated with treatment) are estimated at about D.Kr. 150 million.

513 GEERTS, A. (1976) 'What is the cost of disablement' ('Wat kost invaliditeit'), *Ziekenfondsgids*, **30**, 1, 21–4.

Today, the European Community includes approximately 14 million invalids. However, the various member countries use different norms governing the level of invalidity pensions. In Belgium, the full pension is paid at 66.6% invalidity; in Italy, an invalidity of 50% will qualify for full benefit (50% is the figure recommended by the European Economic Community). Different norms also exist with regard to a classification system. France (like the USSR) recognizes three invalid categories: complete invalidity requiring the help of a third party, complete invalidity, and invalidity that does not exclude all forms of remunerative work. The Netherlands uses a classification with seven categories of invalidity, the degree of invalidity depending on the salary that can still be earned. Benefit payments also differ from country to country. In case of full invalidity, Belgium pays 65% of the last salary received, the Netherlands 80%, and the Federal Republic of Germany 66.66%. The article concludes with a number of statistics that illustrate the considerable increase in the prevalence of invalidity.

514 GOLL, K. (1976) 'Resource use by disease category in general practice' ('Den praktiserende loeges ressourceforbrug fordelt på sygdomskategorier'), *Ugeskrift for Læger*, **138**, 21, 1277–82.

The direct costs of various diseases seen by the GP are estimated. Cost items include details of expenditures on primary health services, hospital services, drugs, and transportation. The estimated total cost is greatest for tumours, accidents, and cardiovascular diseases. The estimated cost per case is greatest for tumours and blood diseases.

515 GUNST, J. and LAURITZEN, N. (1976) 'Alternative means of caring for the elderly' ('Alternative omsorgsforanstaltninger for ældre'), *Social Tidsskrift*, Vol. 52, 89–107.

The authors describe and discuss care of the elderly in the framework of cost–benefit analysis. The discussion relates to a project being undertaken by the authors.

516 HARVALD, B. (1976) 'Screening for hypertension, costs and benefits' ('Hypertensionsscreening omkostringer og gevinst'), *Ugeskrift for Læger*, **138**, 8, 489–90.

In this leading article, the author discusses the costs and benefits of screening for hypertension. Assuming the prevalence of hypertension to be 10% among persons aged over 40 years, the cost of screening and treatment is estimated at about D.Kr. 5,000 per year of life gained. This is compared with the cost, per year of life gained, of D.Kr. 20,000 for treatment in coronary care units, and of D.Kr. 200,000 for dialysis or kidney transplantation.

517 JOHANSEN, L. (1976) 'The epidemiology and treatment of tuberculosis analysed by economic and mathematical models' ('Tuberkuloseutbredelse og -behandling belyst ved økonomiske og matematisk modeller'), *Sosialøkonomen*, **30**, 9–10, 7–11.

A review of Waaler's dissertation on the epidemiology of tuberculosis. There is a striking resemblance between mathematical models describing dynamic developments in biology and in economics. Of special interest is the use of a discount rate in the analysis of health measures yielding outcomes over a long time horizon.
See 507

518 JÖNSSON, B. (1976) *Cost–Benefit Analysis in Public Health and Medical Care*, Lund: University of Lund, Department of Economics (Lund Economic Studies, No. 12) and Stockholm: Institutet för Socialmedicinsk Ekonomi, 141 pp. Also published in Swedish: (1977) *Sjukvårdsekonomi — sociala lönsamhetskalkyler inom hälso- och sjukvården*, Stockholm: AWE/Gebers, 180 pp.

A theoretical discussion of health sector resource allocation and cost–benefit analysis is followed by a review of a large number of studies attempting to estimate the social costs and benefits of health programmes. An attempt is made to organize the different studies into a coherent framework of modern theoretical welfare economics. The book contains chapters on: the market economy, the price system, and cost–benefit analysis; the benefits of poliomyelitis vaccination (a comparison of four different studies); costs and benefits of medical research; costs and benefits of vaccination programmes (poliomyelitis, smallpox, cholera, tuberculosis, measles, rubella, and influenza); early detection of disease (general screening, cervical cancer, and phenylketonuria); choice of treatment (varicose veins, chronic renal disease, early discharge from hospital after gallstone operation, ulcers, treatment with anti-depressants and psychotropic drugs, and treatment of Parkinson's disease with levodopa).

519 KLARMAN, H.E. and GUZICK, D. (1976) 'Economics of influenza' in: SELBY, P. (ed.) *Influenza: Virus, Vaccines, and Strategy. Proceedings of a Working Group on Pandemic Influenza, Rougemont, 26–28 January 1976*, London and New York: Academic Press, 255–68.

This paper attempts to apply cost–benefit analysis to a programme of influenza vaccination in the USA. The difficulty of valuing the intangible benefits of a reduction in the incidence of the disease, especially gains in life expectancy, is discussed. Because of this difficulty, the cost–benefit approach is rejected in favour of cost–effectiveness analysis. For policy purposes, this means that economic analysis cannot indicate whether a programme is worthwhile, or

what priority it deserves among programmes competing for public funds. Because of the antigenic variability of the influenza virus, the analysis is performed over a prolonged period of time, such as a decade, and results are presented for a 'composite' year. It is estimated that, for the aged population of the USA, the net cost per life-year gained is $600-$700 if the vaccine efficacy is 50%, and $300-$400 if it is 70%.
See 22

520 KOCHER, G. (ed.) (1976) Cost–Benefit Analysis in the Health Care System (*Kosten–Nutzen-Analyse im Gesundheitswesen*), Basle: Pharma Information, 67 pp.

This booklet contains the proceedings of a seminar organized in March 1976 in Egerkingen which, probably for the first time in Switzerland, brought together health economists from universities, industry, and government. After defining cost–benefit analysis and outlining its limitations and difficulties, three cost–benefit analyses are presented of anti-depressant drugs, the use of tranquillisers in Germany, and the treatment of alcoholics. These are discussed, together with the use of cost–benefit analysis techniques in preventive medicine and in the health insurance system.

521 MIKKELSEN, M. and NIELSEN, G. (1976) 'Cost–benefit analysis of prevention of Down's syndrome' in: BOUE, A., Prenatal Diagnosis, *Colloques de l'INSERM*, Vol. 61, 283–9.

In Denmark, 21-22 cases of Down's syndrome could be prevented each year through prenatal screening of all women aged 35 years and over. Estimates show that the benefit of screening exceeds its cost for women aged over 40 years and, by interpolation, for women aged over 38 years.

522 MIKKELSEN, M. and NIELSEN, G. (1976) 'Cost–benefit analysis in prenatal diagnosis' in: THE DANISH NATIONAL SERVICE FOR THE MENTALLY RETARDED (ed.), *Flash on the Danish National Service for the Mentally Retarded*, Copenhagen: The Personnel Training School (publication No. 39), 283–9.

New estimates show that prevention of Down's syndrome does not entail a net social cost when amniocentesis is performed on pregnant women aged over 35 years. The total cost is estimated at D.Kr. 7,956,000, composed as follows: amniocentesis D.Kr. 2,223,000, laboratory costs D.Kr. 5,709,000, and therapeutic abortion D.Kr. 24,000. The total benefit in terms of averted cost without prevention is estimated at D.Kr. 8,474,000. The implied net social benefit is D.Kr. 518,000.

523 OLESEN, P. (1976) Public Costs of Alcohol Abuse in Denmark (*Det offentliges omkostninger ved alkoholmisbrug i Danmark*), Copenhagen: P. Olesen, (Dannefoerdsvej 7, 1973 Copenhagen V, Denmark), 105 pp.

The number of alcohol abusers in Denmark (population of 5 million) is estimated at about 200,000, and of persons under treatment at 30,000. In 1973, the tax revenue on alcohol sales amounted to D.Kr. 3.2 billion. Estimates are presented of public expenditure on alcohol-related daily allowances, medical treatment, pensions, road traffic accidents, police and other items. The total cost of alcohol abuse during 1973–74 is estimated at D.Kr. 1.66 billion, of which about D.Kr. 0.5 billion represents the cost of medical care. Various policies to reduce alcohol abuse are discussed.

524 SANTERIAN, M.R. (1976) 'The cost of treatment in a medico-psycho-pedagogical centre' ('Le coût des traitements en centre médico-psycho-pédagogique'), *Revue Economique*, (special number: Health economics), **27**, 3, 483–505.

A study concerning a method of analysing the costs of treatment in medico-psycho-pedagogical centres (informal institutions for child psychology). The costing methods are fully explained. The estimated costs of individual cases are widely dispersed around the mean for each diagnostic category. The author suggests that the method used could also be applied to other ambulatory patients.

525 SWEDEN, STATE MEDICAL RESEARCH COUNCIL (1976) Research on Kidney Diseases — Long-Term Planning (*Njurforskning — Långtidsplanering*), Stockholm: Statens Medicinska Forskningsråd, 247 pp.

This is a report from a working party on cost–benefit analysis and long-term planning of kidney diseases research. The epidemiology and aetiology of the diseases are surveyed, as well as possibilities for treatment and prophylaxis. Research priorities are identified and set out from a cost–benefit standpoint, where possibilities for decreased costs of medical care in the future are of major importance. Three main research areas are proposed: infectious diseases of the urinary tract, glomerulonephritis and related diseases, and renal dialysis.

526 VETERE, C. (1976) 'Decision making techniques in the provision of health care: problems of definition and application' ('Contributi alla definizione ed applicazione di tecniche decisionali alla attività sanitaria'), *I Problemi della Sicurezza Sociale*, **31**, 1/2, 5–33.

The author explains the differences between cost-effectiveness and cost–benefit analysis, and goes on to describe some recent applications of these techniques. These include their use in evaluating comprehensive health care programmes, such as those undertaken by the Kaiser Health Plan, and in assessing the value of particular programmes, such as those designed to control tuberculosis. Applications in the field of hospital economics are also discussed. Finally, some of the problems involved in the application of these techniques in the Italian political and administrative context are discussed.

527 WAMBERG, E. (1976) 'Residential management' in: RAINE, D.N. (ed.) *Medico-social Managment of Inherited Metabolic Disease, Proceedings of the Thirteenth Symposium of the Society for the Study of Inborn Errors of Metabolism*, Lancaster: MTP Press, 63–78.

Presents a cost–benefit analysis of dietary treatment of phenylketonuria. The cost of early detection and treatment is estimated at D.Kr. 276,343, composed as follows: screening D.Kr. 17,143, extra cost of dietary treatment D.Kr. 105,584, and share of expenses of Kennedy Institute D.Kr. 153,616. The benefit, in terms of avoided cost of institutional care from the age of 3 to 67 years, is estimated at D.Kr. 822,571. The net gain is D.Kr. 546,228.

1977

528 KAMPER-JØRGENSEN, F. (1977) 'Cost–benefit analysis and screening' ('Cost–benefit analyse og screening') in: *Medical Yearbook 1977*, Copenhagen: Mungsgaard, 60–8.

This paper discusses some of the basic issues and problems in cost–benefit analysis in relation to screening. The WHO guidelines for screening are introduced. The questions to which cost–benefit analysis can provide answers are raised with reference to a general epidemiological model of disease. The concepts of average and marginal cost are distinguished, and the concept of programme benefits and the epidemiological concepts of sensitivity and specificity are discussed. Some examples of empirical analysis are given. Cost–benefit analysis is described as a 'commentary' rather than a decision-making technique, and the less ambitious cost-effectiveness analysis is recommended. A step-wise procedure using an epidemiological model as the basis for cost-effectiveness and cost–benefit analysis is presented.

529 LAURINKARI, J., NIEMELÄ, P., and ELO, O. (1977) *Costs and Benefits of Influenza Vaccination: a Theoretical Study*, Kuopio: University of Kuopio, Department of Community Health (Series Statistics and Reviews, No. 2), 24 pp.

A theoretical study of the possibility of using vaccination programmes and improving the effectiveness of vaccines. The authors also discuss methods of minimizing disability in the population.

530 Leu, R. and Lutz, P. (1977) Economic Aspects of Alcohol Consumption in Switzerland (*Oekonomische Aspekte des Alkoholkonsums in der Schweiz*), Zurich: Schulthess Polygraphischer Verlag (Basler sozialökonomische Studien, Vol. 7), 638 pp.

The economic cost associated with alcohol consumption in Switzerland is estimated at Sw.Fr. 1.5 billion a year. Economic cost refers to the total cost of alcohol consumption, regardless of who causes and who bears the cost. Total economic cost cannot, therefore, be used as a guide for public policy regarding alcohol consumption. The economic cost caused by alcoholics, which may be avoided through treatment programmes, is estimated separately. Cost–benefit analysis is then applied in order to evaluate treatment of alcoholism and rehabilitation programmes. The social (external) cost of alcohol consumption is estimated at Sw.Fr. 850 million a year, where external cost is defined as the part of total economic cost that is imposed by the alcohol consumption of one individual on other members of society. An externalities model of alcoholic beverages taxation is proposed.

531 Levy, E., Bungener, M., Dumenil, G., and Fagnani, F. (1977) Evaluating the Cost of Sickness (*Evaluer le coût de la maladie*), Paris: Dunod, 296 pp.

The authors consider the costs of sickness in three stages. The first stage consists of preparing as complete and reliable a picture of the disease as possible. The indicators are generally physical ones: the number of individuals affected, the number of deaths, indicators of severity, the duration, etc. The second stage involves determining the cost of producing health; it is claimed that this can easily be estimated in financial terms. In the final and most difficult stage, the cost of sickness is evaluated by preparing a table of its overall consequences, especially in those areas that will suffer losses because of the illness, such as production, welfare, etc. Examples of the approach are given for three diseases: lung cancer, ischaemic heart disease, and chronic bronchitis.

532 Pätiälä, H., Niemelä, P., and Laurinkari, J. (1977) 'Cost–benefit analysis of synovectomy of the knee', *Scandinavian Journal of Rheumatology*, **5**, 4, 227–32.

A follow-up study of the costs and benefits of 225 knee operations carried out in 1973. Information was collected on hospitalization and working ability.

533 Pflanz, M. (1977) 'Cost–benefit analyses of screening: A critique by a non-economist' ('Kosten–Nutzen-Analysen von Untersuchungen zur

Krankheitfrüherkennung: Kritik eines Nichtökonomen') in: ZENTRALINSTITUT FUR DIE KASSNÄRTZLICHE VERSORGUNG IN DER BUNDERSREPUBLIK DEUTSCHLAND, Screening for Malignant Diseases in the Female (*Früherkennung bösartiger Neubildungen bei der Frau*), Cologne: Deutscher Ärtze-Verlag, 68–77.

Almost all papers on cost–benefit analysis in health care come to the conclusion that the benefits of specific programmes by far outweigh the cost. However, such predictions tend not to be evaluated subsequently. The author, an epidemiologist, underlines the need for epidemiological outcome data. Without a fair assessment of the epidemiological effect of a programme such as screening, a cost–benefit analysis has no basis. A paper written by German authors about the tentative effectiveness and efficiency of a 'Cancer Week', a programme of public education about cancer screening, gave a very optimistic relationship between the costs and benefits of such a programme. However, it can be shown that the epidemiological and economic assumptions are wrong or unfounded. It is argued that even cost-effectiveness analysis faces similar problems. The basis of all estimates of cost-effectiveness is the epidemiological data, the assessment of real direct and indirect costs of case detection and treatment, and the development of a mathematical model for the estimation of the relationships between cost and effects under various assumptions.
See 492

46 PFLANZ, M. and GEISSLER, U. (1977) 'Rapid cost expansion in the health care system of the Federal Republic of Germany', *Preventive Medicine*, **6**, 2, 290–301.

718 SCHAEFER, H. (1977) 'Efficiency and effectiveness of medical services in the light of health insurance' ('Effizienz und Effektivität der medizinischen Leistungen im Licht der Krankenversicherung'), *Die Ortskrankenkasse*, **59**, 16, 657–63.

534 SCHICKE, R.K. (1977) Preventive Medicine: Costs and Benefits (*Präventiv-Medizin: Kosten und Nutzen*), Bonn-Bad Godesberg: Friedrich-Thieding-Stiftung des Hartmannbundes (Verband der Ärtze Deutschlands, Schriftenreihe), 55 pp.

A comprehensive outline of the costs and benefits of primary and secondary prevention. The monetary valuation of various programmes in many countries shows the difficulties of comparing published data on costs and benefits. The main problem is the determination of outcome indicators for preventive programmes. Generally, secondary prevention seems to be less cost-effective than primary prevention. Secondary prevention of cancer is more efficient than secondary prevention of heart diseases.

76 UHDE, A.L. (1977) *On the Optimal Allocation of Resources to Health Care; Implications for Cost–Benefit Analysis*, Bergen: University of Bergen (Economic papers, No. 1), 241 pp. (mimeographed document).

1978

535 EKBLOM, M., ELO, O., LAURINKARI, J., and NIEMELÄ, P. (1978) 'Costs and benefits of measles vaccination in Finland', *Scandinavian Journal of Social Medicine*, **6**, 3, 111–5.

In this article, the authors discuss the benefits of vaccination programmes for children aged under 3 years.

536 LAURINKARI, J., NIEMELÄ, P., and ELO, O. (1978) *Vaccination, Health Policy Planning and Decision-Making*, Kuopio: University of Kuopio, Department of Community Health (Series Statistics and Reviews, No. 1), 22 pp.

A summary report of Finnish vaccination studies. It describes the benefits of vaccination programmes in general, and the use of cost–benefit analysis in health policy planning.

4. Measuring the Output of Health Services

1964

197 SPRANZI, A. (1964) Cost Variability (*La variabilità dei costi*), Milan: Antonio Giuffrè, 102 pp.

1967

537 GOOTJES, P. (1967) 'The effectiveness of health protection' ('Het rendement van gezondheidsbescherming'), *Maandschrift Economie*, **31**, 12, 607–16.

Argues that health planning techniques, including cost–benefit analysis, should be carefully applied in the Netherlands, even if the initial results of such an approach in the United States do not appear to be applicable or morally acceptable. All health projects and programmes should first be examined to remove areas of overlap; their benefits, in terms of expenditure savings or national income increases due to reduced mortality and absenteeism, should then be estimated. The results will undoubtedly be challenged and will not be an immediate guide to policy decisions, but this may not always be the case.

1968

538 Bogatyrev, I.D. and Rojtman, M.P. (1968) *Methods of Studying the Economic Benefits of Disease Control*, Copenhagen: World Health Organization, Regional Office for Europe (Original in Russian. Summary in English, No. EURO 0339/4), 5 pp.

Proceedings of a seminar on health economics, held in Moscow from 25 June to 2 July 1968 and organized by the WHO Regional Office for Europe. Outlines a cost–benefit analysis of polio vaccines, the conclusion being that the difference between the total cost of eliminating poliomyelitis in the USSR and the total benefit from the prevention of loss amounts to nearly 3 billion roubles. The cost–benefit ratio is 1:66, i.e., for every rouble spent the economy benefits by 66 roubles.

1969

539 Bourdin, J. (1969) Economic Contribution of the Health Care Sector, Evaluation Methods (*Contribution économique du secteur de la santé, méthodes d'évaluations*), Caen: Université de Caen, Faculté de Droit et des Sciences Economiques (supplementary thesis in economic sciences), 83 pp. (mimeographed document).

The first part of this study deals with the problems of measuring productivity in the health care sector, and factors leading to improvements in productivity. The author concludes that it is possible to increase the technical output of doctors by using auxiliary personnel and by setting up group practices. In the second part, he considers health as an 'input', i.e., as an income-producing resource. He studies the procedure for evaluating the output of a health programme (including the value of human life) and shows that, up to now, medical decisions have generally not been influenced by economic criteria other than overall budgetary limits.

1970

540 Brenna, A. (1970) 'Reflections on economic efficiency in the health care sector, with particular reference to hospitals' ('Alcune considerazioni in materia di efficienza economica del settore sanitario con particolare riguardo al comparto ospedaliero'), *I Problemi della Sicurezza Sociale*, **25**, 3, 425–64.

The author examines the problems encountered when attempts are made to define, measure and promote economic efficiency in the provision of health services in countries such as Italy, where expenditure on these services is, to an increasing extent, financed by public agencies. After analysing the health care system in general, and the problems involved in the provision of health services at no direct cost to the user, the author examines in detail the question of efficiency in the provision of hospital services. He concludes that, in the present situation, institutional aspects assume prior importance, in the sense that improvements in the efficiency of the hospital services are only possible if appropriate changes are made in the structure of the health service as a whole.

541 Felding, F. (1970) Analysis of the Organization of Patient Treatment, Possibilities and Efficiency in Treatment of Older Chronic Patients in Copenhagen (*Analyse af en patientbehandlingsorganisation, muligheder og effektivitet i behandlingen af ældre kronisk syge i Københavns kommune*), Copenhagen: Polyteknisk Forlag, 123 pp.

The organization of treatment is analysed in an operational research framework. Inefficiency is attributed to the lack of an efficient referral system and of coordination with the social services. Optimal organization should cut investment by half, reduce annual current expenditure by D.Kr. 50 million, and eliminate waiting lists in the future.

213 Lodeon, M.C. (1970) Investigation of Qualitative Criteria for Assessing the Management of Hospital Services (*Recherche de critères qualitatifs permettant d'apprécier la gestion des services hospitaliers*), Paris: Ministère de l'Economie et des Finances, Division de la Prévision, Département des Biens Collectifs, 21 pp. (mimeographed document).

1971

542 Fagnani, F. (1971) 'An application of operational research to the organization of emergency treatment' ('Application de la recherche opérationnelle à l'organisation des secours d'urgence'), *Cahiers de Sociologie et de Démographie Médicales*, **11**, 4, 170–6.

A model is proposed for analysing the effectiveness with which different kinds of organizations deal with any type of emergency occurring in a given geographical area. By means of this model, it was possible to simulate the behaviour of various emergency pathological states during the first two hours. These were recorded during an epidemiological survey of all emergencies and accidents occurring in the Côte d'Or between April and July 1968. The various indicators adopted were arranged in programmes, some of which were aimed at reducing waiting time and others at improving the quality of services. The use of the model made it possible to measure the effectiveness of these programmes in terms of the numbers of deaths prevented. The author concludes that this study has provided a viable tool, capable of being used in the field and of being improved on the basis of concrete data.

222 KOCK, S.E. (1971) 'Can the hospital economy be rationalized?' ('Kan sjukhusekonomin rationaliseras?'), *Ekonomiska Samfundets Tidskrift*, **24**, 4, 263–90.

543 POLDERMANS, J.D.G. (1971) 'How do we evaluate the quality of health care?' ('Hoe waarderen we de kwaliteit van de gezondheidszorg?'), *Economisch-Statistische-Berichten*, **56**, 2789, 244–6.

It is suggested that the quality of health care might be measured by examining the trend in laboratory tests, the trend in post-surgical mortality, or the number of deaths per 100 hundred hospitalized patients.

544 VAN LOON, P.C.J. (1971) 'Effectiveness of clinical health care. The need for a rationalization plan for health care' ('Doelmatigheid van de klinische gezondheidszorg. Behoefte aan een rationalisatieplan voor de volksgezondheid'), *Acta Hospitalia*, **11**, 2, 75–104.

The provision of health care, particularly hospital care, results from a series of uncoordinated individual decisions. The goals are patient-oriented and the decisions do not fit into a general framework. As a result, the application of operational research has not been able to rationalize health services. Quality criteria may provide the key to such rationalization. However, the analysis of cost structures of hospitals of different size, with different specialist staff and auxiliary facilities, must receive priority.

420 WHO (1971) *Statistical Indicators for the Planning and Evaluation of Public Health Programmes*, Geneva: World Health Organization (Technical Report Series, No. 472), 40 pp.

1973

545 DELIEGE, D. (1973) 'Concerted medicine, its objectives, its efficacy' ('La médecine concertée, ses buts, son efficacité'), *Médecins de Groupe*, No. 60, 633–43.

This paper sets out various methods for evaluating medical activity: evaluation of the relevance of the objectives pursued, analysis of efficiency, and investigation of utility and efficacy. Such evaluation may be made of action taken, or of the quality of care (based on technical performance, patients' satisfaction, or the nature of the services supplied). A further evaluation could be attempted of the degree to which specified objectives have been met, or the health of the population improved. Specific action may be defined on the basis of the definition of general objectives; to this end, some suggestions applicable to group medicine are made.

459 FELDSTEIN, M.S., PIOT, M.A., and SUNDARESAN, T.K. (1973) *Resource Allocation Model for Public Health Planning. A Case Study of Tuberculosis Control* (supplement to Vol. 48 of the *Bulletin of the World Health Organization*), Geneva: World Health Organization, 110 pp.

546 KAITARANTA, H. and PUROLA, T. (1973) *A Systems-Oriented Approach to the Consumption of Medical Commodities*, Helsinki: The Social Insurance Institution, Research Institute for Social Security, 10 pp. (report); *Social Science and Medicine*, **7**, 7, 531–40.

This paper, presented at the Third International Conference on Social Science and Medicine, held in Elsinore, Denmark, in 1972, outlines a systems-theoretical framework applied in an extensive study of the Finnish health insurance scheme. Consumption is conceptualized as part of a multi-phase process in which perception of illness, initiation of need, derived demand, and finally consumption of medical commodities are the major phases. Each of these phases is described by a model and integrated into a fourth model, which describes the functioning of the public health care system.

242 VAUHKONEN, O. and BÄCKMAN, G. (1973) Hospital Activities in the 1960s (*Sairaalalaitos 1960-luvulla*), Helsinki: The Finnish Hospital Federation, 165 pp. (mimeographed document).

1974

547 Aarby, P. (1974) Evaluation of the Effectiveness of the Hospital (*Effektivitetsvurdering af sygehuse*), Copenhagen: Institutet for Organisation og Arbejdssociologi (Series Nyt fra Samfundsvidenskaberne, No. 74–12), 23 pp.

The purpose of the analysis is to develop a method of measuring the cost-effectiveness of hospitals in Denmark. First, a model of hospital costs is estimated by multiple least squares regression, using data from a large number of Danish hospitals. Second, an index is constructed for each hospital, comparing observed costs with the estimated values.

257 Karlsen, S. (1974) Cost Analysis of General Hospitals (*Kostnadsanalyse av somatiske sykehuse*), Trondheim: Norsk Institutt for Sykehusforskning, 40 pp. + appendix (mimeographed document).

548 Söderström, L. (1974) To Evaluate Health Care (*Att värdera sjukvård*), Lund: University of Lund, Department of Economics (Report 1974:4), 25 pp.

The paper discusses different approaches to evaluating the benefits of medical care, with reference to theoretical welfare economics. The author proposes a method of valuing medical care in terms of its effect on the individual's set of capabilities in performing various activities. He discusses the possibility of using an insurance approach to evaluate consumers' willingness to pay, and compares it to alternative approaches, including the use of health indicators.

549 Westrin, C.G. (1974) 'To measure the effects of health care' ('Att mäta effekter av vård'), *Socialmedicinsk Tidskrift*, **51**, 1, 2–4.

This editorial introduces a special issue of the journal consisting of short contributions and comments on the theme 'To measure the effects of health care'. Participants are research workers in social medicine and hospital administrators. The issue reviews the current debate on evaluation problems, from the viewpoints of social medicine and hospital administration.

1975

273 Coppini, G. (1975) 'An economic function for controlling and distributing hospital expenditure' ('Una funzione economica per il controllo e la

ripartizione della spesa ospedaliera'), *I Problemi della Sicurezza Sociale*, **30**, 2, 215–35.

550 DANISH HOSPITAL INSTITUTE (1975) An Analysis of Resource Consumption in Hospital Health Care (*En Analyse af sygehussundhedsvæsendets ressourceforbrug*), Copenhagen: Danish Hospital Institute, 45 pp. (mimeographed document).

This report, prepared for a working group under a government committee, describes the level of health care expenditure, the increase in resource use, population change, the increase in morbidity, and the change in treatment quality, and explores the functional distribution of treatment in various sectors. It concludes that morbidity has increased and that the quality of care has improved; both factors increase health care expenditure, but available data are insufficient to analyse the trend in detail. It is recommended that a model relating costs to various diagnostic categories be developed. Various cost containment measures are discussed; selective control of hospital sector incomes is not considered relevant, since they have not increased faster than those of other groups.

551 HAKKARAINEN, A. (1975) 'Mathematical model for the production of health services' ('Matemaattinen malli terveydenhuoltajärjestelmän kuvaajana'), *Kansantaloudellinen Aikakauskirja*, **72**, 4, 449–65.

This paper presents a model, developed by a project group in the Finnish National Board of Health, based on Leontief input–output theory and linear programming. The planning problem is formulated as minimization of the deviations of service outputs from service objectives, subject to constraints on different types of resources.

552 KANN, J. (1975) 'Dental care for children — price — product — efficiency' ('Børnetandpleje — pris — ydęlse — effektivitet'), *Danmarks Amtsråd*, **6**, 4, 9–14.

The article compares dental care for children in municipalities providing public dental care and in municipalities with subsidized private dental care. A higher proportion of children were treated, and at a lower cost, in the municipalities with public dental care than in those with subsidized private care.

281 KARLSEN, S. (1975) Cost Analysis of General Hospitals (*Kostnadsanalyse av somatiske sykehus*), Vol. II, Trondheim: Norsk Institutt for Sykehusforskning, 58 pp. + appendix (mimeographed document).

553 Van Zonneveld, R.J., Timmer, M., Petersen, W.G., Sloof, R., and Hatgerink, M.J. (1975) 'Priorities in health care' ('Prioriteiten in de gezondheidszorg'), *Tijdschrift voor Sociale Geneeskunde*, **53**, 3, 76–96

The problem of establishing health care priorities is important, in the Netherlands and elsewhere. One of the groups studying this problem is the working committee on health care priorities of the Council for Health Research of TNO (Nederlandsche organisatie voor toegepast-natuurwetenschappelijk onderzoek). At its request the authors developed, on a theoretical basis, a method to determine the effectiveness of health care. They introduce the concept of 'health benefit', measured in terms of three factors: years of life expectancy, and of health free from invalidity. The method is explained with several examples. Some of the difficulties of its practical implementation are discussed.

559 World Bank (1975) *Health, Sector Policy Paper*, Washington, DC: World Bank, 83 pp. Reproduced in: World Bank (1975) *The Assault on World Poverty: Problems of Rural Development, Education and Health*, Baltimore: John Hopkins University Press, 343–425.

1976

35 Donzé, W. (1976) 'The socio-political aspects of health in Geneva, 1965–1975' ('Aspects socio-politiques de la santé à Genève, 1965–1975') in: Rigoni, R. (ed.) Health Economics, Proceedings of a Workshop, Coppet, 4 October 1975 (*Economie de la santé. Compte rendu d'un colloque, Coppet, 4 octobre 1975*), Geneva: Sandoz Institute for Health and Socio-Economic Studies, 11–7.
See 38.

1977

554 Dahlberg, L. (1977) 'A new method for the economic evaluation of medical treatment — applied to the treatment of scoliosis' in: Dahlberg, L., *Empirical Studies in Public Planning*, Gothenburg: University of Gothenburg, Department of Economics (Memorandum No. 67), 92 pp.

Using an elaborate model, the author studies the development of scoliosis over time and the effectiveness of different treatments. Effectiveness of treatment is estimated by an anatomical curvature measure, which can be related to economic benefits expressed in terms of participation in the labour market. Cost–effectiveness (C/E) and benefit–cost (B/C) ratios are studied over time. Three treatment techniques are analysed: the Harrington operation, treatment with the Milwaukee brace, and a combined treatment. The following conclusions emerge. The Harrington operation has a B/C ratio of 30:1 when done early, before curvature of the spine is too advanced. Both the C/E and the B/C ratios fall the longer the operation is postponed. Early treatment with the Milwaukee brace has an even higher B/C ratio, of between 50:1 and 80:1. If only one of the two treatments is to be used, the Milwaukee brace is the preferred technique if started before the age of 15 years. Thereafter, the Harrington procedure should be chosen. Use of the Milwaukee brace alone is preferable to combined treatment from the viewpoint of economic efficiency. However, the final straightness of spine achieved by combined treatment is usually better than that achieved by the Milwaukee brace alone.

555 HÄRÖ, S. (1977) *Long-Term Evaluation of a Mass BCG Vaccination Campaign: A Study of Thirty Years of Experience in Finland*, Helsinki: Finnish Anti-Tuberculosis Association (Finnish Anti-Tuberculosis Association Yearbook, Vol. 6), 90 pp.

The purpose of this study is to evaluate the overall effectiveness of mass BCG vaccination in a nationwide campaign. Mortality and morbidity are studied in three groups: BCG vaccinated, naturally infected, and non-participants. Census data are used for non-participants. The tuberculosis situation in Finland has developed so favourably that the potential value of BCG vaccination has been reduced.

437 HELBERGER. C. (1977) 'Objectives and results of health policy' ('Ziele und Ergebnisse der Gesundheitspolitik') in: ZAPF, W., Conditions of Life in the Federal Republic of Germany (*Lebensbedingungen in der Bundesrepublik Deutschland*), Frankfurt/Main: Campus, 677–743.

141 HENKE, K.D. (1977) Public Health Expenditures and Distribution, A Contribution toward Measuring and Influencing Group-Specific Welfare in the Health Care Sector (*Öffentliche Gesundheitsausgaben und Verteilung. Ein Beitrag zur Messung und Beeinflussung des gruppenspezifischen Versorgungsniveaus im Gesundheitsbereich*), Göttingen: Vandenhoeck und Ruprecht, 242 pp.

556 ISOKOSKI, M. (1977) Development of Health Centres — the Effects of the Public Health Act (*Terveyskeskus — tutkimus — kansanterveyslain vaikutuksista*), Tampere: University of Tampere, Department of Public Health (research reports).

This research project investigates population contacts with existing health services in Finland before the Public Health Act was implemented (1972), and four years afterwards. The results indicate that developments in communities living in four areas were consistent with the aims of the Public Health Act. The Act has enabled resources to be distributed more flexibily and more equitably.

718 SCHAEFER, H. (1977) 'Efficiency and effectiveness of medical services in the light of health insurance' ('Effizienz und Effektivität der medizinischen Leistungen im Licht der Krankenversicherung'), *Die Ortskrankenkasse*, **59**, 16, 657–63.

5. The Role of Health Care in Economic Growth and Development

1967

557 BRENNA, A. (1967) 'Health care and economic development' ('Tutela della salute e sviluppo economico') in: ECONOMICS INSTITUTE, UNIVERSITÀ CATTOLICA DEL SACRO CUORE (ed.) World Economic Problems in the Light of *Populorum Progressio (I problemi dell'economia mondiale alla luce della* Populorum Progressio), Milan: Vita e Pensiero, 233–49.

After illustrating the increasing importance attached by economists to the concept of human capital, the author analyses the ways in which improvements in human capital may be brought about by adopting appropriate health care measures. The paper concludes with a demonstration of the need by developing countries for substantial international aid to enable an adequate network of health care services to be established. Such assistance can be most effective if provided by international organizations rather than by individual countries.

1973

459 FELDSTEIN, M.S., PIOT, M.A., and SUNDARESAN, T.K. (1973) *Resource*

Allocation Model for Public Health Planning. A Case Study of Tuberculosis Control (supplement to Vol. 48 of the *Bulletin of the World Health Organization*), Geneva: World Health Organization, 110 pp.

558 WHO (1973) *Interrelationships between Health Programmes and Socio-Economic Development*, Geneva: World Health Organization (Public Health Paper, No. 49), 54 pp.

A paper based on technical discussions at the 1972 World Health Assembly. The introductory background paper analyses replies to questions submitted to member States, which demonstrate the lack of integration of the health care sector into the general framework of development planning. The report of the technical discussions amplifies this theme, and recommends measures to achieve closer integration. The paper concludes with an annotated bibliography of relevant sources.

1975

119 DJUKANOVIC, V. and MACH, E.P. (eds) (1975) *Alternative Approaches to Meeting Basic Health Needs in Developing Countries*, Geneva: World Health Organization (Non-Serial Publications), 116 pp.

559 WORLD BANK (1975) *Health, Sector Policy Paper*, Washington, DC: World Bank, 83 pp. Reproduced in: WORLD BANK (1975) *The Assault on World Poverty: Problems of Rural Development, Education and Health*, Baltimore: Johns Hopkins University Press, 343–425.

A concise review of fundamental issues in health care sector policy in developing countries. The introductory discussion of measures and states of health identifies the main health problems, such as the faecally-transmitted and air-borne diseases and malnutrition. The paper argues that health care sector planning should consider health as both a social goal and a productive investment. Yet policies are rarely articulated in these terms. Government health care expenditure is low, generally less than 2% of GNP, and its allocation inefficient and inequitable. Typically, hospital-based curative care absorbs the bulk of expenditure, while coverage is limited to an urban minority at the expense of the rural poor. Health service reform must correct these biases. Concluding chapters discuss recent World Bank lending for health-related projects, and policy alternatives for the future. Annexes review international assistance for health programmes, and present comparative data on health status and sector resource allocation in developing countries.

1976

560 WHO (1976) 'The impact of malaria on economic development', *WHO Chronicle*, **30**, 6, 223–8.

The cost of illness in terms of lost work days, reduced labour efficiency, and lowered GNP is difficult to determine. The problem is particularly important for developing countries, where national planners must often make decisions about allocating scarce resources to the health care sector, without even an approximate idea of what return they can expect from these funds, as opposed to investments in other sectors of the economy. In an effort to find an answer to the problem, the Pan American Health Organization sponsored a 22-month study on the impact of malaria on economic development in Paraguay. Some of the findings are given.

1978

536 LAURINKARI, J., NIEMELÄ, P., and ELO, O. (1978) *Vaccination, Health Policy Planning and Decision-Making*, Kuopio: University of Kuopio, Department of Community Health (Series Statistics and Reviews, No. 1), 22 pp.

V Finance and Organization of Health Services

1. Comparative Studies

1966

561 Birkhäuser, H. (1966) 'Experience with cost-sharing in the health insurance scheme in Switzerland' ('Erfahrungen mit einer Kosten-Beteiligung in der schweizerischen Krankenversicherung'), *Der Landarzt*, **42**, 17, 749–50.

A description of the system of co-insurance practised in Switzerland, its impact on the demand for medical services, and some comparisons with analogous procedures in the health care system of the Federal Republic of Germany.

562 Villani, A. (1966) 'The financing of hospital expenditure' ('Il finanziamento delle spese ospedaliere'), *Rivista Internazionale di Scienze Sociali*, **37**, 7, 326–44.

The article begins with a brief conceptual definition of health service costs, including current and capital expenditure. It then summarizes the sources from which health services are financed, and describes the methods of financing hospital expenditure in selected Western countries. A general relationship is shown between the method of financing adopted and the institutional structure within which the hospitals operate. In countries where the majority of hospitals are nationalized, funding is guaranteed mainly by the state and obtained via taxation (Sweden, Great Britain). In countries where a sizeable proportion are not nationalized (France, the Netherlands, Italy), current expenditure is largely funded through compulsory or voluntary social insurance. The author concludes by examining the pros and cons of the various forms of financing (taxation, social insurance, charitable contributions) for the hospital sector.

1967

563 Abel-Smith, B. (1967) *An International Study of Health Expenditure and* *its Relevance for Health Planning*, Geneva: World Health Organization (Public Health Papers, No. 32), 127 pp.

This paper presents and discusses comparative data on health service expenditure in or about 1961, in 33 countries in five regions: Africa, the Americas, South-East Asia, Europe, the Eastern Mediterranean, and the Western Pacific. Data for 29 of the countries are based on a WHO questionnaire. The introductory chapter compares population, national income, vital statistics, health service resources, and the organization of health services in the study countries. The main part of the study falls into two parts. The first compares current, capital, and total health expenditure, in total and percent of GNP, by source of finance, and by function. The second compares the cost per bed-day and per stay in hospital in different types of hospital: general, maternity, chest, psychiatric, leprosy, and paediatric. Concluding chapters analyse trends in health service expenditure, and discuss the relevance of the study findings for health planning.

1968

653 ILO (1968) *Organization of Medical Care within the Framework of Social Security. Eight monographs on Belgium, Canada, Ecuador, Federal Republic of Germany, India, Poland, Tunisia, and United Kingdom*, Geneva: International Labour Office, 566 pp.

564 Poldermans, J.D.G. (1968) 'Costs of public health care; an experiment in international comparisons' ('De kosten van volksgezondheid; een proeve van internationale vergelijking'), *Economisch-Statistische-Berichten*, **53**, 2671, 1071–4.

Statistical data, and their significance for national health policy, are discussed, and comparisons are made with other countries. The Netherlands performs well on the basis of these indicators, but quality aspects are not taken into account.

1969

565 Muraro, G. (1969) 'Alternative systems of organizing and financing the health care sector and their effects on social welfare' ('Sistemi alternativi di organizzazione e finanziamento del settore sanitario e loro effetti sul benessere sociale'), *Rivista Internazionale di Scienze Sociali*, **40**, 5–6, 439–508.

This paper begins with a consideration of the private market for health services and its deficiencies. Using the tools of welfare economics, it analyses three alternative arrangements for the provision of health care: (1) private organization of both finance and provision, (2) private provision with public financing through compulsory social insurance, (3) public control of both finance and provision (public health service). It concludes that private insurance systems cannot guarantee satisfactory coverage against risk of sickness for the whole population, or produce positive redistributive effects. A system of social insurance, on the other hand, permits the attainment of both these objectives. Only a public health service, however, is capable of offsetting the negative effects that monopolistic suppliers can have upon social welfare. However, even a complete public health service does not automatically solve other problems, such as coordination and rationing of supply and use.

1970

566 ANDERSEN, R., SMEDBY, B., and ANDERSSON, O.W. (1970) *Medical Care Use in Sweden and the United States: A Comparative Analysis of Systems and Behavior*, Chicago: University of Chicago, Center for Health Administration Studies (Research Series, No. 27), 174 pp.

Sets out to investigate differences between the United States and Sweden in the amounts and types of health services utilized. The analysis is based on comparable social surveys carried out in the two countries in 1964.

567 SZAMEITAT, K. (1970) 'How much does health cost? — Data and critique' ('Was kostet die Gesundheit? — Zahlen und kritische Aspekte'), *Das öffentliche Gesundheitswesen*, **32**, 12, 672–90.

Expenditure on health in the Federal Republic of Germany in 1968 is estimated and discussed. Breakdowns are given by sources of funds, such as state, social insurance, and the private sector, and by type of expenditure, such as prevention, therapy, rehabilitation, medical education, and research.

1971

568 ROEMER, M.I. (1971) *The Organization of Medical Care under Social Security*, Geneva: International Labour Office (Studies and Reports, new series, No. 73), 241 pp.

This study examines the organization of medical care under social security provisions in eight countries: India, Poland, United Kingdom, Tunisia, Belgium, Federal Republic of Germany, Canada, and Ecuador. It proceeds from a broad distinction between indirect and direct patterns of medical care organization. Under the former, medical care is provided by personnel and facilities professionally independent of the social security scheme. Under the latter, provision is under the direct control of the scheme itself. This distinction provides the analytical framework for the three parts of the main study, in which the author discusses aspects of the experience of each of the eight countries and evaluates the relative merits of the organizational patterns they have adopted. The first part examines the technical components of medical care: GP care, specialist care, hospitalization, pharmaceutical products and appliances, dental care and other health services, prevention of disease, safeguards for the patient and provider of medical care, and disability certification. The second considers three aspects of resource development and allocation: personnel training and selection, health facilities and their planning, and meeting rural health needs. The final part discusses the quality, cost, and coordination of medical care: influencing the quality of care, financing and controlling costs, and aspects, both national and international, of the coordination of health service schemes.

569 SCHICKE, R.K. (1971), Physician and Health Care in the Social Security Systems of the Federal Republic of Germany, England, and USA (*Arzt und Gesundheitsversorgung im gesellschaftlichen Sicherungssystem — Bundesrepublik Deutschland — England — USA*), Freiburg: Rombach Verlag, 256 pp.

The role of the physician within the organizational framework of health care delivery systems in the Federal Republic of Germany, England, and the USA is analysed from the viewpoint of the individual's need to share risks, and the social and economic aspects of health insurance. The three systems of social security have different historical origins, which partly explain the differences. The available statistical indicators are used to compare the inputs and outputs of the three systems. It is argued that the financing schemes are not the causes but the consequences of the different distribution of risk among the individual, the community, and society. In the FRG, the economic consequences of disease are closely linked with health care, whereas it is rather separated in the other countries. The main topic of the book is the influence of the system on the physician. The functional separation of ambulatory and hospital care in the FRG has distributional consequences, and leads to competition in the ambulatory care sector. This is a challenge to the physician to increase his productivity. However, this is less clear in the USA and England, which have incentives promoting group practice, whereas the FRG does not. The control of the physicians's work is stronger in the FRG than in the other two countries.

1972

570 ANDERSSON, O.W. (1972) *Health Care: Can There Be Equity?,* New York: John Wiley and Sons, 273 pp.

Extensive comparisons are made between the health services of the United States, Sweden, and England; the liberal-democratic context in which the services operate; their performance from 1950 to 1970; and the chronic problems and issues that, to a different extent, have beset all three systems. A substantial bibliography is provided. This book draws on earlier work by the author and others on the health services of these countries.

571 ORRÙ, G. (1972) 'New contribution to the analysis of health care costs' ('Nuovi contributi all'analisi dei costi dell'assistenza sanitaria'), *I Problemi della Sicurezza Sociale*, **27**, 1, 23–40.

The author surveys the results of a number of recent Italian and US research studies on the costs of providing health care. In two such studies, the dynamics of the process are examined and the various factors contributing to the increase in health service expenditure are enumerated. Using basic data from the studies, the author compares the Italian and American systems, and shows that different factors have had substantially similar effects on health care expenditure. In contrast, two further studies form the basis of a static analysis of the differences in costs of treatment and duration of illness. These are found to be related to various background factors, particularly a number of non-medical ones, which the author urges should be further investigated.

721 PERRIN, G. (1972) 'Supplementary systems and social security' ('Les régimes complémentaires et la Sécurité Sociale'), *Revue Française des Affaires Sociales*, **26**, 2, 35–53.

1973

746 BERFENSTAM, R. et al. (1973) *Swedish Medical Care in the 1980s*, Stockholm: Svenska Landstingsförbundet, 66 pp. (mimeographed document).

572 EICHHORN, S. (1973) 'German Federal Republic' in: DOUGLAS-WILSON, J. and MCLACHLAN, G. (eds), *Health Service Prospects, An International Survey*, London: The Lancet Ltd and Nuffield Provincial Hospitals Trust, 81–98.

Health service expenditures and costs in the Federal Republic of Germany are presented and discussed, including the organization of health services, medical education and research, and questions regarding the type of care and the prospects for possible reorganization.

778 GRUNDY, F. and REINKE, W.A. (1973) *Health Practice Research and Formalized Managerial Methods*, Geneva: World Health Organization (Public Health Papers, No. 51), 193 pp.

369 SCHICKE, R.K. (1973) 'The pharmaceutical market and prescription drugs in the Federal Republic of Germany: Cross-national comparisons', *International Journal of Health Services*, **3**, 2, 223–36.

1974

573 BONNET, R. (1974) Social Security Regulations of the Nine Common Market Countries (*Les règlements de Sécurité Sociale de l'Europe des Neuf*), Paris: La Documentation Française (Notes et Etudes Documentaires, No. 4129), 42 pp.

Social Security systems vary greatly among the European Economic Community (EEC) countries, and this may constitute an obstacle to the migration of workers. With a view to protecting the rights of these workers, a European social security law has been adopted that includes regulations to replace the bilateral or multilateral agreements that formerly existed between the member states of the EEC. This document contains a description of how social protection is organized in the EEC, the guiding principles of the move toward coordination, and the different allowances that are available. There is a bibliography of books and articles in the French language dealing with European social security regulations.

574 CLADE, H. (1974) 'The 7-crowns débâcle' ('Das 7-Kronen Debakel'), *Arbeit und Sozialpolitik*, **28**, 3, 79–84.

Summary of the Elan Wilson Report on the 1970 Swedish seven-crowns reform.
See 661, 667, 670

575 FLEISSNER, P. (1974) A Model of the Austrian Health Insurance System (*Ein Modele des Oesterreichischen Gesundheitssicherungssystems*),

Vienna: Institut für Sozio-ökonomische Entwicklungsforschung (Schriftenreihe), 61 pp.

A theoretical simulation model of the health care delivery system in Austria is developed, in which the health care sector is viewed as an integral sub-system interacting with the economic, demographic, and health policy sub-systems.

576 Fulcher, D. (1974) *Medical Care Systems, Public and Private Health Coverage in Selected Industrial Countries*, Geneva: International Labour Office, 178 pp.

This study evaluates aspects of medical care systems in ten industrialized countries: Japan, Federal Republic of Germany, Great Britain, Netherlands, Australia, Belgium, Sweden, Switzerland, Denmark, and New Zealand. The first part examines three specific issues. First, the relative merits of systems based on universal health coverage and separate health insurance schemes; the author concludes that there is no simple choice between universal and pluralist packages, but notes that particular features may affect patterns of delivery (e.g. arrangements for payment of general practitioners and cost-sharing). Second, the continuing extension and role of private health insurance and medical practice, alongside state schemes. Third, questions raised by the introduction of catastrophy (heavy risk) insurance schemes. The author concludes that, if a state scheme is to be sufficiently equitable, comprehensive, and subject to control, it is unlikely to be viable independently of other schemes. The second part of the study considers in detail the following aspects of the medical care systems in each of the ten countries: their history, coverage, organizational structure, medical benefits, financing, medical practitioners and other providers of medical care, methods of payment of medical practitioners, control systems, hospitals, cost and expenditure trends, private medical practice and health insurance, and possible future trends.

683 Illuminati, F. (1974) 'National health service or health insurance? Prerequisites for choice' ('Servizio sanitario o assistenza sociale? Premessa per una scelta'), *I Problemi della Sicurezza Sociale*, **29**, 1, 29–77.

577 Italian Centre for Health and Social Research (1974) The Organization of Health Care in Ten European Countries (*'L'organizzazione sanitaria di dieci paesi europei'*), Rome: Ministero della Sanità, Centro Studi, 413 pp.

Reference is frequently made, during the debate on the reform of the Italian health service, to the organizational experiences of other countries and to their potential relevance for Italy. The choice of countries considered in this monograph was determined by a desire to present a wide range of approaches, even if these are at times contradictory. The National Health Service of the United Kingdom is grouped together with the systems of two socialist countries, the USSR and Yugoslavia. Also included in this group are countries with substantially pluralistic arrangements, modified by public intervention. The Swedish and Danish systems are taken as examples of this latter approach. Both have a long tradition of social commitment, and emphasis on technical efficiency, which have frequently put them in the vanguard in this field. The other countries examined — the Federal Republic of Germany, France, Switzerland, the Netherlands, and Belgium — are for a variety of reasons more similar to Italy in their organization of health care provisions. The account of each country is in two parts: (1) a profile of the health care system, particularly that of the hospital service; (2) health care provision in the general context of social security policy.

578 WEISSENBOECK, H. (1974) Studies on the Economic Efficiency of Health Care Systems (*Studien zur ökonomischen Effizienz von Gesundheitssystemen*), Stuttgart: Georg Thieme Verlag, 189 pp.

An attempt is made to apply the concept of economic efficiency to expenditure on the provision of health care, at the macro-analytical, international level. A comparative study of nine countries (Sweden, Switzerland, the Netherlands, the Federal Republic of Germany, England and Wales, USA, Austria, the German Democratic Republic, and France) is made on the basis of a selected set of input and output data. The author analyses the influence of different degrees of centralization on the technical and economic efficiency of the health care systems. As the drawbacks of such a macro approach are very severe, he undertakes a case study of German hospitals, starting with the assumption that decentralized supply decisions are more efficient than centralized ones. He finds, with the help of a small set of data, that community hospitals are working more cheaply than public hospitals. However, private hospitals could not be included in the comparison.

782 WHO (1974) *Modern Management Methods and the Organization of Health Services*, Geneva: World Health Organization (Public Health Papers, No. 55), 100 pp.

1975

268 BAUHOFER, F. (1975) 'Hospital systems in Europe' ('Krankenhaussysteme in Europa'), *Österreichische Krankenhaus-Zeitung*, **16**, 9, 457–71.

689 BLOHMKE, M. (1975) The Cost of Health Care Systems, Social Ecology, and Social Medicine (*Kosten des Gesundheitswesens, Sozialökologie und Sozialmedizin*), Stuttgart: A.W. Gentner Verlag (Schriftenreihe Arbeitsmedizin, Sozialmedizin, Präventivmedizin, Vol. 56), 135 pp. *See* 584.

579 ROLF, H. (1975) Social Insurance or State Health Service? Comparison of Economic Efficiency of the Health Care Systems of the Federal Republic of Germany and the German Democratic Republic (*Sozialversicherung oder staatlicher Gesundheitsdienst? Ökonomischer Effizienzvergleich der Gesundheitssicherungssysteme der Bundesrepublik Deutschland und der Deutschen Demokratischen Republik*), Berlin: Duncker & Humblot, 219 pp.

The author analyses the influence of the organization of health care, in the Federal Republic of Germany and in the German Democratic Republic, on efficiency, measured as the relation between cost and output. The comparison of the 'financing' and 'consumption' in the two systems allows for the different objectives in the health care systems. The book surveys the most important elements in the two health care systems, and the efficiency of their organization, particularly in the following sub-sectors: ambulatory care, inpatient care, and prescription of drugs. Of central interest to the author is the interdependence of organization and the behaviour of the suppliers and consumers of medical goods and services. He concludes that, in both countries, there are limits to efficiency due to deficiencies in the institutional setting. In the case of the Federal Republic, he refers to the high financial input, which has not induced an equivalent increase in output.

580 SAUER, P. (1975) 'A comparison of health expenditures in the statutory health insurance scheme of the Federal Republic of Germany and the National Health Service in Great Britain' (*Ein Vergleich der Angaben der gesetzlichen Krankenversicherung in der Bundesrepublik Deutschland mit den Ausgaben des National Health Service in Grossbritannien*), Stuttgart: Universität Stuttgart (dissertation), 139 pp. (mimeographed document).

The author analyses health care expenditures in the Federal Republic of Germany and in Great Britain, discusses the differences between the two countries in organization and benefit structure, and concludes that the overall growth in their costs has not differed greatly.

581 SCHICKE, R.K. (1975) An International Study of Group Medicine (*Gruppenmedizin international*), Mainz: Kirchheim, Verlag, 75 pp.

Organizational aspects of the arrangements adopted by cooperating physicians are analysed from an international perspective, and the socio-economic costs and benefits derived from alternative group and cooperative practices are discussed.

582 THIEMEYER, T. (1975) 'Hospital financing' ('Krankenhausfinanzierung') in: LAMPERT, H. (ed.) Current Problems in Health Policies in the Federal Republic of Germany (*Aktuelle Probleme in der Gesundheitspolitik in der Bundesrepublik Deutschland*), Berlin: Duncker & Humblot, 95–157.

Various aspects of hospital financing and the structure of hospital costs are discussed and analysed.

583 VAN LANGENDONCK, J. (1975) *Prelude to harmony on a community theme, health care insurance policies in the Six and Britain*, London: Oxford University Press — Nuffield Provincial Hospitals Trust, 303 pp. Previously published as: VAN LANGENDONCK, J. (1971)Harmonization of Social Health Care Insurance in the EEC (*De harmonisatie van de sociale zekerheid in de EEC*), Leuven: Katholieke Universiteit Leuven, Instituut voor Sociaal Zekerheidsrecht, 182 pp.

The author argues that economic integration in the European Economic Community calls for social integration, taking the form either of coordination or of harmonization of national social laws. Harmonization of social laws, particularly social security, would improve the ability to survey and manage the systems. This report first surveys the six national health insurance systems. It then analyses their common and distinct features, and the converging and diverging features of their evolution. It concludes with a concrete and realistic proposal for harmonization.

584 WEISSENBOECK, H. (1975) 'An international comparison of costs and efficiency in the health services' ('Kosten und Effizienz der Gesundheitswesen im internationalen Vergleich') in: BLOHMKE, M. (ed.) The Cost of Health Care Systems, Social Ecology, and Social Medicine (*Kosten des Gesundheitswesens, Sozialökologie und Sozialmedizin*), Stuttgart: A.W. Gentner Verlag (Schriftenreihe Arbeitsmedizin, Sozialmedizin und Präventivmedizin, Vol. 56), 19–33.

The costs of providing health services in nine countries are compared and efficiency is evaluated by relating inputs used to outputs produced.

See 413, 689

585 WHO (1975) 'Government health expenditures', *World Health Statistics Report*, **28**, 11, 427–49.

This report provides (non-comparable) data for recent years of government health care expenditure in countries in the following regions: Africa, America, Asia, Europe, Oceania, and the USSR. The data, expressed in national currencies, are: total government expenditure, total government expenditure on health care, health care expenditure as percentage of total government expenditure, health care expenditure per capita, and (where possible) the current and capital composition of these expenditure aggregates.

1976

586 CHESTER, T.E. (1976) 'Health care in West Germany and France: a comparative analysis', *Three Banks Review*, No. 112, 66–84.

A comparison of health care financing and costs, in France and the Federal Republic of Germany, is supplemented by data on the health status of their population and on general aspects of health care in the two countries.

587 GULDIMANN, J. (1976) The Limits of the Welfare State (*Die Grenzen des Wohlfahrtsstaates*), Munich: Beck-Verlag, 179 pp.

A discussion of the development of the social security system with particular reference to health insurance, using Sweden and the Federal Republic of Germany as examples.

588 ILO (1976) *The Cost of Social Security. Eighth international inquiry, 1967–1971.* With a supplement on the cost of non-statutory schemes, Geneva: International Labour Office, 189 pp.

These inquiries aim, first, at establishing a consolidated statement of the financial operations of social security schemes existing in various countries and coming within the scope of the inquiry; and second, at providing an international comparison of the data by determining trends in social security costs during the period under review and by comparing the distribution of the cost of social security between different sources of revenue and between different types of social security scheme. The present volume contains ten comparative tables, national accounts data, population data, and consumers' prices indices, and a supplement on the cost of non-statutory schemes.

589 PRIMS, A. (1976) 'Health costs and expenditures in Belgium, Denmark and the Netherlands' in: *International Health Costs and Expenditures*,

Washington, DC: US Department of Health, Education, and Welfare (DHEW Publication No. (NIH) 76–1067), 233–47.

Following a summary review of the major features of the health service systems in Belgium, Denmark, and the Netherlands, non-comparable data are presented on capital and current expenditure on health services in recent years. Concluding comments briefly consider measures being undertaken to restrain the growth in health care expenditure in the three countries.
See 590, 639, 640

590 REINHARDT, U.E. (1976) 'Health costs and expenditures in the Federal Republic of Germany and the United States' in: *Proceedings of the International Conference on Health Cost and Expenditures (John F. Fogarty Center for Advanced Study in the Health Sciences, Bethesda, Md.)*, Washington, DC: US Department of Health, Education, and Welfare (DHEW Publication No. (NIH) 76–1067), 249–80.

A synopsis of the West German and American health care systems shows that they resemble each other more than other systems. The distinction is made between the health care delivery system and the health insurance system in the Federal Republic of Germany. The average physician in the FRG employs more personnel than the American physician, and it is argued that he therefore has a higher productivity than his American colleague. The West German physician also enjoys a higher income. The number of hospital beds is 44% higher in the FRG than in the USA; however, the duration of stay in short-term acute hospitals is 130% higher. The insured have an extended benefit package in West Germany, and the flow of funds in the German statutory health insurance scheme is described. It is argued that a national health insurance system is likely to make both the contract and the flow of funds between consumers and physicians more visible. On paper, at least, the Federal Republic of Germany appears to have struck a more balanced contract between society at large and the medical profession, compared with the USA.
See 589, 639, 640

591 SALOWSKY, H. and SEFFEN, A. (1976) A Comparison of the Structure and Costs of the Health Schemes of Six European Industrial Countries (*System- und Kostenvergleich der Gesundheitssicherung in sechs europäischen Industriestaaten*), Cologne: Deutscher Ärzte-Verlag (Zentralinstitut für die Kassenärztliche Versorgung in der Bundesrepublik Deutschland, Vol. V), 110 pp.

Comparisons of the system and costs in Sweden, the Netherlands, the Federal Republic of Germany, Austria, France, and Great Britain lead to the conclusion that, with respect to health expenditure and cost increases, the Federal Republic of Germany occupies a middle position.

1977

592 KAITARANTA, H. (1977) 'The trend of health care expenditure in Finland 1970–1975' ('Terveydenhuollon kustannusten kehitys Suomessa 1970–1975'), *Sosiaalivakuutus*, **15**, 3, 66–75.

On the basis of the available statistical data from different sources, the paper presents a comprehensive analysis of the trend of health care expenditure in Finland from 1970 to 1975. The data cover the main sources of financing health care in Finland, i.e., the state, the local communes, health insurance, and the patients. The main emphasis is laid on the comparison between the development of hospital inpatient services and of ambulatory care services. The main conclusion is that, owing to deliberate changes in health policy in favour of the development of ambulatory care services, the proportion of health care expenditure on ambulatory care has increased during the years in question.

593 OECD (1977) *Public Expenditure on Health*, Paris: Organization for Economic Cooperation and Development, 137 pp.

This study analyses recent and future trends in the level and structure of public health care expenditure in OECD member countries. Four variables are used to explain these trends: the cost ratio (unit cost of health care), the transfer ratio (public sector share in health care expenditure), the coverage ratio (percentage of population covered by the public health system), and the use ratio (volume of health services consumed per covered person). In 1974, total current health care expenditure averaged 5.7% of trend GDP, and public expenditure 4.4%. By function, expenditure on hospitals accounted for 52% of public expenditure, medical services for 23%, and medical supplies for 12%. Inter-country variations in functional shares are attributable primarily to different cost ratios. Between 1962 and 1974, the average share of public health care expenditure in trend GDP increased by 1.8%, from about 2.6%. Nearly half of this increase was due to a shift from private to public expenditure, with 20% attributable to an increase in the transfer ratio, 22% to the coverage ratio, 36% to the use ratio, and 22% to the cost ratio. By function, expenditure on hospitals accounted for 56% of the increase, medical services for 28%, and medical supplies for 7%. Evidence of the outcome of public health care expenditure is suggestive of both income redistribution and limited health status benefits. Projections of the increase in the GDP share of public health care expenditure by 1985 are based on two alternative assumptions: projection A assumes continuation of existing policies and trends, and projects an increase of 0.68% to 1.19%; projection B assumes a planned reduction in the use ratio for hospitals, and projects a stable share changing by −0.16% to 0.1%. Concluding chapters discuss policy options for containing the rise in health care expenditure, through control of volume (user charges, preventive policies, and supply rationing) and cost (substitution of auxiliaries for doctors, and price of pharmaceuticals).

594 SCHRÄDER, W.F. and VOLKHOLZ, V. (eds) (1977) Regional Analysis of Medical Care (*Regionale Analyse der Medizinischen Versorgung*), Berlin: Technische Universität Berlin, Berliner Arbeitsgruppe Strukturforschung im Gesundheitswesen (Schriftenreihe No. 2), 307 pp.

The book contains a collection of original articles, most of them written by members of the Berlin Working Group on Research in Health Service Structures (Berliner Arbeitsgruppe Strukturforschung im Gesundheitswesen). The main idea is that density indicators (e.g., physician/population ratio, hospital bed ratio) are insufficient for planning purposes. Examples are given that show that equity of physician distribution depends largely on the size of the areas that are statistically analysed. Many examples, from urban and rural areas of the Federal Republic of Germany and of West Berlin, demonstrate the dynamic processes in the relationship between distribution of physicians and socio-economic indicators. It is necessary to supplement the provider indicators with demand indicators. The difficulties of determining the need for medical care are outlined.

595 UNION BANK OF SWITZERLAND (1977) *Social Security in 10 Industrial Nations*, Zurich: Union Bank of Switzerland, 35 pp.

This study compares social security costs and benefits in Austria, Belgium, Canada, the Federal Republic of Germany, Finland, Great Britain, the Netherlands, Sweden, Switzerland, and the USA. It is prepared in collaboration with the Institute of Insurance Economics, St. Gall Graduate School of Economics, and the International Association for the Study of Insurance Economies, Geneva. It covers the following items: objectives and background of the study, pensions and old-age benefits, survivors' insurance benefits, social insurance in case of accident and sickness, unemployment and social security, Switzerland's social security schemes, and future problems of social insurance.

768 WHITE, K.L., ANDERSON, D.O., KALIMO, E., KLECZKOWSKI, B.M., PUROLA, T., and VUKMANOVIC, C. (1977) *Health Services: Concepts and Information for National Planning and Managment*, Geneva: World Health Organization (Public Health Papers, No. 67), 117 pp.

1978

596 BRÜGGEMANN, J., SCHWEFEL, D., and ZÖLLNER, H. (1978) Need and

Planning in the Health Care System. An International Collection of Articles (*Bedarf und Planung im Gesundheitswesen. Eine internationale Aufsatzsammlung*), Cologne: Deutscher Ärzte-Verlag, 269 pp.

This collection of articles is divided into two main parts with two sections each. It is proceded by a survey of the problems and interntional concepts of health planning, and completed by a comprehensive and detailed index of references at the end of the collection. Part one contains articles defining concepts like 'need' and 'demand', followed by articles describing empirical methods to determine need. The articles in part two describe the process of planning in the health care sector, and then illustrate experiences in other countries concerning planning on the basis of need.

597 Leu, R. (1978) 'Measuring the relative efficiency of health care systems empirically' ('Ansätze zur empirischen Messung der relativen Effizienz von Gesundheitssystemen'), *Revue Suisse d'Économie Politique et de Statistique — Schweizerische Zeitschrift für Volkswirtschaft und Statistik*, **114**, 3, 479–503.

The main subject of the investigation is the relation between efficiency in production and state participation in the health care system, especially the influence of state participation in the supply and/or financing of health care, on the health status of the population, and on the costs of the health care system. A multiple regression based on cross-sectional data for OECD-countries (except Iceland, Portugal, and Turkey) for 1973 indicates that: countries with a decentralized organization of the health care sector, and state participation in the supply as well as financing of health services, have higher health care system costs; central decisions on supply and financing (England, New Zealand) significantly lower the costs of the health care system; on the other hand, the inverse relationship between public financing and (post-neonatal) infant mortality indicates that state participation has some positive effects on the health of the population.

2. National Accounts and Surveys

1962

598 Höök, E. (1962) 'The Expansion of the Public Sector — A Study of the Development of Public Civilian Expenditures in Sweden during the

Years 1913–58' ('*Den offentliga sektorns expansion — en studie av de offentliga civila urgifternas utveckling åren 1913–58*'), Stockholm: Almqvist & Wiksell (for Industriens Utredningsinstitut), 572 pp.

Chapter 7 analyses the development of public expenditure on health and medical services in Sweden during the period 1913–58. The greatest increase in public expenditure was for health and medical services. This aspect of consumption grew from 0.9% to 4.2% over the period, with particularly rapid growth during the post-war years. Taking the number of bed-days as a measure of the volume of these services, the volume of hospital care increased by over 150%. In explaining this growth, Höök distinguishes between demand for investment in health and demand for the care of more or less incurable cases. For the former, changes in volume appear to be related to the application of advances in medical knowledge, whereas for the latter they have probably been due to the general rise in the level of incomes, i.e., this type of demand has been characterized by a high income elasticity. Höök also points out the shift in the share of expenditure from the private to the public sector.

1968

599 Foulon A. (1968–1969) The Economic Accounts of Public Hospitals 1961–64 (*Les comptes économiques des hôpitaux publics 1961–1964*), Paris: Centre de Recherches et de Documentation sur la Consommation, Vol. I (1968), 67 pp.; Vol. II (1969), 195 pp. (mimeographed documents).

Volume I of this study seeks to estimate the value of all medical services provided by public hospitals at the widest possible level: the output of hospitals (which is sub-divided into medical costs of inpatient and outpatient services, and hotel costs); the value of physicians' services; and secondary products, such as expenditure on the ambulance service, receipts from sales of waste matter, and miscellaneous services provided for third parties. The second volume assembles the results of the estimates of the total economic accounts, analysed by sources and methods, as described in volume I. Certain characteristic indices of hospital production are established, and compared with the inputs of various factors of production, such as beds and staff. The sources of finance for hospitals and the work of hospital doctors are also considered in the analysis of the behaviour of the indices, and numerous tables and graphs are provided throughout.

600 Gygi, P. and Tschopp, P. (1968) Sociomedical Security (*Sozialmedizinische Sicherung/Sécurité médico-sociale*), Berne: Hans Huber Verlag, 156 pp.

In this bilingual volume (German/French), the authors describe and evaluate the complex Swiss social security system, particularly its health insurance component, under which about 1,000 funds provide a fair measure of protection for 90% of the population, under rules established by the state. They outline the concepts and philosophy, the economic and social aspects, and the financing and roles of private and public institutions. They then examine the 'health market', notably the structures of supply and demand, as influenced by the 'pragmatic' Swiss system, which aims to achieve maximum efficiency of individual efforts. The state intervenes only when private efforts are demonstrably inadequate; but this, the authors argue, has proved costly, particularly with respect to very rapidly rising hospital costs. Finally, they turn to the challenge of the presumably desirable redistribution of income or 'equalization' as goals of insurance. The authors find that injustices are experienced by a relatively small proportion of the low-income population. Noting that the country has long been proud, not only of its direct democracy but also of the community's anonymous assistance to the less fortunate, they propose penetrating measures designed to eliminate, or at least to alleviate, the alleged unfairness to poorer individuals and families.

601 Trappeniers, F. (1968) 'The price of health' ('Le prix de la santé'), *La Revue Nouvelle*, July–August, 28–35.

This article attempts to explain the upward trend in health care expenditure in Belgium, and notes that the 1961 family budget census revealed an income elasticity of demand for health care of about 0.80. It recommends three possible measures to correct the recurrent deficit in the health insurance scheme: an increase in participation rates, an increase in the general tax revenue share of national health insurance, and a decrease in the average rate of reimbursement.

1969

602 Brenna, A. (1969) 'Financing of the national health service in a social security context' ('Il finanziamento del servizio sanitario nazionale in un regime di sicurezza sociale'), *Ospedali d'Italia*, **6**, 5, 581–99.

The author first analyses the characteristics of the Italian social security system, and then identifies areas where it has caused serious malfunctioning, emphasizing in particular its adverse effect upon the composition of expenditure and the provision of health care. He next identifies the potential sources of finance for the hospital service. After demonstrating the difficulties involved in financing this service from direct taxation, he lists a series of indirect taxes that might provide it with revenue.

603 DENMARK, GOVERNMENT OF (1969) Major Trends in the Development of Health Care Institutions and Social Welfare Institutions to 1985 — Expenditures and Manpower (*Hovedtendenser i sundheds- og forsorgs-institutionernes udvikling frem til 1985*), Copenhagen: Statens Trykningskontor, 158 pp.

This report first analyses trends in the development of health care and social welfare institutions in Denmark up to the year 1968. It then attempts to extrapolate these trends to the year 1985. Detailed data on capital and current expenditure, manpower, and productivity are presented.

1970

604 BOSERUP, H. (1970) 'The expansion of hospitals from an economic point of view' ('Udbygningen af sygehusvæsenet i samfundsøkonomisk belysning'), *Ugeskrift for Læger*, **132**, 40, 1897–901 and **132**, 50, 2415–22.

The economic impact of hospital expansion is discussed and illustrated. It is argued that physicians should accept an economic framework for health planning, and that they should help in providing the information it requires. Rational planning presupposes the existence of the necessary planning instruments, including an information system.

87 DENMARK, GOVERNMENT OF (1970) Health Visiting. First Report of a Committee Appointed by the National Health Service of Denmark on Health Visiting and Home Nursing (*Sundhedsplejerskeinstitutionen, betænkning I*), Copenhagen: Statens Trykningskontor (Betænkning No. 573), 98 pp.

605 FRANCE, MINISTRY OF PUBLIC HEALTH AND SOCIAL SECURITY (1970) The Maternity Services: A Study of the Use of Programme Budgeting (General Report) *(La périnalité: étude de la rationalisation des choix budgétaires (Rapport général))*, Paris: Ministère de la SantéPublique et de la Sécurité Sociale (Note d'information No. 28), *Revue Hospitalière de France*, **35**, 239, 335–69.

This report contains the results of a programme budgeting study of the decision making process for maternity services, conducted by the Ministry of Public Health and Social Security from 1 February to 30 June 1970. Annexed to the general report are the methods and detailed results of the study, the list of members of the decision making group, and the new measures that were included in the finance bill of 1971 as a direct result of the study.

1971

606 Brenna, A. (1971) 'Funding the national health service in Italy: major problems' ('Alcuni problemi relativi alle modalità di finanziamento del servizio sanitario nazionale'), *I Problemi della Sicurezza Sociale*, **26**, 2, 237–68.

This article considers some of the fundamental aspects of health service financing, which were rather neglected in the discussions preparatory to the reform of the Italian health services in 1971. It examines the possibilities available for incorporating health insurance contributions into the system of public finance, and makes some tentative proposals. Possible formulae for distributing the National Health Fund among the Regions are considered, bearing in mind that the constitution requires that regional autonomy in the provision of health care must be maintained. The article concludes with some observations on the financial relationships among health care agencies operating within regions (principally local health units and hospitals), and between regions, and makes proposals for dealing with the problems identified.

607 Brunet-Jailly, J. (1971) 'Social security in the life of the nation: an economic point of view' ('La sécurité sociale dans la vie de la nation: un point de vue économique'), *Revue Française des Affaires Sociales*, **25**, 25, 249–80.

The author studies the results of the social security scheme in: ensuring that a greater number of retired persons receive a pension; providing family allowances; and providing health insurance. Numerous tables help to explain how these social expenditures are financed.

608 De Corato, G., Coppini, G., and Nicoletti, G.C. (1971) 'Health service reform: evaluation of services and costs in the Seventies' ('Riforma sanitaria; elementi per una valutazione delle strutture e dei costi negli anni '70'), *I Problemi della Sicurezza Sociale*, **26**, 1, 5–99.

The authors, using the most recent indications of deadlines and procedures for the implementation of the health service reform, seek to define the structure and location of the future local health units, and the optimal number of beds in public hospitals. The study, at regional level, examines the growing financial burden likely to be associated both with the creation of the new structures and with the operation of the entire system, over the decade 1971–80. The final section offers a quantitative analysis of the sources from which expenditure is to be funded, and of the need for medical and paramedical manpower.

609 Höök, E. (1971) 'The development and distribution of health care costs' ('Sjukvårdskostnadernas utveckling och fördelning'), *Landstingens Tidskrift*, **58**, 9, 32–6.

The author describes in general terms the resource allocation problems facing the health care sector. He discusses specifically the possibility of introducing patient fees, or special insurance for road traffic accidents.

610 Sandier, S. (1971) 'Forecasts of the trends in health care expenditure during the VIth Plan. The case of doctors' services' ('Les prévisions de l'évolution des dépenses de santé au cours du VIe Plan. Exemple des services de médecins'), *Cahiers de Sociologie et de Démographie Médicales,* **11**, 4, 185–96.

Following an introduction that presents some data on the consumption of medical services and describes the details of the VIth Plan, this article describes the principal methods used for summarizing expenditure on the provision of medical services and for drawing up projections for 1975, the final year of the VIth Plan. The ways in which the methods may be applied to the services rendered by physicians are then described.

1972

740 Boserup, H. (1972) 'The health care sector in social planning' ('Sygehus og sundhedsvæsenets indplacering i den generelle samfundsplanlægning'). *Danmarks Amtsråd*, **3**, 3, 9–14.

611 Cayla, J.S. (1972) 'Health care expenditure in the social budget of the nation and in the state budget in 1972' ('Les dépenses de santé dans le budget social de la nation et dans le budget de l'Etat en 1972'), *Revue Française des Affaires Sociales*, **26**, 3, 111–19.

The social budget of the nation in 1972, which amounted to Fr. 193,488 million, of which Fr. 45,778 million was for health care, is compared with that of 1970 and 1971. A breakdown is made of the various categories of expenditure on health care in the social budget and in the state budget. The various tables presented in the article show that expenditure on the provision of health services is not increasing any faster than total expenditure on all social services, of which it accounts for 30%.

308 Denmark, Government of (1972) Home Nursing. Second Report of a Committee Appointed by the National Health Services on Health Visiting and Home Nursing (*Hjemmesygeplejen, betænkning II*), Copenhagen: Statens Trykningskontor (Betænkning No. 648), 147 pp.

95 Denmark, Government of (1972) Maternity Care (*Fødselshjælpens tilrettelæggelse*), Copenhagen: Statens Trykningskontor (Betænkning No. 633), 90 pp.

612 Foulon, A. (1972) 'A method for drawing up the national health accounts' ('Les comptes nationaux de la santé, méthode'), *Economie et Santé* (supplement to the *Bulletin des Statistiques de Santé et de Sécurité Sociale*), No. 2, 1–121.

The Committee on Health Accounts, set up by ministerial order in August 1970, was asked to conduct an analysis of the existing accounting methods used in France; to compile retrospective annual accounts that would make it possible to study where health care expenditures go, what needs they satisfy, and which social groups benefit from them; and to estimate the impact of the health care system on the development of the economy. For these purposes CREDOC (Centre de Recherches et de Documentation sur la Consommation) and INSEE (Institut National de la Statistique et des Etudes Economiques) devised a methodology using precise concepts and nomenclature, and a rigorous technique of analysis. The accounts, called 'health satellite accounts', are compiled so that expenditure is shown valued at current prices, at constant prices, and in relative terms for the whole year, half-year, and quarter. Time-series data for the accounts are drawn up, on the basis of the detailed evaluation of the accounts and tables of a particular base year. The frequency with which the series is made available will vary according to need.

613 Kamper-Jørgensen, F. (1972) 'The socio-medical Lorenz curve' ('Den social-medicinske Lorenz-Kasse'), *Ugeskrift for Læger*, **134**, 7, 345–9.

A 'socio-medical' Lorenz curve may be constructed in the same way as that used in the study of income inequality. On the basis of Danish and other research, it is observed that 25% of the population have 50% of all sickness episodes, while a further 10% experience approximately 10% of the total. A 'socio-medical' Lorenz curve consists of three curves describing the distribution of income, education, and sickness, and is considered suitable for describing the distribution of social needs in general.

614 Mollenback, J.E., Rasmussen, J.E., and Rasmussen, P. (1972) 'Growth in selected public expenditures 1960–1970' ('Væksten i udvalgte offentlige udgifter 1960–1970'), *Nationaløkonomisk Tidsskrift*, Vol. 110, 135–60.

As part of this analysis of public sector expenditure trends, the authors estimate that, if the present rate of health care sector growth continues, it will consume the entire net national income by about the year 2000. The problems of health services and of health planning information systems are discussed.

615 Tarquinio, O. (1972) 'What is the cost of health service reform?' ('Qual è il costo della riforma sanitaria?'), *Economia e Lavoro*, **6**, 2, 153–69.

This article discusses methods for estimating the costs of reforming the Italian health care system. It defines the relevant costs and explains how they may be calculated, emphasizing in particular the difference between economic cost and monetary expenditure. It highlights the deficiencies of the methods previously used by the different commissions concerned with the question, both at the ministerial level and that of the health insurance agencies. Consequently, it is difficult to decide whether reform should take place and, if so, which aspects are the most important. In particular, no allowance is made for potential differences in the cost of services under the new structure, as opposed to the expansion of services within the old system. No consideration is given to the opportunity cost of the resources needed for reform. Insufficient attention is paid to estimating the resource costs incurred in, and the benefits accruing to, the implementation of reform, and opportunity costs are not considered.

1973

616 Duriez, M. and Foulon, A. (1973) The National Health Accounts and the Consumption of Medical Services in 1970 (*Comptes nationaux de la santé, la consommation médicale nationale en 1970*), Paris: Centre de Recherches et de Documentation sur la Consommation, Vol. I — Results, 30 pp.; Vol. II — Estimating methods, 89 pp. (mimeographed documents).

Volume I contains: expenditure in the national economic framework; expenditure on the various types of services; expenditure by type of production unit; methods of financing; conclusions. In 1970, national expenditure on the consumption of medical services represented Fr. 45,700 million, or 5.5% of GNP, and 9% of household consumption. Medical services played an increasingly important part in social security expenditure, in terms of both production and consumption. The largest component of medical services production was in hospitals. Of the value of services provided, 95% came from commercial sector enterprises, public or private hospitals, and doctors' surgeries and dispensaries. Financing from collective funds has become increasingly important, and in 1970 coverage under the social security scheme amounted to almost two-thirds of all medical consumption. Volume II contains the principal statistical sources of information about: social security, social assistance, expenditure by the state and local authorities, private mutual benefit societies and insurance companies, the collective provision of medical services by public and private organizations, occupational health, the expenditure of households, supplementary data production, consumption, and fiscal matters. Methods of evaluation are given by type of medical services: physicians' services, laboratory analyses, auxiliary services, dental care, heat treatment, functional rehabilitation, occupational training, and inpatient costs in public and private hospitals. Data are given on medical products, including final consumption of pharmaceuticals and optical and orthopaedic appliances, followed by data on transport services for patients. A summary and conclusions are included. An appendix contains numerous tables showing prices and costs analysed by type of insurance, type of service, and method of financing.

617 GEIL, O.K. (1973) The Flow of Expenditure in Primary Health Services in Århus County in 1970–1971 (*En undersøgelse af udgifterne i sundhedssektoren i Århus amt ekslusiv hospitalsvæsenet 1970–1971*), Århus: Institut for Erhvervs of Samfundsbeskrivelse, Handelshøjskolen i Århus, 120 pp.; *Danmarks Amtsråd*, **4**, 7, 19–24.

The flow of expenditure in primary health services in a Danish county during the year 1970–71 is described. Approximately 30% of total expenditure was allocated to GPs, 20% to dentists, and 24% to drugs. Of expenditure on primary health services, 80% was publicly financed (compared to 100% for hospital services), composed as follows: state 19%, county 3%, community 14%, and health insurance 44%. This investigation was undertaken as part of a wider study of the distribution of expenditure and financing under a tax-financed national health insurance scheme, which was to be introduced in 1973.

618 GOSLINGA, S.S. (1973) Light and Patchwork. The Organisation and Working of Health Care in the Netherlands (*Licht op de Lappendeken. Organisatie en werking van de gezondheidszorg in Nederland*), The Hague: Centraal Planbureau, 532 pp.

This work presents an extensive description of the organization and functioning of health care in the Netherlands in 1973. Chapters deal with legislation, planning, data collection and processing, finance, training, drugs, and preventive and curative care. Though not concerned with quantitative analysis. it has proved to be a useful source of information for mathematical model builders in the field of health care.

619 LÄRSEN, T. and CHRISTENSEN, S.C. (1973) The Development of the Health Care System from an Economic and Statistical Viewpoint 1966–1972 (*Sundhedsvæsenets udvikling i økonomisk-statistisk belysning 1966–1972*), Copenhagen: The National Health Service of Denmark, 32 pp.; *Fra Sundhedsstyrelsen*, **6**, 14, 157–66.

This report, part of a wider economic analysis of the public sector in Denmark, summarizes trends in health service costs, productivity, and manpower use. Several tables describe the development of the hospital sector, the primary health care sector, and drug expenditures. Indicators presented of treatment activity are: number of bed-days, number of inpatients, and number of outpatient examinations. Resource indicators presented are: number of beds, manpower and physicians, current expenditure, and the labour cost share of current expenditure. Data on capital investment are also given.

620 LINDGREN, S.A. (1973) 'Sweden' in: DOUGLAS-WILSON, J. and MCLACHLAN, G. (eds), *Health Service Prospects, An International Survey*, London: The Lancet Ltd and Nuffield Provincial Hospitals Trust, 99–123.

The author surveys the health care system in Sweden and presents data on medical resources, utilization, and the prevalence of diseases.

621 POLDERMANS, J.D.G. (1973) 'Costs and financing of health care in the Netherlands in 1968' ('Kosten en financiering van de gezondheidszorg in Nederland, 1968'). *Tijdschrift voor Sociale Geneeskunde*, **5**, 4, 150–1.

The author comments on two publications of the Central Office for Statistics of the Netherlands, concerning the costs and financing of health care in 1963 and 1968 (published in 1968 and 1973, respectively). He comments on the comparability of the data, the breakdown of costs by province, and the special data on health insurance funds, TB prevention, and mental health programmes. The later report provides a more realistic approach to the costs of scientific research and training. However, still lacking are: data on investment in health care, tables by specialty and by age group, and a complete review of expenditure categories and benefits in the sectors of public health, education, scientific research, housing, social work, and recreation. Nevertheless, the author concludes that these publications are a valuable tool for policy makers, educators, and scientists.

622 PUROLA, T., KALIMO, E., NYMAN, K., and SIEVERS, K. (1973) *National Health Insurance in Finland: Its Impact and Evaluation*, Helsinki: The Social Insurance Institution, Research Institute for Social Security, 12 pp.; *International Journal of Health Services*, **3**, 1, 69–80.

Relationships between medical services research and health policy are examined in the light of a study evaluating a major health policy measure in Finland: the national health insurance scheme, introduced in 1964. A nationwide interview survey was done prior to its introduction, and four years later. The results show that the ratio between care obtained and care needed became more uniform among various population groups. Only a small increase was found in overall utilization rates, and the introduction of daily sickness allowances did not stimulate an increase in days of restricted activity. The results suggested that more ambulatory health services were needed to derive full benefit from the scheme. Finally, the applicability of this approach to evaluation and planning of other health activities is discussed.

1974

573 BONNET, R. (1974) Social Security Regulations of the Nine Common Market Countries (*Les réglements de Sécurité Sociale de l'Europe des Neuf*), Paris: La Documentation Française (Notes et Etudes Documentaires, No. 4129), 42 pp.

623 BRENNA, A. (1974) 'The economics of the Italian health service' ('L'economia del sistema sanitario italiano'), *Le Scienze*, **13**, 73, 110–22.

This article analyses the Italian health care system by its principal economic and structural components, and offers a brief interpretation of the functioning of the system. Its costs, and the reason for their rapid increase, are analysed. The prospects for the implementation of the health plan are discussed, and the problems that will inevitably remain after its implementation are identified.

624 BRUNET-JAILLY, J. (1974) 'Effective financing of health care expenditure' ('Un financement efficace des dépenses de santé'), *Economie et Humanisme*, No. 216, 46–61.

Based on the neo-classical model of welfare economics, this study shows that the private financing of health care expenditures is not necessarily the most efficient method. Even an economic analysis based on the controversial notions of rationality and utility does not lead to the conclusion that private financing is superior. The arguments in favour of the public financing of health care expenditure, along the lines of the social security scheme in France, rest not only on social and political analysis but also on the fact that such methods may be economically optimal and lead to the maximization of welfare. Many hold the view that political experience and belief should be enough to establish the superiority of the public financing of health care expenditure. The author shows that public financing may also be supported on economic grounds.

625 CENTRAL COUNCIL FOR PUBLIC HEALTH OF THE NETHERLANDS (1974) Analysis of Cost Trends in Dutch Health Care for the Period 1950–1980 (*Benadering van de ontwikkeling van de kosten van de Nederlandse gezondheidszorg in de periode 1950–1980*), The Hague: Centrale Raad voor de Volksgezondheid, 40 pp.

This report analyses past, and projects future, volume and cost trends in 14 different sub-sectors: general health care; mental health care; family doctor's care; dental care; medicines, wound-dressings, and medical aids; independent paramedical professional care; specialist care; general, academic, and specialist hospitals; psychiatric hospitals; nursing homes; mental care; management and administration; protection of food and drinking water. These and other expert opinions and statistical examples are used to forecast relevant variances. (See also the two reports: *Benadering van de ontwikkeling van de kosten van de Nederlandse gezondheidszorg*, published on 27 March 1975 and 3 May 1976 by the same office.)

626 CLADE, H. (1974) 'The costliness of the hospital service' ('Die teure Krankenhausmedizin'), *Arbeit und Sozialpolitik*, **28**, 7, 253–9

A discussion of the efficiency of German hospitals, the growth of costs, and its effects in the hospital field. Some methods are suggested for controlling hospital costs.

627 HATTINGA-VERSCHURE, J.C.M. (1974) 'Background to the evolution of cost in health care' ('Achtergronden van de kostenontwikkeling in de gezondheidszorg'), *Maandblad voor Accountancy en Bedrijfshuishoudkunde*, **48**, 1, 466–75.

The increased cost of health care in the Netherlands, from 3.3% of GNP in 1953 to 8.7% in 1975, is analysed. A distinction is made between medico-social, medico-technical, and general social causes, each of which has contributed to the increase in cost.

628 JEAN, P. (1974) 'Expenditure on health care in an economic and financial context' ('Les dépenses de santé dans leur contexte économique et financier'), *Revue Hospitalière de France*, **38**, 271, 781–814.

A file prepared for students at the National School of Public Health, in Rennes, which brings together in tabular form the main statistical data about health economics in France, and general data relating to the French economy. Information is presented on the state budget, the budget of the Ministry of Public Health and Social Security, national expenditure on the social services, and expenditure on the consumption of health goods and services.

629 NAVARRO, V. (1974) *National and Regional Health Planning in Sweden*, Washington, DC: US Department of Health, Education, and Welfare (DHEW Publication No. (NIH) 74–240), 244 pp.

The study details the structures, processes, and methods of national and regional health planning in Sweden, with comparative notes on health planning in the United Kingdom and the experience of the United States. It contains the following chapters: (1) The elements of government in Sweden, (2) Swedish social security and health services, (3) Economic, social, and health planning in Sweden and the relationship between health and economic planning, (4) National health planning, (5) Regional health planning, (6) Further comments on points where the Swedish experience may be relevant to the United States.

263 RHENMAN, E. (1974) *Managing the Community Hospital: Systems Analysis of a Swedish Hospital*, Farnborough: Saxon House, 304 pp. Also: (1969) The District Hospital (*Centrallasarettet*), Lund: Studentlitteratur, 275 pp.

1975

630 BAUDURET, J.F. (1975) 'Conventional budgeting and programme budgeting in the Ministry of Health' ('Budget traditionnel et budget de programmes au Ministère de la santé'), *Cahiers de Sociologie et de Démographie Médicales*, **15**, 2, 46–51.

In 1968, the French government decided that it was necessary to improve the budget preparation process, and therefore invited the various government departments to present their budgetary allocation in programme budget form, in an attempt to classify expenditure so as to facilitate the implementation of budgetary decisions. The paper enumerates the principal concepts that define the traditional budget, then analyses the principal mechanisms of the programme budget, using school health as an example. Five major fields were defined within the framework of this programme budget: the provision of health related services, the provision of social services; the employment of health and social service personnel; expenditure on outside services and miscellaneous activities; and expenditure on medical education and research. At present, 5% of all public expenditure on health care has been organized in a programme budget.

117 BOUCKAERT, L. et al. (1975) Expensive Medicine? Economic Aspects of Health Care in Belgium (*Dure geneeskunde? Ekonomische aspekten van de gezondheidszorg in België*), Leuven: Werkgroep Alternatieve Ekonomie, 112 pp.

631 DURIEZ, M. and FOULON, A. (1975) National Health Care Expenditure in 1970 (*La dépense nationale de santé en 1970*), Paris: Centre de Recherches et de Documentation sur la Consommation, 67 pp. (mimeographed document).

The authors offer a general survey of national health care expenditure, by analysing expenditure on the consumption of medical services and other sizeable items relating to health. The institutional arrangements for administering expenditure on health care are described, and the accounts of the social security scheme, the central government, and the local authorities are discussed. National health care expenditure is then analysed, in the light of national resources, according to the sectors that provide the finance. The authors conclude by showing that, as far as financing is concerned, the public sector plays a very important part. They emphasize the crucial role of social security, which provides 65.23% of the total finance, whereas the state provides finance for only 8.2% of all current expenditure.

632 DURIEZ, M. and FOULON, A. (1975) The National Health Accounts — National Health Care Expenditure 1971, 1972, 1973 (*Comptes nationaux de la santé — La dépense nationale de santé: 1971, 1972, 1973*), Paris: Centre de Recherches et de Documentation sur la Consommation, 100 pp. (mimeographed document).

The first part consists of a discussion of the financing and provision of medical education and research; the budget for therapeutic and preventive services; and the general management of the health services and the accounts relating to their administration in the public sector. Part two presents data on the basic national expenditure on the health services, with estimates for 1971–72 and the trend from 1970 to 1973. The position of expenditure on health care in national economic activity is discussed, and its structure analysed according to the nature of the activities carried out. The sources of finance, both public and private, are described. Basic national health care expenditure, estimated at Fr. 52,000 million (6.44% of GNP) in 1970, increased at an annual average of 14.5% to Fr. 78,000 million (6.83% of GNP) in 1973. In 1973, consumption of medical services represented 10.34% of household consumption as compared to 9.78% in 1970. Salient features in national health care expenditure trends include: the increasingly important role played by the social security system, which financed 65.23% of expenditure in 1970 and 66.62% in 1973; the position of the state and local communities, which account for only about 5% of expenditure on medical consumption but provide most of the finance for research and educational activities (66.50% in 1970 and 72.64% in 1973); and the declining importance of the private sector (26.57% of total expenditure in 1970 and 25.94% in 1973).

633 FORNERO, E. (1975) 'The cost of reforming the health service: Problems of evaluation' ('Problemi nella valutazione dei costi della riforma sanitaria'), *Studi economici*, **30**, 3, 99–150.

The problem of estimating the cost of reforming the health service is tackled using two different working hypotheses. The first envisages that the existing institutional arrangements (based upon a system of health insurance) will remain unchanged, while the second assumes instead that the reform is implemented. In the former case, projected future costs are estimated on the basis of an analysis of trends in expenditure by health insurance agencies in recent years. In the latter case, two estimates of the costs of reforming the health service are described, one made by the Ministry of Health and the other by the Istituto Nazionale per l'Assicurazione contro le Malattie. These estimates are discussed against the background of the guidelines laid down for the reform of the health service. In general, from an economic standpoint, the reform of the system of health care delivery has to be tackled by facilitating the emergence of control mechanisms, which constrain the growth of expenditure while allowing specific health policy goals to be attained. It is therefore necessary to specify the strategic variables to be controlled, namely: the demand for health care, the method of remuneration of doctors, and hospital expenditure.

552 KANN, J. (1975) 'Dental care for children — price — product — efficiency' ('Børnetandpleje — pris — ydelse — effektivitet'), *Danmarks Amtsråd*, **6**, 4, 9–14.

285 PERSSON, E. (1975) 'Hospital costs over 50 years' ('Sygehusomkostningernes udvikling gennem 50 år'), *Tidsskrift for Danske Sygehuse*, **51**, 1, 10–18.

634 REXED, B. (1975) 'How Sweden plans for the 1980s' in: EHRLICH, D.A. (ed.) *The Health Care Cost Explosion: Which Way Now?*, Berne: Hans Huber Verlag, 67–82.

The author describes the present organization of the Swedish health delivery

system, and presents a study by the National Board of Health and Welfare of future organization into the 1980s. The needs of acute somatic inpatient care for the forseeable future are believed to be covered by existing hospital beds. The number of hospital beds in psychiatric care will be greatly reduced. Following the guidelines in the study, the county councils are encouraged to establish a planning organization, and to start work on a comprehensive plan. The planning process is described, and the need for information feedback is stressed. It is pointed out that long-term health planning cannot be effective unless the educational system is adapted harmoniously. The training of physicians and other health professionals is of key importance in planning the performance and direction of the health delivery system. In Sweden, 'specialist training' is used as an instrument of such planning. The author concludes that the costs of medical care will continue to increase to more than 10% of GNP, because some health needs are still inadequately met.
See 26

585 WHO (1975) 'Government health expenditures', *World Health Statistics Report*, **28**, 11, 427–49.

1976

132 CENTRAL OFFICE FOR STATISTICS OF THE NETHERLANDS (1976) The Physically Handicapped in the Netherlands 1971/72. Part 3: Demographic and Physical Data; Special Facilities; Supply of Medical and Social Services (*Gehandicapten wel geteld; lichamelijk gehandicapten 1971/72*), The Hague: Centraal Bureau voor de Statistiek, 69 pp. + appendix 194 pp.

635 DENMARK, GOVERNMENT OF (1976) Ambulance Services Outside Greater Copenhagen (*Betænkning om ambulancetjenesten udenfor storkøbenhavn*), Copenhagen: Statens Trykningskontor (Betænkning No. 766), 117 pp.

The economic, organizational, and health consequences of ambulance services are analysed and discussed. The counties, which own the hospitals, are recommended to develop an overall county-based plan providing publicly financed ambulance services run by licensed private companies. Mobile coronary care units are not recommended.

133 DENMARK, GOVERNMENT OF (1976) Dental Health Status of the Danish Population and Dental Care (*Betænkning om befolkningens tandsund-*

hedsstatus og tandlægevæsenet, afgivet af en af sundhedsstyrelsen nedsat embedsmandsgruppe verdrørende tandlægevæsenet), Copenhagen: Statens Trykningskontor (Betænkning No. 756), 81 pp.

636 GANNIK, D., HOLST, E., and WAGNER, M. (1976) *The National Health System in Denmark, a descriptive analysis*, Washington, DC: US Department of Health, Education, and Welfare (DHEW Publication No. (NIH) 77–673), 85 pp.

The most extensive recent English-language description of the Danish health care system. It contains the following chapters: administrative structure of the national health care system; preventive health care; primary health care; hospital care; rehabilitation services; cost analysis of the health care system. Each chapter ends with 'implications for the United States'.

637 HOUGARDY A. (1976) 'Attempt at evaluation of health care expenditure in Belgium in 1975' ('Essai d'évaluation des dépenses de santé de la Belgique au cours de l'exercice 1975'), *Archives Belges de Médecine Sociale, Hygiène, Médecine du Travail et Médecine Légale*, **34**, 8, 473–96.

The author attempts to estimate Belgian health care expenditures from the viewpoint of both their origin and allocation. This work, which is based on heterogeneous data, is subject to many difficulties and uncertainties; a study of this kind is valuable primarily for indicating orders of magnitude, rather than for its precise data. However, since it is imperative, in our present times of economic instability and recession, to be able to make estimates as accurately as possible, it is desirable that a uniform and functional classification be worked out and adopted by all the bodies involved in this important and complex field.

638 KOCH, J.H., TOFTEMARK, D., and ANDERSEN-ROSENDAHL, P. (1976) *Health Services in Denmark*, Copenhagen: Amtsrådsforeningen i Danmark, 64 pp.

This book provides a brief introduction, in English, to health services in Denmark, with particular emphasis on hospital services. It contains the following chapters: (1) A few facts about Denmark, (2) A very short history of Danish health services, (3) Organization, (4) Admission to hospital and the question of payment, (5) Finance, (6) Hospital staff, (7) Planning.

639 SCHICKE, R.K. (1976) 'Health costs and expenditures in the Federal Republic of Germany' in: *Proceedings of the International Conference on Health Costs and Expenditures (John F. Fogarty Center for Advanced Study in the Health Sciences, Bethesda, Md.)*, Washington,

DC: US Department of Health, Education, and Welfare (DHEW Publication No. (NIH) 76–1067), 291–9.

The distribution of risks and responsibilities in health care and the methods of financing the health services in the Federal Republic of Germany are presented and discussed. Trends in health costs and expenditures are outlined and analysed.
See 589, 590, 640

640 Ståhl, I. (1976) 'Health costs and expenditures in Sweden — the problems of a private good in the public sector' in: *Proceedings of the International Conference on Health Costs and Expenditures (John F. Fogarty Center for Advanced Study in the Health Sciences, Bethesda, Md.)*, Washington, DC: US Department of Health, Education, and Welfare (DHEW Publication No. (NIH) 76–1067), 199–228.

Ståhl surveys the Swedish health care system and presents statistical data for the period 1963–72. He points out the very stable trend in the growth of health consumption and attempts to answer the following question: Is it possible that the elaborate planning system and the complicated political decision process ultimately result only in extremely stable statistical trends or relationships? In a theoretical note, he discusses the optimal voting rule for the consumer in a Swedish-type system, where the total size of the health care system is determined in a political process with a majority decision rule, and where provision is financed by a proportional income tax.
See 589, 590, 639

641 Van Montfort, A.P.W.P., and Spaan, J.M. (1976) 'Hospital costs from 1971 to 1974' ('Kosten over 1971 t/m 1974 van ziekenrichtingen'), *Het Ziekenhuis*, **6**, 4, 98–100.

Data to assess hospital costs were collected by survey questionnaires (85% response). Not included in the total costs are depreciation and interest cost factors of university hospitals. Total costs for 1972/3 and 1974 amounted to Dfl. 6,348 billion and Dfl. 7,704 (an increase of 21.04%). The increase for the period 1971–72 was 22.8%, and for 1972–73 was 17.1%. These increases are broken down for different cost groups and different hospital groups. Finally, a table assesses the relative contribution of price and volume increase to total cost increases. The results show that the volume of services has increased marginally, the majority of cost increases being due to price rises during the period studied.

642 Vlierhuis, A.A.G. (1976) 'Economies in the health service for the sake of the Dutch economy?' ('Bezuinigingen in de gezondheidszorg omwille van de Nederlandse economie?'), *Het Ziekenhuis*, **6**, 8, 205–9.

There must be economies in the health service for the sake of the Dutch economy, but these must be qualified for two reasons. First, the present economic situation, as described in the report of the Central Planning Bureau, does not imply simply that limitations in health care expenditures must take place, but rather that adjustments of the growth of health care provisions are needed to match the limitations of the growth of the Dutch economy. The extent to which these adjustments must occur is not yet known; decisions governing this are part of a balancing process between the different social services. In the second place, the multiplicity of sources financing the health services means that, in addition to the demands for limitation of growth that one might expect from the public sector (health insurance and general taxes), such demands must also come from the private sector.

643 VLIERHUIS, A.A.G. (1976) 'The Dutch health service in figures' ('De nederlandse gezondheidszorg in cijfers uitgedrukt'), *Het Ziekenhuis*, **6**, 6, 146–9.

The following figures are presented: GNP and the growing relative share of health care expenditure, from 1963 (4.5%) to 1975 (8.6%); total number of GPs (4,800, of whom 1,300 have a home pharmacy), specialists (6,600), dentists (4,100), and other health care personnel. Another table presents a breakdown of the nation's budget: education and sciences (14.2 billion guilders), defence (6.3 billion guilders), social benefits (9 billion guilders), and health care (500 million guilders). The total costs of health care are estimated (1974 figure) at 14.6 billion guilders. In addition, the article presents several tables that give the relative costs of different types of hospitals, broken down into various cost groups (medications, running costs, personnel costs, investment costs, reserves), and the expected increase in specialist care with its increasing costs.

1977

644 DENMARK, GOVERNMENT OF (1977) Priority Setting in the Health Care Sector — Report of a Government Committee (*Prioritering i sundhedsvæsenet — betækning fra sundhedsprioriteringsudvalget*), Copenhagen: Statens Trykningkontor (Betænkning No. 809), 440 pp.

The report of a committee set up to establish the basis for priority setting in the health care sector. The first part presents the main part of the analysis, and its conclusions: (1) On the basis of existing information a major change in function between the various health services, or between these and related social services, cannot be recommended; (2) The functions of various health services should be coordinated; (3) Resource use should be critically evaluated; and (4)

Health promotion and preventive activities both within and outside the health services should be increased. Realization of these proposals requires adaptation of the political and administrative system, coordinated planning of the entire health care sector, and an improved health planning information system. The second part describes the existing health services and the major trends in the development of morbidity and the health services, and presents four expert reports dealing with prevention, political and administrative steering, resource use in health services, and the health information system. An extensive list of references to relevant research is included.

645 GYGI, P. and HENNY, H. (1977) The Swiss Health Care System (*Le système suisse de santé — Das schweizerische Gesundheitswesen*), Berne: Hans Huber Verlag, 328 pp.

This bilingual text (French/German) updates to the year 1975 a previous edition. The present edition is a milestone in the Swiss health care system literature for it is the only publication, in a country otherwise known for the paucity of its statistics, to assemble in a coherent form all available data on the different components of the Swiss health care system (statistics, financing, and costs). It covers the suppliers of the health care system and social insurance, studies the evolution of costs since 1960, and analyses the financing of the several elements of the system. One figure alone is revealing: in 1975 Switzerland spent Sw.Fr. 9,900 million (US $3,780 million) on health, or 6.86% of its GNP. A special chapter presents the official viewpoints on the Swiss health care system of the professional associations (medical and paramedical), as well as of the leading political parties.

646 LECOMTE, T. (1977) The Concentration of Medical Expenditure — The Top 10% of Consumers of Services (*La concentration des dépenses médicales — Les 10% plus forts consommateurs de soins*), Paris: Centre de Recherche pour l'Etude et l'Observation des Conditions de Vie, 53 pp. (mimeographed document).

In France, the top 10% of consumers of medical services account for 70% of all expenditure on medical care. An analysis of these heavy consumers reveals the following main facts. Half of the expenditure of the heavy consumers is incurred by young adults, and only 33% by persons over 60 years of age. Although expenditure on the over-sixties is high per person, their share of total medical expenditure is still moderate because they represent only a small proportion of the total population. The heaviest consumers are the culturally and economically privileged classes, and the inhabitants of the Paris area, while the lightest consumers are more likely to be rural inhabitants, members of large households, and persons with few or no educational qualifications. The privileged groups, however, meet a much lower proportion of the expense of their treatment themselves than the poorer groups, since they are larger consumers of services provided out of public funds.

647 NORD-LARSEN, M. and HULTCRANTZ, E. (1977) Health Care Organization in Three Geographical Areas (*Sundhedsvæsenet i tre geografiske områder*), Copenhagen: The Danish National Institute of Social Research (Meddelelse No. 21), Teknik Forlag, 180 pp.

Part of a study of the nuclear primary health team, this paper describes the health and social services in three Danish counties. Data are presented on GPs, home nurses, dental care, maternity care, hospital services, and selected social services during the 1970s.

648 PFLANZ, M. and GEISSLER, U. (1977) 'Rapid expansion in the health care system of the Federal Republic of Germany', *Preventive Medicine*, **6**, 2, 290–301.

In the early 1970s German health care costs expanded at an unprecedented rate of almost 20% per annum, or roughly twice the growth rate of GNP. The search for causes is hampered by the lack of comprehensive health services research and of basic statistics. However, it is safe to say that worldwide trends, as well as national factors, were responsible. Worldwide influence includes such factors as the general progress of medical science and the changing morbidity structure of the population. National factors consist mainly of the introduction of new benefits, such as cancer screening programmes, into statutory health insurance, new legislation concerning hospital financing, the separation between hospital and ambulatory care, and the fee-for-service system in ambulatory care. Although it is generally agreed that the situation is alarming, no decisive remedial action has yet been taken. However, public criticism does seem to have caused hospitals, physicians, and the pharmaceutical industry to exercise some self-restraint, so that the annual rate of cost expansion has been slowed recently to possibly below 10%. Further developments are hard to forecast, but the federal government predicts that health care costs will continue to increase faster than GNP, although at a reduced rate. It is commonly believed in Germany that preventive medicine is one means of restraining the rapid increase in costs. However, few data exist to support this assumption. In 1966, free prenatal care, including laboratory examinations, was introduced into statutory health insurance. In 1971, screening programmes for the early detection of infantile diseases and cancer were added. Screening for cardiovascular and metabolic diseases has been discussed for several years but is still to be decided upon. However, owing to the poor results of treating high-risk populations, enthusiasm for such measures is now fading.

719 SCHWARZ, E. and HANSEN, E.R. (1977) 'Dental services under national health insurance in 1975–76' ('Tandlægelig virksomhed på sygesikringsområdet i 1975–76'), *Tandlægebladet*, No. 81, 262–9.

1978

649 FEDERAL REPUBLIC OF GERMANY, FEDERAL STATISTICS OFFICE (1978) Structure of Expenditures in the Health Field and its Development since 1970 (*Die Struktur der Ausgaben im Gesundheitsbereich und ihre Entwicklung seit 1970*), Bonn: Der Bundesminister für Arbeit und Sozialordnung, 151 pp.

In this comprehensive analysis of expenditures in the health field in the Federal Republic of Germany, official statistics are used for estimating the flow of money. The main sources of economic statistics are institutions, i.e., hospitals, health insurance funds, and other agencies. The services are differentiated into preventive, curative, and rehabilitative. These two dimensions allow a matrix to be assembled giving a clear synopsis of the flows. However, the definitions and boundaries of certain services are not easy to delineate. Total health care expenditure in 1970 was DM 70.3 billion; in 1975 it rose to DM 137.6 billion (all figures including prevention, treatment, rehabilitation, sickness absence benefits, pensions for early invalidity, medical education and training, and medical research). The per capita expenditures rose between 1970 and 1975 from DM 1,160 to DM 2,226. The analysis distinguishes the effect of volume increases and price increases. The advantages and disadvantages of using official statistics, and the difficulties of estimating expenditures in certain fields, are discussed.

650 RUTTEN, F.F.H. and HOOIJMANS, E. (1978) *Financing Medical Care and its Impact on Medical Consumption in the Netherlands*, Leiden: Rijksuniversiteit Leiden, Centrum voor Onderzoek van de Economie van de Publieke Sector (Report 77.03); Leidschendam: Ministerie van Volksgezondheid en Milieuhygiëne, 25 pp.

Regional differences in the medical consumption of both the publicly and privately insured are considered. A cross-section analysis is performed, relating medical consumption to supply of medical facilities, population characteristics, and regional characteristics. Remuneration systems of physicians differ under the public and private insurance systems; the difference in medical consumption between the publicly and privately insured could be partly explained by the differences in financial incentives.

3. Public Health Schemes

1964

725 BERLINGUER, G. (1964) Health Care in Economic Planning, 1964–1978 (*La sanità pubblica nella programmazione economica, 1964-1978*), Rome: Leonardo Edizioni Scientifiche, 174 pp.

1967

726 DELOGU, S. (1967) Health Care, Social Security, and Economic Planning (*Sanità pubblica, sicurezza sociale e programmazione economica*), Turin: Einaudi, 156 pp.

1968

651 BERLINGUER, G. (1968) Social Security and Insecurity (*Sicurezza e insicurezza sociale*), Rome: Leonardo Edizioni Scientifiche, 607 pp.

This three-part volume collects together the result of research on social security, conducted in different periods by the trade union movement and by scholars from various disciplines (economics, sociology, medicine). Part one is dedicated to public health. Part two deals with specific themes in the more important and complex sectors: work, the city and the country, the condition of women, and the aged. Part three covers social insurance and theoretical aspects of social security.

652 DEBRAY, J.R. et al. (1968) Social Security: Evolution or Revolution? (*Sécurité Sociale à évolution ou révolution?*), Paris: Presses Universitaires de France, 230 pp.

This study has two purposes: first, to analyse the ways in which protection against social risks have developed in France; and second, to define the present meaning and likely future evolution of the term 'social risks'. Although it is undoubtedly true that the organization set up in 1945 has failed to achieve all the objectives specified at the time, particularly regarding health insurance, it is nevertheless necessary to plan its future, to adapt the social security scheme to deal with the kinds of social risk that currently exist, and to reconsider the classic notion of social transfers. This book contains information about family allowances, longevity, health insurance, industrial accidents, occupational diseases, and methods of financing social needs.

653 ILO (1968) *Organization of Medical Care within the Framework of Social Security. Eight monographs on Belgium, Canada, Ecuador, Federal Republic of Germany, India, Poland, Tunisia, and United Kingdom*, Geneva: International Labour Office, 566 pp.

This series of monographs describes the organization of medical care under social security provisions in eight countries, within the following framework: methods by which members of the population may obtain medical care and other personal health services; provisions of the statutory insurance scheme(s) concerning medical care; experience and problems with the application of the statutory insurance scheme(s); methods of remunerating members of the medical and allied professions, and of paying for hospital facilities, pharmaceuticals, and other medical and surgical supplies; relations between the statutory social insurance scheme(s) and the public health authorities (including planning and coordination of services); attitudes of interested parties; special problems; and statistical data. The UK monograph describes the National Health Service prior to its reorganisation in 1974.

1. Rajan, V. *India*, (SOC. SEC, 1968/D, 1), 51 pp.
2. Kozusznik, B. *Poland*, (SOC. SEC. 1968/D. 2), 66 pp.
3. ILO Social Security Branch *The United Kingdom National Health Service*, (SOC. SEC. 1968/D. 3), 65 pp.
4. Balma, A. *Tunisia*, (SOC. SEC. 1968/D. 4), 58 pp.
5. Dejardin, J. *Belgium*, (SOC. SEC. 1968/D. 5), 66 pp.
6. Andrade Marin, C. *Ecuador*, (SOC. SEC. 1968/D. 6), 74 pp.
7. Kastner, F. *Federal Republic of Germany*, (SOC. SEC. 1968/D. 7), 74 pp.
8. Hastings, J.E.F. *Canada*, (SOC. SEC. 1968/D. 8), 112 pp.

654 Predetti, A. (1968) 'Economic implications of health care with particular reference to the National Institute of Health Insurance' ('L'economia della sanità pubblica con particolare riferimento all'operato dell' Istituto Nazionale per l'Assicurazione contro le Malattie'), *I Problemi della Sicurezza Sociale*, **23**, 2, 189–228.

The article begins by identifying the salient characteristics of the market for health services in Italy. The chief economic implications of public health care are then examined, with particular emphasis on the income losses caused by illness among the population of working age. Attention is next given to the operations of the Istituto Nazionale per l'Assicurazione contro le Malattie in the decade 1956–65. Trends in the number of persons insured with the agency, and the morbidity patterns (with particular reference to illness involving hospitalization), are analysed. The study contains an extensivc examination of the behaviour over time of the price indices implicit in the calculation of expenditure on general medical services, pharmaceuticals, and hospital care. The article concludes with a brief list of suggestions on how the serious deficit registered by the health and social insurance system might be reduced.

1969

602 BRENNA, A. (1969) 'Financing of the national health service in a social security context' ('Il finanziamento del servizio sanitario nazionale in un regime di sicurezza sociale'), *Ospedali d'Italia*, **6**, 5, 581–99.

655 BROUN, G. (1969) 'Financing the costs of illness — a proposed economic analysis' ('Le financement des coûts de la maladie — essai d'analyse économique'), *Revue Française des Affaires Sociales*, **23**, 1, 3–18.

After noting the general difficulties involved in applying the principles of financing health insurance, the author considers the ways in which universal insurance is ill-suited to the community as a whole, and the problems that inevitably result from such a scheme. He examines the effects of illness on economic life, and develops proposals concerning the economic functions performed by the health care sector. He tries to show that economic analysis does not automatically recommend a single system of financing preferable to all others but that, on the contrary, the collective coverage of health care costs may take different forms for different age groups, as long as excessive complexity is avoided.

1970

656 BRENNA, A. (1970) 'Health policy at a turning point' ('Sanità al bivio'), *Relazioni Sociali*, **10**, 3/4, 1–49.

The central theme of this article is the specification of financial instruments that would bring about a decisive shift in the direction of health care policy in Italy. The author explains the significance of the objectives contained in official documents (and constantly referred to by politicians). He then suggests the implementation of a number of short-term measures that would represent a concrete start to the organization of a national health service.

657 JAMBU-MERLIN, R. (1970) Social Security (*La Sécurité Sociale*), Paris: Armand Colin (Collection U), 90 pp.

A description of the basic problems and principles of social security, which offers the reader a general idea of administrative regulations scattered throughout the relevant literature. Each part of the book is accompanied by documents, of necessity in an abbreviated form, and a bibliography, to enable the student to do his own research. Copious references to texts and legal decisions provide useful supplementary sources on problems where the author's treatment has been constrained by space. The contents include: the organization of social security in France; the major categories of allowance; the relations between social security and civil law; economic and financial problems of social security; systems of social protection outside the social security scheme; and the international problems of social security.

658 NEUBAUER, G. (1970) The National Health Service: Socio-Economic Problems of a State-run Health Service (*National Health Service, sozialökonomische Probleme eines staatlichen Gesundheitsdienstes*), Würzburg: Universität Würzburg, 193 pp.

The concept of health service provision is examined, with reference to the organization, structure, and financing of the National Health Service in England. The market for health services and the determinants of behaviour in the market by its monopolistic elements are analysed, and the effectiveness of the National Health Service is assessed.

659 SCHREIBER, W. and ALLEKOTTE, H. (eds) (1970) Cost Explosion in the Statutory Health Insurance Scheme (*Kostenexplosion in der gesetzlichen Krankenversicherung*), Cologne: Wison Verlag (Kölner Schriften zur sozialwissenschaftlichen Forschung, Vol. II), 93 pp.

A number of contributors deal with topics relating to expenditure under the statutory insurance scheme, including: the importance of physicians' remuneration, the influence of medico-technological developments, the effect of pharmaceutical consumption, the role of cash benefits, and the organization and expenditure of the statutory health insurance funds.

1971

660 DUPEYROUX, J.J. (1971) 'The national agreement between the social security scheme and the medical profession' ('La convention nationale entre la Sécurité Sociale et le corps médical'), *Droit Social*, No. 9–10 (supplement), 1–75.

The texts and documents concerning the national contract between the social security scheme and the medical profession, from 1971 to 1975, are set out. A preamble presenting the ideas advanced by those responsible for the social security scheme and by the medical profession, concerning the contract, indicates the individual agreements that have existed since 1960. In 1961, for example, approximately 75% of all doctors were parties to a contract, while by 1965 this figure had risen to 85.6%, and by 1970 to 90.3%.

661 GABRIELLI, B. and SERNER, U. (1971) 'The effects of the "seven-crowns" reform' ('Sjukronorsreformens effekter'), *Läkartidningen*, **68**, 11, 1205–11.

On 1 January 1970 the Swedish system of health insurance was changed, and the out-of-pocket price for outpatient care standardized to Sw.Kr. 7. The authors compare the changes, between 1969 and 1970 (after the reform), in the following variables: waiting time for non-acute visits in outpatient care, time spent on each patient, number of visits, number of remittances, and number of laboratory and X-ray tests. They conclude that waiting times have increased but that productivity has not changed.
See 574, 667, 670

568 ROEMER, M.I. (1971) *The Organization of Medical Care under Social Security*, Geneva: International Labour Office (Studies and Reports, new series, No. 73), 241 pp.

662 SCHLAUSS, H.-J. (1971) 'Expenditure by the statutory health insurance scheme on hospital care in the decade 1958–1967; development, analysis, and possibilities for restraining hospital costs' (*Die Ausgaben der gesetzlichen Krankenversicherung für Krankenhauspflege im Jahrzent 1958–1967; Entwicklung, Analyse und Beeinflussbarkeit der Krankenhauskosten*), Marburg: Universität Marburg (dissertation), 263 pp. (mimeographed document).

Hospital sector expenditure for the insured population, including pension recipients, is examined historically. Variables such as personnel costs, duration of hospital stay, degree of utilization, and structural factors that might affect cost increases are not taken into consideration.

663 VAN DEN HEUVEL, R. (1971) 'The health insurance deficit' ('Het deficit van de ziekteverzekering' / 'Le déficit de l'assurance maladie invalidité'), *Kontakten/Contacts*, **71**, 3, 158–63 and 174–80.

This paper presents some reflections of a predominantly social nature in the context of the 1971 health insurance deficit. The author argues that the problems of health insurance will only be solved permanently when it is viewed as part of a broad health care policy. This should be regarded, in turn, as part of a broader social policy, the main objective of which is a balanced improvement in health and prosperity. The author questions whether investment in industry is more appropriate than investment in a more specialized health care system. He argues that the efficacy of the health care system can be improved, in part by automation.

664 VITALI, L. (1971) 'Aspects and problems of the English National Health Service' ('Aspetti e problemi del servizio sanitario inglese'), *I Problemi della Sicurezza Sociale*, **26**, 3, 447–64.

The study outlines the organization and economics of the British health service. The author argues that the fundamental weakness of the British system lies in the lack of real planning of objectives, and in the absence of ways in which standards might be raised, particularly in certain geographical areas. The current problems of the health care system require the adoption of a planning strategy that takes full account of resource availability and of economic and social priorities.

1972

665 DOUBLET, J. (1972) Social Security (*Sécurité Sociale*), Paris: Presses Universitaires de France (Collection Thémis), 5th edition, 816 pp.

This book reviews the historical and legal aspects of the social security system in France, and describes the various kinds of social provision for employees, the resources of the social security system, and the various allowances available. The general and specific systems are considered successively. One chapter is devoted entirely to foreign social security legislation and to international law regarding social security.

666 HERDER-DORNEICH, P. (1972) 'Provision of services or monetary reimbursement in the statutory health insurance scheme?' ('Sachleistungsprinzip oder Erstattungsprinzip in der gesetzlichen Krankenversicherung?'), *Arbeit und Sozialpolitik*, **26**, 3, 87–90.

The author discusses the issues of service benefits versus monetary reimbursement for services rendered in the statutory health insurance scheme. The financial consequences of each mode are examined for the voluntarily and statutorily insured population groups within the general social health insurance scheme of the Federal Republic of Germany.

667 JOHANSSON, K. and SERNER, U. (1972) 'The effects of the "seven-crowns" reform (II)' ('Sjukronorsreformens effekter (II)'). *Läkartidningen*, **69**, 51, 6069–72.

This article follows an earlier one (see 661) and confirms that waiting times increased following the reduction in the out-of-pocket price for outpatient care, instituted under the health insurance reform of 1 January 1970. The authors also find a slight decrease in the amount of time spent on each patient. *See* 574, 661, 670

668 Kastner, F. (1972) 'The financial situation and current problems of local health insurance funds' ('Finanzlage und aktuelle Probleme der Ortskrankenkassen'), *Die Ortskrankenkasse*, **54**, 10, 397–405.

The income and expenditure of local health insurance funds in the Federal Republic of Germany are discussed. The analysis covers general trends in expenditure, including spending on such sectors as physicians' services, dental care, preventive services, and cash benefits paid to patients.

669 Martel, P., Launay, J.P., and Perdriau, H. (1972) 'The planning model for social security operations' ('Le modèle de projection des opérations de Sécurité Sociale'), *Statistiques et Etudes Financières* (Série orange, No. 6), 3–23.

This model deals with the operations of all institutions coming under the general heading of 'social security', as defined in the national accounting system. It is useful from the macroeconomic point of view, because the sheer volume of transfers, and their rate of increase, are such that it has proved necessary to prepare highly reliable methods of planning. It is also useful as a means of studying the institutions it includes. As instruments of social policy, governed by a complex and gradually evolving legislative mechanism, the operations of social security present problems, particularly of financing, which are of great concern to the public authorities.

721 Perrin, G. (1972) 'Supplementary systems and social security' ('Les régimes complémentaires et la Sécurité Sociale'). *Revue Française des Affaires Sociales*, **26**, 2, 35–53.

670 Thulesius, K. (1972) 'Economic aspects of health care against the background of the "seven-crowns" reform' ('Ekonomiska aspekter på sjukvården mot bekgrund av sjukronorsreformen'), *Läkartidningen*, **69**, 35, 3881–9.

In 1970 the Swedish health insurance system was changed. Prior to the reform, approximately 75% of the price of outpatient care was reimbursed to the patient. The reform fixed a low uniform price of Sw.Kr. 7 per visit, irrespective of actual costs. The author analyses the effects of the change with reference to data from Växjö hospital. It shows that the reform has achieved some of its

objectives, such as a simplified payment system and the channelling of physicians payments. However, one of its major objectives, a shift from inpatient to outpatient care, has not been achieved.
See 574, 661, 667

1973

362 Busca, L. (1973) The Cost of Drug Consumption under social security (*Le coût de la consommation pharmaceutique dans la Sécurité sociale*), Brussels: Commission of the European Communities (Report No. V/442/73-F), 41 pp.

671 Commission of the European Communities (1973) Synthesis of Three Investigations of the Main Items of Health Insurance Expenditure Covered by Social Security (*Rapport de synthèse concernant trois études sur les principaux postes des dépenses de l'assurance maladie couvertes par la sécurité sociale*), Brussels: Commission of the European Communities, General Directorate of Social Affairs (Report No. V/396/73-F), 38 pp. (mimeographed document).

In this report, three experts (M.C. Michel, M.F. Illuminati, and A. Jolivet) analyse the main items of health insurance expenditures, and national experts report on: relations between the medical profession and social security; the cost of pharmaceutical consumption; and hospital care and treatment covered by social security. The report concludes by insisting on a number of checks including drawing up 'medical profiles' based on statistical data in order to detect anomalous medical expenditure patterns.

672 Denmark, Government of (1973) Income Limits for Public Health Insurance (*Betækning om indtægtsgrænsen ved offentlig sygesikring*), Copenhagen: Statens Trykningskontor (Betænkning No. 676), 90 pp.

The report of a working group established to analyse and propose models for income limits in future reform of the Danish national health insurance scheme. The existing compulsory system, introduced in 1960, provides free access to most health services to individuals below a specific income level, and a co-payment system to individuals above that level. The advantages and disadvantages of five alternative models are discussed, and it is recommended that either of two should be adopted. The first provides a uniform system to the whole population. The second provides a voluntary system under which individuals can opt either for free services, but must select their GP each year, or for co-payment with unrestricted choice of GP (hospital services are free to both groups). A voluntary system was introduced in 1976.

673 DUE, J. (1973) 'Distribution and development of sickness among members of the health insurance system 1967–1972' ('Fordeling og udvikling af sygeligheden blandt sygekassemedlemmer, der var dagpengeforsikrede 1967–1972'), *Socialt Tidsskrift*, **49**, 8, 209–24.

The author analyses the trends in registered sickness in Denmark. The number of sickness episodes has been increasing, with a tendency towards shorter episodes. The distribution of length of episodes is bimodal; this can only be explained by the compensation rules of the sickness insurance, with an increase in compensation for longer episodes.

674 GUIBERT, B. (1973) Methods of Protecting the Population by Social Systems in 1970 (*Les modes de protection de la population par les systèmes sociaux en 1970*), Paris: Centre de Recherches et de Documentation sur la Consommation, 58 pp. (mimeographed document).

An INSEE–CREDOC sample survey (Institut National de la Statistique et des Etudes Economiques — Centre de Recherches et de Documentation sur la Consommation), carried out from January 1970 to January 1971, on the consumption of medical services. It showed that: the social security system covered 95.5% of the population under its various schemes; the mutual insurance societies accounted for 50.6%; free medical assistance (AMG) or Article 115 covered 1.8%; and private insurance schemes covered 6.6%. There were, however, about 800,000 persons, or 1.6%, with no protection at all. The demographic and social characteristics of the insured and those entitled to allowances are presented, including: age and sex (the percentage of persons protected declines with age); type of household; educational level and socio-occupational category; areas and categories of communities; and income per 'consumption unit'. These results are then compared with those of the 1960 survey, and the 1965–66 pilot survey, to show that: the level of social security coverage has increased by 2.3% annually; the number of mutual society members not protected by social security has declined by 17.3% annually; the number of beneficiaries of AMG and Article 115 has declined by 4.6% annually; and the number of persons who are privately insured has decreased by 2.1% annually.

675 HÖÖK, E. (1973) 'A comment on social insurance' ('Ännu en synpunkt på socialförsäkringarna'), *Ekonomisk Debatt*, **1**, 2, 129–30.

This short report on a previous article by Ståhl (see 681) points out that the present Swedish health insurance system has a tendency to cover small risks, for example by paying sickness benefits from the first day of a sickness episode, but that it does not properly cover large risks, such as life-long incapacity due to rheumatism.
See 681.

676 KALIMO, E., NYMAN, K., PUROLA, T., and SIEVERS, K. (1973) 'Effects of the health insurance scheme in Finland. An evaluation based on health interviews' ('Effekter av sjukförsäkringen i Finland. En utvärdering med hjälp av hälsointervjuer'), *Socialmedicinsk Tidskrift*, **50**, 10, 583–9.

In Finland a compulsory health insurance scheme was introduced in 1964, compensating for 45%–100% of all costs in ambulatory health care. A survey based on interviews was done before the insurance scheme was introduced and four years later. The results confirm that consumption of health services increased mainly in the low-income groups.

677 LENOIR, C. and SANDIER, S. (1973) Trends in the Structure of the Medical services 1959–1972 — Health Insurance 1973 (*Evolution de la structure des soins médicaux 1959–1972 — Assurance maladie 1973*), Paris: Centre de Recherches et de Documentation sur la Consommation, 58 pp. (mimeographed document).

This study contains a detailed analysis of expenditures for health insurance in the general social security system, between 1959 and 1972, with the twofold purpose of providing greater knowledge about the structure and trends in various kinds of medical care consumption, and of relating the trend in insurance expenditures to various causal factors, such as consumption, prices, method of coverage, and financing. The study is in two parts: the first concerns the methodology used, and recent trends in medical consumption from 1970 to 1972; the second deals with trends in the consumption of services from 1968 to 1972.

678 MEIER, A. (1973) General Economic Considerations on Health Insurance (*Generelle wirtschaftliche Ueberlegungen zur Krankenversicherung*), St. Gallen: Interdisziplinäres Forschungszentrum für die Gesundheit, 124 pp. + appendix 40 pp.

The introduction contains some reflections on humanism versus economism in health care, especially the inhibitions of doctors in taking costs into account. In the second chapter, the author discusses special features of demand and supply in the health care sector, looking for starting points in containing cost inflation. The third chapter has a similar function for hospital management and pricing of hospital services. After briefly summarizing foreign experience with health care schemes (a somewhat larger but still very short presentation is given in an appendix), the author deals in the fifth chapter with his main objective: to develop basic features of a health care system, and especially of a health insurance mechanism, that is not only reasonable by medical standards but economically sound.

679 NYMAN, K. and KALIMO, E. (1973) *National Sickness Insurance and the Use of Physicians' Services in Finland*, Helsinki: The Social Insurance Institution, Research Institute for Social Security (E 76/1973), 13 pp.; *Social Science and Medicine*, **7**, 7, 541–53.

The implementation of a national health insurance programme in Finland, in 1964, was accompanied by a two-phase evaluation study, before and after the implementation. In this paper, the changes in sickness behaviour as reflected in the utilization of the ambulatory services of physicians are examined. Basic utilization rates, as well as results concerning the determinants of seeking ambulatory care, are given. The results suggest that the changes in sickness behaviour are in accordance with the main aims of the reform.

680 STÅHL, I. (1973) 'Social insurance — the end of a reform era?' ('Socialförsäkringarna — en avslutad reformepok?'), *Ekonomisk Debatt*, **1**, 1, 43–52.

The economic theory behind social insurance systems, such as health insurance and pension schemes, is presented. The main purpose of these systems is to cover certain health risks and to make possible a safe redistribution of income during a lifetime. Many systems also implicitly redistribute income between high- and low-income earners. The proposal for a new dental care insurance scheme is analysed and compared with a perfect private insurance system. The possibility of reforming present-day health insurance in the direction of theoretically optimal insurance system is discussed.

681 STÅHL, I. (1973) 'The possibilities of the market economy in social welfare and health care' ('Marknadsekonomins möjligheter inom social- och hälsosektorerna'), *Sosialøkonomen*, **27**, 1, 35-41.

The causes of different types of market failure, leading to different types of government intervention in the social welfare and health care sectors, are discussed. The possibilities of using more elaborate insurance and pricing systems, without violating political aims concerning just distribution, are discussed as an alternative to present pricing and insurance policies.
See 675

1974

576 FULCHER, D. (1974) *Medical Care Systems. Public and Private Health Coverage in Selected Industrial Countries*, Geneva: International Labour Office, 178 pp.

682 Herder-Dorneich, P. (1974) 'The Federal Trade Commission and social politics' ('Kartellamt als Sozialpolitiker'), *Arbeit und Sozialpolitik*, **28**, 10, 355–8.

A description of the duties of the Federal Trade Commission relating to the non-market area of the provision of health services.

683 Illuminati, F. (1974) 'National health service or health insurance: prerequisites for choice' ('Servizio sanitario o assistenza sociale? Premessa per una scelta'), *I Problemi della Sicurezza Sociale*, **29**, 1, 29–77.

The author argues that Italian health service reform must take account of foreign experience. Specifically, it is essential to analyse the situation in highly industrialized countries, where the social insurance and social service systems have undergone radical restructuring, and to observe the trends in the systems of the EEC member states. The author provides a set of guidelines for reforming the Italian social security system.

684 Laumay, P. and Worms, G. (1974) 'The influence of growth on social security' ('L'influence de la croissance sur la Sécurité Sociale'), *Statistiques et Etudes Financières* (Série orange, No. 13), 21–60.

The technical projection studies carried out in preparation for the VIth Plan predicted a large deficit for 1975 in the general social security system. However, the results from 1971 to 1973 did not confirm this trend, and the possibility of a deficit seems less and less likely. The reason for this is that overall economic forecasts underestimated the rate of growth and the level of inflation. The projected trend in social security operations is subject to similar errors. If legislation on benefits remains unchanged, the underestimate of assessments is greater than that of benefits, with the result that financing difficulties are exaggerated. The analysis was carried out in detail, with the aid of the projection model of social security operations presented in No. 6 of this review.
See 669

685 Nordström, E., (1974) 'The relationship between rule changes and changes in sickness registration' ('Sambandet mellan lagändringar och förändringar is sjukbeteende'), *Nordisk Medicin*, **89**, 9, 269–70.

The article compares registered sickness in the health insurance system in Sweden during five periods with different compensation rules. A significant increase in registered sickness occurs when compensation levels are increased or when self-insurance decreases.

113 PUROLA, T., KALIMO, E., and NYMAN, K. (1974) *Health Services Use and Health Status under National Sickness Insurance*, Helsinki: The Social Insurance Institution, Research Institute for Social Security, 317 pp.

686 SCHAAD, R. (1974) 'Medical costs and provisions for social security' ('Medizinische Kosten und Sozialvorsorge'), *Politische Rundschau — Revue Politique*, **53**, 1–2, 52–8.

A brief description of cost developments in the Swiss health care and hospital system, and of measures for restraining medical costs, is followed by a review of the efforts made to reorganize the health insurance system. A shift in effort from curative to preventive medicine seems to be indicated. An attempt must always be made to preserve and support individual interest in health care. There must be a balanced distribution of the burden between social security and the individual.

687 VAN DEN HEUVEL, R. (1974) 'The changing role of health insurance funds' ('De rolverschuiving van de ziekenfondsen'), *Tijdschrift voor privaat recht*, **11**, 2–3, 381–7.

The system of health insurance funds in Belgium has undergone a profound change. The cost of health care and the increasing social consciousness of the population have led to a widening of its scope, and the health insurance funds have developed into welfare institutions engaged in health care. The author argues that the funds are able to act as efficient representatives of the insured vis-à-vis the authorities and the health professions, provided they combine expertise and continuity with frequent contact with their members.

1975

688 ANDEL, N. (1975) 'Distributional effects of the social security system, exemplified by the statutory health insurance scheme in the Federal Republic of Germany' ('Verteilungswirkungen der Sozialversicherung am Beispiel der gesetzlichen Krankenversicherung in der Bundesrepublik Deutschland') in: DREISSIG, W., Public Finance and Distributtion III (*Öffentliche Finanzwirtschaft und Verteilung III*), Berlin: Duncker & Humblot (Schriften des Vereins für Sozialpolitik, Gesellschaft für Wirtschafts und Sozialwissenschaften, Neue Folge Band 75/III), 39-82.

In order to analyse the distributional effects of statutory health insurance in the Federal Republic of Germany, the insurance benefits, according to age, sex, and the number of insured members per family, are linked with the income-related insurance contributions (for the year 1971). The differential incidence of variations is analysed, relating contributions to benefits. As detailed data needed for the analysis of the contribution side are not available, rough calculations have to be made using specific indicators. After discussing briefly the preferential treatment given to statutory health insurance by third parties, and the health insurance of pensioners, the distributive efficiency of the German national health insurance scheme is analysed critically, and methods of securing improvement are discussed.

689 BLOHMKE, M. (1975) The Cost of Health Care Systems, Social Ecology, and Social Medicine (*Kosten des Gesundheitswesens, Sozialökologie und Sozialmedizin*), Stuttgart: A.W. Gentner Verlag (Schriftenreihe Arbeitsmedizin, Sozialmedizin, Präventivmedizin, Vol. 56), 135 pp.

Of the seventeen papers presented, seven are on health economics, covering respectively: health service costs, cost and efficiency in an international context, WHO activities in health economics, health service cost in the Federal Republic of Germany, hospital cost problems, the costs of prevention, and the economic costs of smoking. The other contributions are concerned with social ecology and social medicine.
See 413, 584.

118 CLOSON, J.P. (1975) 'Influence of national health insurance on the accessibility of care and on income distribution' ('Influence de l'assurance maladie-invalidité sur l'accessibilité des soins et sur la distribution des revenus'), *Orientation Mutualiste*, **28**, 3–4, 186–207.

25 CLOSON, J.P. (1975) Public Health Care and Social Security: An Economic Approach (*Santé publique et prévoyance sociale: une approche économique*), Louvain: Université de Louvain, Faculté des Sciences Economiques, Sociales et Politiques (PhD thesis, Nouvelle série des thèses de doctorat, No. 127), 105 pp.

690 DAHLBERG, L. (1975) 'Next patient please' ('Tack nästa'), *Ekonomisk Debatt*, **3**, 1, 65–8.

Sickness and early retirement pensions are formally approved on medical grounds. However, an analysis of scoliosis shows that the medical criteria become very weak for old persons who have difficulty in securing employment. There is evidence that sickness pensions are used as an alternative to labour market measures.

691 DUPEYROUX, J.J. (1975) Social Security Law (Legal Systems, Supplementary Systems, Unemployment) (*Droit de la Sécurité Sociale, (régimes légaux, régimes complémentaires, chômage)*), 6th edition, Paris: Dalloz, 1102 pp.

This work on social security law gives an overall view of the basic problems of the subject, as well as a systematic analysis of the increasingly complex laws. Considerable space is devoted to the latest developments in the French system. It includes an extensive bibliography.

692 FAUSTO, D. (1975) 'The effectiveness of a national health service' ('L'efficacia di un servizio sanitaria nazionale'), *I Problemi della Sicurezza Sociale*, **30**, 4, 501–17.

The author explains how the market characteristics of health care relate to the goals of public intervention, and states the case for a national health service in preference to a health care delivery system based on private ownership and control. Although the health service in Italy needs reform, even greater priority should go to more rational resource utilization under the existing health insurance arrangements. A realistic approach to the problem must necessarily involve the elimination of abuses associated with the existing system, since any further resource increase for the provision of health care is unlikely in the foreseeable future.

693 FRANCE, DIRECTORATE OF SOCIAL SECURITY (1975) Social Security in France (*La Sécurité Sociale en France*), Paris: La Documentation Française, (Les cahiers français, No. 172), 104 pp.

A booklet on the French social security system, published for the 38th anniversary of the French social security plan. It documents and summarizes concisely the problems of social security in 1975: organization, financing, and benefits.

694 GORI, A. (1975) 'Methods and criteria for the allocation of funds to regions: the case of hospitals' ('Metodologie e tecniche di redistribuzione tra diversi livelli di governo: il caso del settore ospedaliero'), *Rivista di diritto finanziario e scienza delle finanze*, **34**, 3, 319–40.

An attempt to specify methods and criteria for the regional allocation of a given sum of public money. The method by which funds are redistributed aims at a more equitable distribution of resources relative to the socio-economic characteristics of the region. Such methods and criteria can now be tested practically in the distribution among the Italian Regions of the National Hospital Fund, created by Law no. 386/1974. Output and input indicators must be chosen, for use both in the construction of allocative parameters and as a means of monitoring the results of the intervention programme. A distributional system can then be specified, which will operate more or less automatically, depending upon the extent to which objective indices are used as opposed to political judgments. The article concludes with an example in which per capita levels of health care expenditure are equalized (within a given time period) by the redistribution of both current and capital expenditure funds.

695 GRUND, J. (1975) 'The role of financing systems in social policy' ('Finansieringsordningenes rolle i sosialpolitikken'), *Sosialøkonomen*, **29**, 9–10, 21–6.

The present financing systems for social security in Norway result from a long process of historical development, and are far from rational solutions based on economic analysis. The author points out that a system where the state finances a given share of the expenditures of local authorities is inferior to a system with lump sum transfers based on estimates of need. It is also suggested that insurance premiums for occupational injuries should be differentiated according to risk of injury.

696 INSTITUTE FOR SOCIAL RESEARCH, MILAN (1975) Health Care Expenditure at the Regional Level (*La distribuzione regionale della spesa sanitaria*), Rome: Ministero della Sanità, Centro Studi, 259 pp.

Reform of the Italian health care system will transfer functions from the state to the regions. This makes it extremely important to know both the levels of health care expenditure so far borne at the regional level, and the dynamics of that expenditure over time. This is particularly the case for expenditure by the health insurance agencies, which, at the regional level, make by far the largest contribution. The study is composed of three parts. Part one presents data for the years 1970–1971–1972 of health care expenditure by the major health insurance agencies in the various Italian regions. Part two measures the degree of dispersion of regional expenditure around the national average. The data are also compared to major economic aggregates. Part three uses the results of the earlier sections as a basis for the formulation of concrete proposals for the allocation of the future National Health Fund.

697 LECCISOTTI, M. (1975) 'Relative income redistribution effects of health insurance and of a national health service' ('Gli effetti sulla distribuzione del reddito dell'assicurazione malattia o del servizio sanitario nazionale'), *I Problemi della Sicurezza Sociale*, **30**, 5, 661–82.

In assessing the consequences of health insurance or a national health service upon the distribution of income, it is necessary to distinguish the direct effects, on those who bear the cost and enjoy the benefits of health care, from the indirect effects on individuals' income, which stem from the functioning of each system. The distribution of direct benefits depends on a variety of factors: size of economic unit; structure and composition of family; pattern of demand for health care services by individuals according to income group. In general, the evidence suggests that the benefits of both health insurance and a national health service are progressive. The article analyses the income of the medical profession relative to that of other professions, and the distribution of income among doctors.

698 LECOMTE, T., MIZRAHI, A., MIZRAHI, A., and VILLENEUVE, A. (1975) 'Methods of social protection in 1970' ('Les modes de protection sociale en 1970'), *Economie et Statistique*, No. 64, 35–40.

The medical expenses of private individuals are analysed, using data from the health survey carried out by CREDOC and INSEE (Centre de Recherches et de Documentation sur la Consommation and Institut National de la Statistique et des Etudes Economiques) in 1970 among 8,000 households. These expenses are, for the most part, either paid directly by a third party or reimbursed. Of those persons protected by social security (95% of the population), more than half also benefit from mutual society payments, 1.8% are beneficiaries of free medical aid or of Article 115, and 6.6% of some private insurance scheme. However, 1.6% of the population do not benefit from any system of medical protection.

699 NEUBAUER, G. (1975) Socio-Economic Problems of the National Health Service in Great Britain (*Sozioökonomische Probleme eines staatlichen Gesundheitsdienstes — Grossbritannien*), Heidelberg: Alfred Hüthig Verlag, 144 pp.

The organization and financial structure of the National Health Service are described and analysed. The supply of, and demand for, services are considered against the background of the monopolistic features of the system, and of the relationships between the providers and consumers of health care.

700 OLDIGES, F.J. (1975) 'Problems in the financial development of the health insurance scheme' ('Krankenversicherung, Probleme der finanziellen Entwicklung'), *Bundesarbeitsblatt*, No. 26, 157–61.

Various issues that have affected the financing of the German health insurance scheme are discussed. Trends in the growth of cost are analysed in the light of the constituents of costs, and such contributory factors as morbidity levels.

701 ROLIGHED-LAURIDSEN, T. (1975) 'What are the effects of Danish health insurance reforms?' ('Hvordan virker de danske sygesikrings- og dagpengereformer?'), *Nordisk Medicin*, **90**, 1, 28–9.

A short communication on the experience of the new Danish health insurance and sickness benefit system. Sickness absence has increased but not to a serious level, according to the author.

702 RUFFOLO, G. (1975) 'Irrationality and health care: An unlikely system' ('Sanità e follia: un sistema improbabile') in: RUFFOLO, G., Reforms and Counter-Reforms (*Riforme e Controriforme*). Bari: Laterza (Collona Litri del Tempo No. 144), 1–22.

This is the first of three essays by the author on 'failed reforms' (the others deal with housing and schooling). It contains a brief description of the Italian health care system, and of the major causes of its inefficiency. Although an inefficient health care structure involves social losses that are likely to increase over time, the implementation of the health service reform project faces serious difficulties. The major barriers to progress are, however, political rather than financial. Reforms are opposed by particular groups and institutions, whose interests would be adversely affected by implementation of the reform.

703 SACREZ, A. (1975) 'The problem of health insurance' ('Le problème de l'assurance maladie'), *Orientation Mutualiste*, No. 1, 7–54.

This paper presents a number of key statistics concerning health insurance in Belgium, in order to emphasize the problems with which it has to deal. Particular attention is given to the elderly, health insurance, hospitals, and remuneration for technical medical services.

704 SCHMITZ, A. (1975) 'Problems of increasing health service costs' ('Zum Problem der Kostensteigerung im Gesundheitswesen'), *Krankenhaus-Umschau*, **44**, 10, 775–9.

Trends in the cost of providing health services in the Federal Republic of Germany are analysed against the background of contributory factors, such as detrimental life styles and family circumstances. Both short- and long-term measures are suggested to curb health care costs.

583 VAN LANGENDONCK, J. (1975) *Prelude to harmony on a community theme, health care insurance policies in the Six and Britain*, London: Oxford University Press — Nuffield Provincial Hospitals Trust, 303 pp. Previously published as: VAN LANGENDONCK, J. (1971) Harmonization of Social Health Care Insurance in the EEC, (*De harmonisatie van de sociale zekerheid in de E.E.C.*), Leuven: Katholieke Universiteit Leuven, Instituut voor Sociaal Zekerheidsrecht, 182 pp.

289 VARIOUS AUTHORS (1975) 'Special issue on the health care sector' ('Speciale sanità'), *Prospettive Sociali e Sanitaria*, **5**, 17/18, 1–34.

1976

705 BAUER, G. (1976) 'Financing of health insurance' ('Die Finanzwirtschaft in der Krankenversicherung') in: BLOHMKE, M. et al. (eds) Handbook of Social Medicine (*Handbuch der Sozialmedizin*), Vol. III, Stuttgart: F. Enke Verlag, 492–515.

The financial aspects of statutory health insurance in the Federal Republic of Germany are examined in a historical perspective, over the period 1885–1972.

706 BRUNET-JAILLY, J. (1976) 'Some evidence concerning the development of the health care system' ('Quelques évidences sur l'évolution du système de santé'), *Revue Economique*, **27**, 3, 343-401 (special number: Health Economics).

Examination of trends that characterize the economic development of the health care system over a period of, say, twenty years is valuable for international comparisons and for improving our understanding of current problems. Four topics are discussed from this viewpoint: the extension of health insurance; its effectiveness in reducing the economic obstacles to access to health services; the incomes of professional health personnel; and the structure of the hospital system. It is likely that the tendencies that have been observed in these four areas are interdependent and that the connections between them help to explain such features of the health services as the rapid increase in expenditure on health care, the persistence of important inequalities, and the increase in profit-oriented measures.

707 GUSTAFSSON, C. (1976) 'Changes in sickness absence — according to health insurance statistics' ('Förändringar i sjukfrånvaro — enligt försäkringsstatistiken'), *Socialmedicinsk Tidskrift*, **53**, 4, 231–6.

Absence due to illness has increased over a long period in Sweden. The article presents a detailed description of the development of sickness registration under health insurance in the Gothenburg region, from 1955 to 1973. The investigation suggests that there may be large regional variations. The recent decrease in registered sickness for older men is mainly due to an increase in early retirement pensions.

708 HERDER-DORNEICH, P. (1976) 'Cost explosion — a problem of steering' ('Kosten explosion — ein Steuerungsproblem'), *Medizin, Mensch, Gesellschaft*, **1**, 1, 22–7.

The use of systems analysis reveals possibilities for regulative measures to curb the growth in costs.

416 KUEHN, H. (1976) 'Some statistical reflections on cost inflation in the health care system' ('Statistische Ueberlegungen zur Kostenentwicklung im Gesundheitswesen') in: Yearbook for Critical Medicine (*Jahrbuch für kritische Medizin*), Vol. I, Berlin: Argument Verlag, 179–96.

709 MUELLER, H.W. (1976) 'The hospital and the statutory health insurance scheme: cost saving possibilities' ('Das Krankenhaus und die gesetzliche Krankenversicherung: Möglichkeiten einer Kostenbeschränkung'), *Krankenhaus-Umschau*, **45**, 5, 317–28.

The relationship between statutory health insurance and hospitals in the Federal Republic of Germany is outlined, and suggestions for containing the growth in hospital costs are discussed.

710 SCHICKE, R.K. (1976) 'Co-insurance in other countries: between health policy and social policy' ('Kostenselbstbeteiligung im Lichte ausländischer Erfahrungen: zwischen Gesundheits- und Sozialpolitik'), *Das öffentliche Gesundheitswesen*, **38**, 9, 569–74.

A discussion of the nature and effects of co-insurance. Utilization was found not to be very sensitive to co-insurance, but the effect on utilization may depend upon the possibilities for substituting other types of care.

711 SCHOEPF, A. (1976) 'On the development of health care expenditures' ('Zur Entwicklung der Gesundheitsausgaben'), *Wirtschaftspolitische Blätter*, No. 23, 59–69

A historical analysis of the economic aspects of health care, showing the costs of health care in Austria (1955–74) and other selected countries, as a percentage of their GNP. Factors contributing to the growth in costs are discussed.

712 SEFFEN, A. (1976) Costs of Illness, their Growth, and Possibilities for Control (*Krankheitskosten, Entwicklung und Begrenzungsmöglichkeiten*), Cologne: Deutscher Instituts-Verlag (Beiträge zur Wirtschafts- und Sozialpolitik, Institut der Deutschen Wirtschaft, Vol. 37), 60 pp.

The author examines the cost of health service development in the years 1965–75, and makes estimates of its development to 1980. Possibilities for curbing the rising cost of health services in the Federal Republic of Germany are explored.

713 SIEBECK, T. (1976) Cost Trends in Health Insurance (*Zur Kostenentwicklung in der Krankenversicherung*), Bonn: Verlag der Ortskrankenkassen, 145 pp.

A variety of factors contributing to the increase in cost of statutory health insurance are examined from a historical perspective. The causes of cost increases are analysed in a similar manner for the individual sectors in the health service.

714 THIEMEYER, T. (1976) 'Proposals for controlling the cost explosion' ('Vorschläge zur Bewältigung der Kostenexplosion'), *Medizin, Mensch, Gesellschaft*, **1**, 1, 14–21.

The author analyses the proposals most frequently cited in the literature for damping the cost explosion. The pros and cons of co-payment, along with the cost reimbursement principle, are set against each other. Suggestions for rationalization in the field of ambulatory care are discussed.

1977

715 JAHN, E. (1977) 'Cost trends in medical care' ('Zur Kostenentwicklung in der medizinischen Versorgung'), *Pharma Dialog*, No. 49, 21 pp.

The author considers how changes in nursing charges, length of stay, and the prices of pharmaceutical products have affected the cost of medical care.

716 KLECZKOWSKI, B.M., MACH, E.P., and THOMAS, R.G. (1977) 'Containing the rising cost of medical care under social security', *WHO Chronicle*, **31**, 10, 408–12.

This paper attributes the rising cost of health care under social security systems to a bias towards hospital care, inappropriate use of advanced technology, and associated high labour costs. It recommends a series of measures to contain the trend: revised benefit structures to de-emphasize unjustified hospital care; improved cost-accounting for selection of cost-effective specific health services; encouragement of medical cost-consciousness; rational use of drug therapy; promotion of guided self-care; and greater emphasis on preventive services.

717 KOCHER, G. (ed.) (1977) Cost Reduction in the Health Care System (*Kosteneindämmung im Gesundheitswesen*), Solothurn: Verlag Konkordat der Schweizerischen Krankenkassen, 162 pp.

Proceedings of a symposium organized by the federation of Swiss health insurance agencies. Switzerland does not have a ministry of health, but the central government helps to finance the deficit of many of the hundreds of Swiss health insurance agencies. The progressive reduction of this federal subsidy led the insurance agencies to consider future cost reduction measures. Representatives of the state, the health insurance agencies, the Swiss federation of physicians, the director of a large hospital, a professor of preventive medicine, and a professor of economics presented papers. A record of the ensuing discussions is given, together with the concluding recommendations to the authorities and other interested bodies.

718 SCHAEFER, H. (1977) 'Efficiency and effectiveness of medical services in the light of health insurance' ('Effizienz und Effektivität der medizinischen Leistungen im Licht der Krankenversicherung'), *Die Ortskrankenkasse*, **59**, 16, 657–63.

Effectiveness in the health care system results from the behaviour of the patient; the opportunities to reduce illness, and the theory of health. If effectiveness is understood as a measure of the fit between the changes in health status and the services to attain this status, the main problem is measurement. The precondition for it is adequate knowledge of the cause–effect relationships involved. Despite the tremendous increase in expenditures in the health care system in the Federal Republic of Germany, the life expectancy of middle-aged males decreased between 1960 and 1970. It is estimated that, in 1971, the health services had to spend about DM 35,000 in order to save a life, with uncertain further life expectancy; in 1977, the corresponding sum was possibly DM 300,000. The cost increase is a question of humanity and not of economic benefit. In many cases heart operations, unnecessary surgery, treatment in intensive care units, and screening are of doubtful effectiveness and efficiency.

719 SCHWARZ, E. and HANSEN, E.R. (1977) 'Dental services under national health insurance in 1975–76' ('Tandlægelig virksomhed på sygesikringsområdet i 1975–76'), *Tandlægebladet*, No. 81, 262–9.

In Denmark, the national health insurance scheme reimburses a proportion of the fee for a limited number of dental services: examination, descaling, fillings, extractions, X-rays, and root-canal treatment. Approximately 11 million such services were delivered to adults, and 1.5 million to children, during 1975–76. The most frequently used service was fillings (43%), followed by examination (26%) and descaling (15%). Differences in utilization were identified, both between regions and between population groups. The cost of dental services to the insurance scheme was approximately D.Kr. 0.5 billion (or D.Kr. 130 per adult Dane, all of whom are covered by the scheme). The total direct cost of dental services, including the patients' share of service fees, is estimated at D.Kr. 1.5 billion.

595 UNION BANK OF SWITZERLAND (1977) *Social Security in 10 Industrial Nations*, Zurich: Union Bank of Switzerland, 35 pp.

1978

720 LAURINKARI, J. (1978) *Economic Health Security as a Whole*, Kuopio: University of Kuopio, Department of Community Health, 24 pp.

A study of the development of health insurance and other insurance compensation schemes in Finland.

4. Private Insurance Schemes

1972

721 PERRIN, G. (1972) 'Supplementary systems and social security' ('Les régimes complémentaires et la Sécurité Sociale'), *Revue Française des Affaires Sociales*, **26**, 2, 35–53.

The paper begins with a definition of supplementary systems, i.e., any system intended to provide benefits in addition to those of a legal social security system. This is followed by an analysis of the different existing types (legal system, inter-occupational systems, business firm systems, etc.). The roles of these supplementary systems are explored, revealing a defect in the basic systems. The ways in which these systems have developed are examined, particularly by comparing the French system with those of other countries.

1973

674 Guibert, B. (1973) Methods of Protecting the Population by Social Systems in 1970 (*Les modes de protection de la population par les systèmes sociaux en 1970*), Paris: Centre de Recherches et de Documentation sur la Consommation, 58 pp. (mimeographed document).

1974

576 Fulcher, D. (1974) *Medical Care Systems. Public and Private Health Coverage in Selected Industrial Countries*, Geneva: International Labour Office, 178 pp.

1975

722 Lange, H. (1975) 'Private health insurance, present rules, alternatives, and supplements' ('Die privaten Krankenversicherung liefern Masstäbe, Alternativen und Ergänzungen'), *Arbeit und Sozialpolitik*, **29**, 8/9, 348–52.

A comparison is drawn between statutory health insurance and private health insurance, in terms of the costs of progress in medical technology and of increasing the volume of treatment.

723 Tervooren, F. (1975) 'Insurers should examine the efficiency of the services they offer' ('Die Kassen sollten die Effizienz ihres Leistungsangebotes prüfen'), *Arbeit und Sozialpolitik*, **29**, 6, 216–18.

Suggestions, made by the manager of the federal association of incorporated health insurance agencies, for more efficient health insurance.

1976

710 Schicke, R.K. (1976) 'Co-insurance in other countries: between health policy and social policy' ('Kostenselbstbeteiligung im Lichte ausländi-

scher Erfahrungen: zwischen Gesundheits- und Sozialpolitik'), *Das öffentliche Gesundheitswesen*, **38**, 9, 569–74.

1977

724 GRIESEWELL, G. (1977) 'Strategy on cost curbing in health insurance — control of supply or demand? A status report on the topic "co-insurance"' ('Strategien der Kostendämpfung in der sozialen Krankenversicherung — Angebots- oder Nachfragesteuerung? Eine Bestandaufnahme zum Thema "Selbstbeteiligung"'), *Sozialer Fortschritt*, **26**, 4, 84–9 and **26**, 5, 110–12.

Outlines the historical, political, and economic context of the present debate on co-insurance, to show the background and motivations of the approaches now favoured. Drawing on studies and surveys in the Federal Republic of Germany, France, and Great Britain, the author concludes that co-insurance is not only unlikely to stop cost inflation, but that its effects are difficult to quantify.

717 KOCHER, G. (ed.) (1977) Cost Reduction in the Health Care System (*Kosteneindämmung im Gesundheitswesen*), Solothurn: Verlag Konkordat der Schweizerischen Krankenkassen, 162 pp.

VI Planning Whole Systems

1964

725 BERLINGUER, G. (1964) Health Care in Economic Planning, 1964-1978 (*La sanità pubblica nella programmazione economica, 1964-1978*), Rome: Leonardo Edizioni Scientifiche, 174 pp.

The study seeks to respond to the need, widely recognized in Italy, for a health service plan that will provide for the quantitative development of services, the reorganization and improvement of provision, and the reform of public health institutions. Such a plan cannot be effective unless it forms an integral part of economic planning to improve welfare. This plan is divided into five-year phases: 1964-68, 1969-73, and 1974-78. While some of its provisions refer to single regions or geographical zones, most are at the national level. Its objectives are: to ensure health care protection to the entire population; to emphasize the preventive character of health care programmes, with the aim of reducing the incidence of those illnesses that have the greatest impact on society; and to eliminate the insurance principle for health care services creating a national health service, financed by the public according to their income level and directed by the state through the Ministry of Health, the regions, the provinces, and the municipalities.

1967

563 ABEL-SMITH, B. (1967) *An International Study of Health Expenditures and its Relevance for Health Planning*, Geneva: World Health Organization (Public Health Papers, No. 32), 127 pp.

726 DELOGU, S. (1967) Health Care, Social Security, and Economic Planning (*Sanità pubblica, sicurezza sociale e programmazione economica*), Turin: Einaudi. 156 pp.

The launching of the first Italian five-year economic development plan presented an opportunity to revise the social security system. Because of its economic import, this system conditions the process of social development, in terms of more efficient utilization of available resources and of qualitative changes in health care services and social security. This study traces the evolution of social security during the last twenty years, through four major stages: charity, legal aid, mutual aid, and social insurance, and then considers the current situation, including political and social trends and pressures. It goes on to examine the relationship between different social security policies and planned economic growth.

727 WHO (1967) *National Health Planning in Developing Countries*, Geneva: World Health Organization (Technical Report Series, No. 350), 40 pp.

This report of a WHO Expert Committee presents a very general review of basic aspects of health planning in developing countries. It discusses and makes recommendations in three areas: preparation of planning through collection of basic data and establishment of a planning unit, methods of planning, and training of planning staff.

1969

728 DEBOECK, G. (1969) Health Care Planning: a macroeconomic analysis of health care (*Gezondheidsplanning: een macro-ekonomische analyze van de volksgezondheidszorg*), Leuven: Katholieke Universiteit Leuven, Centrum voor Economische Studien, 200 pp.

The purpose of this study is to demonstrate the need for systematic planning of the health care sector. The first part presents correlations between health indicators and per capita income in several countries. The multiple economic effects of disease eradication are analysed, and the economic cost of diseases quantified. The author argues that evaluation of health programmes reveals an inefficient use of limited health care sector resources, and that a systematic approach to health care planning needs to be developed. The second part analyses the health care planning methodology used primarily in Latin American countries, and finds it to be both time and money consuming. Some techniques for analysing alternative health care strategies, including cost–benefit and cost–effectiveness analysis, are discussed. The study concludes by stressing the need for a pragmatic but systematic approach to health care planning.

729 FRANCE, MINISTRY OF SOCIAL AFFAIRS (1969) Thoughts on the Future of the Health Care System. Contribution to the Presentation of a Health Care Policy (Report of a Working Group on the Outlook for Health)

(*Réflexions sur l'avenir du système de santé. Contribution à l'élaboration d'une politique de santé (rapport d'un groupe de travail sur la perspective sanitaire)*), Paris: La Documentation Française, 107 pp.

Report of a committee set up late in 1967 by the Ministry of Social Affairs and the General Commissioner for the Plan, chaired by the head of the Department of Studies and Revisions in the Ministry of Public Health, to generate ideas and information about the organization of medicine in modern society. Its reflections are varied, including: the expected characteristics of French society in 1985; integrated information processing; the major functions of a rational health care system (general, specialized, and hospital medicine); health care systems structures (university and continuous medical training, group medicine, hospital structures); coordination of the public and private sectors; prevention aimed at the individual and at the social and natural environment; the pharmaceutical industry and drug requirements, marketing, and distribution; and the methodology for defining a health care policy and for health care planning.

50 GILLIAND, P. (1969) Demographic Ageing and Hospital Planning (*Vieillesse démographique et planification hospitalière*), Lausanne: Département Cantonal de l'Intérieur, Service de la Santé Publique, 342 pp.

206 VÄÄNÄNEN, I., BÄCKMAN, G., PERÄLÄ, J., and VAUHKONEN, O. (1969) Study of Hospital Use by Regression Models (*Väestön sairaalankäytön selittäminen ja ennakoiminen regressiomallien avulla*), Helsinki: The Finnish Hospital Federation, 98 pp.

1970

730 BOPP, S. (1970) Regional Hospital Planning. A Theoretical Attempt to Conceptualize and Analyse its Practical Application in the Federal Republic of Germany, the USA, and England (*Regionale Krankenhausplanung, Versuch ihrer theoretischen Erfassung und Untersuchung der Praxis in der Bundesrepublik, in den USA und in England*), Berlin: Duncker & Humblot, 115 pp.

A theoretical approach to the regional hospital planning concept, including the use of cost–benefit analysis as an auxiliary tool in deciding the distribution of hospitals, is followed by an analysis of the situation in the Federal Republic of Germany, the USA, and England.

731 British Medical Association (ed.) (1970) *Health Services Financing*, London: British Medical Association, xvi + 605 pp.

The second section contains fourteen papers examining the finance and organization of health services in the developed world (Appendices D–Q):

Seldon, A., 'Organisation and financing of medical care in Australia', 309-24.
Kohlmaier, H., 'The organisation and financing of health insurance in Australia', 325-42.
Ruderman, A.P., 'The organisation and financing of medical care in Canada', 343-58.
Sirc, L., 'Organisation and financing of medical care in East European Communist countries', 359-72.
Rösch, G., 'The economics of medical care in France', 373-402.
Schreiber, W., 'Health insurance in the German Federal Republic', 403-20.
Duncan, G., 'The organisation and financing of medical care in Ireland'. 421-30.
Ahlbaun, H., 'Sickness insurance in the Grand Duchy of Luxembourg'. 431-8.
Van Langendonck, J., 'Organisation and financing of medical care in the Netherlands and Belgium', 439-70.
Ward, J.T., 'Organisation and financing of medical care in New Zealand'. 471-84.
Evang, K., 'The organisation and financing of health services in Norway'. 485-506.
Thorburn, T., 'Organisation and financing of medical services in Sweden'. 507-20.
Hauser, M., 'Organisation and financing of medical services in Switzerland', 520-34.
Lindsay, C.M. and Buchanan, J.M., 'The organisation and financing of medical care in the United States', 535-85.

209 Cappelli, A., Gugliomella, G., Pellicelli, G., and Scanagatta, A. (1970) Methodology of Hospital Planning (*Elementi di metodologia della programmazione ospedaliera*), Rome: Federazione Italiana Associazioni Regionali Ospedaliere, xv + 212 pp.

732 Engler, H. (1970) Planning Problems in the Health Care System (*Planungsprobleme im Gesundheitswesen*), Zurich: Schulthess Polygraphischer Verlag, 165 pp. A modified summary of this book is also published under: Frey, R.L. and Engler, H. 'Forecasting in the health sector' in: Paeling, J.H. (ed.) (1970) *Programming for Europe's Collective Needs*, Amsterdam: North-Holland (Series ASEPELT [Association Scientifique Européenne pour la Prévision Economique à Moyen et à Long Terme], Vol. IV), 285-308.

This book examines several peculiarities of decision making and planning in the health care sector. Above all, it is the dominant position of doctors (who decide on both demand and supply), and their special relationship to their patients (a kind of trusteeship), which make it difficult to separate consumption and production functions (supply produces its own demand). This leads to an extreme tendency to risk aversion and inefficient allocation of resources. The consequences of these peculiarities in, for example, medical research and training, preventive medicine, and social security are examined and policy measures outlined.

733 WHO (1970) *National Environmental Health Programmes: Their Planning, Organization and Administration*, Geneva: World Health Organization (Technical Report Series, No. 439), 56 pp.

This report of a WHO Expert Committee reviews current trends in environmental health and the major categories of environmental health problems, both national and international. It argues that health care agencies have a responsibility for coordinating environmental health policy, and discusses aspects of planning and evaluation of environmental health programmes within this framework.

1971

734 Denmark, Government of (1971) 'The health care sector' ('Sundhedsvæsenet') in: Perspective Planning 1970-1985 (*Perspektivplanlægning 1970-85*), Copenhagen: J.H. Schultz Forlag, 80-97.

In 1968, the Danish government appointed a working group to analyse sectoral trends in a 15-year perspective. The analysis of the health care sector raises important planning questions. The paper emphasizes the need for overall health sector planning on the basis of economic criteria. It recommends that future planning should consider increased preventive activity, a shift from inpatient to outpatient treatment, improved functional distribution of work between hospitals, and rationalization of activities within hospitals. Continued growth of the health care sector at its present rate is recognized to be unlikely. Basic resource data are presented.
See 747.

735 France, Committees of the VIth Plan (1971) Report of the Health Committee (*Rapport de la Commission Santé*), Vol. I, 276 pp.; Vol. II, 188 pp. Report of the Committee on Social Benefits (*Rapport de la Commission Prestations Sociales*), Vol. I, 300 pp.; Vol. II, 187 pp., Paris: La Documentation Française.

These four volumes contain all the conclusions reached in the studies carried out by the Health Committee and the Committee on Social Benefits, in preparation for the VIth Plan, and give the proposals made. The actual policies and strategies adopted are given only in the Plan itself. Extensive tables and statistics are included, concerning medical goods and services and the social security system.

736 France, Ministry of Public Health and Social Security (1971) Towards a Health Policy, The Major Health Campaigns (*Pour une politique de santé, les grandes actions de santé*), Paris: La Documentation Française, Vol. I, 253 pp; Vol. II, 345 pp.

The collection 'Towards a Health Policy' consists of three volumes. The first two cover the major health campaigns, and the third covers hospitals. They present the ideas of several working groups that assisted the Ministry of Public Health, between 1969 and 1971, in the formulation of a health policy. Volume I consists of six reports on: medical progress, perinatality, emergency services, the medical aspects of ageing, cardiovascular diseases, and peripheral vascular pathology. Volume II contains the reports of seven working groups on: suicide, rheumatology, dental services and prevention, thermal springs, everyday life and health, public hygiene, and pollution and nuisances.

737 Popov, G.A. (1971) *Principles of Health Planning in the USSR*, Geneva: World Health Organization (Public Health Papers, No. 43), 172 pp.

This paper provides a detailed exposition of the principles of health planning, together with extensive data (some comparative) on health status, and health services resources and utilization in the USSR. Following a review of the theory of health planning, it discusses measures of health status and methods of health forecasting, and the availability, distribution, and utilization of outpatient and hospital care facilities and medical manpower. Concluding chapters discuss methods of planning, the training of medical manpower, and the specification of the norms and standards for medical care and manpower, which constitute the core of the planning method. An annex lists 300 indices for use in health planning and evaluation.

738 Schicke, R.K. (1971) 'Health service research and methodologies in planning for medical care facilities: some international comparisons', *Methods of Information in Medicine*, **10**, 3, 163–8.

Methods in planning for stationary health facilities in the context of different national settings are presented and discussed, as a basis for selecting appropriate methods in planning and research. Part one deals with conceptual issues. Part two is empirical, providing illustrative material on national and regional planning methods, using computer-processed data collection instruments.

739 WHO (1971) *Planning and Programming for Nursing Services*, Geneva: World Health Organization (Public Health Papers, No. 44), 123 pp.

This paper is intended to help nurses participate effectively in national health planning. Introductory chapters review, at a general level, principles, trends, and training in health planning. The substance of the paper discusses aspects of the planning process relevant to nursing services. Annexes review the PAHO-CENDES (Pan American Health Organization — Center for Development Studies), PPBS (Planning, Programming, and Budgeting Systems), and USSR approaches to health planning, and some techniques in planning nursing services. The paper concludes with a glossary of terms and a bibliography of relevant sources.

420 WHO (1971) *Statistical Indicators for the Planning and Evaluation of Public Health Programmes*, Geneva: World Health Organization (Technical Report Series, No. 472), 40 pp.

1972

740 BOSERUP, H. (1972) 'The health care sector in social planning' ('Sygehus og sundhedsvæsenets indplacering i den generelle samfundsplanlægning'), *Danmarks Amtsråd*, **3**, 3, 9–14.

The role of the health care sector in the economy and in social planning is discussed, and its increased rate of growth is illustrated. The development of a detailed health sector budget covering both capital and current expenditure, over a time horizon of several years, is recommended as an integral element of national planning.

229 BRENNA, A. and CESARINI, F. (1972) Contributions to the Lombardy Hospital Plan — Economic and Financial Aspects (*Contributi per il Piano Ospedaliero della Lombardia — Gli spetti economico-finanziari*), Milan: Giunta Regionale della Lombardia, Assessorato alla Sanità, 105 pp.

741 COUDER, B., SANDIER, S., and TONNELLIER, F. (1972) 'The study of coherent projections by interdependent variables' ('Recherche de projections cohérentes par des variables interdépendantes'), *Consommation*, No. 3, 34–67.

The authors show that the study of compatible projections can, in certain cases, lead to the resolution of a series of linear programmes that take account of the relative increases in the variables. This procedure was used to predict trends in medical services and hospitalization during the VIth French Plan.

742 HILLEBOE, H.E., BARKHUUS, A., and THOMAS, W.C. (1972) *Approaches to National Health Planning*, Geneva: World Health Organization (Public Health Papers, No. 46), 108 pp.

This paper surveys different health planning approaches practised in developing and developed countries. The introductory chapters distinguish between systematic and pragmatic planning, and argue that the pragmatic approach is inevitable in developing countries constrained by existing resource commitments and lack of data. Among the developing countries, the paper reviews health planning in India, health manpower planning in Peru, Taiwan, and Turkey, and the PAHO-CENDES (Pan American Health Organization — Center for Development Studies) methodology developed for Latin America. Among the developed countries, it reviews health planning in the USSR, Sweden, and the USA.

743 KRYSMANSKI, R. and SCHAEFERS, B. (eds) (1972) Planning and Interests in Health Services (*Planung und Interessen im Gesundheitswesen*), Düsseldorf: Bertelsmann Universitäts-Verlag, 178 pp.

Various authors deal with the general theme of health service planning. They compare planning systems in the Federal Republic of Germany with those in England, the USA, and the USSR, and conclude with an analysis of planning in North Rhine–Westphalia.

744 LEVY, E. (1972) 'The future of the health care system. An economist's views' ('L'avenir du système de santé. Vues d'un économiste'), *Revue Française des Affaires Sociales*, **26**, 2, 118–29.

The paper reviews three approaches for exploring the future beyond the medium-term prospects of the French Plan. It extrapolates from past trends, assuming present conditions continue. A functional analysis is made of a research 'model' of the health care system, using 'heavy trends' (those alredy begun and practically irreversible) and 'harbingers of the future' (early tendencies still not very extensive, but likely to direct change into fruitful new channels). Future scenarios are constructed, with a rational health care system as end-point and progressive alterations in the present system to bring it closer to this ideal image. In evaluating health system development over the next 20 years, general socio-economic factors, and developmental factors peculiar to the health care system, are considered and conclusions are drawn, including an estimate that medical consumption will quadruple by 1985, to 20% of the French GNP.

669 MARTEL, P., LAUNAY, J.P., and PERDRIAU, H. (1972) 'The planning model for social security operations' ('Le modèle de projection des opérations de Sécurité Sociale'), *Statistiques et Etudes Financières* (Série orange, No. 6). 3–23.

745 WHO (1972) *Health Planning and Organization of Medical Care*, Copenhagen: World Health Organization, Regional Office for Europe (Public Health in Europe Series, No. 1), 131 pp.

This collection contains papers by individual contributors on the following subjects: French studies in health economics; health economics and cost–benefit analysis; current developments and trends in rehabilitation in Europe; systems of prevention in dental care; organization of occupational health services; evaluation of health laboratory services; objectives of medical computing in the hospital; reasons for failure and factors making for success (in hospital computer systems); future prospects for the application of mathematical methods and computer techniques to the control of hospital admission services in large cities; measuring the effectiveness of public health services. The concluding chapter presents comparative demographic, health status, and health manpower statistics for countries in the European region in or around 1969.

1973

746 BERFENSTAM, R. et al. (1973) *Swedish Medical Care in the 1980s*, Stockholm: Svenska Landstingsförbundet, 66 pp. (mimeographed document).

This report, based on a study tour, discusses decisions and policy considerations in the planning and programming of future health and medical care systems in England, Scotland, Canada, and the USA, in comparison with Sweden. The final part presents the authors' predictive view of typical Swedish society in the 1980s, and of the problems that are likely to characterize health and medical care.

747 DENMARK, GOVERNMENT OF (1973) 'The health care sector' ('Sundhedsvæsenet') in: Perspective Planning II, 1972-1987 (*Perspektivplanredegørelse II, 1972-1987*), Copenhagen: Statens Trykningskontor, 482-506.

This contribution to the Danish government's continued analysis of long-term economic planning summarizes the important sector resource indicators,

estimates the outcomes of various policies, and discusses the elements of a long-term policy. Estimates are based on a restraint in hospital expansion, growth in primary health care services, and increased preventive activity. No definite conclusions are drawn. The average annual sector growth rate is assumed to fall from its previous value of about 5.5% to 1.7% throughout the period to 1987. Basic data are presented for the period analysed.
See 734.

748 Destanne de Bernis, G. (1973) 'Health planning — introductory questions' ('La planification sanitaire — questions introductives'), *Tiers-Monde*, **14**, 53, 19–45.

The author argues that health planning is indispensable and should be integrated with general socio-economic planning. He reviews the objectives of a public health plan and the means for establishing such a plan, and distinguishes between the industrialized countries and those of the Third World.

459 Feldstein, M.S., Piot, M.A., and Sundaresan, T.K. (1973) *Resource Allocation Model for Public Health Planning. A Case Study of Tuberculosis Control* (supplement to Vol. 48 of the *Bulletin of the World Health Organization*), Geneva: World Health Organization, 110 pp.

749 France, Ministry of Public Health and Social Security (1973) 'The problem of decision making in health matters' ('Les problèmes de la décision en matière de santé'), *Economie et Santé* (supplement to the *Bulletin des Statistiques de Santé et de Sécurité Sociale*), No. 3, 1–63.

Documents prepared during the work of the think-tank on the 'science of decision making in health matters', set up in 1971. The review begins with decision making problems in health matters in general, particularly basic difficulties of interdisciplinary communication, e.g., between medicine, sociology, and economics. It contrasts the way in which practising physicians see and understand choices facing them, compared to economists' views of the same choices: the former centring on individual patients, the latter more on aggregated groups. Mutual understanding and appreciation of each other's viewpoints and concerns is urged. Three illustrations are given of decision making problems. The discrepancies between the conclusions of a Planning Programming and Budgeting Study on perinatal services, and the policies actually adopted, are analysed. Problems of defining and evaluating the benefits of a health campaign are identified in analysing the treatment of arterial hypertension. Health examination programmes are used to illustrate the development of a decision making process and the respective parts played by the social partners involved.

750 SPRI (1973) Programme Budgeting in Public Health Care — A Feasibility Study (*Programbudgetering inom sjukvården — an förstudie*), Stockholm: The Swedish Planning and Rationalization Institute for the Health and Social Services (SPRI Report 9/73), 35 pp

Rapidly rising costs of public health care in Sweden make it urgently necessary to consider economic and administrative reforms in the public health care sector. SPRI therefore decided to study the validity of programme budgeting in public health care, and did a feasibility study with the Malmöhus County Council. The issues considered in the study involve the background and concepts in programme budgeting, and an outline of conceivable applications. Diseases of the locomotor system serve as an illustration.

1974

751 BUHAUG, H. (1974) Planning and Control Systems in Health Care (*Planleggings og styringssystemer i helsevesenet*), Trondheim: Norsk Institutt for Sykehusforskning, 52 pp. (mimeographed document).

A general introduction to an investigation of the use of new planning and control systems in health care, in Norway.

752 LEMPERS, F.B. (1974) A Health Care Model for the Netherlands (*Een model voor de gezondheidszorg in Nederland*), The Hague: Centraal Planbureau, 43 pp.

This paper outlines an econometric model of the Dutch health care system. The model consists of three parts: a set of equations describing the flow of patients through the system; manpower aspects; and price equations. The paper is theoretical and is intended to provide a framework for empirical research.

753 POLDERMANS, J.D.G. (1974) 'Some remarks on the implications for future health care facility needs of the latest population forecast in 1973' ('Enige opmerkingen inzake de toekomstige behoefte aan enkele voorzieningen in de gezondheidszorg, mede aan de hand van de nieuwste bevolkingsprognose 1973'), *Tijdschrift voor Sociale Geneeskunde*, **52**, 20, 715–19; **52**, 21, 761–5, and **52**, 22, 833–8.

The author analyses the implications of the 1973 population forecast for the planning of general and special hospitals, manpower, financing, and compulsory and optional health insurance in the Netherlands.

754 SPRI (1974) Economic forecast models for health services (*Ekonomiska prognosmodeller för sjukvården*), Stockholm: The Swedish Planning and Rationalization Institute of the Health and Social Services (SPRI Report 11/74), 41 pp.

Describes the SPRI model for cost calculation in long-term health care planning. The model aims to indicate the resource requirements of the proposed health care organization, and to determine the financial implications. It uses projected estimates of the staff necessary to realize the objectives of the health care plans. The average salary for different staff categories is determined, and the cost of the staff plan as a whole is calculated. Other types of costs are calculated as percentage increments of the total wage amount. It is proposed that calculations be performed in two steps, with different price assumptions: in unchanged (fixed) prices, and in current (rising) prices. This makes it possible to separate volume effects from price effects in the evaluation of cost trends. The report proposes that the financial calculation be extended to include capital expenditure, and describes a general model in which capital expenditures are financed to some extent by new loans, depreciation, and additional tax financing, with the option of using alternative assumptions about the degree of self-financing.

267 VARIOUS AUTHORS (1974) Regional Hospital Planning (*Programmazione regionale ospedaliera*), Florence: Le Monnier, xiii + 223 pp.

783 WHO (1974) *New Approaches in Health Statistics*, Geneva: World Health Organization (Technical Report Series, No. 559), 40 pp.

755 WHO (1974) *Planning and Organization of Geriatric Services*, Geneva: World Health Organization (Technical Report Series, No. 548), 46 pp.

This report of a WHO Expert Committee reviews general issues in the organization of geriatric services. The number of elderly persons (over 60 years) is projected to double between 1970 and 2000, representing an increase from 8% to 9% of the world population. In the developing countries, the proportion of elderly persons would increase faster, from 5.4% to 7% over the same period; in these countries the problems of the elderly have received little attention, but are likely to be accentuated by rapid social change. The report identifies the health problems of the elderly, and argues that their needs are inadequately served by existing services. It emphasizes that efficient organization requires systematic planning and integration of geriatric services, and describes a model programme coordinating a general practitioner health centre and domiciliary, hospital, and community services.

1975

756 BAILEY, N.T.J. and THOMPSON, M. (eds) (1975) *Systems Aspects of Health Planning. Proceedings of the International Institute for Applied Systems Analysis (IIASA) Conference, Baden, Austria, August 20-22, 1974*, Amsterdam: North-Holland, 347 pp.

Systems analysis has different meanings for observers in different contexts. For the managers of complex health care systems, the discipline focuses upon ways of optimizing system operation. Among the several papers in this volume discussing such optimization, special emphasis is put on the information sub-system and the ways in which it should be structured to enhance overall system performance. Other papers define systems analysis following the International Institute for Applied Systems Analysis: the application of a rational way of thinking and of scientific methodology to resolve complex decision problems. They cover such problems as: determining the proper supply of acute care hospital beds, improving guidance of biomedical research, and evaluating possible large-scale screening programmes. Three papers show the potential of econometric regression analysis: one in identifying the minimal information set needed for health planning, a second for aid in modelling a national health care system, and a third in resolving a difficult question on the cumulative effects of health care expenditures. The role of precise numerical modelling is displayed and discussed in a number of problem-oriented papers. Others emphasize the role of scientifically based projections and of prognosis in health planning.

757 BROOKE, E.M. (1975) 'Planning for mental health statistics, Basic document', *World Health Statistics Report*, **28**, 2, 77-87.

This paper argues the need for international planning of functional, rather than (existing) descriptive, mental health statistics, in order to improve the planning of mental health services. It compares the advantages and disadvantages of two alternative approaches: the use of existing statistics, and the execution of special studies of specific topics. It discusses the difficulties peculiar to mental health statistics, and concludes with a series of proposals for the collection and dissemination of mental health statistics.

758 MERAUD, J. (1975) 'Report of the Committee on 'Social Inequalities'. Preparation of the Preliminary Orientation of the VIIth Plan' (*Rapport de la Commission "Inégalités Sociales". Préparation de l'orientation préliminaire du VIIe Plan*), Paris: La Documentation Française, 114 pp.

A report on social inequalities, introducing preliminary directives for the VIIth plan, including several chapters on health and physicians. It discusses the need for change in the allocation of resources, to achieve a more egalitarian geographic distribution of services in France. Differences in health insurance provisions lead to unequal provision of health care. It is argued that the question of the beneficiary's contribution ('ticket modérateur') must be considered, as well as the development of medico-social prevention. It is proposed that the improvement of working conditions, and the tracing of occupational diseases, be taken up by the social security. The report also considers social inequalities due to differences in income, and the need to analyse the redistributive effect of social transfers. For example, it recommends the revision of a minimum old-age pension, the abolition of unwarranted charges borne by the general social security system, and the gradual removal of a ceiling for employers' health insurance contributions, with a view to the long-term removal of a ceiling on the financing of benefits in kind.

759 MOE, T. (1975) 'Programme analysis as a step in further development of a governmental planning and budget system' ('Programanalyser som et ledd i den videre utvikling av statens planleggings- og budsjettsystem'), *Sosialøkonomen*, **29**, 3, 40–8.

In 1974, the Norwegian government proposed a budget reform including programme budgeting. Some features of a programming system are discussed in connection with examples from health care, in particular the treatment of tuberculosis.

634 REXED, B (1975) 'How Sweden plans for the 1980s' in: EHRLICH, D.A. (ed.) *The Health Care Cost Explosion: Which Way now?*, Berne: Hans Huber Verlag, 67–82.
See 26.

760 WHO (1975) *European Conference on the Planning of a National Health Service (Bucharest, March 1974),* Copenhagen: World Health Organization, Regional Office for Europe (EURO 4107), 72 pp.

Report of a conference attended by representatives of 25 countries in the European region. Key aspects of provincial health planning systems in three countries (Austria, the Federal Republic of Germany, and the USSR) are very briefly reviewed. The key elements in the planning process are outlined, and its scope and perspective discussed, in different planning contexts. Next, some of the practical requirements for planning are considered, including: organizational arrangements; participation by the health professions, other disciplines, and the public; information requirements; techniques; limitations; and evaluation. Training and research are then discussed, and conclusions and recommendations are made on the above aspects. Of the six annexes, four are technical papers: two on health planning in general, one on planning techniques, and one on education and training for planning.

787 WHO (1975) *Organization of Mental Health Services in Developing Countries*, Geneva: World Health Organization (Technical Report Series, No. 564), 41 pp.

559 WORLD BANK (1975) *Health, Sector Policy Paper*, Washington, DC: World Bank, 83 pp. Reproduced in: WORLD BANK (1975) *The Assault on World Poverty: Problems of Rural Development, Education and Health*, Baltimore: Johns Hopkins University Press, 343–425.

1976

57 GILLIAND, P. (ed.) (1976) Medical Demography in Switzerland. Public Health Care and Prospects 1900–1974–2000 (*Démographie médicale en Suisse, santé publique et prospective 1900–1974–2000*), Lausanne: Office de Statistique de l'Etat de Vaud, 290 pp.

761 JØRGENSEN, E. et al. (1976) 'Long-term health policy' ('Langsigtet sundhedspolitik), *Ugeskrift for Læger*, **138**, 49, 3133–58.

At the annual meeting of the Danish Medical Association, discussions took place on the setting of long-term priorities, both within the health care sector and between the health care sector and other social sectors. It was generally agreed that greater emphasis should be placed on preventive services within and outside the health care sector, and that changes in health services should be considered in a long-term perspective.

795 KLECZKOWSKI, B.M. and PIBOULEAU, R. (eds) (1976) *Approaches to Planning and Design of Health Care Facilities in Developing Areas* (Vol. I), Geneva: World Health Organization (Offset Publication, No. 29), 145 pp.

762 LUCIONI, C. (1976) 'Reflections on a seminar on the utility of social indicators as guidelines in decision making in health care policies' ('Considerazioni a proposito di un Seminario sugli Indicatori Sociali quali strumento di orientamento delle scelte di politica sanitaria'), *Epidemiologia e prevenzione*, **1**, 0, 54–6.

Reports the main conclusions of a seminar on social indicators, organized by the Institute for Research in Health Economics, in Milan. The following themes were considered: need; expressed demand and social indicators; the filter function of social indicators and 'social validation of demand'; social indicators and information systems; limitations of health registers; social indicators and the 'quality of life'; social indicators and planning; social indicators and participation.

763 MAHLER, H. (1976) 'The application of economic techniques to health planning, and its limits' ('Le recours aux techniques économiques en planification sanitaire et ses limites') in: RIGONI, R. (ed.) Health Economics, Proceedings of a Workshop, Coppet, 4 October 1975 (*Economie de la santé. Compte rendu d'un colloque, Coppet, 4 octobre 1975*), Geneva: Sandoz Institute for Health and Socio-Economic Studies, 18–27.

In this paper, the WHO Director-General stresses the importance of an interdisciplinary and multi-sectoral approach to studies that will have to be undertaken on a very large scale. The health planner will increasingly have to take into account education, environmental protection, energy production, agriculture, and other essential elements in seeking to preserve the health of mankind.
See 38.

764 SPRI (1976) *Health service chiefs' plans up to 1985: comparison in figures*, Stockholm: The Swedish Planning and Rationalization Institute of the Health and Social Services (SPRI Report, No. 5), 156 pp.

A homogeneous data base covering strategic decisions on the provision of services for general sick care, mental health and handicap, and dental care, as envisaged by health service chiefs. Compilation by SPRI (the Swedish Planning and Rationalization Institute of the Health and Social Services), the Department of Social Security, and the Association of Regional Councils.

765 SPRI (1976) *Hospital Buildings 3. Cost Projection Method. Linear Regression Analysis*, Stockholm: The Swedish Planning and Rationalization Institute of the Health and Social Services (SPRI Report 10/76), 21 pp.

The report presents an improved cost projection method, intended primarily for use in the early stages of planning the construction of hospitals and other closely related health and social service institutions. It is more accurate than the standard methods of early cost estimation based on average cost per unit of floor area, which tend to provide only gross estimates. The new formula is the result of linear regression analysis of data from approximately 200 hospitals and health and social service institutions, completed in Sweden during the years 1966–72. Tested on data not included in the original data base, it was not particularly efficient when applied to small, specialized institutions. The report concludes with an applied example demonstrating the use of the method.

766 WHO (1976) *Planning and Evaluation of Public Dental Health Services*, Geneva: World Health Organization (Technical Report Series, No. 589), 35 pp.

In different countries economic, social, and political structures, as well as structures and mechanisms for dealing with health matters, are in different stages of development. Moreover, many countries accept the concept and value of national health planning, but few actually carry it out effectively. While recognizing that existing health planning systems vary, this report by a WHO Expert Committee notes that there are certain specific principles and steps in planning that are applicable to almost all situations, regardless of the political and social situation, and that these should be applied.

767 WHO (1976) *Planning and Organization of Services for Alcoholism and Drug Dependence*, Copenhagen: World Health Organization. Regional Office for Europe, 49 pp.

The Mental Health Unit of the WHO Regional Office for Europe has devoted special attention to activities relating to problems of alcohol and drug dependence. The Office's long-term programme in mental health, approved by the WHO Regional Committee, includes activities related to these problems every year from 1971 to 1980. Epidemiology is of major interest because of its importance to aetiology and prevention, but treatment, rehabilitation, and prevention have also received much attention. In 1975, scheduled activities included a symposium on the planning and organization of services for alcoholism and drug dependence. This report presents the deliberations of the symposium. The meeting, held in Albi, France, was attended by 37 participants from 22 countries, including staff of WHO Headquarters and the Regional Office for Europe, and representatives of the United Nations Division of Social Affairs, the World Psychiatric Association, and the International Council on Alcohol and Addictions. Participants included public health administrators, psychiatrists, nurses, social workers, psychologists, and sociologists. The purpose of the meeting was to consider the nature and extent of information required to plan and organize a range of services for the prevention of alcohol and drug dependence, to examine the experience derived from current service programmes, and to identify trends and directions for future planning.

796 WHO (1976) *Use of Operational Research in European Health Services*, Copenhagen: World Health Organization, Regional Office for Europe, 68 pp.

1977

768 DAHLBERG, L. (1977) 'A simple model for planning short-term inpatient medical care' in: DAHLBERG, L., *Empirical Studies in Public Planning*, Gothenburg: University of Gothenburg, Department of Economics (PhD thesis, memorandum No. 67), 23 pp. Also published in Swedish: (1975) 'En enkel modell för planering av den slutna akutsjukvårdens produktion', *Sosialøkonomen*, **29**, 5, 21-31.

A model for planning short-term inpatient medical care is presented. The individual clinic is treated as a production unit, which produces different kinds of treated ward cases with a given production technique. The model seeks to maximize the yearly number of treated ward cases, subject to three constraints: the yearly demand for different kinds of treated ward cases, which is assumed to be proportional to the number of citizens within the clinic's catchment population; the yearly budget assigned by public authorities, which has to cover all costs as medical care is supplied free of charge; and the clinic's physical capacity, measured by the number of beds. The model has been applied to the specialty of internal medicine, using the production-cost structure estimated for an existing clinic.

769 FRANCE, G. (1977) 'Social Statistics' ('Statistiche sociali'), *Epidemiologia e prevenzione*, **1**, 1, 71–4.

The attention of researchers in the area of social policy has recently been directed toward the definition of three interrelated phases of investigation; the construction of socio-economic accounts, the development of social indicators, and the collection of social data. The publication in Italy of the volume 'Statistiche Sociali', by the Istituto Centrale di Statistica, falls into this third phase. The author critically examines the contents of this volume, testing the statistics presented for relevance with respect to four categories of indicators that are considered central in the formulation and evaluation of a social programme: informative, predictive, evaluative, and problem-oriented indicators.

770 GILLIAND, P. (1977) Public Health Planning — A Few Plausible Bases and Trends (*Planification de santé publique — Quelques bases et tendances plausibles*), Aarau: Institut Suisse des Hôpitaux (Cahier d'études, No. 5), 99 pp.

An up-to-date summary of the author's preceding works. He has tried to assemble the data needed for the establishment of a practical system of public health planning in Switzerland. In addition to many tables and graphs, he gives his views about the problems involved in public health planning, points out

plausible trends and long-term prospects, and concludes by suggesting a 'scenario' for the target period 1990–2000.
See 50, 57.

534 SCHICKE, R.K. (1977) Preventive Medicine: Costs and Benefits (*Präventiv-Medizin: Kosten und Nutzen*), Bonn–Bad Godesberg: Friedrich-Thieding-Stiftung des Hartmannbundes, (Verband der Ärzte Deutschlands, Schriftenreihe), 55 pp.

771 VARIOUS AUTHORS (1977) A New Model for Health and Social Services (*Un nuovo modello per i servizi socio-sanitari*), Potenza: Regione Basilicata, Dipartimento Sicurezza Sociale, 454 pp.

Results of pilot research projects on the organization of health and social services in the southern Italian region of Basilicata, conducted by SAGO (Sistema Automatico Governo Organizzazione Sanitaria) and funded by the Ministry of Budget and Economic Planning and the Basilicata regional government. The coordinators were B. Angeletti, A. Brenna, A. Cappelli, O. Carnevali, I. Nicoletti, S. Paderni, and F. Tavazza. The volume is divided into five parts: demographic and economic factors that influence the health needs of the population; analysis of the various levels of government involved in the planning process, including the functions and territories of these levels and their planning procedures; the tools for constructing a new model of health and social services; application of the new model to the Basilicata region; and priority measures aimed at building up the new service.

772 VUORI, H. (1977) 'The use of automated health information systems in the management and planning of health services', *Public Health*, **9**, 1, 33–43.

The term 'health information system' is often used without a clear definition of its objectives, components, and area of application. This paper reviews the types and major uses of systems designed for collecting, processing, analysing, and distributing information required for organizing and operating health services. Theoretical considerations based on information theory, systems theory, and the prevailing planning ideology for the development of the data base of such systems, as well as practical guidelines for the inclusion of specific data items into the data base, are presented.

773 WHITE, K.L., ANDERSON, D.O., KALIMO, E., KLECZKOWSKI, B.M., PUROLA, T., and VUKMANOVIC, C. (1977) *Health Services: Concepts and Information for National Planning and Management*, Geneva: World Health Organization (Public Health Papers, No. 67), 117 pp.

This paper presents and discusses the principal conceptual, empirical, and methodological findings of the WHO International Collaborative Study of Medical Care Utilization. Its central purpose is to propose and illustrate useful approaches to the need for information appropriate to the planning and management of health services. The WHO study collected comparative data on indicators of perceived need, resource availability, and resource use in 12 study areas in 7 countries, in 1968–69. On the basis of this study, the authors propose key analytical areas in health care planning: the balance between needs, resources, and use; substitution among resource inputs; productivity of health care systems; identification of target groups and unmet need. The concluding chapter proposes a set of guiding principles in health care planning, chief among which is that data should be population-based rather than institution-based.

1978

596 BRÜGGEMANN, J., SCHWEFEL, D., and ZÖLLNER, H. (1978) Need and Planning in the Health Care System. An International Collection of Articles (*Bedarf und Planung im Gesundheitswesen. Eine internationale Aufsatzsammlung*), Cologne: Deutscher Ärzte-Verlag, 269 pp.

145 VAN DER GAAG, J. (1978) *An Econometric Analysis of the Dutch Health Care System*, Leiden: Rijksuniversiteit, Economisch Instituut (PhD. thesis), 180 pp.

VII Utilization and Management Studies

1968

774 VAN LOON, P.C.J. (1968) 'Modern social health care' ('*Moderne maatschappelijke gezondheidszorg*'), in: HORNSTRA, R. (1968) Social Health Care in Perspective (*Maatschappelijke gezondheidszorg in perspectief*), Assen: Koninklijke Van Gorcum, 227–45.

The tendency of health economics to concern itself with the existing situation, and with macro rather than micro questions, leads to a neglect of preventive action. Further it tends to be concerned only with the efficiency of hospital care, despite its diminishing marginal productivity in improving the health status of the population. Training of medical and auxiliary personnel in unlimited numbers, has caused medical over-consumption, especially in sectors with sophisticated clinical care. Other sectors are understaffed because the relevant indicators are insufficiently amenable to economic analysis.

1969

85 KALIMO, E. (1969) Determinants of Medical Care Utilization (*Lääkintäpalvelusten käyttöön vaikuttavat tekijät*), Helsinki: The Social Insurance Institution, Research Institute for Social Security, 253 pp.

1970

733 WHO (1970) *National Environmental Health Programmes: Their Planning, Organization and Administration*, Geneva: World Health Organization (Technical Report Series, No. 439), 56 pp.

1971

775 LEVY-LAMBERT, H. and GUILLAUME, H. (1971) Rationalization of Budgetary Choices (*Rationalisation des choix budgétaires*), Paris: Presses Universitaires de France (Collection L'Economiste), 213 pp.

Chapter VII of this book deals particularly with public health care (pp. 160–77). It quotes and summarizes the Planning Programming and Budgeting System applied to health services in France, including: the treatment of fractures in two public assistance wards in Paris, mass BCG vaccination of persons under 25 years of age, systematic screening for cervical cancer, and a study of perinatality.

420 WHO (1971) *Statistical Indicators for the Planning and Evaluation of Public Health Programmes*, Geneva: World Health Organization (Technical Report Series, No. 472), 40 pp.

1972

776 LACRONIQUE, J.F. (1972) 'Data processing, health, and economics' ('Informatique, santé et économie'), *Cahiers de Sociologie et de Démographie Médicales*, **12**, 1, 36–8.

Discusses the dissemination of technical progress in the health care field, particularly the special features of the development of medico-hospital data processing. The author defines the field of application of computers in health matters, and gives statistics concerning equipment that show the scope of the trend towards automation in hospitals. A complex administrative apparatus is responsible for developing this new specialty. The author finds that there is competition between various pressure groups that are active in the health care field.

777 SMEDBY, B., KJELLSTRÖM, T., and BERFENSTAM, R. (1972) The Utilization of Hospital Care (*Sjukhusvårdens konsumenter*), Stockholm: The Swedish Planning and Rationalization Institute of the Health and Social Services (SPRI Report 18/72), 69 pp.

This study uses person-based statistics, to investigate how different people utilized hospital care from 1965 to 1968 in the Uppsala region. To describe the effect of linking different stays referring to the same person, the number of discharges per person is calculated for different sub-groups. This number increases with age and is higher for men than for women. The use of hospital care is shown to be highly skewed. A small group of patients (0.4% accumulated more than two years in hospital and used 20% of the total number of bed-days. A group of heavy users of hospital care were subject to particular investigation.

745 WHO (1972) *Health Planning and Organization of Medical Care*, Copenhagen: World Health Organization, Regional Office for Europe (Public Health in Europe Series, No. 1), 131 pp.

1973

618 GOSLINGA, S.S. (1973) Light and Patchwork. The Organization and Working of Health Care in the Netherlands (*Licht op de Lappendeken. Organisatie en werking van de gezondheidszorg in Nederland*), The Hague: Centraal Planbureau, 532 pp.

778 GRUNDY, F. and REINKE, W.A. (1973) *Health Practice Research and Formalized Managerial Methods*, Geneva: World Health Organization (Public Health Papers, No. 51), 193 pp.

This paper reviews a wide range of quantitative techniques applicable to the planning and management of health services. Following an introductory discussion of basic concepts and terminology, the paper describes and illustrates the major techniques of operational research: inventory modelling, scheduling, linear programming, estimation, regression and correlation analysis, queuing theory, simulation, decision analysis, and dynamic programming. It then presents illustrative applications of quantitative techniques to specific problems: health care in the community, hospital service utilization and planning, resource allocation in disease control (typhoid, tuberculosis, and cholera), health manpower requirements, and work study (in hospitals). The concluding chapter discusses the need for training health professionals in quantitative methods. An annotated bibliography of relevant sources is included.

779 KOHLER, F. (1973) 'The economic and organizational aspects of health care in Europe and their influence on hospital management', *Hospital and Health Services Review*, **69**, 8, 296–302.

Aspects of hospital services in some European countries are briefly outlined, including: the total health care system of the Eastern European countries, the nationalized British system, the socialized Swedish system, and the centralized

French system. Some middle-of-the-road countries are Austria, the Federal Republic of Germany, and Switzerland.

1974

780 BAINBRIDGE, J. and SAPIRIE, S. (1974) *Health Project Management: A manual of procedures for formulating and implementing health projects*, Geneva: World Health Organization (Offset Publication, No. 12), 280 pp.

This manual is intended 'to offer health planners and administrators a set of procedures for managing . . . health projects'. It presents the health project management method, developed by a project systems analysis team established in 1970 by the World Health Organization. Part I describes the project formulation procedures designed for use in the planning stage of health projects. Part II presents the project implementation procedures, designed to be used when the projects are actually being carried out.

781 BORGENHAMMAR, E. and MARGUELIS, A. (1974) To Organize Care (*Att organisera vård*), Stockholm: Natur och Kultur, 272 pp.

This book is intended as a text on medical care administration. A description of the organization of health services in Sweden, at both micro and macro levels, is combined with a discussion of problems of medical care administration. What are the determinants of the demand for medical care? How can need for medical care be assessed? The chapter on health economics consists mainly of a description of the budget process for a county council. A chapter on manpower, which accounts for 70% of the costs of hospital care, points out that this factor has doubled between 1950 and 1970. It also describes the duties of different kinds of personnel in health services, and reviews questions about democracy and participation in decision making for different staff categories. The growth of administrative staff, and possible explanations for it, are discussed. According to official statistics, the number of administrative staff increased from 1,350 in 1950 to 4,300 in 1972, or from 1.7% to 2.2% of total health manpower. A concluding chapter discusses the future of medical care. Different models for planning are reviewed, and critical factors in future developments are pointed out. The authors forecast that a dramatic increase in the numbers of the aged, improved education, the fast growing public sector, urbanization, and changes in attitudes will have a great impact on medical care in the future.

371 DENMARK, GOVERNMENT OF (1974) Drug Distribution in Denmark (*Lægemiddeldistribution i Danmark*), Copenhagen: Statens Trykningskontor (Betænkning No. 725), 250 pp.

113 PUROLA, T., KALIMO, E., and NYMAN, K. (1974) *Health Services Use and Health Status under National Sickness Insurance*, Helsinki: The Social Insurance Institution, Research Institute for Social Security, 317 pp.

782 WHO (1974) *Modern Management Methods and the Organization of Health Services*, Geneva: World Health Organization (Public Health Papers, No. 55), 100 pp.

This paper is based on technical discussions at the 1973 World Health Assembly. An outline paper discusses the relevance of modern management techniques to the delivery of health services. Comments on the outline paper form the basis of a background paper, which discusses management problems experienced by member states. The technical discussions elaborate these themes, and conclude with recommendations for WHO support in the development of managerial skills.

783 WHO (1974) *New Approaches in Health Statistics*, Geneva: World Health Organization (Technical Report Series, No. 559), 40 pp.

This report of the Second International Conference of National Committees on Vital and Health Statistics discusses recent progress and future requirements in health statistics. It identifies significant progress in the previous 20 years in the collection of health manpower, health resource, and population statistics, but little progress in the collection of vital and health (morbidity) statistics, particularly in developing countries. It recommends that future work concentrate on meeting five basic requirements for internationally comparable statistics: health status indicators; health service utilization rates; health service resource availability; health care expenditure related to specific objectives; and demographic, social, and environmental data. The central theme is that health statistics must serve the planning and evaluation of health services, and it urges close cooperation between health statisticians and planners.

755 WHO (1974) *Planning and Organization of Geriatric Services*, Geneva: World Health Organization (Technical Report Series, No. 548), 46 pp.

1975

759 MOE, T. (1975) 'Programme analysis as a step in further development of a governmental planning and budget system' ('Programanalyser som et ledd i den videre utvikling av statens planleggings- og budsjettsystem'), *Sosialøkonomen*, **29**, 3, 40–8.

125 NYMAN, K. (1975) Dental Care Consumption and Dental Status (*Hammaslääkärin palvelusten käyttö ja hampaiden kunto*), Helsinki: The Social Insurance Institution, Research Institute for Social Security, 198 pp.

126 PRIMS, A. and QUAETHOVEN, P. (1975) 'The cost of medical and paramedical care. Scientific research methods and an outline of the basic statistical material' ('Le coût des soins médicaux et paramédicaux. Méthode de recherche scientifique avec indication du matériel statistique de base'), *Revue Belge de Sécurité Sociale*, **17**, 5, 432–593 and **17**, 6–7, 609–69.

287 RUTTEN, F.F.H., VAN DER GAAG, J., and VAN PRAAG, B.M.S. (1975) The Hospital in Health Care. An Econometric Analysis of the Use of Hospital Beds (*Het ziekenhuis in de gezondheidszorg*), Leiden: Stenfert Kroese b.v., 117 pp.

784 VAN DER GAGG, J., RUTTEN, F.F.H., and VAN PRAAG, B.M.S. (1975) 'Determinants of hospital utilization in the Netherlands', *Health Services Research*, **10**, 3, 264–77. Also: *An Inquiry into the Determinants of Hospital Utilization, with Reference to Government Intervention, The Dutch Case*, Leiden: Rijksuniversiteit Leiden, Economisch Instituut, 28 pp. (mimeographed document).

Hospital use in the Netherlands is examined in a cross-sectional analysis of 1969 and 1971 data for 120 service regions. Elasticities of admissions with respect to the supply of beds and of general practitioners are calculated, and the substitutability of first-level care (by general practitioners) for hospital care is considered. Substitution effects found indicate that the Dutch government's plan to reduce the ratio of hospital beds to population is feasible.

785 VERHEYEN, P.A. (1975) 'Hospital model or model hospital' ('Ziekenhuismodel of modelziekenhuis'), *Maandschrift Economie*, **40**, 1–2, 104–15.

This paper deals with management information system techniques. It shows how the input–output method can be used for hospital budgeting, and analyses criteria for defining hospital divisions. A mathematical model is described and its possible implementation discussed.

786 WHO (1975) *Health Services in Europe*, second edition, Copenhagen: World Health Organization, Regional Office for Europe, 299 pp.

This volume provides an extensive survey of health services in the WHO European region. The first part describes recent developments in methods of public health administration, preventive services, the organization of medical care, and the role and training of health personnel. The second part describes the organization and financing of health services, and the supply and training of health personnel, in each of the member states in the early 1970s, and the international organizations concerned with health care in Europe. The final part presents comparative demographic, social, economic, health status, health manpower, hospital facilities, and utilization data for member states in or about 1970.

787 WHO (1975) *Organization of Mental Health Services in Developing Countries*, Geneva: World Health Organization (Technical Report Series, No. 564), 41 pp.

This report of a WHO Expert Committee reviews issues in the organization of mental health services in developing countries. It argues that mental disorders constitute a serious problem in developing countries, yet mental health receives low priority in the health care sector. Facilities and trained staff are scarce, and limited in coverage. The report emphasizes the need for rational planning in relation to specified objectives, and recommends that mental health services be decentralized and integrated into the general framework of health and welfare services.

1976

788 BLANPAIN, J.E. (1976) 'Survey of medical organization patterns in hospitals' ('Overzicht van samenwerkingsverbanden'), *Acta Hospitalia*, **16**, 1–2, 84–91.

The 'workshop' view of hospitals is responsible for the fact that physicians still perform in splendid isolation within them. Such transfer, of the outside 'solo practice' performance model to the in house structural design of hospitals, is subject to increasing pressure, aimed at integrating the activities of physicians into the overall organization of the hospital. Interdependence of physicians resulting from rapid development of medical specialization, and the need for continuity in patient care, demand an adequate organizational response, requiring individual physicians to cooperate and share responsibility in order to improve effectiveness and efficiency. Comprehensive medical staff organization, as an encompassing structural design and process, appears to deserve priority over *ad hoc* set-ups of specialists in the form of partnerships or special-purpose teams, both of which may be a threat to complete development of medical staff organization unless they are supported specifically by all medical staff members.

789 BLANPAIN, J.E., BROTHERSTON, J., CHAVES, M.M., et al. (1976) *Application of systems analysis to health management*, Geneva: World Health Organization (Technical Report Series, No. 596), 69 pp.

The systems approach to problem-solving has become well established in various economic enterprises and is being applied increasingly in government planning. WHO has carried out work in this field since 1970, in an effort to improve health management practice in member states and to link health planning more effectively with socio-economic development. A WHO Expert Committee, convened to review the work done during the first five years and to explore future lines of development, confirms the success of the WHO project, which has generated a useful set of procedures suitable for widespread application in member states. These procedures have helped national authorities to deal with the most pressing problem of contemporary health administration: the devising and managing of policies that utilize scarce resources to achieve the maximum impact on health status. The report gives a full account of the systems approach and of the history of the WHO project, and makes a number of suggestions for the further development of the subject in so far as it applies to health management. It also considers ways in which knowledge of systems analysis can be disseminated. WHO's contributions to the subject are described in an annex to the report, and two further annexes examine the development of WHO's procedures and the technique of cost-benefit analysis.

790 EMBRECHTS, G. (1976) Growth and Evolution of Hospital Organizations (*Groei en Evolutie van Ziekenhuisorganisaties*), Antwerp: Rijksuniversitair Centrum, Leerstoel Bijzondere Sociologie (thesis in applied economics), 220 pp.

The hospital is considered from different viewpoints: its relationship to society, legislation, and as a non-profit institution. The different types of hospital, and the health care system in which they operate, are surveyed. Analysis of changes in hospital organization is based on a literature review and on specific investigation of changes in four public hospitals in Antwerp, using annual reports and statistical data for the period 1969–75. Particular attention is given to the roles of various groups and to some recent trends in hospital organization.

791 HATTINGA-VERSCHURE, J.C.M. (1976) 'The influence of physician payment systems and medical staff organization on the quality of health care' ('Betekenis van betaalsystemen en samenwerkingsverbanden voor de kwaliteit van zorgen'), *Acta Hospitalia*, **16**, 1–2, 153–62.

The author distinguishes between two types of factors determining the quality of health care: those related to specific items of medical care, such as the physician's know-how, his manual skills, available time, technology, and personnel; and those related to the medical care process, such as indication for hospital admission, indication for specific items of medical care, and integrated care. In comparing a fee-for-service payment system with a salary system, the author argues that the former gives an incentive to maximise the number of services with a minimum use of time, technology, personnel, postgraduate training, etc., whereas the latter has the opposite effect. The author is convinced that, so far as the organizational aspects of medical work are concerned, a salary system has limited effects on the medical care process, whereas a fee-for-service system induces neglect of thorough assessment of indications for admission, or for specific items of care, and tends to bring about partnerships between two or three physicians at the expense of the overall medical staff organization.

792 HECKMAN, J. (1976) 'Payment systems and ethics' ('Betaalsystemen en ethica'), *Acta Hospitalia*, **16**, 1–2, 74–83.

Argues that the method of remuneration is immaterial to the physician, since it does not detrimentally affect the physician–patient relationship. Whatever the system, it should provide for a satisfactory quality of health care, protection of patients against excessive fees, and adequate remuneration for the physician. Medical ethics and deontology are determined to a considerable extent by influences exercised by society, and the autonomy of the medical profession rests essentially on a mandate given by society. Because of the trust bestowed on them, physicians are committed to take the initiative in eliminating any abuse of the remuneration system provided for them, though abuse is a marginal phenomenon inherent in any payment system. Possible forms of abuse in different payment systems do not therefore necessarily affect the choice of a payment system as such.

793 HERDER-DORNEICH, P. (1976) Expansion of costs in the health services and their steering (*Die Kostenexpansion und ihre Steuerung im Gesundheitswesen*). Cologne: Deutscher Ärzte-Verlag (Zentralinstitut für die Kassenärztliche Versorgung in der Bundesrepublik Deutschland, Vol. IV), 212 pp. Also appears under the title: Growth and Equilibrium in the Health Sector (*Wachstum und Gleichgewicht im Gesundheitswesen*), Opladen: Westdeutscher Verlag (1977).

The author analyses the health service cost increases in the Federal Republic of Germany, and proposes steering mechanisms at the 'middle level' to contain such increases. A special role in such endeavours is allotted to cooperation between physicians' organizations on the one hand, and health insurance funds on the other.

794 ILO (1976) *The Organization of Occupational Health Services in Developing Countries*, Geneva: International Labour Office (Occupational Safety and Health Series, No. 7), 187 pp.

The first part of this volume reports on discussions of the fifth session of the joint ILO/WHO Committee on Occupational Health (1966), in four areas of occupational health in developing countries: existing resources for the protection of workers' health, basic needs and special problems of the developing countries, characteristics and functions of occupational health services, and the role of paramedical and auxiliary personnel. The second part contains related papers by individual contributors, under the following title headings: scope for occupational health services in developing countries; specific factors influencing industrial health and its practice in developing countries; some practical considerations in the organization of industrial hygiene programmes in developing countries; the present state of organization of occupational health services in Nigeria, as an example of a developing country; and occupational health for developing countries.

795 Kleczkowski, B.M. and Pibouleau, R. (eds) (1976) *Approaches to Planning and Design of Health Care Facilities in Developing Areas* (Vol. I), Geneva: World Health Organization (Offset Publication, No. 29), 145 pp.

This collection is the first of a series planned to discuss aspects of the planning and design of health care facilities appropriate to developing countries. It contains five papers by individual contributors, under the following title headings: the importance of legislation and administration for medical care facilities, with special reference to developing countries; the rôle of area-wide planning and functional programming in the planning process of medical care; rationalization of planning and construction of medical care facilities in developing countries; advanced building techniques and their utilization in developing countries; and the influence of climate on buildings.

195 May, A.R. (1976) *Mental Health Services in Europe. A Review of Data Collected in Response to a WHO Questionnaire*, Geneva: World Health Organization (Offset Publication, No. 23), 59 pp.

135 Prims, A. and Quaethoven, P. (1976) 'Analysis of factors determining the consumption of medical care' ('Analyse des facteurs qui déterminent la consommation des soins'), *Gestions Hospitalières*, No. 159, 761–74.

767 WHO (1976) *Planning and Organization of Services for Alcoholism and*

Drug Dependence, Copenhagen: World Health Organization, Regional Office for Europe, 49 pp.

796 WHO (1976) *Use of Operational Research in European Health Services*, Copenhagen: World Health Organization, Regional Office for Europe, 68 pp.

This paper contains a report of a working group convened by the WHO Regional Office for Europe to examine the use of operational research in European health services. It considers: the nature of operational research; application of operational research in the health services; the context and role of operational research; education and training. The annexes contain papers on the development of mass screening in Romania, the development of resources and services for the long-term care of the elderly; the use of hospital beds and the factors influencing hospital costs; the conceptual basis of a model for the optimization of a regional public health service; and the relationship between the policy maker and the operational research scientist.

1977

773 WHITE, K.L., ANDERSON, D.O., KALIMO, E., KLECZKOWSKI, B.M., PUROLA, T., and VUKMANOVIC, C. (1977) *Health Services: Concepts and Information for National Planning and Management*, Geneva: World Health Organization (Public Health Papers, No. 67), 117 pp.

List of Journals and Periodicals

Acta Hospitalia
Acta Medica Scandinavica
Acta Universitatis Tamperensis
Analyse et Prévisions
Annales de la Société Belge de Médecine Tropicale
Arbeit und Sozialpolitik
Archiv for Pharmaci og Kemi
Archives Belges de Médecine Sociale, Hygiène, Médecine du Travail et Médecine Légale
Arzt und Krankenhaus

Basler sozialökonomische Studien
Beiträge zur Wirtschafts- und Sozialpolitik
Bild der Wissenschaft
Bolletino dell'Economia Pubblica (Economia Pubblica)
British Journal of Preventive and Social Medicine (Journal of Epidemiology and Community Health)
Bulletin de l'Institut National de la Santé et de la Recherche Médicale
Bulletin des Statistiques de Santé et de Sécurité Sociale
Bulletin of the World Health Organization
Bulletin Trimestriel de l'Ecole Nationale de la Santé Publique
Bundesarbeitsblatt
Bundesgesundheitsblatt

Cahiers d'Etudes de l'Institut Suisse des Hôpitaux
Cahiers de Sociologie et de Démographie Médicales
Cahiers du Séminaire d'Econométrie
Colloques de l'INSERM
Community Dentistry and Oral Epidemiology
Concours Médical
Consommation

Das Öffentliche Gesundheitswesen
Das Schweizer Spital — L'Hôpital Suisse
Der Deutsche Arzt
Der Landarzt (Zeitschrift für Allgemeinmedizin)
Der Praktische Arzt
Deutsche Apotheker Zeitung
Deutsches Aerzteblatt
Die Medizinische Welt

Die Ortskrankenkasse
Die Weltwirtschaft
Droit Social

Economia e Lavoro
Economia Pubblica (*Bolletino dell'Economia Pubblica*)
Economie et Humanisme
Economie et Santé
Economie et Sociétés
Economie et Statistique
Economisch-Statistische-Berichten
Ekonomisk Debatt
Epidemiologia e Prevenzione

Fra Sundhedsstyrelsen
Furtibles 2000 (*Futuribles*)

Geburtshilfe, Frauenheilkunde
Gestions Hospitalières

Health Services Research
Het Ziekenhuis
Heures de France
Hospital and Health Services Review (*The Hospital*)

ILO Occupational Safety and Health Series
ILO Studies and Reports Series
In Zet (*Ziekenfondsgids*)
International Journal of Health Services
International Labour Review

Jahrbuch für Sozialwissenschaften
Journal de la Société de Statistiques de Paris
Journal of Epidemiology and Community Health (*British Journal of Preventive and Social Medicine*)

Kansantaloudellinen Aikakauskirja
Kölner Schriften zur Sozialwissenschaftlichen Forschung
Kontakten/Contacts
Krankenhaus-Umschau
Krankenpflege — Soins Infirmiers (*Revue Suisse des Infirmières*)

L'Evolution Médicale
L'Hôpital et l'Aide Sociale à Paris
L'Industria
La Documentation Française

La Revue Nouvelle
Läkartidningen
Landstingens Tidskrift
Le Scienze
Les Cahiers Français

Maandblad voor Accountancy en Bedrijfshuishoudkunde
Maandschrift Economie
Médecins de Groupe
Medicinsk Forum
Medisch Contact
Medizin, Mensch, Gesellschaft
Methods of Information in Medicine

Nationaløkonomisk Tidsskrift
Niedersächsiches Ärzteblatt
Nordisk Medicin
Notes et Etudes Documentaires

Orientation Mutualiste
Ospedali d'Italia
Österreichische Krankenhaus-Zeitung

Pharma Dialog
Pharmazeutische Zeitung
Politische Rundschau — Revue Politique
Presse Médicale
Preventive Medicine
Prospective et Santé Publique
Prospettive Sociali e Sanitarie
Public Health

Relazioni Sociali
Research Series of the Center for Health Administration Studies, University of Chicago
Revue Belge de Sécurité Sociale
Revue d'Economie Politique
Revue d'Epidémiologie, Médecine Sociale et Santé Publique
Revue Economique
Revue Française d'Automatique, d'Informatique et de Recherche Opérationnelle (*Revue Française de Recherche Opérationnelle, Revue Française d'Informatique et de Recherche Opérationnelle, Revue Française d'Automatique, Informatique, Recherche Opérationnelle*)
Revue Française de Recherche Opérationnelle (Revue Française d'Automatique, d'Informatique et de Recherche Operationnelle)
Revue Française de Sociologie

Revue Française des Affaires Sociales
Revue Hospitalière de France
Revue Internationale de Sécurité Sociale
Revue Médicale de Bruxelles
Revue Suisse d'Economie Politique et de Statistique — Schweizerische Zeitschrift für Volkswirtschaft und Statistik
Revue Suisse des Infirmières (Krankenpflege — Soins Infirmiers)
Revue Trimestrielle de Droit Sanitaire et Social
Rivista degli Ospedali
Rivista di Diritto Finanziario e Scienza delle Finanze
Rivista di Economia e Politica Industriale
Rivista Internazionale di Scienze Economiche e Commerciali
Rivista Internazionale di Scienze Sociali

Scandinavian Journal of Rheumatology
Scandinavian Journal of Social Medicine
Schmollers Jahrbuch für Gesetzgebung, Verwaltung und Volkswirtschaft
Schriften der Gesellschaft für Sozialen Fortschritt
Schriften des Vereins für Sozialpolitik
Schriftenreihe Arbeitsmedizin, Sozialmedizin, Präventivmedizin
Schriftenreihe der Friedrich-Thieding-Stiftung des Hartmannbundes
Schriftenreihe des Instituts für Sozio-ökonomische Entwicklungsforschung
Schriftenreihe des Schweizerischen Krankenhausinstituts
Schriftenreihe Strukturforschung im Gesundheitswesen
Semaine des Hôpitaux
Social Science and Medicine
Socialmedicinsk Tidskrift
Socialt Tidsskrift
Sosiaalivakuutus
Sosialøkonomen
Soziale Sicherheit
Sozialer Fortschritt
Special Studies, Official Statistics of Finland
SPRI Reports
Statistics and Reviews, University of Kuopio
Statistiques et Etudes Financières
Studi Economici
Studien zur Wirtschafts- und Sozialforschung des Wirtschafts- und Sozialwissenschaftlichen Instituts des Deutschen Gewerkschaftsbundes

Tandlægebladet
Techniques Hospitalières
The Hospital (Hospital and Health Services Review)
Three Banks Review
Tidsskrift for Danske Sygehuse
Tiers-Monde

Tijdschrift voor Privaat Recht
Tijdschrift voor Sociale Geneeskunde

Ugeskrift for Læger

WHO Chronicle
WHO Non-Serial Publications
WHO Offset Publications
WHO Public Health in Europe Series
WHO Public Health Papers
WHO Technical Report Series
Wirtschaft und Statistik
Wirtschaftspolitische Blätter
World Health Statistics Reports

Zeitschrift für Allgemeinmedizin (*Der Landarzt*)
Ziekenfondsgids (In Zet)

List of Publishers, Editors, Journals, and Periodicals

Country name abbreviations;

A	Austria
B	Belgium
CH	Switzerland
D	Federal Republic of Germany
DK	Denmark
F	France
GB	Great Britain
I	Italy
N	Norway
NL	Netherlands
S	Sweden
SF	Finland
USA	United States of America

The addresses given in this index are current for 1979/80.

N.B. Where the place of publication cited in the reference differs from that given in the index, this may be due to:

(a) a change of address by the publisher (e.g., Athenäum Verlag moved from Frankfurt to Königstein);

(b) different addresses for the administrative office (cited in the index) and the registered office or printing works (cited in the reference) (e.g., Westdeutscher Verlag is registered and printed in Opladen, but its administrative office is in Wiesbaden);

(c) the exact postal address being given in the index whereas the main town is cited in the reference (e.g., Voorburg is a suburb of The Hague, and Sollentuna, Vällingby, and Solna are all suburbs of Stockholm).

Academic Press Inc.
24-28, Oval Road, GB–London NW1

Acta Hospitalia
Centrum voor Ziekenhuiswetenschap, 102, Decosterstraat, B–3000 Leuven

Acta Medica Scandinavica
Almqvist & Wiksell, Box 2102, S–103 13 Stockholm 2

Acta Universitatis Tamperensis
Tampere University, 4, Kalevantie, SF–33101 Tampere 10

ADVANCED SCHOOL FOR HOSPITAL ADMINISTRATION
See: Scuola Superiore di Disciplina e Tecnica dell' Amministrazione

ALFRED HÜTHIG VERLAG
315, Wilckenstrasse, Postfach 10 28 69, D–6900 Heidelberg 1

ALLIANCE NATIONALE DES MUTUALITÉS CHRÉTIENNES
121, rue de la Loi, B–1040 Bruxelles

ALLMÄNNA FÖRLAGET
c/o Liber Förlag AB, Fack, S–162 89 Vällingby

ALMQVIST & WIKSELL FÖRLAG AB
Box 2102, S–103 13 Stockholm 2

AMTSRÅDSFORENINGEN I DANMARK
10, Landemærket, DK–1119 København K

ANALYSE ET PRÉVISIONS
Société d'Etudes et de Documentation Economique, Industrielle et Sociale, 44, rue François ler, F–75008 Paris

ÅNDSSVAGEFORSORGEN SOCIALSTYRELSEN SAERFORSORGSAFDELINGEN
6, Kristineberg, DK—2100 København Ø

ANNALES DE LA SOCIETE BELGE DE MÉDECINE TROPICALE
J. Goemaere, 21, rue de la Limite, B–1030 Bruxelles

ANTONIO GIUFFRÈ EDITORE
2, Via Statuto, I–20121 Milano

ARBEIT UND SOZIALPOLITIK
21, Am Jägersteig, Postfach 547, D–4010 Hilden
Nomos Verlagsgesellschaft GmbH, 3-5, Waldseestrasse, Postfach 610, D–7570 Baden-Baden

ARCHIV FOR PHARMACI OG KEMI
Danmarks Apotekerforening, 14, Hammerichsgade, DK–1611 København K

ARCHIVES BELGES DE MÉDECINE SOCIALE, HYGIÈNE, MÉDECINE DU TRAVAIL ET MÉDECINE LÉGALE
Archives de Médecine Sociale et d'Hygiène, Cité administrative, 6, Quartier Esplanade, B–1010 Bruxelles

ARGUMENT VERLAG
6, Tegeler Strasse, D–1000 Berlin 65

ARMAND COLIN
103, Boulevard Saint-Michel, F–75005 Paris

ARNOLD BUSCKS BOGHANDEL
49, Koebmagergade, DK–1150 København K

ARSCIA UITGAVEN N.V.
Presses Académiques Européennes, 60, rue de l'Etuve, B–1000 Bruxelles

ARZT UND KRANKENHAUS
Verband der Leitenden Krankenhausärzte Deutschlands e.V., 9, Tersteegenstrasse, D–4000 Düsseldorf

ASSOCIATION DES CONSOMMATEURS
27, rue Royale, B–1000 Bruxelles

ASSOCIAZIONE PER L'INFORMAZIONE SANITARIA
24, Via XX Settembre, I–20123 Milano

ATHENÄUM VERLAG
2, Adelheidstrasse, Postfach 1220, D–6240 Königstein
(Formerly: Frankfurt)
AWE/GEBERS
Almqvist & Wiksell Förlag AB, Box 2120, S–103 13 Stockholm 2

BASLER SOZIALÖKONOMISCHE STUDIEN
Schulthess Polygraphischer Verlag A.G., 2, Zwingliplatz, CH–8001 Zürich
BECK-VERLAG
9, Wilhelmstrasse, Postfach 40 03 40, D–8000 München 40
BEITRÄGE ZUR WIRTSCHAFTS- UND SOZIALPOLITIK
Institut der Deutschen Wirtschaft, Abteilung Wirtschafts- und Sozialwissenschaften, 84-88, Oberländer Ufer, D–5000 Köln 51
BERGER-LEVRAULT
1, Avenue de l'Observatoire, F–75006 Paris
BERTELSMANN GMBH
1, Steinhauserstrasse, Postfach 80 03 60, D–8000 München 80
BERTELSMANN UNIVERSITÄTS-VERLAG
c/o Westdeutscher Verlag, 12-16, Gustav-Stresemann-Ring, Postfach 58 29, D–6200 Wiesbaden 1
(Formerly: D–4000 Düsseldorf)
BILD DER WISSENSCHAFT
121-125, Neckarstrasse, Postfach 209, D–7000 Stuttgart 1
Bollettino dell'Economia Pubblica
See: ECONOMIA PUBBLICA
(A.) BONNIERS FÖRLAG AB
Fack, S–191 20 Sollentuna
British Journal of Preventive and Social Medicine
See: JOURNAL OF EPIDEMIOLOGY AND COMMUNITY HEALTH
BRITISH MEDICAL ASSOCIATION
Tavistock House, Tavistock Square, GB–London WC1H 9JR
BULLETIN DE L'INSTITUT NATIONAL DE LA SANTÉ ET DE LA RECHERCHE MÉDICALE
Institut National de la Santé et de la Recherche Médicale, 101, rue de Tolbiac, F–75645 Paris Cedex 13
BULLETIN DES STATISTIQUES DE SANTÉ ET DE SÉCURITÉ SOCIALE
Ministère de la Santé et de la Sécurité Sociale, 8, Avenue de Ségur, F–75007 Paris

La Documentation Française, 31, Quai Voltaire, F–75340 Paris Cedex 07
BULLETIN OF THE WORLD HEALTH ORGANIZATION
World Health Organization, Avenue Appia, CH–1211 Genève 27
BULLETIN TRIMESTRIEL DE L'ECOLE NATIONALE DE LA SANTÉ PUBLIQUE
Avenue du Professeur-Léon-Bernard, F–35043 Rennes
BUND-VERLAG
46, Deutz-Kalker-Strasse, Postfach 21 01 40, D–5000 Köln 21

BUNDESARBEITSBLATT
Bundesministerium für Arbeit und Sozialordnung, 1, Rochusstrasse, D–5300 Bonn

BUNDESFACHVERBAND DER HEILMITTELINDUSTRIE
1, Breitestrasse, D–5000 Köln 1

BUNDESGESUNDHEITSBLATT
Bundesgesundheitsamt, 88-92, Thielallee, D–1000 Berlin 33

BUNDESMINISTERIUM FÜR ARBEIT UND SOZIALORDNUNG
1, Rochusstrasse, D–5300 Bonn

BUREAU UNIVERSITAIRE DE RECHERCHE OPÉRATIONNELLE
Faculté des Sciences, 9, Quai Saint-Bernard, F–75007 Paris

CAHIERS D'ETUDES DE L'INSTITUT SUISSE DES HÔPITAUX
Institut Suisse des Hôpitaux, 29, Bahnhofstrasse, CH–5001 Aarau

CAHIERS DE SOCIOLOGIE ET DE DÉMOGRAPHIE MÉDICALES
Centre de Sociologie et de Démographie Médicales, 60, Boulevard Latour-Maubourg, F–75007 Paris

CAHIERS DU SÉMINAIRE D'ECONOMÉTRIE
Editions du Centre National de la Recherche Statistique, 15, Quai Anatole-France, F–75007 Paris

CALMANN-LÉVY
3, rue Auber, F–75009 Paris

CAMPUS GMBH
65, Schumann Strasse, D–6000 Frankfurt 1

CENTRAAL BUREAU VOOR DE STATISTIEK
428, Prinses Beatrixlaan, NL–2270 Voorburg

CENTRAAL PLANBUREAU
14, Van Stolkweg, NL–Den Haag

CENTRAL COUNCIL FOR PUBLIC HEALTH OF THE NETHERLANDS
See: Centraale Raad voor de Volksgezondheid

CENTRAL OFFICE FOR STATISTICS OF THE NETHERLANDS
See: Centraal Bureau voor de Statistiek

CENTRAALE RAAD VOOR DE VOLKSGEZONDHEID
5, J.C. Van Markenlaan, P.B. 226, NL–2285 Rijswijk

CENTRE D'ETUDES PROSPECTIVES DE L'ECONOMIE MATHÉMATIQUE APPLIQUÉE A LA PLANIFICATION
142, rue du Chevaleret, F–75013 Paris

CENTRE DE RECHERCHE ECONOMIQUE SUR L'EPARGNE
45, Boulevard Vincent-Auriol, F–75013 Paris

CENTRE DE RECHERCHE POUR L'ETUDE ET L'OBSERVATION DES CONDITIONS DE VIE
45, Bd. Vincent-Auriol, F–75634 Paris Cedex 13
(Until July 1976: Centre de Recherches et de Documentation sur la Consommation)

CENTRE DE RECHERCHE SUR LE BIEN-ÊTRE
140, rue du Chevaleret, F–75013 Paris

CENTRE DE RECHERCHES ET DE DOCUMENTATION SUR LA CONSOMMATION
See: Centre de Recherche pour l'Etude et l'Observation des Conditions de Vie
CENTRE DE RECHERCHES MATHÉMATIQUES POUR LA PLANIFICATION
See: Centre d'Etudes Prospectives de l'Economie Mathématique Appliquée à la Planification
CENTRE DE SOCIOLOGIE ET DE DÉMOGRAPHIE MÉDICALES
60, Boulevard Latour-Maubourg, F–75007 Paris
CENTRE FOR PHARMACEUTICAL RESEARCH
See: Centro per Ricerce Farmaceutice
CENTRE INTERNATIONAL DE GÉRONTOLOGIE SOCIALE
3, Place des Etats-Unis, F–75013 Paris
CENTRE NATIONAL DE LA RECHERCHE SCIENTIFIQUE
15, Quai Anatole-France, F–75007 Paris
CENTRO PER RICERCE FARMACEUTICE
I–Roma
(This Centre no longer exists)
CENTRO ITALIANO PER LA RICERCA SANITARIA E SOCIALE
3, Piazza Gandhi, I–00144 Roma
CIACO
16 A, Parijsstraat, B–3000 Leuven
CLUB EUROPÉEN DE LA SANTÉ
9, Boulevard des Capucines, F–75002 Paris
COLLOQUES DE L'INSERM
Institut National de la Santé et de la Recherche Médicale, 101, rue de Tolbiac, F–75645 Paris Cedex 13
COLOMBO CURSI EDITORE
109, Via Vespucci, I–56100 Pisa
COMMISSION OF THE EUROPEAN COMMUNITIES, GENERAL DIRECTORATE OF SOCIAL AFFAIRS
200, rue de la Loi, B–1040 Bruxelles
COMMUNITY DENTISTRY AND ORAL EPIDEMIOLOGY
Munksgaard, 35, Noerre Soegade, DK–1370 København K
CONCOURS MÉDICAL
37, rue Bellefond, F–75441 Paris Cedex 09
CONFÉDÉRATION DES SYNDICATS MÉDICAUX FRANÇAIS
60, Boulevard Latour-Maubourg, F–75007 Paris
CONSOMMATION
Centre de Recherche pour l'Etude et l'Observation des Conditions de Vie, 45, Bd. Vincent-Auriol, F–75634 Paris Cedex 13
CUJAS
6, rue Victor-Cousin, F–75005 Paris

DALLOZ
11, rue Soufflot, F–75240 Paris Cedex 15
DANISH HOSPITAL INSTITUTE
10, Landemærket, DK–1119 København K

DANMARKS AMTSRÅD
10, Landemærket, DK–1119 København K
DAS ÖFFENTLICHE GESUNDHEITSWESEN
Georg Thieme Verlag, 63, Herdweg, Postfach 732, D–7000 Stuttgart 1
DAS SCHWEIZER SPITAL — L'HÔPITAL SUISSE
(Offizielles Organ der Vereinigung Schweizerischer Krankenhäuser)
Postfach 149, CH–5001 Aaran
DAUSSE
60, rue de la Glacière, F–75621 Paris Cedex 13
DEN ALMINDELIGE DANSKE LÆGEFORENING
12A, Kristianiagade, DK-2100 Kæbenhavn O
DÉPARTEMENT CANTONAL DE L'INTÉRIEUR, CANTON DE VAUD, SERVICE DE LA SANTÉ PUBLIQUE
4, Place du Château, CH–1005 Lausanne
DER BUNDESMINISTER FÜR ARBEIT UND SOZIALORDNUNG
1, Rochusstrasse, D–5300 Bonn
DER DEUTSCHE ARZT
(Die Zeitschrift des Hartmannbundes, Verband der Ärzte Deuschlands e.V.)
54, Godesberger Allee, D–5300 Bonn–Bad Godesberg
Der Landarzt
See: ZEITSCHRIFT FÜR ALLGEMEINMEDIZIN
DER PRAKTISCHE ARZT
Berufsverband der Praktischen Ärzte für Allgemeinmedizin Deutschlands e.V., 9, Belfortstrasse, D–5000 Köln 1
DEUTSCHE APOTHEKER ZEITUNG
Deutscher Apotheker Verlag, 44, Birkenwaldstrasse, D–7000 Stuttgart 1
DEUTSCHER ÄRZTE-VERLAG
2, Dieselstrasse, Postfach 40 04 40, D–5000 Köln 40
DEUTSCHER INSTITUTS-VERLAG GMBH
84-88, Oberländer Ufer, Postfach 51 06 70, D–5000 Köln 51
DEUTSCHES AERZTEBLATT
Bundesärztekammer und Kassenärztliche Bundesvereinigung, 5, Hädenkampstrasse, D–5000 Köln 41
DIE MEDIZINISCHE WELT
F.K. Schattauer Verlag, 3, Lenzhalde, Postfach 2945, D–7000 Stuttgart 1
DIE ORTSKRANKENKASSE
Bundesverband der Ortskrankenkassen, D–5300 Bonn-Bad Godesberg

Verlag der Ortskrankenkassen, 60, Euskirchener Strasse, Postfach 14 02 12, D–5300 Bonn-Endenich
DIE WELTWIRTSCHAFT
(Halbjahresschrift des Instituts für Weltwirtschaft an der Universität Kiel)
120-122, Düsternbrooker Weg, D–2300 Kiel

J.C.B. Mohr (Paul Siebeck), 18, Wilhelmstrasse, D–7400 Tübingen
DIRECTION DE LA SÉCURITÉ SOCIALE
Ministère de la Santé et de la Sécurité Sociale, 8, Avenue de Ségur, F–75007 Paris

DROIT SOCIAL
Librairie Sociale et Economique, 3, rue Soufflot, F–75005 Paris
DUNCKER & HUMBLOT
9, Dietrich-Schäfer-Weg, Postfach 41 03 29, D–1000 Berlin 41
DUNOD
17, rue Rémy-Dumoncel, F–75680 Paris Cedex 14

ECOLE NATIONALE DE LA SANTÉ PUBLIQUE
Avenue du Professeur-Léon-Bernard, F–35043 Rennes
ECOLE POLYTECHNIQUE, CENTRE DE RECHERCHES EN GESTION
17, rue Descartes, F–75005 Paris
ECONOMIA E LAVORO
48, Via Tevere, I–00198 Roma
ECONOMIA PUBBLICA
6, Via Fratelli Gabba, I–20133 Milano
(Until December 1969: *Bolletino dell'Economia Pubblica*)
ECONOMIC AND SOCIAL INSTITUTE OF THE GERMAN TRADE UNION CONGRESS
See: Wirtschafts- und Sozialwissenschaftliches Institut des Deutschen Gewerkschaftsbundes
ECONOMICS INSTITUTE, UNIVERSITÀ CATTOLICA DEL SACRO CUORE
5, Via Necchi, I–20100 Milano
ECONOMIE ET HUMANISME
99, Quai Clémenceau, F–69300 Caluire
ECONOMIE ET SANTÉ
(Supplément au *Bulletin des Statistiques de Santé et de Sécurité Sociale*)
Ministère de la Santé et de la Sécurité Sociale, 8, Avenue de Ségur, F–75007 Paris

La Documentation Française, 31, Quai Voltaire, F–75340 Paris Cedex 07
ECONOMIE ET SOCIÉTÉS
Cahiers de l'Institut des Sciences Mathématiques et Economiques Appliquées, 11, Boulevard de Sébastopol, F–75001 Paris
ECONOMIE ET STATISTIQUE
Institut National de la Statistique et des Etudes Economiques, 41, Quai Branly, F–75007 Paris
ECONOMISCH-STATISTISCHE-BERICHTEN
Stichting Nederlands Economisch Instituut, 50, Burgermeester Oudlaan, NL–Rotterdam
EDITIONS DE L'ASSISTANCE PUBLIQUE DE PARIS
3, Avenue Victoria, F–75004 Paris
EDITIONS DE L'UNIVERSITÉ DE BRUXELLES
Parc Léopold, B–1040 Bruxelles
EDITIONS DU SEUIL
27, rue Jacob, F–75261 Paris Cedex 06
EDITIONS MÉDICALES ET UNIVERSITAIRES
40, rue Pascal, F–75013 Paris

EDITIONS SANDOZ
14, Boulevard de Richelieu, F–92505 Rueil-Malmaison
EINAUDI EDITORE
1, Via Biancamano, I–10121-Torino
EKONOMISK DEBATT
Fack, S–103 20 Stockholm 16
EKONOMISKA FORSKNINGSINSTITUTET
Handelshögskolan i Stockholm, Box 6501, S–113 83 Stockholm
EKONOMISKA SAMFUNDETS TIDSKRIFT
Svenska Handelshögskolan, 22, Arkadiag., SF–00100 Helsinki 10
(F.) ENKE VERLAG
63, Herdweg, Postfach 1304, D–7000 Stuttgart 1
EPIDEMIOLOGIA E PREVENZIONE
Istituto de Biometria e Statistica Medica, Facoltà di Medicina e Chirurgia dell'Università di Milano, 1, Via Venezian, I–20133 Milano
ERICH SCHMIDT VERLAG
30 g, Genthiner Strasse, D 1000 Berlin 30.
10, Herforder Strasse, D–4800 Bielefeld
ESSELTE AB
24, Scheelegatan, S–112 85 Stockholm
EUROPEAN CLUB OF HEALTH
See: Club Européen de la Santé

FEDERAL REPUBLIC OF GERMANY, FEDERAL STATISTICS OFFICE
See: Statistisches Bundesamt
FEDERATION OF SWEDISH COUNTY COUNCILS
See: Svenska Landstingsförbundet
FEDERAZIONE ITALIANA ASSOCIAZIONI REGIONALI OSPEDALIERE
46, Via dei Prefetti, I–00186 Roma
FELTRINELLI EDITORE
6, Via Andegari, I–20121 Milano
FINANSDEPARTTEMENTET, PLANLEGGINGSAVDELNINGEN
42, Akersgt., N–Oslo 1
FINNISH ANTI-TUBERCULOSIS ASSOCIATION
9, Kalevank, SF–00100 Helsinki 10
FINNISH GOVERNMENT PRINTING CENTRE
P.O. Box 516, SF–00101 Helsinki 10
FLAMMARION
26, rue Racine, F–75278 Paris Cedex 06
FRA SUNDHEDSSTYRELSEN
Sundhedsstyrelsen, 1, Store Kongesgade, DK–1264 København K
FRANCE, DIRECTORATE OF SOCIAL SECURITY
See: Direction de la Sécurité Sociale
FRANCE, MEDICAL HIGH COMMISSION OF THE SOCIAL SECURITY
See: Haut-Comité Médical de la Sécurité Sociale

FRANCE, MINISTRY OF HEALTH AND SOCIAL SECURITY
MINISTRY OF PUBLIC HEALTH
MINISTRY OF PUBLIC HEALTH AND SOCIAL SECURITY
See: Ministère de la Santé et de la Sécurité Sociale
FRANCE, MINISTRY FOR INDUSTRIAL AND SCIENTIFIC DEVELOPMENT
See: Secrétariat d'Etat auprès du Premier Ministre (Recherche)
FRANCE, MINISTRY OF SOCIAL AFFAIRS
See: Secrétariat Général, Conseil Economique et Social
FRANCO ANGELI EDITORE
106, Viale Monza, I–20127 Milano
FRIEDRICH-THIEDING-STIFTUNG DES HARTMANNBUNDES
Verband der Ärzte Deutschlands, 54, Godesberger Allee, D–5300 Bonn–Bad Godesberg 1
FUTURIBLES 2000
(Revue Mensuelle de l'Association Internationale Futuribles)
55, rue de Varenne, F–75007 Paris
(Formerly: *Futuribles*)

GEBURTSHILFE, FRAUENHEILKUNDE
Georg Thieme Verlag, 63, Herdweg, Postfach 732, D–7000 Stuttgart 1
GENERAL PRACTITIONERS ORGANIZATION
See: Den Almindelige Danske Lægeforening
(A.W.) GENTNER VERLAG
131, Forststrasse, Postfach 688, D–7000 Stuttgart
GEORG THIEME VERLAG
63, Herdweg, Postfach 732, D–7000 Stuttgart 1
GESELLSCHAFT FÜR SOZIALEN FORTSCHRITT E.V.
17, Münsterstrasse, D–5300 Bonn
GESTIONS HOSPITALIÉRES
2, rue Jules-Verne, F–78200 Mantes-la-Jolie
GIUNTA REGIONALE DELLA LOMBARDIA, ASSESSORATO ALLA SANITÀ
10, Via Pontaccio, I–20121 Milano
GÖTEBORGS STADTSKONTOR
S–400 00 Göteborg

HANDELSHØJSKOLEN I KØBENHAVN
7, Fabrikvej, DK–2000 København F
HANS HUBER VERLAG A.G.
76, Länggasse, CH–3012 Bern
HAUT-COMITÉ MÉDICAL DE LA SÉCURITÉ SOCIALE
5, Avenue Bosquet, F–75007 Paris
HEALTH SERVICES RESEARCH
Hospital Research and Education Trust, 840, North Lake Shore Drive, USA–Chicago, Ill. 606 11

Allan Press Inc., USA–Lawrence, KS 6600 44

HERAL
23, rue Tronchet, F–75008 Paris
HET ZIEKENHUIS
Nationale Ziekenhuisraad, 4, Bourgermeester Oudlaan, NL–Utrecht
HEURES DE FRANCE
30, rue des Saints-Pères, F–75007 Paris
HOFFMAN–LA ROCHE
122, Grenzacherstrasse, CH–4058 Basel
Hospital and Health Services Review
(The official journal of the Institute of Health Service Administrators)
75, Portland Place, GB–London W1N 4AN
(Until December 1971: *The Hospital*)

I PROBLEMI DELLA SICUREZZA SOCIALE
Via Colombo, I–00144 Roma
IL CROGIOLO
(This publication no longer exists)
IL PENSIERO SCIENTIFICO
48, via Panama, I–00198 Roma
ILO OCCUPATIONAL SAFETY AND HEALTH SERIES
International Labour Office, 4, Route des Morillons, CH–1211 Genève 22
ILO STUDIES AND REPORTS SERIES
International Labour Office, 4, Route des Morillons, CH–1211 Genève 22
IN ZET
Federatie van door Verzekerden en Medewerkers Bestuurde Ziekenfondsen, 3, Wilhelminenlaan, NL–De Bilt
(Until December 1976: *Ziekenfondsgids*)
INDUSTRIENS UTREDNINGSINSTITUT
Box 5037, S–102 41 Stockholm
INSTITUT FOR ERHVERVS OF SAMFUNDSBESKRIVELSE, HANDELSHØJSKOLEN I ÅRHUS
4, Fuglesangs Alle, DK–8210 Århus V
INSTITUT FÜR SOZIO-ÖKONOMISCHE ENTWICKLUNGSFORSCHUNG
20, Fleischmarkt, Stiege 1, A–Wien 1
INSTITUT NATIONAL DE LA SANTÉ ET DE LA RECHERCHE MÉDICALE
101, rue de Tolbiac, F–75645 Paris Cedex 13
INSTITUT NATIONAL DE LA STATISTIQUE ET DES ETUDES ECONOMIQUES
41, Quai Branly, F–75007 Paris
INSTITUT SUISSE DES HÔPITAUX
29, Bahnhofstrasse, CH–5001 Aarau
INSTITUTE FOR RESEARCH IN HEALTH ECONOMICS
See: Istituto per la Ricerca di Economia Sanitaria
INSTITUTE FOR SOCIAL RESEARCH, MILAN
See: Istituto per la Ricerca Sociale
INSTITUTET FOR ORGANISATION OG ARBEJDSSOCIOLOGI
60, Howitzvej, DK–2000 København F

INSTITUTET FÖR SOCIALMEDICINSK EKONOMI
Box 1319, S–113 83 Stockholm
INSTITUTT FOR ANVENDT SOSIALVITENSKAPELIG FORSKNING
31, Munthes gt., N–Oslo 2
INTERDISZIPLINÄRES FORSCHUNGSZENTRUM FÜR DIE GESUNDHEIT
103 c, Rorschacher Strasse, CH–9006 St. Gallen
INTERNATIONAL CENTRE FOR SOCIAL GERONTOLOGY
See: Centre International de Gérontologie Sociale
INTERNATIONAL JOURNAL OF HEALTH SERVICES
Dr Vicente Navarro, Johns Hopkins University, 615, North Wolfe Street, USA–Baltimore, Md. 21205

Baywood Publishing Company Inc., 120, Marine Street, Farmingdale, USA–New York, N.Y. 11735
INTERNATIONAL LABOUR OFFICE
4, Route des Morillons, CH–1211 Genève 22
INTERNATIONAL LABOUR REVIEW
International Labour Office, 4, Route des Morillons, CH–1211 Genève 22
ISTITUTO PER LA RICERCA DI ECONOMIA SANITARIA
7, Piazza Cadorna, I–20123 Milano
ISTITUTO PER LA RICERCA SOCIALE
24 Via XX Settembre, I–20123 Milano
ITALIAN CENTRE FOR HEALTH AND SOCIAL RESEARCH
See: Centro Italiano per la Ricerca Sanitaria e Sociale
ITALIAN FEDERATION OF REGIONAL HOSPITAL ASSOCIATIONS
See: Federazione Italiana Associazioni Regionali Ospedaliere

JAHRBUCH FÜR KRITISCHE MEDIZIN
Kommission für Medizin, 48A, Alpensteinstrasse, D–1 Berlin 33
JAHRBUCH FÜR SOZIALWISSENSCHAFTEN
Vandenhoek und Ruprecht, 13, Theaterstrasse, Postfach 77, D–3400 Göttingen
JOHN WILEY AND SONS INC.
605, Third Ave, USA–New York, N.Y. 10016
JOHNS HOPKINS UNIVERSITY PRESS
USA–Baltimore, Md. 21218
JOURNAL DE LA SOCIÉTÉ DE STATISTIQUES DE PARIS
118, Rue de Tocqueville, F–75017 Paris
JOURNAL OF EPIDEMIOLOGY AND COMMUNITY HEALTH
British Medical Association, Tavistock House, Tavistock Square, GB–London WC1
(Until December 1977: *British Journal of Preventive and Social Medicine*)

Oxford University Press, Ely House, 37, Dover Street, GB–London W1
JURIST- OCH SAMHÄLLSVETAREFÖRBUNDET FÖRLAGS AB
Box 5167, S–102 44 Stockholm 5

KANSANTALOUDELLINEN AIKAKAUSKIRJA
Union Bank of Finland, Department of Economic Research, 30, Aleksanterinkatu, SF–00100 Helsinki 10

(S.) KARGER A.G.
25, Arnold-Böcklin-Strasse, Ch–4011 Basel

KATHOLIEKE UNIVERSITEIT LEUVEN, CENTRUM VOOR ECONOMISCHE STUDIEN
2 B, van Evenstraat, B–3000 Leuven

KATHOLIEKE UNIVERSITEIT LEUVEN, INSTITUUT VOOR SOCIAL ZEKERHEIDSRECHT
41, Tiensestraat, B–3000 Leuven

KATHOLIEKE UNIVERSITEIT LEUVEN, SOCIOLOGISCH ONDERZOEKSINSTITUUT
2 B, van Evenstraat, B–3000 Leuven

KIRCHHEIM VERLAG GMBH
41, Kaiserstrasse, Postfach 2524, D–6500 Mainz

(W.) KOHLHAMMER VERLAG
69, Hessbrühlerstrasse, Postfach 80 04 30, D–7000 Stuttgart 80

3, Philipp-Reis-Strasse, Postfach 42 11 20, D–Köln 1

KÖLNER SCHRIFTEN ZUR SOZIALWISSENSCHAFTLICHEN FORSCHUNG
Wison Verlag, 59, Weyertal, Postfach 41 09 48, D–5000 Köln 41

KOMMISSION FÜR WIRTSCHAFTLICHEN UND SOZIALEN WANDEL
(ceased activities in 1977)

KONINKLIJKE VAN GORCUM & CO.
P.O.B. 43, NL–Assen

KONTAKTEN/CONTACTS
Caritas Catholica, 1, Rue Guimard, B–1040 Bruxelles

KRANKENHAUS-UMSCHAU
(Zeitschrift für das gesamte Krankenhauswesen, Fachvereiningung der Verwaltungsleiter Deutscher Krankenanstalten)
79, Bremserstrasse, D–6700 Ludwigshafen

E.C. Baumann Verlag, 5, E.-C. Baumann-Strasse, Postfach 1149, D–8650 Kulmbach

KRANKENPFLEGE–SOINS INFIRMIERS
(Revue officielle de l'Association Suisse des Infirmières et Infirmiers Diplômés)
1, Choisystrasse, CH–3006 Bern (Until July 1979: *Revue Suisse des Infirmières*)

Imprimerie Vogt-Schild, CH–4501 Soleure 1

L'EVOLUTION MÉDICALE
1, rue de Courcelles, F–75008 Paris

L'HÔPITAL ET L'AIDE SOCIALE À PARIS
7, rue des Minimes, F–75003 Paris

L'INDUSTRIA
5, Piazza Cadorna, I–20123 Milano

LA DOCUMENTATION FRANÇAISE
31, Quai Voltaire, F–75340 Paris Cedex 07

LA REVUE NOUVELLE
305, Avenue van Volxem, B–1090 Bruxelles
LABORATOIRE D'ECONOMIE ET DE SOCIOLOGIE DU TRAVAIL
Chemin du Coton-Rouge, F–13100 Aix-en-Provence
LÄKARTIDNINGEN
(Organ för Sveriges Läkarförbund)
5, Villagatan, Box 5610, S-114 86 Stockholm 5
LANDSTINGENS TIDSKRIFT
Box 6606, S–113 84 Stockholm
LARCIER
Rue des Minimes, B–1000 Bruxelles
LATERZA EDITORE
51, Via Dante, I–70121 Bari
LE MONNIER EDITORE
100, Via Scipione Ammirato, I–50136 Firenze
LE SCIENZE
2, Via Hugo, I–20123 Milano
LEONARDO EDIZIONI SCIENTIFICHE
5, Via Baglivi, I–00161 Roma
LES CAHIERS FRANÇAIS
La Documentation Française, 31, Quai Voltaire, F–75340 Paris Cedex 07
LIBER FÖRLAG AB
Fack, S–162 89 Vällingby
LIBRAIRIE ARNETTE
2, rue Casimir-Delavigne, F–75006 Paris

MAANDBLAD VOOR ACCOUNTANCY EN BEDRIJFSHUISHOUDKUNDE
J. Muusses, Postbus 13, NL–1440 AA Purmerend
MAANDSCHRIFT ECONOMIE
H. Gianotten, NL–Tilburg
MACMILLAN PUBLISHERS LTD.
4, Little Essex Street, GB–London WC2
MASSON EDITEUR
120, Boulevard Saint-Germain, F–75006 Paris
MÉDECINS DE GROUPE
Société d'Editions de Publications Médicales, F–80620 Domart-en-Ponthieu
MEDICINSK FORUM
25, Landemærket, DK–1119 København K
MEDISCH CONTACT
Vitgeveesing Kruyt b.v., 28, Groot Hertogirmelan, NL–Bussum
MEDIZIN, MENSCH, GESELLSCHAFT
F. Enke Verlag, 63, Herdweg, Postfach 1304, D–7000 Stuttgart 1
MEDIZINISCH PHARMAZEUTISCHE STUDIENGESELLSCHAFT
94, Humboldstrasse, D–6000 Frankfurt

METHODS OF INFORMATION IN MEDICINE
(The official journal of the European Federation of Medical Informatics)
F.K. Schattauer Verlag, 3, Lenzhalde, Postfach 29 45, D–7 Stuttgart 1

MINISTÈRE DE L'ECONOMIE ET DES FINANCES, DIVISION DE LA PRÉVISION
9, rue Croix-des-Petits-Champs, F—75001 Paris

MINISTÈRE DE LA SANTÉ PUBLIQUE

MINISTÈRE DE LA SANTÉ ET DE LA FAMILLE
See: Ministère de la Santé et de la Sécurité Sociale

MINISTÈRE DE LA SANTÉ ET DE LA SÉCURITÉ SOCIALE
8, Avenue de Ségur, F–75007 Paris
(Formerly successively until July 1979: Ministère de la Santé Publique, Ministère de la Santé et de la Sécurité Sociale, Ministère de la Santé et de la Famille)

MINISTÈRE DU DÉVELOPPEMENT INDUSTRIEL ET SCIENTIFIQUE
See: Secrétariat d'Etat auprès du Premier Ministre

MINISTERIE VAN SOCIALE ZAKEN EN VOLKSGEZONDHEID
See: Ministerie van Volksgezondheid en Milieuhygiëne

MINISTERIE VAN VOLKSGEZONDHEID EN MILIEUHYGIËNE
12, Dokter Reijersstraat, NL–Leidschendam (Formerly: Ministerie van Soziale Zaken en Volksgezondheid)

MINISTERO DELLA SANITÀ, CENTRO STUDI
20, Viale dell'Industria, I–00144 Roma

(J.C.B.) MOHR (PAUL SIEBECK)
18, Wilhelmstrasse, D–7400 Tübingen

MTP PRESS
Falcon House, Cable Street, GB–Lancaster LA1 1PE

MUNKSGAARDS BOGHANDEL
6, Noerregade, DK–1165 København K

NATIONAL ALLIANCE OF CHRISTIAN MUTUAL INSURANCES
See: Alliance Nationale des Mutualités Chrétiennes

NATIONAL INSTITUTE FOR HEALTH AND MEDICAL RESEARCH
See: Institut National de la Santé et de la Recherche Médicale

NATIONALØKONOMISK TIDSSKRIFT
Det Kgl. Bibliotek, 8, Chr. Brygge, DK–1219 København K

NATUR OCH KULTUR FÖRLAGSEXPEDITIONEN
6, Gårdsvägen, S-171 52 Solna

NAUWELAERTS
10, Muntstraat, B–3000 Leuven

NIEDERSÄCHSICHES ÄRZTEBLATT
Ärztekammer Niedersachsens und der Kassenärztlichen Vereinigung, 20, Berliner Allee, D–3000 Hannover 1

NOMOS VERLAGSGESELLSCHAFT GMBH
3-5, Waldseestrasse, D–7570 Baden-Baden

NORDISK MEDICIN
Harlang og Toksvig Bladforlag A/S, 30, Dr Tvaergade, DK–1302 København K

NORSK INSTITUTT FOR SYKEHUSFORSKNING
11, Øvre Allé, N–7000 Trondheim
NORTH-HOLLAND PUBLISHING CO.
335, Jan van Galenstraat, P.O. Box 211, NL–1000 AE Amsterdam
NOTES ET ETUDES DOCUMENTAIRES
La Documentation Française, 31, Quai Voltaire, F–75340 Paris Cedex 07
NUFFIELD PROVINCIAL HOSPITALS TRUST
3, Prince Albert Road, GB–London NW1
NYT FRA SAMFUNDSVIDENSKABERNE
Institutet for Organisation og Arbejdssociologi, 60, Howitzvej, DK–2000 København F

OFFICE DE STATISTIQUE DE L'ETAT DE VAUD
11 bis, rue de la Caroline, CH–1003 Lausanne
OFFICIAL STATISTICS OF FINLAND, SPECIAL STUDIES
Finnish Government Printing Centre, P.O. Box 516, SF–00101 — Helsinki 10
ORGANIZATION FOR ECONOMIC COOPERATION AND DEVELOPMENT
2, rue André-Pascal, F–75775 Paris Cedex 16
ORIENTATION MUTUALISTE
(Organe bimestriel de l'Alliance Nationale des Mutualités Chrétiennes)
121, Rue de la Loi, B–1040 Bruxelles
(A Dutch edition, *Leiding*, is also available)
OSPEDALI D'ITALIA
46, Via dei Prefetti, I–00186 Roma
ÖSTERREICHISCHE KRANKENHAUS-ZEITUNG
D. Göschl Verlag, 34, Klopstock-Gasse, A–1170 Wien
OXFORD UNIVERSITY PRESS
Ely House, 37, Dover Street, GB–London WC1

PHARMA DIALOG
Bundesverband der Pharmazeutischen Industrie, 21, Karlstrasse, D–6000 Frankfurt
PHARMA INFORMATION
4, Birsigstrasse, Ch–4054 Basel
PHARMAZEUTISCHE ZEITUNG
Arbeitsgemeinschaft der Berufsvertretungen Deutscher Apotheken, 1-3, Beethovenplatz, Postfach 97 01 08, D–6000 Frankfurt 97
POLITISCHE RUNDSCHAU — REVUE POLITIQUE
(Zeitschrift für Kultur, Politik und Wirtschaft),
Generalsekretariat der Freisinning-Demokratischen Partei der Schweiz
Postfach 2642, 10, Bahnhofstrasse, CH–3001 Bern
Willy Gassmann Verlag, 11, Freiestrasse, CH–2501 Biel
POLYTEKNISK FORLAG
1, Anker Engelundsvej, DK–2800 Lyngby

PRESSE MÉDICALE
120, Boulevard Saint-Germain, F–75006 Paris
PRESSES UNIVERSITAIRES DE FRANCE
49, Boulevard Saint-Michel, F–75005 Paris
PRESSES UNIVERSITAIRES DE GRENOBLE
B.P. 47, F–38040 Grenoble Cedex
PREVENTIVE MEDICINE
(Official journal of the American Health Foundation)
1370, Avenue of the Americas, USA–New York, N.Y. 10019

Academic Press Inc., 111 Fifth Avenue, USA–New York, N.Y. 10003
PROSPECTIVE ET SANTÉ PUBLIQUE
Association Prospective et Santé Publique, 5 rue Clément-Marot, F–75008 Paris
PROSPETTIVE SOCIALI E SANITARIE
7, Piazza Cadorna, I–20123 Milano
PUBLIC HEALTH
(The Journal of the Society of Community Medicine)
The Royal Institute of Public Health and Hygiene, 28, Portland Place, GB–London W1

Academic Press Inc., 24-28, Oval Road, GB–London NW1

REGIONE BASILICATA, DIPARTIMENTO SICUREZZA SOCIALE
Parco Aurora, I–85100 Potenza
RELAZIONI SOCIALI
24, Via XX Settembre, I–20123 Milano
REVUE BELGE DE SECURITÉ SOCIALE
Ministère de la Prévoyance Sociale, 3 c, rue de la Vièrge-Noire, B–1000 Bruxelles (A Dutch edition, *Belgisch Tijdschrift voor Sociale Voorzorg*, is also available)
REVUE D'ECONOMIE POLITIQUE
22, rue Soufflot, F–75005 Paris
REVUE D'EPIDÉMIOLOGIE, MÉDECINE SOCIALE ET SANTÉ PUBLIQUE
Masson, 120, Boulevard Saint-Germain, F–75006 Paris
REVUE ECONOMIQUE
103, Boulevard Saint-Michel, F–75005 Paris
REVUE FRANÇAISE D'AUTOMATIQUE, D'INFORMATIQUE ET DE RECHERCHE OPÉRATIONNELLE
Association Française pour la Cybernétique Economique et Technique, 92, Rue Bonaparte, F–75006 Paris
(Formerly successively: *Revue Française de Recherche Opérationelle* (1959–66), *Revue Française d'Informatique et de Recherche Opérationnelle* (1967–71), *Revue Française d'Automatique, Informatique, Recherche Opérationnelle* (1972–76)

Centrale des Revues Dunod, Gauthier Villars, B.P. 119, F–93104 Montreuil Cedex

Revue Française de Recherche Opérationnelle
See: Revue Française d'Automatique, d'Informatique et de Recherche Opérationnelle

REVUE FRANÇAISE DE SOCIOLOGIE
15, Quai Anatole-France, F–75007 Paris

REVUE FRANÇAISE DES AFFAIRES SOCIALES
Ministère de la Santé et de la Sécurité Sociale, 8, Avenue de Ségur, F–75007 Paris
La Documentation Française, 31, Quai Voltaire, F–75340 Paris Cedex 07

REVUE HOSPITALIÈRE DE FRANCE
(Organe officiel de la Fédération Hospitalière de France)
83-87, Avenue d'Italie, F–75013 Paris.

REVUE INTERNATIONALE DE SECURITÉ SOCIALE
Association Internationale de Securité Sociale, 4, Route des Morillons, CH–1211 Genève 22

REVUE MÉDICALE DE BRUXELLES
Association des Médecins, Anciens Etudiants de l'Université Libre de Bruxelles, 7, rue Heger-Bordet, B–1000 Bruxelles 02

REVUE SUISSE D'ECONOMIE POLITIQUE ET DE STATISTIQUE – SCHWEIZERISCHE ZEITSCHRIFT FÜR VOLKSWIRTSCHAFT UND STATISTIK
Verlag Stämpli A.G., Postfach 2728, CH–3001 Bern

Revue Suisse des Infirmières
See: Krankenpflege – Soins Infirmiers

REVUE TRIMESTRIELLE DE DROIT SANITAIRE ET SOCIAL
3, rue Soufflot, F–75005 Paris

RIJKSUNIVERSITAIR CENTRUM
1, Middelheimlaan, B–2020 Antwerpen

RIJKSUNIVERSITEIT LEIDEN, CENTRUM VOOR ONDERZOEK VAN DE ECONOMIE VAN DE PUBLIEKE SECTOR
32, Hugo de Grootstraat, P.O. Box 9521, NL–2300 RA Leiden

RIJKSUNIVERSITEIT LEIDEN, ECONOMISCH INSTITUUT
32, Hugo de Grootstraat, NL–2300 Leiden

RIVISTA DEGLI OSPEDALI
48, Via Panama, I–00198 Roma

RIVISTA DI DIRITTO FINANZIARIO E SCIENZA DELLE FINANZE
Istituto di Finanza dell'Università di Pavia, 65, Strada Nuova, I–27100 Pavia

RIVISTÀ DI ECONOMIA E POLITICA INDUSTRIALE
6, Via S. Stefano, I–00198 Roma

RIVISTA INTERNAZIONALE DI SCIENZE ECONOMICHE E COMMERCIALI
Via Teuliè, I–20136 Milano

RIVISTA INTERNAZIONALE DI SCIENZE SOCIALI
1, Largo Gemelli, I–20123 Milano

ROMBACH VERLAG
3, Lörracher Strasse, Postfach 13 49, D–7800 Freiburg

SANDOZ INSTITUTE FOR HEALTH AND SOCIO-ECONOMIC STUDIES
5, Route de Florissant, CH–1206 Genève

SAXON HOUSE, LEXINGTON BOOKS
c/o Teakfield Ltd., 1, West Mead, GB–Farnborough

SCANDINAVIAN JOURNAL OF RHEUMATOLOGY
c/o Dr Olle Lövgren, S:t Eriks Sjuhus, P.O. Box 12600, S–112 82 Stockholm

SCANDINAVIAN JOURNAL OF SOCIAL MEDICINE
Socialmedicinska Institutionen, Karolinska Institutionen, S–104 01 Stockholm

SCHMOLLERS JAHRBUCH FÜR GESETZGEBUNG, VERWALTUNG UND VOLKSWIRTSCHAFT
Gesellschaft für Wirtschafts- und Sozialwissenschaften, Verein für Sozialpolitik, 24-42, Adenauerallee, D–5300 Bonn 1

SCHRIFTEN DER GESELLSCHAFT FÜR SOZIALEN FORTSCHRITT
Gesellschaft für Sozialen Fortschritt e.V., 17, Münsterstrasse, D–5300 Bonn

Duncker & Humblot, 9, Dietrich-Schäfer-Weg, Postfach 41 03 29, D–1000 Berlin 41

SCHRIFTEN DES VEREINS FÜR SOZIALPOLITIK
Duncker & Humblot, 9, Dietrich-Schäfer-Weg, Postfach 41 03 29, D–1000 Berlin 41

SCHRIFTENREIHE ARBEITSMEDIZIN, SOZIALMEDIZIN, PRÄVENTIVMEDIZIN
A.W. Gentner Verlag, 131, Forststrasse, Postfach 688, D–7000 Stuttgart 1

SCHRIFTENREIHE DER FRIEDRICH-THIEDING-STIFTUNG DES HARTMANNBUNDES
Verband der Ärzte Deutschlands, 54, Godesberger Allee, D–5300 Bonn-Bad Godesberg 1.

SCHRIFTENREIHE DES INSTITUTS FÜR SOZIO-ÖKONOMISCHE ENTWICKLUNGSFORSCHUNG
Institut für Sozio-Ökonomische Entwicklungsforschung, 20, Fleischmarkt, Stiege 1, A–Wien 1

SCHRIFTENREIHE DES SCHWEIZERISCHEN KRANKENHAUSINSTITUTS
Schweizerisches Krankenhausinstitut, 29, Bahnhofstrasse, CH–5001 Aarau

SCHRIFTENREIHE STRUKTURFORSCHUNG IM GESUNDHEITSWESEN
Technische Universität Berlin, Berliner Arbeitsgruppe Strukturforschung im Gesundheitswesen, 135, 17. Juni Strasse, D–1000 Berlin 12

SCHULTHESS POLYGRAPHISCHER VERLAG A.G.
2, Zwingliplatz, CH–8001 Zürich

(J.H.) SCHULTZ FORLAG
19, Moentergade, DK–1116 København K

(O.) SCHWARTZ VERLAG
7, Annastrasse, D–3400 Göttingen

SCHWEIZERISCHES KRANKENHAUSINSTITUT
29, Bahnhofstrasse, CH–5001 Aarau

SCUOLA SUPERIORE DI DISCIPLINA E TECNICA DELL'AMMINISTRAZIONE
Università degli Studi di Milano, Igiene e Medicina Preventiva, 7, Via Festa del Perdono, I–Milano

SECRÉTARIAT D'ETAT AUPRÈS DU PREMIER MINISTRE (RECHERCHE)

35, rue Saint-Dominique, F–75007 Paris
(Formerly: Ministère du Developpement Industriel et Scientifique)
SECRÉTARIAT GÉNÉRAL, CONSEIL ECONOMIQUE ET SOCIAL
35, rue Saint-Dominique, F–75007 Paris
(Formerly: Ministère des Affaires Sociales)
SEMAINE DES HÔPITAUX
15, rue Saint-Benoît, F–75278 Paris 06
SOCIAL SCIENCE AND MEDICINE
Pergamon Press, Headington Hill Hall, GB–Oxford OX3 0BW
SOCIALFORSKNINGSINSTITUTTET
28, Borgergade, DK-1300 København K
SOCIALMEDICINSK TIDSKRIFT
Fack, S–104 01 Stockholm
SOCIALT TIDSSKRIFT
45, Sankt Peders Straede, DK–1453 København K
SOSIAALIVAKUUTUS
Kansaneläkelaitos, Sosiaaliturvan tutkimuslaitos, 1 B, Olavinkatu, SF–00100 Helsinki 10
SOSIALØKONOMEN
26, Storgt., N–Oslo 1
SOZIALE SICHERHEIT
(Die sozialpolitische Monatszeitschrift der Gewerkschaften)
Bund-Verlag GMBH, 46, Deutz-Kalker-Strasse, Postfach 21 01 40, D–5000 Köln 21
SOZIALER FORTSCHRITT
Gesellschaft für Sozialen Fortschritt e.V., 17, Münsterstrasse, D–5300 Bonn

Duncker & Humblot, 9, Dietrich-Schäfer-Weg, D–1000 Berlin 41
SPRI REPORTS
The Swedish Planning and Rationalization Institute of the Health and Social Services, Fack, S–102 50 Stockholm
SPRINGER VERLAG
50, Kochstrasse, D–1 Berlin 33
STATENS BAKTERIOLOGISKA LABORATORIUM
S–105 21 Stockholm
STATENS MEDICINSKA FORSKNINGSRÅD
166, Sveavägen, S–113 46 Stockholm
STATENS TRAFIKSÄKERHETSRÅD
1, Roda Vagen, S–78186 Borlange
STATENS TRYKNINGSKONTOR
20, Bredgade, DK–1260 København K
STATISTIQUES ET ETUDES FINANCIÈRES
Ministère de l'Economie, Direction de l'Economie, 93, rue de Rivoli, F–75005 Paris RP

Imprimerie Nationale, 27, rue de la Convention, F–750015 Paris

STATISTISCHES BUNDESAMT
11, Gustav-Stresemann-Ring, Postfach 55 28, D–6200 Wiesbaden 1
STENFERT KROESE
38, Pieterskerkhof, NL–Leiden
STUDENTLITTERATUR
Fack, S–221 01 Lund
STUDI ECONOMICI
Facoltà di Economia e Commercio, 36, Via Partenope, I–80121 Napoli
STUDIEN ZUR WIRTSCHAFTS- UND SOZIALFORSCHUNG DES WIRTSCHAFTS- UND SOZIALWISSENSCHAFTLICHEN INSTITUTS DES DEUTSCHEN GEWERKSCHAFTSBUNDES
Bund-Verlag, 46, Deutz-Kalker-Strasse, Postfach 21 01 40, D–5000 Köln 21
SVENSK FARMACEUTISK TIDSKRIFT
Box 1136, S–111 81 Stockholm
SVENSKA HANDELSHÖGSKOLANS PUBLIKATIONER
22, Arkadiag., SF–00100 Helsinki
SVENSKA LANDSTINGSFÖRBUNDET
Box 6606, S–113 84 Stockholm
SVERIGES KOMMUNALTJÄNSTEMANNAFÖRBUND
27, Grevtutegatan, Box 5101, S–102 43 Stockholm
SWEDEN, STATE MEDICAL RESEARCH COUNCIL
See: Statens Medicinska Forskningsråd

TANDLÆGEBLADET
Dansk Tandlægeforening, 14, Oslo Plads, DK–2100 København O
TECHNIQUES HOSPITALIÈRES
17-19, rue Danton, F–94270 Kremlin-Bicêtre
TECHNISCHE HOGESCHOOL
Afdeling Bedrijfskunde, Postbus 513, NL–Eindhoven
TECHNISCHE UNIVERSITÄT BERLIN, BERLINER ARBEITSGRUPPE STRUKTURFORSCHUNG IM GESUNDHEITSWESEN
135, 17. Juni Strasse, D–1000 Berlin 12
TEKNISK FORLAG A/S
4, Skelbackgade, DK–København 5
THE DANISH NATIONAL INSTITUTE OF SOCIAL RESEARCH
28, Borgergade, DK–1300 København
THE DANISH NATIONAL SERVICE FOR THE MENTALLY RETARDED
See: Åndssvageforsorgen Socialstyrelsen Særforsorgsafdelingen
THE FINNISH HOSPITAL FEDERATION
6, Rautatieläisenk, SF–00520 Helsinki 52
The Hospital
See: Hospital and Health Services Review
THE LANCET LTD.
7, Adam Street, GB–London WC2
THE NATIONAL HEALTH SERVICE OF DENMARK
1, Store Kongensgade, DK–1264 København

THE PERSONNEL TRAINING SCHOOL
83A, Islands Brygge, DK–2300 København S
THE SOCIAL INSURANCE INSTITUTION, RESEARCH INSTITUTE FOR SOCIAL SECURITY
1B, Olavink., SF–100100 Helsinki 10
THE SWEDISH PLANNING AND RATIONALIZATION INSTITUTE OF THE HEALTH AND SOCIAL SERVICES
Fack, S–102 50 Stockholm
THREE BANKS REVIEW
National and Commercial Banking Group Ltd., 3, Bishopsgate, GB–London EC2
TIDSSKRIFT FOR DANSKE SYGEHUSE
Koebenhavns Amts Sygehus i Glostrup, DK–2600 Glostrup
TIERS-MONDE
12, rue Jean-de-Beauvais, F–75005 Paris
TIJDSCHRIFT VOOR PRIVAAT RECHT
Story-Scientia, 8, Pr. Van Duysplein, B–9000 Gent
TIJDSCHRIFT VOOR SOCIALE GENEESKUNDE
Algemene Nederlandse Vereniging voor Sociale Geneeskunde, Tijlmedia B.V., 76-80, Texelstraat, P.O. Box 384, NL–Amsterdam

UGESKRIFT FOR LÆGER
Den Almindelige Danske Lægeforening, 12A, Kristianiagade, DK–2100 København O
UNION BANK OF SWITZERLAND
45, Bahnhofstrasse, CH–8021 Zürich
UNIVERSITÄT MARBURG
10, Biegenstrasse, D–3550 Marburg
UNIVERSITÄT SAARBRÜCKEN
Stadtwald, D–6600 Saarbrücken
UNIVERSITÄT STUTTGART
7, Keplerstrasse, D–7000 Stuttgart
UNIVERSITÄT WÜRZBURG
2, Sanderring, D–8700 Würzburg
UNIVERSITÉ D'AIX-MARSEILLE, FACULTÉ DE DROIT ET SCIENCES ECONOMIQUES
3, Avenue Robert-Schuman, F–13621 Aix-en-Provence
UNIVERSITÉ DE CAEN
Esplanade de la Paix, F–14032 Caen
UNIVERSITÉ DE DIJON
Campus Universitaire de Montmuzard, B.P. 138, F–21004 Dijon
UNIVERSITÉ DE LOUVAIN, ECOLE DE SANTÉ PUBLIQUE
30, Clos de la Chapelle-aux-Champs, B–1200 Bruxelles
UNIVERSITÉ DE LOUVAIN, FACULTÉ DES SCIENCES ECONOMIQUES, SOCIALES ET POLITIQUES
Place de l'Université, B–1340 Louvain-La-Neuve
UNIVERSITÉ DE PARIS, FACULTÉ DE DROIT ET DES SCIENCES ECONOMIQUES
See: Université de Paris II

UNIVERSITÉ DE PARIS I, PANTHÉON-SORBONNE
12, Place du Panthéon, F–75005 Paris
UNIVERSITÉ DE PARIS II
12, Place du Panthéon, F–75005 Paris
UNIVERSITÉ DE PARIS X, PARIS–NANTERRE
200, Avenue de la République, F–92001 Nanterre
UNIVERSITÉ DES SCIENCES SOCIALES DE GRENOBLE
Domaine Universitaire St.-Martin-d'Hères, F–38000 Grenoble
UNIVERSITÉ LIBRE DE BRUXELLES
44, Avenue Jeanne-d'Arc, B–1050 Bruxelles
UNIVERSITETSFORLAGETS TRYKNINGSCENTRAL
Blindern, N–Oslo 3
UNIVERSITY COLLEGE OF KARLSTAD
Fack, S–650 09 Karlstad
UNIVERSITY OF BERGEN
1, Muséplass, N–5000 Bergen
UNIVERSITY OF CHICAGO, CENTER FOR HEALTH ADMINISTRATION STUDIES
5720, Woodlawn Avenue, USA–Chicago, Ill., 60637
UNIVERSITY OF COPENHAGEN, INSTITUTE OF SCOCIAL MEDICINE
32, Mariesvej, DK–2100 København Ø
UNIVERSITY OF GOTHENBURG, DEPARTMENT OF ECONOMICS
Fack, S–400 10 Göteborg 3
UNIVERSITY OF HELSINKI, DEPARTMENT OF SOCIOLOGY
13, Franzenink., SF–00500 Helsinki 50
UNIVERSITY OF KUPIO, DEPARTMENT OF COMMUNITY HEALTH
SF–70101 Kupio 10
UNIVERSITY OF LEIDEN, ECONOMIC INSTITUTE
See: Rijksuniversiteit Leiden, Economisch Instituut
UNIVERSITY OF LUND
Fack, S–220 05 Lund 5
UNIVERSITY OF TAMPERE
4, Kalevantie, SF–33101 Tampere 10
US DEPARTMENT OF HEALTH, EDUCATION, AND WELFARE
USA–Washington, DC 20009

US Government Publications, Superintendent of Documents, US Government Printing Office, USA–Washinton, DC 20402

VANDENHOECK UND RUPRECHT
13, Theaterstrasse, Postfach 77, D–3400 Göttingen
VERBAND DER ÄRZTE DEUTSCHLANDS (HARTMANNBUND) E.V.
54, Godesberger Allee, D–5300 Bonn–Bad Godesberg
VERLAG DER ORTSKRANKENKASSEN
60, Euskirchener Strasse, Postfach 14 02 12, D–5300 Bonn 1
VERLAG KONKORDAT DER SCHWEIZERISCHEN KRANKENKASSEN
20, Römerstrasse, Ch–4500 Solothurn

VITA E PENSIERO
1, Largo Gemelli, I–20123 Milano
VSA-VERLAG
7, Erkelenzdamm, Postfach 36 03 07, D–1000 Berlin 36

(B.) WAHLSTRÖMS BOKFÖRLAG AB
Förlagsexpeditionen, Fack, S–791 01 Falun
WELTARCHIV GMBH
21, Neuer Jungfernstieg, D–2000 Hamburg 36
WERKGROEP ALTERNATIEVE EKONOMIE
c/o Noël Molisse, 64, Bogaardenstraat, B–3000 Leuven B
WESTDEUTSCHER VERLAG GMBH
12-16, Gustav-Stresemann-Ring, Postfach 58 29, D–6200 Wiesbaden 1
WHO CHRONICLE
WHO NON-SERIAL PUBLICATIONS
WHO OFFSET PUBLICATIONS
WHO PUBLIC HEALTH PAPERS
WHO TECHNICAL REPORT SERIES
World Health Organization, Avenue Appia, CH–1211 Genève 27
WHO PUBLIC HEALTH IN EUROPE SERIES
World Health Organization, Regional Office for Europe, 8, Scherfigsvej, DK–2100 København Ø
WIRTSCHAFT UND STATISTIK
Statistisches Bundesamt, 11, Gustav-Stresemann-Ring, Postfach 55 28, D–6200 Wiesbaden 1
W. Kohlhammer Verlag, 69, Hessbrühlerstrasse, Postfach 80 04 30, D–7000 Stuttgart 80
WIRTSCHAFTS- UND SOZIALWISSENSCHAFTLICHES INSTITUT DES DEUTSCHEN GEWERKSCHAFTSBUNDES
46, Deutz-Kalker-Strasse, D–5000 Köln 21
WIRTSCHAFTSPOLITISCHE BLÄTTER
Bundeskammer der Gewerblichen Wirtschaft, 12, Stubenring, A–1010 Wien
WISON VERLAG
59, Weyertal, Postfach 41 09 48, D–5000 Köln 41
WORKING PARTY OF THE SOCIETY FOR SOCIAL PROGRESS
See: Gesellschaft für Sozialen Fortschritt
WORLD BANK
1818 H Street, N.W., USA–Washington DC
WORLD HEALTH ORGANIZATION
Avenue Appia, CH–1211 Genève 27
WORLD HEALTH ORGANIZATION, REGIONAL OFFICE FOR EUROPE
8, Scherfigsvej, DK–2100 København Ø
WORLD HEALTH STATISTICS REPORTS
World Health Organization, Avenue Appia, CH–1211 Genève 27

ZEITSCHRIFT FÜR ALLGEMEINMEDIZIN
Hippokrates Verlag GmbH, 121, Neckarstrasse, D–7000 Stuttgart 1
(Until 1969: *Der Landarzt*)
ZEITSCHRIFT FÜR ORGANISATION
Dr Th. Gagler, Betriebswirtschaftlicher Verlag, D–6200 Wiesbaden
ZENTRALINSTITUT FÜR DIE KASSENÄRZTLICHE VERSORGUNG IN DER BUNDESREPUBLIK DEUTSCHLAND
5, Haedenkampstrasse, D–5000 Köln 41 (Lindenthal)
Ziekenfondsgids
See: In Zet

Author Index